Thomas Edward Cliffe Leslie

Essays in political and moral Philosophy

Thomas Edward Cliffe Leslie

Essays in political and moral Philosophy

ISBN/EAN: 9783337073565

Printed in Europe, USA, Canada, Australia, Japan

Cover: Foto ©ninafisch / pixelio.de

More available books at **www.hansebooks.com**

POLITICAL AND MORAL PHILOSOPHY.

BY

THOMAS EDWARD CLIFFE LESLIE, LL.D.,

OF LINCOLN'S INN, BARRISTER-AT-LAW.

DUBLIN: HODGES, FOSTER, & FIGGIS, GRAFTON-ST.
LONDON: LONGMANS, GREEN, & CO., PATERNOSTER-ROW.
1879.

PREFACE.

In some of the Essays in this volume, which the Provost and Senior Fellows of Trinity College have honoured the author by publishing in the Dublin University Press Series, slight changes of phrase have been made, but for the most part they are reprinted without alteration. Written at different times and on different subjects, they naturally exhibit some diversities of view, and readers who dissent from the author's reasoning on some questions may concur with it in the main on others. Yet threads of connexion will be found in the method of investigation, and in some fundamental ideas. The conception, for example, is followed throughout that every branch of the philosophy of society, morals and political economy not excepted, needs investigation and development by historical induction; and that not only the moral and economic condition of society, but its moral and economic theories and ideas, are the results of the course of national history and the state of national culture. Contemporary social phenomena, such as the statistician explores, though indispensable to the researches and verifications of the economist and the moralist, are regarded in these Essays as but the latest links in chains of sequence connecting the past and the future, and as marking steps in a movement in which there is both continuity and change.

The author desires gratefully to acknowledge that Mr. Mill, though not concurring in all his views, always warmly encouraged his endeavours to bring the light of inductive research to bear on the problems of Political and Moral Philosophy.* Whatever differences exist between Mr. Mill's treatment of some of those problems and his own—for example, in relation to the Utilitarian theory of morals, and the economic theories of profits and prices—are, he believes, in a great measure attributable to the fact, that whereas Mr. Mill in his youth attended the lectures of Mr. Austin, the author had the good fortune to attend those of Sir Henry Maine at the Middle Temple, and to learn first from them the historical method of investigation, followed with such brilliant success in Ancient Law, Village Communities in the East and West, and the Lectures on the Early History of Institutions. Holding a Professorship of both Jurisprudence and Political Economy, he was led to apply that method to the examination of economic questions, and to look at the present economic structure and state of society from Sir Henry Maine's point of view, as the result of a long evolution. Further investigation has convinced him that the English economist of the future must study in the schools of both Mr. Stubbs and Sir Henry Maine, as well as in that of Mr. Mill. Mr. Thorold Rogers'

---

* The following passage in a letter from Mr. Morley, the distinguished Editor of the *Fortnightly Review*, accepting a proposal of the Essay on Auvergne in this volume, shows how cordially Mr. Mill welcomed such investigations at a time when they were coldly regarded by the majority of English economists:—" September 17, 1874. No letter could have given me more pleasure than one containing such a proposal as yours. A long time ago, Mr. Mill said to me that no one wrote accounts at once so instructive and so interesting as your narratives of your foreign visits. Believe, therefore, how heartily I shall welcome your Paper on Auvergne for my November number."

History of Agriculture and Prices—'heroicum sane opus'—is an admirable example of original investigation of the sources of economic history. The Essay in this volume on Utilitarianism and the Summum Bonum, written in 1863, is from its brevity necessarily an imperfect presentation of the historical method in relation to morals, but it is an application of that method which the author believes had not been made before, and which disposes of some long controverted questions.

The two earliest Essays in point of date in the volume, entitled 'The Question of the Age—Is it Peace'? and 'The Future of Europe Foretold in History,' will, it is submitted, if read in connexion with the one entitled 'Political Economy and Sociology,' written nearly nineteen years later, and with the political history of the interval, be found to establish the conclusion that the economy of modern Europe—including therein the occupations of its inhabitants, the motives determining the directions of their energies, and the constituents, amount, and distribution of their wealth—cannot be adequately interpreted without reference to the warlike tendencies of the age and their causes. Another conclusion which, it is believed, several of the Essays establish, is that 'the desire of wealth,' from which some eminent economists have attempted to deduce economic laws, is but an abstraction, and that one of the main problems of Political Economy is to investigate the changes which the desires, sentiments, and motives of which different kinds of wealth are the objects, undergo.

The reader is respectfully referred to a forthcoming Essay by the author in the *Fortnightly Review* (June 1, 1879), entitled 'The Known and the Unknown in the Economic World,' **for** proof of the following propositions:—

1. That the full knowledge and foreknowledge claimed by **Mr.** Lowe for the political economist in modern commercial society, can exist only at an opposite stage of development at which human business and conduct are determined, not by individual choice, or the pursuit of wealth, or commercial principles, but by immemorial ancestral custom.

2. That **Mr.** Ricardo, **in his** exposition of 'the laws which regulate natural prices, natural wages, and natural profits,'* ignored **the** essential difference between stationary and progressive society, between the ancient economic world, **with its** simple and customary methods and prices, and the modern, with its vastness, complexity, incessant movement, and sudden vicissitudes and fluctuations. .

3. That the distinction which Mr. Mill has drawn between home trade and international trade in respect of the transferability of labour and capital, and the equalization of wages and profit, if it had once some foundation when trade at home was simpler and better known, and when foreign trade **was** almost wholly unknown, can no longer be sustained. In **both** home trade and international trade, the migration of **labour and** capital has now some effect on wages **and** profits, and the comparative cost of producing different commodities has some effect on their comparative value and price, but in both cases the effect is uncertain and irregular, and incalculable. In neither case is there an equalization of either wages or profits; **in neither case do** prices conform to the Ricardian law of cost.

* Ricardo's Works, M'Culloch's Ed., p. 49.

4. That Mr. Ricardo's doctrine that the 'rate of profits can never be increased but by a fall in wages'—and 'is never increased by a better distribution of labour, by the invention of machinery, by the establishment of roads or canals, or by any means of abridging labour either in the manufacture or in the conveyance of goods'*—is erroneous. Mr. Mill made an important correction of his predecessor's language in saying that the rate of profit depends, not on wages but on the cost of labour. Yet the cost of labour is only one of several conditions affecting the result.

The author is under much obligation to Mr. Ingram, F.T.C.D., Secretary of the Dublin University Press Series Committee, for aid in reading and correcting proofs.

T. E. C. LESLIE.

21, DELAHAY-STREET, STOREY'S GATE,
  LONDON, S.W., *May*, 1879.

* Ricardo's Works, M'Culloch's Ed., p. 75.

CONTENTS.

		PAGE.
I.	The Love of Money,	1
II.	The Celibacy of the Nation,	9
III.	The Individual and the Crowd,	16
IV.	Utilitarianism and the Summum Bonum,	36
V.	The Wealth of Nations and the Slave Power,	51
VI.	The Question of the Age—Is it Peace?	62
VII.	The Future of Europe foretold in History,	94
VIII.	Nations and International Law,	111
IX.	The Military Systems of Europe in 1867,	128
X.	The Political Economy of Adam Smith,	148
XI.	The History of German Political Economy,	167
XII.	'Some Leading Principles of Political Economy newly expounded, by Professor Cairnes,'	179
XIII.	The Incidence of Imperial and Local Taxation on the Working Classes,	192
XIV.	On the Philosophical Method of Political Economy,	216
XV.	John Stuart Mill,	243
XVI.	Professor Cairnes,	248
XVII.	Mr. Bagehot,	251
XVIII.	The Reclamation of Waste,	254
XIX.	British Columbia in 1862,	259
XX.	The Distribution and Value of the Precious Metals in the Sixteenth and Nineteenth Centuries,	264

		PAGE
XXI.	THE NEW GOLD MINES AND PRICES IN EUROPE IN 1865,	296
XXII.	PRICES IN GERMANY IN 1872,	326
XXIII.	PRICES IN ENGLAND IN 1873,	349
XXIV.	THE MOVEMENTS OF AGRICULTURAL WAGES IN EUROPE,	356
✓ XXV.	ECONOMIC SCIENCE AND STATISTICS,	375
✓ XXVI.	POLITICAL ECONOMY AND SOCIOLOGY,	383
XXVII.	AUVERGNE,	412
XXVIII.	M. DE LAVELEYE ON PRIMITIVE PROPERTY,	435
XXIX.	MAINE'S EARLY HISTORY OF INSTITUTIONS,	448
XXX.	HEARN'S ARYAN HOUSEHOLD,	469

APPENDIX.

| TWO BOOKS ON INTERNATIONAL LAW, | 477 |

ESSAYS
IN
POLITICAL AND MORAL PHILOSOPHY.

I.

THE LOVE OF MONEY.*

The Love of Money has always been in more or less disrepute with moralists. They have almost universally assigned to it nearly the lowest place in the scale of human affections. We say of human affections, for it is one which distinguishes man from all other animals, however intelligent. 'You call me dog,' said Shylock to the Christian merchant; 'hath a dog money?' Phrenologists have indeed laid down that all the propensities—combativeness, destructiveness, philoprogenitiveness, alimentiveness, love of life, &c.—are 'common to man with the lower animals;' but we are surprised that they have not discovered a peculiar protuberance on the outside of the human head corresponding with a peculiar propensity for money inside it. It is the more to be regretted that they have not ascertained the locality of this organ, since a claim has been set up on behalf of the lower animals to a close relationship to the human family. If a bump of philargyriveness or philonomismativeness could be shown on the human head, a conspicuous absence of this manifestation on the cranium of the former would enable us to disprove the connection, to the satisfaction at least of believers in phrenology. It would not, however, enable us, without further inquiry, to determine whether

---

* This Essay was published in November, 1862, in a periodical which has ceased to exist.

the love of money, which distinguishes us from the brutes, places us above or below them in moral character. To satisfy ourselves on this point, we must begin by inquiring what this thing 'Money,' of which men, and men only, are so fond, consists of. Sir Robert Peel's celebrated question—'What is the meaning of that word, a Pound, with which we are all familiar?'—was answered by himself in terms to the effect that a pound of money is a fixed quantity of gold or silver. But this answer, though highly appropriate to a discussion on the currency, is irrelevant to our present inquiry, whether money is a good or an evil; and whether the love of it is a good or a bad quality in mankind. Sir Robert Peel very justly ridiculed the definition given by one writer on the currency of a pound, as 'a sense of value in reference to currency as compared with commodities.' Yet in practical life this is really something like what men generally mean and want by money. They mean so much goods; so much of the commodities for sale in the market of the world. A pound to a 'navvy,' for instance, is so much beer and tobacco; to his mother it is so much tea and sugar. But these two cases are sufficient to show the extreme difficulty of pronouncing any moral judgment whatever upon the love of money, considered as a general human propensity; for the love of tea and sugar is universally admitted to be in itself an innocent affection, while the love of beer and tobacco is often condemned as combining two most pernicious desires. The love of money is really only a phrase for the love of a vast number of different things, which may be good, bad, or indifferent, regarded from a moral, religious, æsthetical, political, or medical point of view, but which are alike in one respect—namely, that they are all to be had for money, and are not to be had without it. As Solomon said, 'A feast is made for laughter, and wine maketh merry; but money answereth all things.' The love of money is that universal desire of wealth from which political economists have deduced a theory of commercial values, along with several important truths respecting the conditions of industrial energy and prosperity. Everybody wishes for some kind of wealth, and money is convertible into every other kind; and therefore everybody loves money for some purpose or other, from which we get the laws of competition, prices, wages, profits, and rent. Yet this general principle of pecuniary interest or love of riches by no means explains all the phenomena of the economic world. For it is, as we have said already, only a single expression for a great variety of wants, wishes, and tastes, which are not always the same from age to age, or from country to country, nor felt alike by every individual in any one age or country, and which, moreover, lead to very different consequences as regards the nature, amount, and distribution of wealth, and as regards the material as well as the moral welfare of human society.

That disease of language which metaphysicians call the realism of the schools, still infests many of the terms and phrases which philosophy must employ. A host of different things are alike in some one respect, and a common name is given to them in reference to the single quality or circumstance which they have in common. It is simply a name for their common feature, but it puts their numerous differences out of sight and out of mind, and they come to be thought of in a lump as one sort of thing. Those moralists, accordingly, who feel themselves the better for heartily denouncing the general principle of the love of money or pursuit of wealth with which political economy sets out, confound, in their horror of a mere abstraction, the love of health, cleanliness, decency, and knowledge, with sensuality, avarice, and vanity. And perhaps political economists have not escaped a bias from their own phraseology, and are apt to imagine in their scientific discussions, a much fuller explanation of the complete phenomena of wealth, and a much closer approximation to the complete philosophy of the subject, than lies within their province as commonly circumscribed by themselves at present.

It is obvious that the love of money includes a demand for various things, the production of which variously affects both the material interests of the consumers and the quality and distribution of the revenue of the whole community. It includes a love of pictures, toys, jewellery, plate, furniture, clothing, opium, soap, bibles, brandy, and, in short, everything in the International Exhibition, and many things not exhibited there. It includes a love of eating and drinking, both in moderation and in excess; of literature and science; of architecture; of the fine arts; of indolence and ease, and of business and sport; of foreign travel, and of a country house; of music; of charity, sensuality, cruelty, and power; of horses and dogs. It expresses sometimes a desire for the comforts of an old bachelor, and sometimes an inclination for matrimony; and when it takes the latter direction, it means with one young lady love in a cottage, and with another a palace without love; in one man it is fortune-hunting—in another, a disinterested attachment to Miss Aurora Penniless. The disciples of Malthus know how to discriminate between the economic consequences of these diverse matrimonial tendencies, and the important differences of their influence on the price of beef. Napoleon III. seems to behold in money the sinews of war; his friend Mr. Cobden connects it with commerce and peace. The poor man's love of money is a different feeling from the rich man's, and, accordingly, the writer of this essay never throbs with the emotions which must animate the breasts of Baron Rothschild and Lord Overstone. The American Southerner worships in the almighty dollar the giver of African slaves; the negro slave of Brazil adores it chiefly as the purchaser of liberty. The wealth which is coveted by men in the East is not that which is most prized by the men of the West. An Indian Rajah's chief wealth is a plurality of wives, personal attendants and elephants, and a load of gold trappings on both his elephant's body and his own—all which, not exclusive of the wives, would be more than an English duke or prince could bear. An old writer gives an account of a religious ceremony which he witnessed in Turkey, at which Prince Mustapha—a boy of eleven years old—'was so overloaded with jewels, both himself and his horse, that one might say he carried the value of an empire about him.' That is to say, the wealth which, in the hands of English capitalists, would have made a whole territory prosperous, and been distributed in wages through many hundred families, was concentrated upon making one small Turkish child vain and uncomfortable. And the oriental lust for jewels not only has effects upon the economic condition of the world which merit the attention of the political economist, but it has also, in a great measure, sprung from the absence, for many ages, of the conditions essential to general prosperity, and the accumulation of wealth in really useful forms. Wherever insecurity has long prevailed, a spirit of hoarding must exist, with a desire for that sort of wealth which contains much value in a durable and portable form, and which is easily hidden, easily removed, and none the worse for being buried for months or years in the ground. It is probable, therefore, that the love of gold chains and jewels for which the European Jew is remarkable has a European as well as an Asiatic origin, being inherited from his persecuted, plundered, and usurious ancestors in the middle ages, who found it necessary to pack their wealth into the smallest possible compass.

The existence of security, banks, and paper currency, have long exterminated from England that curious animal the genuine miser, with his treasure in a strong box, doing no good to any one. Dr. Johnson, talking of misers to Boswell, said, 'A man who keeps his money has, in reality, more use of it than he can have by spending it. Why, Sir, Lowther, by keeping his money, had the command of the county, which his family has lost by spending it.' But an English millionaire does not keep his money to himself, as the ancient miser, whether he spends it or not. If he saves it, instead of locking it up or carrying it about on his body, he puts it in a bank, and the banker's customers make use of the wealth he does not himself consume.

But when we say that the form of the love of money which displays itself in a love of dress, ornaments, and jewels, is almost confined to the men of Eastern countries, we must be understood as speaking of men in the narrowest sense, and as making no allusion in that comparison to the ladies of the two hemispheres. Women have everywhere their own peculiar notions of the value of money; and a world of either men alone or of women alone would contain a very different assortment of articles of wealth from that in the great mundane shop for both sexes which exists. With most species of animals, the male is more gorgeously dressed than the female; but so it seems to be with the human species generally, only in its less civilized forms. For we may perceive, with the growth of European civilization, a marked decline in the taste of men for the display of wealth on the body. A mediæval baron was much more expensively got up than his wife or daughter. Even in the last century, the toilette of a gentleman was nearly as elaborate and splendid as that of a lady. Now, a gentleman thinks he makes a smart appearance with a flower in his button-hole, at an assembly at which the ladies are blazing with diamonds. It might be an instructive inquiry how far this difference in the desire for wealth is traceable to a radical difference in the natural mental constitutions of the sexes, and how far to restraints which confine the ambition of women in general to paltry objects, leading them to waste their time in hunting husbands, while men hunt seats in parliament, and foxes. Addison remarks, in the Spectator, that 'One may observe that women in all ages have taken more pains than men to adorn the outside of their heads.' Perhaps one reason for this is, that men have in all ages prevented them from taking so much pains to adorn the inside. While we are on the subject of dress as one of the equivalents of money, and one of the objects of its pursuit, we may make a remark upon that singular revolution of the human mind through which it has come to be thought, by all men of a certain rank, in the Western world, becoming to attire themselves every evening in black from head to foot, as if for a funeral; and by most men, of all ranks, in that civilized region, becoming to clothe themselves in the dingiest hues all day long. The male apparel which is the last product of civilization appears to display a remarkable mixture of good sense and bad taste. The mistake made by the ladies of our time seems to be that of aiming at show and accomplishing waste; while the mistake of the gentlemen is that of aiming at plainness and accomplishing gloom.

Many other illustrations might be given of the curious turns taken by the fancy for clothing, as one of the uses of money. In the north of Ireland, for example, it is common to see a girl on the road with a smart bonnet, an extensive petticoat, and a gay parasol carried in the usual manner, but with a pair of shoes not upon her feet, but in her hands. Five and twenty years ago such a girl would have no more minded the effect of the sun on the skin of her face, than she now minds the effect of the earth on the skin of her foot; and five and twenty years hence it may be safely predicted that such a girl will not only **think** it advisable to wear her shoes on her feet, but will discover that they really hurt less there, when one is used to them, than the stones upon the road. At the same time, we must admit that the shoemakers of mankind—and of womankind, too, we presume—have left nothing undone to perpetuate a prejudice against their own particular production and to weaken the force of the love of money for the sake of obtaining it. There is, again, in the inventory of modern wealth, and among the civilized uses of money, another article of dress of so obvious and simple a character that many persons may naturally suppose that it descends from the most remote antiquity. Yet, some centuries ago, all the wardrobes in England did **not comprise a** single night-dress for lady or gentleman, king or queen. Take again, another institution **of the modern** dressing-room—the **bath.** There is a history of civilization in the Tale of a Tub. There is a letter to the old Spectator, on the effects of the love of money, in which the writer says that it is to that we owe the politician, the merchant, and the lawyer; 'Nay,' he adds, ' I believe to that also we are indebted for our Spectator.' We are not prepared to explain the various motives which inspire the pens of authors. **Did** Shakspeare write for money? Did Pope? Did Dr. Johnson? **Did Lord** Macaulay? Does Sir Edward Bulwer Lytton? We are concerned at present with the motives of consumers rather than producers; and one thing at least is clear, that it is highly to the credit of the former to elicit such productions from the latter, **and that** the love of money **in** the modern world **is to** a great extent the love of good, **elevating, and instructive** objects—a love which meets with **its** return. **New desires for** health, decency, knowledge, refinement, and intellectual **pleasures, have,** in fact, revolutionised production. **The** antithesis to modern wealth is not so much poverty as **a** different kind of wealth. The change **is** more remarkable in the quality than **in** the quantity. No inconsiderable part of human wealth, it is true, still **consists of** the means of unhappiness rather than of happiness, and of the gratification of vice rather **than of** virtue. On the whole, however, there is a transformation in the moral character of wealth, and of the desires involved in the general love of money. For the most part, instead of representing wickedness, brutal delight, and idle pomp, or conquest, tyranny, and plunder, the wealth of Europe represents peace, culture, liberty, and the comfort of the many rather than the magnificence of the few. Where man's treasure is, there his heart is also; and the treasures of modern civilization seem to us to show as remarkable an improvement in the moral as in the intellectual and physical condition of society. 'Riches,' said Milton, ' grow in hell;' for even in his time much of the wealth that grew on earth bore many marks of being the property of bad and unhappy beings. But we may venture now to ask those well-meaning persons who, without regard to time and place, and without discrimination between good and evil, repeat ancient warnings against the love of money and the pursuit of wealth, whether they mean to praise dirt under the name of poverty, and whether they think idleness better than industry, ignorance better than science and art, and barbarism better than civilized progress? To political economists, on the other hand, we venture to suggest the cultivation of a department of the philosophy of riches which has never been scientifically investigated. The laws which regulate the value of the supply forthcoming from producers have been almost exhaustively developed in political economy; but the deeper laws which regulate the demand of the consumers, and which give the love of money all its force and all its meaning, have never yet received the regular attention of any school of philosophers.

II.

THE CELIBACY OF THE NATION.*

WHAT are the causes of Celibacy? Is it the inevitable lot of millions of persons in this country? It was found in 1851 that three in seven of all the women in Great Britain, of the age of twenty and upwards, were without husbands; and of every hundred women between twenty and forty years of age, forty were set down in the Population Tables of that year as 'spinsters.' The Census Commissioners of 1851 predicted that a definite and very large percentage of the population then living would never marry, and there is every reason to believe that their prediction was only under the mark. The tables of the Census of 1861 may probably show that a larger proportion of a larger population than at the end of the previous ten years remained unmarried, and that there are not only many more 'spinsters' now than there were ten years ago, but that there are more in comparison with the total number of women; so that celibacy is increasing in rate as well as in amount. Is this the fault of the men, or, as we ought to say, of the unmarried men of our time? According to a late eminent writer, men have no choice at all about the matter. He reasoned from statistics that the number of marriages is determined 'not by the temper and wishes of individuals, but by facts over which individuals can exercise no authority.'† 'They have,' he said, 'a fixed and definite relation to the price of corn;' and in England the experience of a century has proved that, 'instead of having any

* This Essay was published in February 1863, in the same periodical as the one preceding.
† Buckle's History of Civilization.

connection with personal feelings, they are simply regulated by the average earnings of the great mass of the people.' The statistics of the year which has just closed seem to afford a sad confirmation of the premises of this argument, if not of its conclusion; for the Registrar General's returns show that the number of marriages in Lancashire declined with the rate of wages. Yet we should say that the natural inference from such facts is the reverse of that which Mr. Buckle drew. If the annual number of marriages were, contrary to what happens, wholly unaffected by variations in the circumstances of individuals, it might then be legitimately inferred that their conduct in the matter is governed by some influence which they have no power to resist. But the fact, on the one hand, that men for the most part marry when they think they can afford it, goes to show that 'personal feelings' have something to do with the result; and, on the other hand, the fact that there are fewer marriages when there are fewer men able to support a wife and family, goes to prove that the attractions to marriage, powerful as they are, are not altogether irresistible, and that celibacy is, at least in a great number of cases, the result of an exercise of individual discretion. We cannot, therefore, acquit our unmarried men of all responsibility, whether they are free from blame in the matter or not. The circumstances of the case cannot, however, be summed up in either of Mr. Buckle's two short and easy formulas. Marriages have not, in point of fact, a constant relation to the price of corn, or to any fixed standard of wages or income. It is needless to say that the amount of the baker's bill is about the last thing a man in the upper or middle classes would think of as an obstacle to his marriage. But even the marriages of the labouring classes are not found to vary uniformly, either with the size of the loaf or with the amount of their earnings. Malthus himself, the chief exponent of the relation between food, wages, marriages, and population, has remarked that from 1720 to 1750 'the price of the loaf had so fallen, while wages had risen, that instead of two-thirds, the labourer could purchase the whole of a peck of wheat with a day's labour.' But this greatly increased command of bread did not, he adds, produce a proportionate increase of marriages and population; instead of which, to a considerable extent, an improvement took place in the houses and dress **of** the lower classes, and the quality of their food. Mr. Buckle's measures seem not to fit either of the two extremes of social progress. Savages don't consider whether they are likely to be able to support a family before they undertake to rear one; **and** men accustomed to some of the habits and comforts of civilization have generally a higher standard for the requisites of married life than a certain quantity of corn, or bare subsistence of any sort. And as there is, on the whole, a steady increase in the wages of labour in Great Britain, there is reason to expect that the whole community will, at no very distant period, be placed above the necessity of watching the price of flour for the signal to marry. But are we to conclude that, as civilization and general prosperity advance, and as the mass of men become emancipated from the control of such restraints upon marriage as we have been talking of, celibacy will become rarer, until it finally disappears from the notice of the statistician? On the contrary, the conclusion to which the evidence points is, that celibacy without vows or compulsion is a form of human existence which is commonly to be seen only in civilized society, and which becomes commoner as civilization goes forward and spreads.

Some writers, struck by the increasing number of unmarried women, have asked 'Why are women redundant?' The question seems to us to partake of the nature of the 'fallacy of interrogation,' which Archbishop Whately illustrates by the instance of the witness who was asked 'whether he had left off beating his father?' At least, if the real gist of the inquiry is simply **why** are so many women unmarried, the assumption of their 'redundancy' in the same proportion is mere rhetoric and sophistry, not to say impertinence. But why are so many women unmarried? The stubbornness or eccentricity of a few men, the perversity or unloveliness of a very few women, may be disregarded altogether, as producing no perceptible effect upon the Census, or the Registrar General's returns. A certain untowardness in the local and social distribution of individuals is perhaps a cause of celibacy of more importance. A and B,

who are exactly suited to each other, perhaps never meet, or don't meet often enough **to** bring things to a **crisis.** But even this obstruction to marriage is hardly worth taking into account, partly because it is one of an essentially unpractical **nature,** which nothing short of human ubiquity could entirely **remove; and** partly because, after all, few men need go out of **their parish for** a suitable wife. Witness the parochial clergy, compared with whom itinerant barristers and roving officers are a **set** of monks. We pass on, therefore, to the main causes of celibacy, which we affirm to be two—namely, marriage and civilization. Let us say a few words on each. The most obvious and immediate answer to **the question** ' **Why are so** many women unmarried?' is—Because so many women are married. To illustrate this, let us suppose that the Legislature had gallantly granted the 'Petition of the Ladies of London and Westminster,'* in **1693,** 'that for the utter discouragement of celibacy it should **be enacted** that all men, of what quality or degree soever, should be obliged to marry as soon as they are one-and-twenty.' Had a law to this effect been in force down to the passing of the Reform Bill thirty years ago, the population of Great **Britain,** in the absence of Malthusian plagues and famines, would now, instead of being 24 millions,† be more than 124 millions. But estates **would not have** increased with the **number** of eldest sons, nor 'places' with the number of younger sons; church livings and curates' stipends **would not** have grown with the number of clergymen: **briefs and guineas** would not have multiplied in proportion to the multiplication of barristers. **The** streets would be filled with really hungry attorneys. The public offices could contain no more clerks than they do now, but the candidates would be six times as many. Acres would not have increased with the number of ploughmen, nor cotton and wages with the number of operatives. There would be many more men, but fewer men able to marry. **Instead of two** million single women, there would be more than two-and-twenty million, and there would not be even as much work for the two-and-twenty million as there is now for the two million.

---

* Printed as such in the Harleian Miscellany.
† **Ireland not** included.

Men would take the work out of their hands, and the bread out of their mouths. **Men** can do the work of governesses, milliners, sempstresses, and housemaids, as well as of parlourmaids and shopwomen, and they would do it if competition **were** greater and wages were lower; just as men-servants have been commoner in Ireland than in England, because they have been cheaper.

But the world is wide, it has been said; the room for British families is not bounded by the British shores. The earth, as **a** whole, is underpeopled, and much of it is wholly uninhabited. This argument strangely assumes for our own countrymen **a** monopoly of the privilege **of** universal **marriage.** Had all nations been multiplying at the rate supposed, **the whole world** would be full. Already the Chinese have **found themselves** *de trop* in California and Australia, as well as at home. Moreover, a great part of the earth **is no** more available for the immediate support of the British population than the moon. Food, clothing, houses, roads, shops, and money are not ready waiting in every new country for a swarm of emigrants. In British Columbia, for example, thousands of Englishmen have found that they cannot live on rocks and forests, nor even upon rich unbroken meadows and gold-fields; and emigration, even when **it** succeeds, is so far from always making an immediate provision for marriage, that it has considerably increased the number of unmarried women in Great Britain, because men can go where women cannot follow. The number of women in the country accordingly exceeds the number of the men by more than **half** a million.

It has been argued that marriages and population have increased with civilization, and that the people now in England are better off than their ancestors, whose number was comparatively small. But although civilization has made it possible for increased numbers to live, it has not made it possible for all our present numbers to live in health, comfort, and decency; and there is hardly a cottage in the kingdom in which there are not too many people to be properly lodged, clothed, fed, and educated, **or** even to breathe freely. And it is a misconception of **the part** civilization has played in increasing our numbers, to suppose that it has increased the rate of marriages. It has, on the contrary, greatly checked the **rate of marriages**, but it has also checked in a still greater degree the rate of deaths; so that, **married and** unmarried together, we greatly outnumber our ancestors, and a goodly number of us are what the sneering **world** calls 'old bachelors' and 'old maids,' as if celibacy were something stale and antiquated, instead of being something quite fresh and modern. The Census Commissioners of 1851 probably took credit to themselves for liberality and indulgence when they said, 'If those of the age of 20 and under 40 years are called 'young,' and those of the age of 40 and upwards are called 'old,' **it will be found that there are in the** kingdom* about 1,407,225 'young' and 359,969 'old' **maids**; 1,413,912 'young' **and** 275,204 **'old'** bachelors.' But we object to this classification altogether, as an abuse of terms. Unmarried **people** do not become suddenly 'old' at **40; and** those whose **forbearance is** the chief reason why their married neighbours **are** not starving, should at least be spoken of respectfully. **Only** for the celibacy of one part of the community, marriage **would** have to stop altogether for a quarter of a century every **now and** then; and, accordingly, our unmarried ladies ought to be held in honour as the bridesmaids of the nation. We might borrow instruction from a people of much **longer experience** in these matters than our own. **In overpopulated China,** as M. Huc relates, if a girl will not **marry she is** honoured after death with peculiar pomp, and subscriptions are raised for a **monument to her virtue.** At Ningpo, **he adds,** when the English took **the** town, **they** found a **long** street entirely composed of such triumphal **arches,** and they talked of carrying them all **off and making of them a** complete street in London. M. Huc remarks that such an enterprise would have been worthy of English eccentricity. **We** should say, on the contrary, that it would have been worthy of English prudence and patriotism to have brought home so excellent a model. Celibacy should be carefully fostered in England, as the effect of marriage and civilization, by all those who are not prepared to put a stop to either.

---

* Great Britain, exclusive of Ireland.

We appeal on behalf of celibacy, likewise, to all whose love of country leads them to hope that England will never be all town and market garden, of which it begins to show some signs already. There are some unreasoning beings whose doctrine, if it were carried into practice, would soon make England one great poorhouse. If these people are not paupers already, they owe it to those whom they call old bachelors and old maids before their time. Every form of expression which tends to bring the meritorious status of celibacy into disrepute should be especially discountenanced by all those who, like the writer of this essay, wish to be happily married themselves.

III.

THE INDIVIDUAL AND THE CROWD.

(Frazer's Magazine, May, 1861.)

Two interesting questions have been lately raised respecting the relation between society at large and its individual members. One is, whether the structure of the modern world tends to merge the individual in the crowd, to suppress originality and diversity of thought, character, and pursuit, to make all men closely alike, and history henceforward that of common rather than uncommon men. The other question is one closely related. It is, whether the history of nations, or of the human race, is susceptible of scientific interpretation, disclosing the action of general laws; or whether it is more properly a narrative of so many distinct beings, each in some respects unlike any other of the species, subject to no discoverable laws of variation, and including from time to time individuals who not only widely deviate from anything like a common type, but leave their own stamp upon the race instead of being moulded by it.

I. The first inquiry does not seem to involve a difficult argument. To the multitude, at least, the social economy of our own times must afford a freer scope for the exhibition of natural varieties of disposition and ability than the institutions of former ages permitted. For what was the condition of the bulk of the people, that is to say, of the whole rural population except the proprietary class, in the feudal period? From the village in which he was born, a peasant could seldom escape, unless by the gate of death. He was made prisoner there by the law of the land, by his own poverty and ignorance, by the dangers and difficulties of the road, and by the scarcity of other than agricultural occupations. His bodily powers were his lord's, and the priest took charge of those of his soul. His imagination might be stirred by the pictures of saints and angels in his church, or by the sight of nobles, knights, and ladies belonging to a sphere almost as much above his own, or even by deep draughts of holiday ale; but these temporary emotions excepted, his life must have been nearly as monotonous and thoughtless as that of a beast of burden. If indeed he lived close to a monastery, and had an uncommon aptitude for learning Latin, he might be admitted into a spiritual corporation, which regulated his minutest actions and his inmost thoughts, and regarded any display of what is now called individuality as rebellion or heresy. Or if he lived near a city, he might, after a year's concealment, defy the suit of his lord to recover him as a fugitive serf. But he was by no means sure of a welcome within the city walls; and the regulations of the old municipal guilds were far from being nursing mothers of originality. The industry of towns was then in a constant state of siege, and their inhabitants formed a sort of garrison, which had to be kept in order by stringent discipline. Had the towns, however, favoured individual liberty more than we are justified in supposing, the vast majority of the mediæval population lived in the country, and to this day we find that rural life, until broken in upon by innovations emanating from towns, is a perpetual servitude to custom. In a small island like ours, studded with populous cities, and intersected with railways, rustic usages have long ceased to exist in their purity; but on the Continent we still find the peasantry in many places mere stereotyped copies of their ancestors, with little even of physical diversity between individuals. The true German peasant, for example, is an individual only in a numerical sense. He is merely a common specimen of his race and class; so much so that his immobility has been panegyrised as the grand security against revolution, by a writer whose descriptions of his countrymen are always faithful and instructive, although they will appear to most English minds suggestive of a different moral. The following passage is from his pages :*—

* Die Bürgerliche Gesellschaft. Von W. H. Riehl. Dritte Auflage, pp. 43-4.

'Among the townspeople of Germany, the original form of body, as well as of mind and manners, is lost in a type of individuality. The peasantry, on the contrary, vary, even in bodily appearance, only by groups, according to locality and class of life. In one rural district you find a tall, long-boned frame general, in another, a squat, broad-shouldered figure, transmitted for centuries by an unadulterated race. So in Hesse, at this day, you will meet those lengthy visages with broad, high foreheads, small eyes, arched eyebrows, long, straight noses, and big lips, just as they are painted by Jacob Becker in his village tales. Comparing these rustic faces with the sculptures of the thirteenth century in the Church of Elizabeth at Marburg, you perceive that the old Hessian cast of countenance has remained unaltered for six hundred years; with, however, this distinction, that while on those monuments the heads of princes and nobles are carved, showing in their lineaments the genuine stamp of the race, *that* is now to be found among the peasantry alone. Whoever would portray mediæval forms with historical fidelity, must look to the peasants for his models. This affords a natural explanation of the fact that the old German artists, of an age when it was far less the custom than in our time to draw from a model, have so generally given one uniform cast to their heads. The human figure had at that time reached no greater individuality. And the fact that this uniformity is still preserved among the peasantry, suggests the following observation. In the so-called educated world, the human being lives and works, for the most part, as an individual; the peasant, on the other hand, lives and works as one of a group, as a unit of an aggregate class. Hans drives the plough, and lives and thinks just like Karl; but that amongst so many thousands, one lives, thinks, and ploughs like another, is a fact of no light weight in the political and social scale. In the educated world, the individual has his style, and style is the index to the man. With the peasantry it is the race, the locality, the province, that have their style, that is to say, their peculiar dialect, idioms, phrases, and songs; and this style is the index to whole communities. It is an historical heir-loom to which the peasant clings with tenacity. There are districts in Hungary where the rustic descendants of German colonists of the twelfth and thirteenth centuries continue to sing the old Saxon songs and tunes, while the educated German immigrant in a very short time forgets the language of his home, and takes to the Hungarian. In America, too, it is seen how long the peasant emigrant preserves the inheritance of his own provincial dialect, while the townsman has the sorry ambition to adapt himself to his new abode by forgetting his mother tongue.'

Such are the effects of rural life even now that the peasants of Germany are emancipated from feudal bondage, and are brought near the ferment and progress of the towns of Western Europe. But in the middle ages, the restrictions of villenage combined with many other causes to suppress originality and the development of individual powers. 'Slaves,' says Adam Smith, 'are very seldom inventive, and all the most important improvements have been the discoveries of free men.' But invention is simply a phase of individuality; and the majority of mankind were formerly a kind of slaves.

Every great social and economical change in modern Europe has helped to clear a passage through the crowd, and through the world, for the humblest man with any real individuality. Information is easily got, travelling is safe and cheap, people may go almost where they like, the choice of occupations is considerable. Every man may be said to be born with a more active brain, a swifter foot, a less vulnerable body, than his ancestors, and with many more modes of turning to account his superior powers. The roads to eminence are more numerous; there is a lane off them to every cottage; and an ingenious boy of humble birth may aspire to become as remarkable an individual as Watt, Stephenson, or Faraday. 'Freedom and a variety of situations,' says Mr. J. S. Mill,* adopting the language of Baron W. von Humboldt, 'are the two requisites from the union of which arise individual vigour and manifold diversity.' But practical freedom involves much more than the absence of legal and social restraint; every limitation of power is an abridgment of positive liberty. A man is not free to go from

---

* Essay on Liberty, p. 103.

Shropshire to London, or from Liverpool to New York, if the journey is too long and expensive for him; nor is he actually free to develop a powerful intellect if education lies beyond his reach. The present multiplicity of occupations, pursuits, and paths of thought, affords the requisite variety of situations; and a nominal freedom has arisen from the abolition of many feudal, municipal, and religious disabilities; but it is the facility of information and locomotion, the accessibility of books, newspapers, and places, that give real freedom to the poor.

Hence a vast addition to the stock of individuality in the market of the world. A hundred thousand men, it has been very justly said, can never produce as many energetic characters as ten millions. And this country, at least, now draws its energetic characters from the millions, instead of as formerly only from the thousands. Nor is the latitude of scope for individuality confined to the world of business; it is almost as wide in the world of thought, so great are the facilities which every man enjoys for making up his mind for himself on all important subjects, and for the avowal of his opinions. He may read Bishop Butler or Mr. Holyoake; and he may get a Sunday audience in Hyde Park either for a loyal and orthodox discourse, or for a sermon against Christianity and the British Constitution.

This view of the enlargement of the sphere of individuality in modern times is quite consistent with Mr. Mill's observation, that the characteristic of a bygone state of society was 'the utmost excess of poverty and impotence in the masses; the most enormous importance and uncontrollable power of a small number of individuals;'[*] but it is only in a sense to which attention will be drawn in the second part of this Essay, that it is fully reconcileable with another observation of the same distinguished philosopher, namely, that 'the most remarkable of those consequences of advancing civilization which the state of the world is now forcing upon the attention of thinking minds, is this: that power passes more and more from individuals to masses; that the importance of the masses becomes constantly greater, that of individuals less.'[†]

---

[*] Dissertations and Discussions, vol. i. p. 164.   [†] Ib. vol. i. p. 163.

Doubtless over most of Europe the noble classes have lost some exclusive powers and means of gratifying their natural impulses, and of displaying their personal strength and ability. Yet, not to mention that this sphere of liberty or licence was due to the force of conventionality, rather than of individuality, the opportunities which even a nobleman formerly had of making himself felt in his generation, were comparatively few. He had perhaps an open career for his passions; but of employment for his talents, and of pursuit, he had but little choice. A courtier, a gallant knight, a dignitary of the Church, he might be; or he might be a petty tyrant, a freebooter, and a libertine. But an accomplished scholar, a poet, a historian, an improver of his estates, he could not be. Hence, while the masses had no scope for originality, the nobility and gentry had but little; and one nobleman or gentleman was very much like another in his pursuits, tastes, education, and opinions, taking his character simply from his birth and station in society. Lord Derby, Lord Palmerston, Lord John Russell, and Lord Dufferin, had they lived in the twelfth century, would have differed chiefly in the size of their armour, and the force of their lances; and the third named nobleman, notwithstanding his personal courage, could never have overthrown his rivals.

It is true that when government and military command were the only occupations of distinction open to the laity, and the sovereign was by natural position at the head of both, if he happened to possess considerable abilities, he enjoyed a range for their display which few men, even monarchs, now possess. One great and conspicuous individual was thus developed, but he shone almost alone; as we may judge from the fact that from the arrival of the Saxons in Britain to the accession of Edward III., a period of nearly nine centuries, the only very remarkable names in English history are those of Alfred, William the Conqueror, Anselm, Henry II., Becket, Roger Bacon, and Edward I.—four kings, two priests, and one philosopher. In the last sixty years alone, how many new sciences, new arts, new directions of scholarship and art, new roads to prodigious wealth and influence, have been created, each affording to many individuals a place above the crowd.

In every century, in every generation, **there** must be born some men with more than average **ability** for some special purpose, **and a few** with extraordinary genius or force of character. Civilization can have no tendency to prevent such births, and it has **every** tendency to disclose them. Whereas formerly there **were few** ladders of ascent for the few, and none, or almost none, **for the** many; now, superior and original capacity can emerge at numerous points from the whole population.

In one sense, nevertheless, 'the variety of situations' appears to be less than it **was.** '**The** circumstances which surround different classes and individuals and shape their characters, are daily becoming more **assimilated.** Formerly, different ranks, different neighbourhoods, different **trades and** professions, lived in what **might be called** different worlds; **at** present, to a great **degree, in** the same. Great **as** are the differences of position **which remain,** they are as nothing to those which have ceased.'*

The truth appears to **be, that** artificial varieties of situation **have** been superseded **by natural** ones, conventional and **local** differences by individual ones; and that personal ability, personal energy, peculiar genius and taste, are yearly more favourably circumstanced. **One** might even **go** so far as to say that the gradual **disappearance of** national diversities of life and character, however **undesirable at** present, **would prove in** the end an accession **to the triumphs of individual bent and** power over traditional and **topical limitations. When** every county had its own dialect, every trade its **own** laws and government, every class its own peculiar dress, there were many visible distinctions **among** the crowd which are now effaced, but they were so many **positive** restraints upon individual liberty, **and** the symbols of many **more.** The education of the people of Europe by nations has **been** one **of** the chief means of their improvement; but it has been so, not **by its** exclusions, but by **its** inclusions; not by dividing **men from each other** as foreigners, but by uniting them as fellow-citizens; by giving to friendship and sympathy the noble area of **patriotism,** and inspiring every man with a grand theme of daily thought.

* Essay on Liberty. By John Stuart Mill. Page 131.

The mechanical revolution **which** the world has undergone and is still undergoing, the close proximity of states, their easy intercourse and common politics, although not unattended **with** grave immediate dangers, combine with commerce, science, and literature to enlarge the sphere of every individual's interests and choice of **life** and habitation. The juxtaposition, too, of **a** variety of conflicting opinions has always been found in the long run conducive to the toleration of each, as our own religious history remarkably exemplifies. Recollections **of** the Roman Empire, described by Gibbon **as one vast** prison, may lead to misapprehensions respecting the prospects of liberty from the tendencies to ultimate assimilation perceptible in modern nations. That a great common country may be a free **one for all** its citizens, the condition of the British Empire proves. **Even** in France, under the present monarchy, the majority of the inhabitants have far more real liberty than when it was divided into numerous petty tyrannies, when the weak were always at the mercy of the strong, and the poor man was plundered with impunity by the rich, when abject wretchedness, ignorance, and superstition were **the** inheritance of the millions, and knowledge and independent **thought were** passports to the flames. Moreover, if France **is** yearly coming closer to England with **a** centralized despotism and an **army** of conscripts, England is approaching France at the same pace with a House of Commons, a free press, and a nation, as one may **say,** of volunteers, since the voluntary principle prevails in every **department of** British life.

Meantime the approximation of the **countries** has had one result which Adam Smith, though a **political** economist, would have rejoiced to witness. 'In barbarous societies of hunters and shepherds, every man **is** a warrior (he said), and every man **too is in some measure a** statesman.' But the division of labour, by confining the industry of the masses to mechanical and sedentary operations, tended, he thought, 'to render them incapable of any generous and noble sentiment, **or** of forming any judgment upon the great interests of the country, and to corrupt both the courage of their minds and the activity of their bodies.'*

* Wealth of Nations, book **v., c. i.**

As regards the public **spirit which animates** each individual of the body, a hunting tribe or **nomad horde might** perhaps be compared more justly with a **herd of buffaloes** or a pack of wolves, **than** with a society of warriors and statesmen. But the **structure** and situation of English society really tend to render 'every man in some measure a statesman,' and, **if necessary,** 'every man a warrior.' And this takes place, not **as in the** republics of antiquity, through the interference and compulsion of the State, but by the deliberate choice and voluntary action of the individual citizen.

II. **But if we admit that the** character or volition **of** individuals exercises **a powerful and increasing** influence upon the progress **of** society, **must we conclude that human history is placed beyond the reach of human science?** To put the **interposition of** individuality in its most forcible instance, must **we incline to** the belief '**that** the one **fact** that genius **is** occasionally present in the world, is enough **to** prevent our ever discovering any regular **sequence in human** progress, past **or** future?'*

That the frequent intervention of persons of extraordinary genius or power does not render a scientific interpretation of **the history of mankind im**possible, is the main proposition to the support **of which the** following arguments **are** meant **to** contribute **something. Two** or three preliminary observations must, however, be made. **In the first** place, science never explains the whole **order or** sequence of things. It is always **only a** partial explanation. Being always progressive, it always **leaves** much for future discovery. Moreover, **no science,** as such, **predicts** events unconditionally, or asserts unqualified **or undisturbed** sequences to **come,†** least of all should a science

---

* **The Limits of** Exact Science as applied to History, p. 42. In this lecture Mr. Kingsley had not confined his arguments to the establishment of the incontrovertible proposition that history cannot be made, by any conceivable method, the subject matter of an *exact* science, properly so called, that is, of a science which treats of laws or forces, the action of which can be explained with numerical precision. In this sense metaphysics, political economy, geology, botany, physiology, and several other branches of human knowledge and inquiry, are *inexact* sciences.

† Sir George Lewis, in his chapter 'On Predictions in Politics,' has put this **with great clearness.** 'The anticipations of science are general, and merely

of history, which is by its very terms only an explanation of the past, be challenged to read the future with absolute prescience. If indeed, from their comparatively short and partial study of human nature and experience, statesmen and legislators can to a certain extent foretel events, can provide for remote generations, and foresee the operation of human laws and passions, it might well be hoped from philosophy, acting systematically and by the joint and successive labours of many men of genius, undisturbed by personal and transient interests, to look still farther into distant time; but that extraordinary visitations of various kinds—earthquakes, famines, pestilences, wars, revolutions, accidents so called*—are in the present state of human knowledge beyond scientific prevision, seems to be a fact quite consistent with the possibility of tracing a regular sequence in the past career of nations, of measuring the character of mankind from a great variety of instances, and of judging how they will be affected and act under circumstances analogous to those of which we have a full account. There may be a science of geology, though it does not presume to assert that no changes in the earth's surface will ever take place from causes below its depths and above its sphere; and some predictions, founded on the experienced stability of nature, may notwithstanding be drawn from it. No astronomer can absolutely insure to the world the continuance of its present climate and seasons, or even the light of the sun, for the next thousand years; yet

affirm that in a hypothetical and abstract state of things, a certain cause will produce a certain effect. . . . In comparing the powers of physical and political science, we must bear in mind that no science can properly be said to predict anything. The general affirmations of a science apply indeed equally to the future and to the past; but this is true of political as well as physical science, so far as human nature, the subject matter of politics, is unchangeable. . . . In strictness of speech, scientific astronomy merely determines and describes the relations of the heavenly bodies, and the laws of their real and apparent motions, and predicts nothing. By the aid of these laws and general formulæ the practical astronomer and almanac maker calculate the future events of astronomy, and refer them to their computed terms. But astronomical theory itself makes no predictions. . . Political history, though it does not itself predict the future, furnishes the materials out of which political predictions are constructed.'—On the Method of Observation and Reasoning in Politics, vol. ii., pp. 329, 332, 338, 350, &c.

* Hume. Essay xiv.

astronomy is a science upon which we may build many calculations with the best possible human security.

In like manner, and with the same qualified certainty, we may, from the past conduct of our race, foretel that the distance in time between all the capitals of Europe **will** be shortened **before** the termination of this century, and that so long as men **are men,** their approximation and intercourse with each other will have some results of a well-known character.

But the proper business of historical philosophy is the interpretation of the **past career,** not the anticipation of the future progress, of our species; and **in this, its** proper business, it provides ample and worthy occupation for the most capacious scientific genius. Already, for **example, we can trace a** regular sequence **on** the one hand in the **events which** led to the fall of **the** Roman Empire; and on the other, in those which have built **up the** Empire of Great Britain ; **but it remains for future** researches **to** explain the mystery of race, and account for the different fortunes and **mental constitution of** the Celtic and Teutonic offspring of **a** common ancestry. **Of this** and similar discoveries the student of history should not despair ; nor should he forget that wherever he is met by inexplicable difficulties, which for the present **he** must accept as ultimate facts, he is still in the true path **of** science, whose mission it is to separate the discoverable from the undiscovered, and the operations of the known from those of **the unknown laws** of nature. Thus, **for** example, it is possible—and **this is the** main proposition **on which** the present argument turns—that **the** appearance, **employment,** and influence of men of extraordinary genius may **be** subject to ascertainable social **conditions,** although the secret **of their** birth may be for ever undiscovered, and although **mankind may never acquire** the art **which** the bees possess, of producing **on emergency an** individual **of** their species gifted with inherent sovereign qualities.

If, then, it be suggested that human science can give no solution of the career of prodigies of human genius, can trace no sequence between their epochs, we are brought to a question of fact. We may undoubtedly conceive the apparition of human beings superhuman in **their natural** powers, **and** exercising, uncontrolled by their fellows, a permanent influence upon the fortunes of the race. But the proper inquiry for science is, not what may be conceived, but what has really taken place. **Have** men of extraordinary power, as a matter of fact, determined their own career, and the contemporary and subsequent condition of the world? Or can it be shown, on the contrary, that antecedent and surrounding circumstances have uniformly determined the quality of genius which has made itself known and felt, and the direction which it has taken; and that its permanent effects fall **likewise** within the cognizance of science?

Take, for example, Julius Cæsar. Is he an unaccountable phenomenon? Did his will or genius overthrow the Commonwealth and introduce autocracy? So Brutus thought when he endeavoured to restore the Republic by the death of the usurper. But modern philosophy would convince us that Cæsar could no more have destroyed the Republic, than Cato and Cicero could save it, or Brutus and Cassius restore it; and that if Cæsar owed his abilities to nature, we must ascribe the use he made of them, and his supremacy at Rome, to its previous history, and the times he lived in. The Republic was destroyed already before Cæsar had **attained** to manhood; and we can trace a clear connexion between the character and situation of the founders of the city, the military career of their descendants, the decline of industry and patriotism in a later age, the rise of individuals such as Marius, Sylla, Catiline, and Cæsar, and of such as Cato, the representative of an ancient cause.

When the conquests of the Romans had spread beyond Italy, and **no** formidable rival kept the safety of the Commonwealth in mind; **when the** soldiers had been but too naturally corrupted by debauchery in Asia, and the citizens by idleness and public maintenance at home, or by **the bribes of** wealthy candidates for office; when, too, the laws and administration depended on the votes of men who were Roman citizens only in name, 'the public assemblies became so many conspiracies against the State; the soldiers were no longer the soldiers of the Commonwealth, but of Sylla, of Marius, of Pompey, and of Cæsar; and as the Republic was fated to destruction, **the only** material question was who should have the credit of overthrowing it.'* Order could only be restored by some one who could **make** himself master of all **the** factions; a general wish for such an arbiter **was generated**; and, as Hume expresses it, the greatest happiness the Romans could look for was the despotic power of the **Cæsars.†**

At the end of the second Punic war, when the dictatorate ceased for a hundred and twenty years, a Cæsar could no more have made himself the sovereign of Rome than could a Scipio; no more than the Duke of Wellington could have made himself the monarch of Great Britain after the victory **of Waterloo**. But revolution, faction, and anarchy ever create, first their leaders and then their conquerors; **and the passions**, emergencies, and opportunities of disorderly and desperate times **place** a ladder to bad eminence under the feet of men like Cæsar, Cromwell, and Napoleon, who, in a tranquil and patriotic State, would have **been** good and peaceable citizens. Had O'Connell been born **the** year he died, he might have proved a blessing to Ireland, and an object of admiration and esteem in England. England has at this hour her guiltless Cromwells as well as her Wellesleys and Nelsons. A nation cannot be permanently great which has not at all times in reserve a stock of genius, energy, and resolution; which has not many children always ready for any emergency and every opportunity. Happy is the nation which, like England, has its quiver full of them. That England always has this vital element of greatness, every crisis **in her** history proves — the Great Rebellion, the war with **France**, the Indian mutiny; and in civil life, the literature, philosophy, commerce and invention of the last three hundred **years, have proved it.**

Mankind in the mass want leaders always, and they may count on such as they will follow. They want them in the ship, the regiment, the factory, the shop, at school, in Parliament, in courts of justice, in science and opinion; and they have them. It is the wants, the feelings, the temper, and the condition of

---

* Montesquieu. Declension of the Roman Empire. Translation. Chapter 9-11.

† Essay iii.

the crowd that determine the calling, the station, and the following of the individual. England evokes her Pitts, Wellingtons, and Peels; and France her two Napoleons. And the number of great men, good and bad, whom the world has known and loved or hated, is as nothing compared with those of equal or greater genius for whom it has found no place above obscurity.

Vasquez de Gama and Columbus changed the paths of commerce and its chief seats in Europe.* But their discoveries were inevitable and necessary, if the actual discoverers were not. It was an age of maritime adventure. For eighty years before De Gama's voyage, the Portuguese had laboured to find a road to the East Indies by the Southern Ocean; and Bartholomew de Diaz had already turned the Cape. Columbus was bound on the same popular errand by another road. He thought to find a Western passage to the Indies, relying on ancient authorities, rumours, and reasoning, which must have stimulated other minds. A long series of naval enterprises—from that of Sebastian Cabot, who reached the continent of North America a year before Columbus entered the Gulf of Paria, to that of Magellan, who in the next generation sailed through the strait which bears his name—afford conclusive proof that the discovery of America was the inevitable result of its actual existence at one side of the Atlantic, and of the spirit which at the other side animated Europe towards the close of the fifteenth century.

But the Reformation,—was not it the work of a single man? On the contrary, the Reformation must have happened in England, in Bohemia, and in Switzerland, had Luther never been born; and it is hard to see how it could happen in them without easily finding a champion in Saxony, where so many things conspired to produce and favour it, from the Elector to the state of the Empire, and from Tetzel, the vender of indulgences, to the state of the Papacy. The rolls of the English Parliament, the popular ballads, the writings of Wicliffe and Chaucer, must convince every careful student that from the death of Edward III., the temporal power and establishment of the Church in this

---

* 'The ports of the Mediterranean were deserted as soon as those on the western coast of Europe were opened to fleets from both the Indies.'—Heeren's Historical Researches. General Introduction.

island were doomed, so soon as any circumstance should separate the Crown from its alliance; and that **its spiritual** power was doomed so soon as the cessation of war should leave the nation free to accomplish a great revolution, to avail itself of the new lights of the age, to vent the moral indignation accumulating for three hundred years, and to bring to bear upon the problems of the next world the same zeal and inquiry which it showed in navigation respecting the distant realities of this world. Luther was but a single crater of **a** volcano which must have burst through a hundred **smaller orifices,** had not one chief vent been provided **for its fury.**

A great reformer **is** the best interpreter of his age and crisis. He owes his power chiefly **to the fact that he better** understands than other men its natural **drift, or is more deeply** and enthusiastically moved by the cause of the people he represents. **Often** he but foresees what he appears to the world **to** accomplish, confident of and proving the existence of law **and** sequence in the affairs of men. And often when the battle is over, and the conqueror is no more, the position of his followers is not that to which he led them, but that which **the more** lasting forces of society decide. The authority of Luther could not fix the creed **of** Protestantism. Napoleon I. carried the boundaries of France to the Elbe, but they are now what they would have been had no Corsican adventurer ever found his way to Paris. And not the **will** of Napoleon III., but the will of France upon the one hand, **and** of the rest of Europe on the **other,** and the balance of European power, will determine, **whether** the French flag shall float over Antwerp, Coblentz, **Genoa, and** Alexandria at the end of the present century.

Nor is it in war, politics, commerce, and religion only, that we may trace the influence of paramount laws of human progress upon the appearance, bent, and consequence of genius, and even discern a regular sequence in the applications of the human intellect to the satisfaction of human wants, in the order of their urgency and importance. In its early life a nation can accomplish but few things at a time, and must do those things first for which there is the greatest need. It has to secure itself **against its enemies, to** form a polity, establish order, fix the rights of property, settle its code of morals and religious worship, to build, to till its fields, and manufacture, as well as a rude people can, before it can have a literature or a literary tongue. The forests of Canada must be cleared before they can be cultivated, or towns be built upon their ashes; and the woodman, the farmer, and the builder, the butcher, and the grocer, must have houses and food before the author or the artist.

'It is' (says Hallam), 'the most striking circumstance in the literary annals of the dark ages, that they seem still more deficient in native than in acquired ability. It would be a strange hypothesis that no man endowed with superior gifts of nature lived in so many ages. Of military and civil prudence, indeed, we are now speaking. But though no man appeared of genius sufficient to burst the fetters imposed by ignorance and bad taste, some there must have been who in a happier condition of literature would have been its legitimate pride. We perceive, therefore, in the deficiencies of these virtues, the effect which an oblivion of good models, and the practice of a false standard of merit, may produce in repressing the natural vigour of the mind.'*

But, in truth, the cause of these deficiencies lay much deeper. 'The condition of literature' was the result of the condition of society. How could there be a burst of literary genius when the vernacular language was unfit for literary use, when the masses were engrossed in war or **agriculture,** when 'military and civil prudence' absorbed the minds of the chief laity; and the only educated portion of society—the clergy—lived in cloisters, wrote in Latin, were subject to rapine, had a daily round of sacerdotal and ministerial offices, were governed by theology in their studies, and were not only the priests, but the schoolmasters, the physicians, and the lawyers of mankind?

The law especially demanded all the intellectual energies of our ancestors which theology could spare; and Glanville, Bracton, Fleta, were of necessity much earlier products of the English mind than Gower and Chaucer, because protection **and** justice seem more necessary to men than refined amusement,

---

* History of Literature, **chapter i. part I.**

and because ruder minds can supply the former than the latter. This phenomenon has exhibited itself in every country which has run a historical career. The Romans applied to Greece for help in law some centuries before they sought its art and literature,* and in America there were numerous native lawyers before there was one native author deserving of the name.† Hence we need to be at no loss to understand the futile complaint of Innocent IV., in 1254, 'to all the prelates of France, England, Scotland, Wales, Spain, and Hungary, that his ears had been stunned with reports that great multitudes of the clergy, neglecting theology, crowded to hear lectures on secular laws; and that bishops advanced none but such as were either advocates or professors of law.' Roger Bacon, in the same age, lamented that natural science had no followers, while those of civil law were numberless; and his own exception confirms the rule that the occupations and success of genius are determined not by, but for it, through conditions not beyond detection. Why did he strive in vain to found a school of physical inquiry? Why were the mental powers of Europe given for centuries either to forensic art, or to endless controversy respecting the nature of abstractions? Why did the second Bacon withhold his inductive power in a flattering Court, and on the eve of a revolution, from political speculation? What accounts for the late appearance of such philosophers as Newton, Davy, Faraday, Adam Smith, and John Stuart Mill? The age must be ripe for the man. Roger Bacon's instance, a marvellous anomaly in history, proves the incapacity of the most powerful and fertile genius to lead the energies of a people into a channel for which they are unfitted by previous education, by hereditary and prevailing taste, by more urgent wants, fanciful or real, by personal

* 'To the close of the Republic the law was the sole field for all ability, except the special talent of a capacity for generalship.'—Cambridge Essays, 1856, p. 27; where the fact is eloquently explained by Mr. Sumner Maine. And see his Ancient Law, p. 361.

† In 1775, Burke said, in his speech on conciliation with America,—'In no country in the world, perhaps, is the law so general a study. The profession is numerous and powerful, and in most provinces it takes the lead. All who read endeavour to obtain some smattering in that science. I have been told by an eminent bookseller that in no branch of his business, after tracts of popular devotion, were so many books as those on the law exported to the plantations.'

interests, and by the general structure of society. On a threadbare and unprofitable argument the schoolmen of his epoch lavished an amount of intellectual **activity** and power which at **a** later period would have sufficed to rear a true and fruitful philosophy of nature. Necessity seems surely not too strong a **term to** designate the stress of all the forces which sway the movements of the human faculties. The dominant ideas and associations of the time and place, the help or hindrance which individual genius meets from other minds, the appliances **at** hand, the things already done, the reward **and countenance,** or the condemnation **or** organized resistance of the **world around, are** inevitable guides or masters. There could be no **Demosthenes** or Socrates without an Athens ; no Cicero without **a Roman** forum, a senate, and the aid of Greek philosophy. **There could** be no Shakespeare in a rude and illiterate, a priest-ridden **or a** puritanical age, **nor among** a fierce democracy or a servile populace, nor in a nation without a history and a heart, **nor** yet in one without some mixture of Paganism with Christianity. There could have been no Newton before Kepler, Galileo, and the telescope ; no Adam Smith until trade, wealth, and civil liberty had reached a high development; no Mill before Adam Smith and Francis Bacon. Until the eighteenth century geology had neither eyes nor tongue; **in the fourteenth, Davy,** Herschel, and Faraday would have been alchemists, astrologers, **sorcerers,** or nothing; and before the twelfth a Walter Scott **or** Bulwer **Lytton** must have embellished lives of saints with marvellous fiction to achieve a literary reputation. In 1849, Garibaldi fought **in** vain ; three years ago he would have died obscure ; **and** without the Italy, **France,** and England of his time, his **power** would be less at this hour than that of any priest in Naples. What he might have been as the child of **nature, we** cannot guess; as the child of history, he is what he **is. All** the memories of his country, **all** the aspirations of his age for national and human freedom, have inspired his heroic soul.

These are but a few faint indications of the nature of the proofs that might **be collected** in a longer argument. They tend, **it** is hoped, to show that although the purposes and aims of **society** have become more numerous and its machinery more complex, yet individual energy does not disturb the order of history, and that the science contended for remains as possible when it has to account for great numbers of men, each with a definite function and a distinct character, as when the phenomena to which it is applied consist merely of a vast level crowd upon the one hand, and a few tyrants or protectors on the other. The time may come when an exhaustive analysis of the memorials of our race shall enable us to explain as easily the causes which now elicit the most varied genius from the multitude in Western Europe, as those which once stifled it in England, and still stifle it in China, Turkey, and Russia.

But this view of history, as disclosing law and sequence throughout the progress of mankind, proceeds on a conception of the causes of the movement differing widely from the intellectual theory of a learned writer.* What the acquisitions of the human intellect, what the progress of knowledge would have been, without human interests and wants, without the passions, impulses, and hopes which actuate mankind, it is impossible even to surmise. We can frame no idea what motives would stimulate the labour and direct the inquiries of purely intellectual beings. In truth, civilization comes of a most promiscuous origin; and we can discover in the career of nations the co-operation towards a common end of the most heterogeneous forces. To make men noble and enlightened citizens of an opulent and happy commonwealth, is the work of civilization viewed as a result. But as a process what has it been? How has it been, in fact, accomplished? By men uncivilized at first; by instinct and necessity, more often than by reason or forethought; by the conflict and eventual reconciliation of many passions and ideas; by courage, enterprise, and patient industry; by experience, suffering, a thousand failures, and by exhausting all the paths of error; by chivalry and commerce, war and peace, by the dispersion and aggregation of mankind, and the mixture of hostile races; by the overthrow of ancient empires, and the occupation of their seats, sometimes by fresh and vigo-

---

* 'The advance of civilization solely depends on the acquisitions of the human intellect, and on the extent to which those acquisitions are diffused.'—Buckle's History of Civilization, vol. i. p. 307.

rous barbarians, sometimes by the soldiers of a highly cultivated people ; by crimes and virtues, sordid cares and generous aims ; by homely affections and by public spirit ; by faith and doubt ; by learning and material wealth ; by the useful and the sublime and beautiful ; by soaring genius and by common sense. Such and so various have been the human agencies which have contributed to the improvement of the human world. Beneath the seeming chaos of its current history, philosophy detects already some evidence of general order.

IV.

UTILITARIANISM AND THE SUMMUM BONUM.

(Macmillan's Magazine, June 1863.)

THE two questions—what is right? and, what are the motives to do right?—or, what is the foundation of the moral sentiments? and, what rule should regulate their dictates?—or, again, what is the summum bonum? and what leads men to pursue it?—are now generally opposed as philosophically distinct. They are not so, indeed, according to the theory of an innate sense of right and wrong which assumes that every man's conscience informs him of his duty. But it is of more importance to observe that neither can the two questions properly be opposed according to the theory of moral progress suggested by the study of history upon the plan illustrated in Mr. Maine's Ancient Law. The conclusion to which that historical theory would seem to lead—and it is one to which other considerations also tend—is, that no complete and final philosophy of life and human aims has been constructed; that the world abounds in insoluble problems, and man's ideal of virtue is both historical and progressive; and that the circumstance at which Mr Mill has expressed a mournful surprise—namely, that 'neither thinkers nor mankind at large seem nearer to being unanimous on the subject of the summum bonum than when Socrates asserted the theory of utilitarianism against the popular morality,'* is what might have been expected, and could not have been otherwise, from the nature of the subject. Another conclusion to which the considerations referred to lend at least a probability is, that happiness is not the sole nor even the chief

---

* Utilitarianism, page 1

constituent of the summum bonum, as the utilitarian doctrine asserts. Moral progress may be taken to mean an improvement either in men's knowledge and ideas of duty, or in their dispositions and practice. Taken in either sense, it has been often denied. The reasons given by Sir James Mackintosh for denying it in the former sense, and for asserting that morality, in fact, admits of no discoveries, deserve attention. 'More than 3,000 years have elapsed since the composition of the Pentateuch; and let any man, if he is able, tell me in what important respects the rule of life has varied since that distant period. Let the books of false religions be opened, and it will be found that their moral system is, in all its grand features, the same. Such as the rule was at the first dawn of history, such it continues till the present day. Ages roll over mankind; mighty nations pass like a shadow; virtue alone remains the same, immortal and unchangeable. The reasons of this fact it is not difficult to discover. It will be very plain, on the least consideration, that mankind must so completely have formed their rule of life in the most early times that no subsequent improvements could change it. This is the distinction between morality and all other sciences. The facts which lead to the formation of moral rules are as accessible, and must be as obvious to the simplest barbarian as to the most enlightened philosopher. The motive which leads him to consider them is the most powerful that can be imagined. It is the care of his own existence. The case of the physical and speculative sciences is directly opposite. There the facts are remote, and the motive that induces us to explore them is comparatively weak. It is only curiosity or, at most, a desire to multiply the conveniences and ornaments of life. From the endless variety of the facts with which these sciences are concerned, it is impossible to prescribe any bounds to their future improvement. It is otherwise with morals. They have hitherto been stationary, and, in my opinion, are likely to remain so.'* A later reasoner has not only acquiesced in this view of the stationary character of speculative morality, but has denied that any improvement has taken place upon the

---

* Life of Mackintosh.

whole in the disposition or practical virtue of mankind, and has attempted to construct a philosophy of civilization by reference to the merely intellectual progress of the race. It is particularly remarkable that this writer should have argued forcibly that mental philosophy can be successfully studied only by historical methods, and yet should have overlooked the application of historical investigation to moral philosophy, and the contradiction which it gives to the doctrine of the unchangeable nature of human morals, either speculative or practical. The absence in the records of very ancient society of anything resembling our standard of right and wrong, and the entirely different direction given to the sentiments of approbation and disapprobation from what we deem just and reasonable, can hardly fail to strike any reader of Homer. An individual, in heroic Greece, was good or bad in reference not to his personal character and conduct, but to his birth and station in society. The chief was estimable because, however cruel, licentious, and treacherous, he possessed the esteemed qualities of rank and power; the common man was base, vile, and bad because the class to which he belonged was despised.* To this day the moral ideas of barbarous communities have the same peculiar aspect which Mr. Maine discovers in the vestiges of primitive society. There is hardly a conception of individual responsibility, merit, or demerit. 'The moral elevation and abasement of the individual appears to be confounded with or postponed to the merits and offences of the group to which the individual belongs.'† The offence of a Red Indian is the offence of his

---

* 'The general epithets of good, just, &c., signify (in legendary Greece) the man of birth, wealth, influence, and daring, whatever may be the turn of his moral sentiments, while the opposite epithet bad designates the poor, lowly and weak.' . . . 'The reference of these words ἀγαθός, ἐσθλός, κακός, to power and not to worth, is their primitive import in the Greek language descending from the Iliad downwards. The ethical meaning of the words hardly appears until the discussions raised by Socrates.' . . . 'Throughout the long stream of legendary narrative to which the Greeks looked back as their past history, the larger social virtues hardly ever come into play. There is no sense of obligation there between man and man as such, and very little between each man and the entire community of which he is a member; such sentiments are neither operative in real life, nor present to the imagination of the poet.'— Grote's History of Greece.

† Maine's Ancient Law, p. 127.

whole tribe, and to be visited upon the whole tribe. And, so far from the moral sentiments of mankind having been always and everywhere alike, there are living languages which lack names for the feelings essential to the rudiments even of a low morality. Affection, benevolence, gratitude, justice, and honour, are terms without equivalents in the speech of some savage societies, because they have no existence in their minds. The Englishman is so early taught that he should love his neighbour, that he is ready to think the knowledge of that duty comes to him by intuition. The African savage thinks that he, too, has intuitive knowledge—but it is of the art of rearing cattle and of making rain; and he cannot believe that God meant him to love any one but himself.* Yet the nations of Africa can recognise the duty of hospitality; and among the Makololo, says Dr. Livingstone, so generally is it admitted, that 'one of the most cogent arguments for polygamy is, that a respectable man, with only one wife, could not entertain visitors as he ought.' The facts upon which the modern morality of Europe is based are not, in truth, as Sir James Mackintosh argued, before the eyes of the barbarian; nor, if they were, would they attract his observation. The structure of the society in which he lives is based upon radically different rules from those by which a civilized society is kept together, and his ideas are generated almost exclusively by his appetites, antipathies, and ceremonial customs. If he has treacherously murdered many men of another tribe in this world, the Fijian thinks he will be happy in the next world, for that is his idea of virtue. His wife or daughter will, he believes, be fearfully punished hereafter, if she has not been properly tattooed in this life, for that is his estimate of wickedness and sin.*' The idea of consummate virtue entertained by

* 'God told us differently. He made black men first, and did not love us as he did the white men. He made you beautiful, and gave you many things about which we know nothing. He gave us nothing except the assegai, and cattle, and rainmaking, and He did not give us hearts like yours. We never love one another. God has given us one little thing about which you know nothing. He has given us the knowledge of certain medicines by which we can make rain. We do not despise those things which you possess, though we are ignorant of them. You ought not to despise our little knowledge, though you are ignorant of it.'—Livingstone's South Africa.

our own ancestors is described in the famous death-song of Lodbrog, the Scandinavian chief. Shut up in a dungeon filled with venomous serpents, he sings, as a viper tears his breast— 'From my youth I have shed blood, and desired an end like this. The goddesses sent by Odin to meet me call to me, and invite me. I go, seated among the foremost, to drink ale with the gods. The hours of my life are passing away. I shall die laughing.' How could the human mind, while carnage was the highest enjoyment and the noblest occupation, conceive or comprehend the moral creed of our time? The laws of this country show how slow the descendants of the fierce Northmen were to acquire the mild temper and humane spirit which characterize Englishmen now: and they fully refute the position of the historical writer referred to before, that although there may be an ebb and flow in the good and bad feelings and habits of mind of successive generations, the tide of good never gains ground in the end. Daines Barrington, commenting on our ancient statutes, observes, that they prove that the people of England were formerly more vindictive and irritable than they are now, and asks whether it can be supposed that, in the thirteenth century, any one would have thought of subscribing for the relief of the inhabitants of Lisbon after an earthquake, or to clothe the French prisoners? There is scarcely, again, a page of the history or literature of the seventeenth century, says Lord Macaulay, which does not prove that our ancestors were less humane than their posterity. The code of honour, in the eighteenth century, we may add, commanded a gentleman to commit murder; and drunkenness was then little short of a duty to male society.

It has been urged, however, as a decisive proof of the stationary character of moral principles, that 'the only two principles which moralists have ever been able to teach respecting war, are that defensive wars are just, and that offensive wars are unjust.'* But it is sufficiently obvious that the words defensive and offensive have no fixed and definite meaning, and may mean one thing in one age, and another thing in another.

* Buckle's History of Civilization.

The same verbal proposition does not always carry the same import. The law of Moses commanded the Israelite to love his neighbour as himself; but, fifteen hundred years after, the Jew asked 'who is my neighbour?' and learnt for the first time the length and breadth of the duty of humanity. By the justice of defensive wars, might be understood, wars like the Crusades, for the defence of the Christian faith; or, wars for the defence of one's country; or, again, wars for the defence of humanity, human liberty, and civilization. The fundamental doctrine of the present code of nations—that of the right of independence— as on the one hand, it had a purely technical origin, so, on the other, there is nothing in it of immutable expediency or justice. Men have talked, indeed, and still talk vaguely of the law of nature and nations; but so they have talked and talk of the natural rights of individuals to life, liberty, and property, although there has never been any fixed or general rule respecting the just limitations of human liberty, or the nature and degree of the sacrifices which society may, in the last resort, exact from its members. May a man be compelled to fight against his conscience, for his country? if so, where is the recognition of his right to life and liberty? if not so, where is the immutable line to be drawn between the domain of individual independence, and that of public authority? If there were a natural right to private property, how are taxes, poor-laws, and railway acts to be justified, or the communism of the first Christians? By analogy, it follows that nothing but the good of mankind at large, according to the estimation of the time, entitles the Government of any single nation to exclusive dominion within its territory. And it is surely conceivable that convictions of public policy and duty, different from those now entertained, and deeper sympathies between mankind, may lead civilized states to make territorial sovereignty conditional upon not making the territory over which it extends the scene of outrages sickening even to read of. As humane sentiments gain ground, as international jealousies and antipathies wear out, as the interests of countries are perceptibly reconciled, may we not reasonably suppose that a clearer and better code of international morality will commend itself to the public conscience of the world, than any of which even wise men dream at present? **Or is there any** probability that the conceptions of the nineteenth century respecting individual duty have reached perfection; that no new duties, now unthought of, will hereafter be recognised; and that no claims of man upon man, as of nation upon nation, other than those at present allowed, will be hereafter entertained?

But, if progress in both public and private morals can be proved in the past and shown to be probable in the future, can the Utilitarian formula of general happiness be accepted as the final measure of **right** and wrong, and **the** sole guide of human conduct? **If Mr. Mill has failed to** establish this, there is antecedent reason to believe **that the theory** is essentially defective, and that, if it **could have been** proved, it would have **been** proved by the reasoning of so powerful and persuasive an **advocate.** The common objections to **the** doctrine must, in fairness, be admitted **to be** weak. **For** example: when M. Victor Cousin says that **the** ideas of justice **and** expediency—if they often go together—are sometimes opposed, he instances the answer of Aristides to the proposal of Themistocles, **to burn the** ships of the allies in the port of Athens to secure supremacy to the Athenian State. 'The project would be expedient,' said Aristides; 'but it is unjust.' The Utilitarian denies that it would have been expedient, even **for** the interests of **the** Athenians themselves, to establish **a** precedent for treachery toward confiding neighbours and friends, and to make the citizen of **Athens,** wheresoever he went, **the** object of suspicion, retaliation, **and** cunning and cruel surprises. Or, again, when it is argued **that a** piece of furniture, or any other inanimate object, may be **useful,** yet that no one ascribes **to** it moral rectitude or virtue, and that it follows, that intention and not utility is the criterion of morality, **the** Utilitarian fairly replies that things without feeling are not **fit objects,** however useful, for gratitude or indignation, for reward or punishment, because they cannot feel either, and neither is therefore expedient; because such things tend to do harm as well **as** good, to hurt or inconvenience as well as to do service; and because no praise or censure bestowed upon senseless matter tends to make the class to which it belongs contribute to the happiness of life. In the Utilitarian estimate intention is of great importance, because of its consequences or tendencies. The Utilitarian blames a small act of malignity, not in proportion only to the actual pain it causes, but to the general mischiefs to which malignity tends. He does not, on the other hand, blame a person who sets fire to a house by reading in bed, as he does an incendiary; because the general tendency of midnight study is wholly different from that of vindictiveness and treachery; and because, again, the reader in bed is not so likely to burn the house by accident as the person who tries to do so of malice intent. Yet the former is blamed according to the doctrine of utility, and blamed just in proportion to the probability that his negligence will do harm: if he reads by a perfectly safe light, he is not blamed at all. Or take a higher example. 'At the cavalry combat at El Bodon, a French officer raised his sword to strike Sir Felton Harvey, of the 14th Light Dragoons; but, perceiving that his antagonist had only one arm, he stopped, brought down his sword before Sir Felton in the usual salute, and rode on.'* Was this proceeding right or wrong? The first duty of a citizen is to his country, and of an officer to his army. War, too, is not a duel, and the combatants do not measure their swords. Sir Felton Harvey had not lost his head, and the head of an officer is more dangerous to an enemy in battle than his arm. The Frenchman, therefore, ought, it seems, to have cut him down. Yet the Utilitarian would admit that the magnanimous intention alters the character of the act, because it is of supreme importance to human happiness that a spirit should exist among the strong to spare the weak, and that even enemies should show mercy and courtesy to each other. Take yet another case. It has been argued that the negroes in America are happier as slaves than as free labourers, and, therefore, upon Utilitarian principles, slavery is not a crime. But—apart from the fact that a view of slavery which looks only at the slave at play instead of at work (that is, in his moments of liberty), so far as it goes, supplies evidence only in favour of liberty—a just Utilitarian estimate of slavery includes not only the consequences of oppression and debasement

* Maurel's Life of Wellington.

to the slave, but also the consequences to his master of the possession of tyrannical power and ill-gotten gain, and the consequences to the world at large of an empire being founded on the principle that the strong may lawfully trample on the weak. Finally, the theory of Utility, as Mr. Mill describes it, is as free from the vulgar reproach of materialism as it is from that of selfishness; for it not only enjoins on every man to seek the happiness of all mankind, and of himself, only as one of their number, but it insists that the highest pleasures are not those of the body, but those of the intellect and of the best affections of the heart, and that it is these which the individual should chiefly pursue, both for others and for himself. These doctrines are, however, urged upon grounds, and they have applications, which seem to point to the conclusion, that happiness is not the sole end of human conduct, ethically regarded, and that 'the happiness principle' is not 'a comprehensive formula, including all things which are in themselves good.'

To prove that happiness is the summum bonum at which virtue aims, Mr. Mill concedes the necessity of showing that the greatest human happiness results from the employment of the highest faculties of humanity; but of this he gives no other proof than the following: 'Of two pleasures, if there be one to which all, or almost all, who have experience of both give a decided preference, irrespective of any feeling of moral obligation to prefer it, that is the more desirable pleasure. Now, it is an unquestionable fact that those who are equally acquainted with and equally capable of appreciating and enjoying both, do give a most marked preference to the manner of existence which employs their highest faculties. Few human beings would consent to be changed into any of the lower animals for the fullest allowance of a beast's pleasures; no intelligent human being would consent to be a fool; no instructed person would be an ignoramus; no person of feeling or conscience would be selfish or base, even though they should be persuaded that the fool, or dunce, or the rascal is better satisfied with his lot than they are with theirs. It is better to be a human being dissatisfied than a pig satisfied; bettter to be Socrates dissatisfied than a fool satisfied. And, if the fool and the pig are of a different opinion, it is because they only know their own side of the question. The other party to the comparison knows both sides. From this verdict of the only competent judges I apprehend there can be no appeal. On a question, which is the best worth having of two pleasures? or which of two modes of existence is the most grateful to the feelings, apart from its moral attributes and its consequences? the judgment of those who are qualified by knowledge of both, or, if they differ, that of the majority among them, must be admitted to be final.'*

It might be asked, where is the **testimony to be** found of all those who are competent to judge? and, if they differ, why should their opinions be counted rather than **weighed**? Or what proof **have** we that those who have volunteered evidence were competent to testify not only for themselves but **for others?** The heart knoweth its own bitterness, and a **stranger** intermeddleth not with its joys. The philosopher **has** not the experiences of the fool, nor can the fool have the experiences of the philosopher. The unselfish and spiritually minded man may find his greatest happiness in pursuits from which less generous and lofty minds could derive nothing but weariness. Even Alcibiades would have found the life which Socrates preferred —if Socrates indeed preferred it for the sake of happiness alone —an intolerable **burden ; yet Alcibiades had** great genius, and most men **have** none. **There is an** illusive semblance **of** simplicity in the Utilitarian formula. **The** tendency **to** produce happiness seems **to** be an easy test ; **but it** assumes **an** unreal concord about the constituents of **happiness and an** unreal homogeneity of human minds in point of sensibility **to** different pains and **pleasures.** The things that make life a pleasure or a pain **are not the same for the** Hindoo, the Englishman, the Chinaman, **the Arab, the Italian,** the Red Indian, the Frenchman, and the Turk, nor yet for all Englishmen, or all Frenchmen. There **is a** uniformity of character in a tribe of savages, as there is in a flock of sheep or a pack of wolves; but in proportion as society has advanced beyond the simplicity of barbarism, individuality is developed, and diversities of tastes and temperaments baffle **the** Utilitarian **measure.** Nor is it possible **to** weigh

* Utilitarianism, p. 14.

bodily and mental pleasures and **pains one** against the other; no single man can pronounce with certainty about their relative intensity even for himself, far less for all his fellows. And, if it is better to be a sad philosopher than a merry fool, better to be a dissatisfied man than a satisfied pig, it must be so because there is really something better and more to be desired **by the** elevated soul than happiness, and something worse and more to **be** shunned than suffering **or** grief. If the unhappy sage will not change places with the happy brute or idiot, it must **be** either because he does **not, as** Mr. Mill supposes, 'know **both** sides of the question,' or else because **he** knows or believes that happiness is not the summum bonum. Few men, perhaps, would change their lot with any other earthly being. **Partly, this** arises from a fallacy of the imagination; they carry in thought **all their** present hopes and aspirations into a new state of being, **in which those** hopes and aspirations would be baffled, but the metamorphosis excludes them **altogether; partly, it** arises **from** 'the absurd presumption in **their own** good fortune,' which, according to Adam Smith, is common to **the greater** part of men. But, if the choice of his own sad lot in preference to **the** happier lot of the beast is made by the philosopher on rational principles, it must **be** because he will not descend in the scale of being, although the descent would be unconsciously made, and he would pass at once **from a** painful **into a** pleasurable existence. It must be, in short, because the wise and virtuous man does not, nor does Mr. Mill, accept in practice the theory **of** the summum bonum on which the Utilitarian morality is built —**namely,** that pleasure and freedom from pain are the only **things desired** or desirable as ultimate ends. For, if the wise and good man thinks there are things better for himself than happiness, and that pleasure is **not his** highest and most worthy aim in life, must he not think so for his fellow-men also? 'In an improving state of the human mind,' Mr. Mill justly observes, 'the influences **are constantly** on the increase which tend to generate in each individual a feeling of unity with all the rest; which, if perfect, would make him never think of or desire any beneficial condition for himself in the benefits of which they are **not included.' And surely** it follows that, as men become wiser and better, the highest benefits they will seek **to confer upon** others will be those which they desire for themselves—namely, those modes of life which ennoble and exalt humanity, and which discipline and strengthen the highest faculties, at whatever cost of toil and suffering. It is no doubt impertinent bigotry 'to inveigh against the doctrine of Utility as a godless doctrine.' Nevertheless **there** seems no warrant for 'the belief that God desires above all things the happiness of his creatures, and that this was his purpose in their creation.'* So far as we may presume the purpose of creation from **all that** science can discover **or** suggest, it would rather seem that the **development, improvement, and elevation of** the faculties **of** terrestrial beings is **the** plan apparent on the face of nature. It is not **indeed easy to see how** in the happiest conceivable world there **could be** any schooling or developing of some of the noblest faculties, or any practice of some of the noblest virtues. Heroism, self-sacrifice, **and** compassion, imply the existence of pain and suffering. And **the** growth of intelligence brings with it cares, anxieties, and sorrows, which never disturb the happiness **of the** thoughtless animals.

> **The lamb thy riot** dooms to bleed to-day,
> **Had he thy reason,** would he skip and play?

Every step in the progress of civilization **has by no means been attended by an increase of human happiness; yet the** step was a thing **desirable in** itself, irrespective **of ultimate ends.** The 'merry England,' of which it pleases the laudator temporis acti to speak, is, **no doubt, in a** great measure, **an historical** fallacy; yet **an England of** Miltons and Hampdens, if **ever so grave** and sad, **were better than** an England of Falstaffs, if ever **so merry on cakes and ale. And if** the good **man would not choose** the lower and more animal life, however pleasant, either **for** himself or for mankind, **does it not seem that the summum** bonum and the aim and end **of virtue is what disciplines and** ennobles **humanity, and** elevates **it more and more above the** condition of the brute, rather **than what may serve** to annihilate most **pains and** provide most pleasures? Is not the progressive **improvement of** living creatures the best purpose the world seems to **contain or** disclose?

* Utilitarianism, **p. 301.**

The chief quality in the character of virtue is, in truth, not usefulness, **but excellence,** rarity, nobleness. If **all** men were benevolent, and equally so, benevolence would not be thought of **as a virtue.** The pecuniary value of things in the market depends, not on their utility, but on their comparative scarcity, difficulty of attainment, and superiority; and so the moral worth of actions and qualities is estimated by their rare and peculiar merit and extraordinary dignity and sublimity, rather than their pleasure-giving effects. What we most admire in man is what sets him above the brute; and what we most admire and approve in men is ascent above their fellow-men in intellectual and moral rank; and these sentiments of admiration **and esteem** supply ample motives to sacrifice pleasure to improvement, and tend to make the standard or criterion of virtue the tendency to elevate and ennoble human nature rather than to promote the happiness of human life; **so that,** for example, in **our** dealings with inferior races, such as **those** of Africa and Polynesia, **we** might be influenced by other **and** higher considerations of their advantage than their ease **and enjoyment.**

In a **noble** passage, Mr. Mill observes that 'all the grand sources of human suffering are, in a great degree—many of them almost entirely—conquerable by human care **and** effort; and though **the** removal **is** grievously slow—though **a long** succession of generations **will perish in the** breach before **the** conquest is completed, and this **world becomes all** that, if will and knowledge **were** not wanting, **it might easily** be made—yet every mind **sufficien**tly intelligent **and** generous to bear a part in the endea**vour,** will draw a noble enjoyment from the contest itself, which **he would not** for any bribe, **in the form** of selfish indulgence, consent **to be** without.' **Whether such a** contest could afford what **may fairly be called enjoyment to all** competent to take part **in it, might be doubted; and** still more doubtful is it whether**, from less arduous and** less philanthropic occupations, most **men** might **not derive** more pleasure in their day. Yet the contest may **be good, in a** sense appreciable to our present moral sentiments, even **for those** to whom it brings little but care and sorrow and broken health, and loss of ease and rest. **It** may, too, be better towards the true advantage of the human race that such a contest should take place than that it should have been altogether unnecessary. 'Life is neither a pleasure nor a pain, but a serious business, which it is our duty to carry through, and terminate with honour.' Such was the serious and solemn theory of life which commended itself to the judgment of M. de Tocqueville; and whoever accepts it for himself must repudiate also for others the theory, that earthly happiness is the goal of human effort. But different theories of life must, in this world of mystery and doubt, present themselves to different minds, and the just weight to be attached to earthly happiness can be determined by no human measure. It is in itself a good, but not the sole good. And, in truth, it seems that, as on the one hand the moral sense is not a single sentiment, but a plurality of affections, emotions, and ideas, of different complexion in different ages and different men, so there is no sole and universal criterion either of virtuous actions or of human good. We love, approve, admire, respect, and venerate different qualities respectively; and virtue is, in short, not an abstract name of a single attribute, but a noun of multitude, which includes not only the useful and the loveable, but the exalted, the excellent, the noble, and the sublime, and the beautiful to the eye of the soul. All virtue aims, indeed, at human good; but human good seems manifold. It is innocent pleasure and innocent escape from pain, but it is also improvement; it is enjoyment, but it is also discipline, energy, and action. And, if a conflict should arise between the two, if the progressive should become less happy than the stationary state, the virtuous man may be expected to make the choice of Hercules both for himself and for others. The great changes which have taken place, however, in the moral sentiments of successive generations of mankind, and in their estimates of the worth of qualities and actions, might in reason warn us from attempting to fix for ever the standard and ideal of virtue, or to determine the aims of life for all future generations. It was held in ancient Rome, 'that valour is the chiefest virtue,' and humanity would then have been held nearly akin to vice. So it seems not for us to make certain that our present theories of the right and good are not dwarfed by the imperfection of our sentiments and our knowledge. **For this reason** alone the claims of Utilitarianism to be received **as** 'a comprehensive formula, including all things **which are** in themselves good,' would seem open to question. The moral progress of mankind is in itself a **good,** which makes the final determination of the summum bonum improbable ; and **it is too** in itself a good which is probably better than happiness.

V.

THE WEALTH OF NATIONS AND THE SLAVE POWER.

(Macmillan's Magazine, February, 1863.)

It has long been a prevalent notion, that Political Economy is a series of deductions from the principle of selfishness or private interest alone. The common desire of men to grow rich by the shortest and easiest methods—to obtain every gratification with the smallest sacrifice on their own part, has been supposed to be all that the political economist desires to have granted in theory, or to see regulating in practice the transactions of the world, to insure its material prosperity. A late eminent writer has described as follows the doctrine of Adam Smith, in the Wealth of Nations: 'He everywhere assumes that the great moving power of all men, all interests, and all classes in all ages and in all countries, is selfishness. He represents men as pursuing wealth for sordid objects, and for the narrowest personal pleasures. The fundamental assumption of his work is that each man follows his own interest, or what he deems to be his interest. And one of the peculiar features of his book is to show that, considering society as a whole, it nearly always happens that men, in promoting their own, will unintentionally promote the interest of others.'*

But, in truth, the acquisitive and selfish propensities of mankind, their anxiety to get as much as possible of everything they like, and to give as little as possible in return, are in their very nature principles of aggression and injury instead of

---

* Buckle's History of Civilization, vol. ii.

mutual benefit: the mode of acquisition to which they immediately prompt, is that of plunder or theft, and the competition which they tend to induce is that of conflict and war. Their first suggestion is not, 'I will labour for you,' but 'you shall labour for me;' not, 'Give me this, and I will give you what will suit you better in exchange,' but, 'Give it to me, or else I will take it by force.' The conqueror rather than the capitalist, the pirate rather than the merchant, the brigand rather than the labourer, the wolf rather than the watch-dog, obey the impulses of nature. The history of the pursuit of gain is far from being the simple history of industry, with growing national prosperity; it is the history also of depredation, tyranny, and rapine. One passage in it is thus given, in the early annals of our own country: 'Every rich man built his castle, and they filled the land with castles. They greatly oppressed the wretched people by making them work at their castles, and, when they were finished, they filled them with evil men. Then they took those whom they suspected to have any goods, seizing both men and women by night and day; and they put them in prisons for their gold and silver, and tortured them with pains unspeakable. . . . The earth bare no corn; you might as well have tilled the sea; for the land was all ruined by such deeds.'

But, if misery and desolation are the natural fruits of the natural instincts of mankind, how has the prosperity of Europe steadily advanced in spite of the enemy to it which nature seems to have planted in every man's breast? How has the predatory spirit been transformed into the industrial and commercial spirit? Under what conditions are individual efforts exerted, for the most part, for the general good? These are the chief problems solved in Adam Smith's 'Inquiry into the Nature and Causes of the Wealth of Nations.' He has been careful to point out that 'the interests of individuals and particular orders of men, far from being always coincident with, are frequently opposed to, the interests of the public;' and he observes that 'all for themselves and nothing for other people, seems to have been, in every age, the vile maxim of the masters of mankind.' The effort of every man to improve his own condition is, it is true, in Adam's Smith's philosophy, a principle of preservation in the body politic; but his aim was to demonstrate that this natural effort is operative for the good of society at large only in proportion to the just liberty secured to every member of it to employ his natural powers as he thinks proper, whether for his own advantage, or for that of others. Every infraction of, and every interference with, individual liberty, he denounced as being as economically impolitic as morally unjust. His systematic purpose was to expose the losses which a nation suffers, not only from permission of the grosser forms of violence and oppression, but from every sort of restriction whatever upon voluntary labour and enterprise. Of laws regulating agriculture and manufactures for the supposed advantage of the public, he said, 'both were evident violations of natural liberty, and therefore unjust, and they were as impolitic as they were unjust.' That security, he added, which the laws in Great Britain give to every man, that he shall enjoy the fruits of his own labour, is alone sufficient to make any country flourish. The history of Europe, in so far as it is the history of the progress of opulence, is not, in his pages, the history of selfishness, but of improving justice; of emancipated industry, and of protection for the poor and weak. It is, accordingly, the history of strengthening restraints upon the selfish disposition of mankind to sacrifice the happiness and good of others to their advantage or immediate pleasure. The fundamental principles on which the increase of the wealth of nations rests are thus summed up, at the end of Adam Smith's Fourth Book: 'All systems, either of preference or restraint, being thus completely taken away, the obvious and simple system of natural liberty establishes itself of its own accord. Every man, so long as he does not violate the laws of justice, is left perfectly free to pursue his own interest his own way, and to bring both his industry and his capital into competition with those of any man or order of men.'

The treatise on the Wealth of Nations is, therefore, not to be regarded, as it was by Mr. Buckle, as a demonstration of the public benefit of private selfishness. Adam Smith denies neither the existence nor the value of higher motives to exertion.

The springs of industry are various. Domestic affection, public spirit, the sense of duty, inherent energy and intellectual tastes, make busy workmen, as well as personal interest. And personal interest is itself a phrase for many different motives and pursuits, deserving the name of selfishness or not according to their nature and degree; just as wealth under a single term includes many things of very different moral quality, according to their character and use. The aims of men in life may be high or low; they may seek for riches of very different kinds and for very different purposes. In a recent essay in the 'Revue des Deux Mondes,' the eminent economist, M. de Lavergne, maintains that political economy and religion are, though essentially distinct, related to each other as the soul and body are. Wealth, he says, means food, clothes, and houses; and religion, though it treats of higher things, does not teach that men should be left to perish of hunger and cold. Political economy has for its special end the satisfaction of the bodily wants, and religion that of the spiritual wants of man. M. de Lavergne seems to have been led astray by the economic use of general terms, such as material wealth, material interests, and material progress. For wealth is not really or properly limited in political economy to such things as satisfy the bodily or material wants of humanity. It comprehends many things, the use of which is to minister to man's intellectual and moral life, but which have, notwithstanding, a price or value. Books, for example, as well as bread and meat, are wealth. Spiritual and other instructors are paid for as well as butchers and doctors. Wealth means, in fact, many different things, more or less material or immaterial, in different ages and countries. The highest kinds of wealth will be found where there is most general freedom for the development of the highest powers of humanity, and where no class have a licence for the gratification of their selfish passions at the expense of any other class. But what Adam Smith contended for was, that no class of men, be their motives good or bad, should be suffered, under any pretext, to encroach upon the industrial liberty of other men. The true moving power of the economic world, according to his system, is not individual selfishness, but individual energy and self-control. His fundamental principle is perfect liberty. The 'Wealth of Nations' is, in short, an exhaustive argument for free labour and free trade, and a demonstration of the economical policy of justice and equal laws. Arguing against the law of apprenticeship, the philosopher said: 'The property which every man has in his own labour, as it is the original foundation of all other property, so it is the most sacred and inviolable. The patrimony of a poor man lies in the strength and dexterity of his hands, and to hinder him from employing his strength and dexterity in what manner he thinks proper for his own advantage is a plain violation of that most sacred property. It is a manifest encroachment upon the just liberty both of the workman and of those who might be disposed to employ him. As it hinders the one from working at what he thinks proper, so it hinders the others from employing whom they think proper.'

The system, therefore, which is most subversive of the doctrines of political economy, as taught by Adam Smith, is that most selfish of all possible systems—slavery. The political economist must condemn it as loudly as the moralist. It attacks the life of industry, and prevents the existence of exchange. It robs the labourer of his patrimony; it robs those who would hire him in the market of their lawful profits; and it is a fraudulent abstraction from the general wealth of nations, the quantity and quality of which depend upon the degree of industrial liberty secured to every individual throughout the world for the exercise of his highest powers. Of the property of the slaveholder in the industry of his slaves, the paradox, 'la propriété c'est le vol,' is a literal truth according to political economy as well as common morality, and as regards not only the slaves, but the whole commercial world. Yet slavery is a system within the legitimate range of economic inquiry, which is by no means limited, as has sometimes been contended, to the phenomena of an imaginary world of free exchanges, but extends to all the economic phenomena of the real world, in which wealth is produced and distributed according to very different systems. Injustice and oppression have their natural train of economic consequences as well as liberty and equal laws, and the economist is concerned with both, as the physician studies the laws of disease as well as health. 'Writers on political economy,' says the chief among them in our time, 'propose to investigate the nature of wealth, and the laws of its production and distribution, including, directly or remotely, the operation of all the causes by which the condition of human beings is made prosperous or the reverse.' There is not a country in Europe at this day, not excepting our own, the economic phenomena of which the principle of exchange would be sufficient to interpret. But, even if pure commercial competition now regulated, throughout the whole of Europe, the production and distribution of every article of wealth, the whole domain of history, and the breadths of Asia, Africa, and America would remain for the economist to explore, and to account on other principles for the direction and results of human industry, the use of natural resources, and the division of the produce. The economy of the Slave States of America, for example, afforded an opportunity for this inquiry, of which Mr. Cairnes availed himself in his admirable Essay on the Slave Power. In an earlier Essay, he described political economy as belonging to 'the class of studies which includes historical, political, and social investigations,' and defined it as 'the science which traces the phenomena of the production and distribution of wealth up to their causes in the principles of human nature, and the laws and events of the external world.'* In the later Essay, instead of deducing unreal consequences from the hypothesis of industrial liberty, he has traced the origin and consequences of the opposite order of things. Instead of the theory of wages, profit, and rent, applicable to a free society, he lays bare the structure of a society which excludes wages, for the labourer is fed and flogged like a beast of burden; in which there is no profit, according to the economist's definition, for labour is not hired, but stolen; in which there is little or no rent, for only the best soils can be cultivated, and they are constantly becoming worthless instead of growing in value; in which fear is substituted for the hope

---

* Logical Method of Political Economy. By J. E. Cairnes, Professor of Political Economy in the University of Dublin.

of bettering his condition, and torment for reward, as the stimulus to the labourer's exertion; and in which wealth exists only in its rudest forms, because the natural division of employments has no place, and only the rudest instruments of production can be used. Adam Smith had previously examined the milder conditions of feudal servitude, demonstrating that the backwardness of mediæval Europe was attributable to these and similar discouragements to industry, and showing how it was forced into unnatural channels by such obstructions. For, through every part of his philosophy, 'Dr. Smith sought,' as Dugald Stewart relates, 'to trace, from the principles of human nature and the circumstances of society, the origin of the positive institutions and conditions of mankind.' The Wealth of Nations contains the substance of the last division of a complete course of lectures upon moral science, in which Adam Smith expounded, in succession, Natural Theology, Ethics, Jurisprudence, and Political Economy. His lectures on Jurisprudence have not survived; but his pupil Dr. Millar states, that 'he followed in them the plan suggested by Montesquieu, endeavouring to trace the gradual progress of jurisprudence from the rudest to the most refined ages, and to point out the effect of those arts which contribute to subsistence and to the accumulation of property, in producing corresponding improvements or alterations in law and government.' From this it is clear that his conception of the true scope and method of jurisprudence agreed with his conception of the true scope and method of economic inquiry. And in the Wealth of Nations, accordingly, he traced the operation both of the causes which rescued Europe from barbarism and occasioned its progress in opulence, and of those which impeded the action of the natural principles of preservation and improvement. In short, his treatise included an inquiry into the causes of the poverty as well as of the wealth of nations, and an investigation of the actual constitution and career of industrial society. He showed how rural industry and progress were thwarted in the middle ages by such impediments; that, but for the happier circumstances of its towns, Europe could never have emerged from the calamities which befel it after the dissolution of the Roman Empire. The servile and insecure position of the cultivators of the soil **prevented** industry from achieving its first triumphs **in the country according to the course of nature,** which makes agriculture the primary, **because the** most necessary, business of mankind. 'Order and good government, on the other hand, and along **with them** the liberty and security of individuals, were established in cities **at** a time **when** the occupiers of land in the country were exposed **to** every **sort of** violence. But men in this defenceless condition naturally content themselves with a bare subsistence, because to acquire more might only **tempt the** injustice of their oppressors. On the contrary, when they are secure of enjoying the fruits of their industry, they **naturally exert it** to better their condition, and to **acquire, not only the necessaries, but** the comforts and elegancies of life. **That industry, therefore, which aims at something more** than necessary subsistence, was established in cities **long** before it was commonly practised by the occupiers of land **in the** country.' In this manner, Adam Smith has traced the causes of the actual and, **as he** calls it, the 'unnatural' **course** of industry in the slow and chequered progress of modern Europe. He investigated the phenomena of what was, **happily** for us, on the whole, a progressive society. Mr. Cairnes, on the contrary, has investigated those of a retrograde one.

In the Slave **States of** America Mr. **Buckle** might have seen the economical results of a society based upon selfishness instead of justice. **The negro** shows elsewhere* his capacity to take

---

* The following statement, affording evidence as to the character, capacity, **and enterprise** of the negroes, is contained in a letter to the writer of this paper **from one of** the principal English residents in Victoria, the capital of Vancouver's **Island. It formed** part of a general description of the Colony, furnished without **any reference to the** question **of** slavery :—' Before the gold excitement, but **during the same year** (1858), **the** Legislature **of** California passed a law forbidding **the immigration** of negroes. This caused **the latter** to appoint a deputation, which visited the **British** Possession of Vancouver's Island; and so favourable was their report, that it not only caused many coloured **people to** leave California, but also aroused general attention, particularly that of **British subjects**; for by all who had occasionally heard of the island before, it was considered a sort of petty Siberia. While people were reading accounts of the climate, soil, and low price of town lots in Victoria, there **came rumours of rich** gold sands on the banks of the Frazer River in British **Columbia. Two or** three small coasting vessels had previously sailed with coloured passengers; but the demand for passages by white people became so great, that large steamships departed every

his part in the free division of labour, and the **consequent** multiplication of the productions of the different **arts,** which occasions, in the words of Adam Smith, in a well-governed society that universal opulence which extends itself to the lowest ranks of the people. In the squalid and comfortless homes even of the higher ranks of the people in the American Slave States, we see the consequence of oppressed and degraded industry. 'It may be,' says Adam Smith again, 'that the accommodation of a European prince does not always so much exceed that of an industrious and frugal peasant, **as** the accommodation of the latter exceeds that of an African king, the absolute master of the lives and liberties of ten thousand naked savages.' The American slave-owner is, as it were, a petty African king, **and** in real penury, as well as in power, resembles such a ruler. It is said, indeed, that we owed to slavery the produce which supplied the principal manufacture of Great Britain. But the whole of this production was in truth to be credited to free industry, while all the waste and ruin which accompanied it must be ascribed to slavery. The possibility of the profitable growth of so much cotton was caused by the commerce and invention of liberty, **while the** barbarism of the poor whites, the brutifying of **the** negro population, and the exhaustion of the

few days with from 300 to 1,000. Among them were some coloured people, and they have increased in number until, I think, **we may** safely estimate them at 500. The occupations of these coloured people **in Victoria** are, to the best of my recollection, porters, sawyers, draymen, day-labourers, barbers, **and** bathkeepers; eating-house keepers; one hosier, as black as **a coal,** with the best **stock** in the town; and two or three grocers. Some of them went **to** the mines, and were moderately successful. Their favourite investment is in a **plot** of ground, on which they build a neat little cottage and cultivate vegetables, raise poultry, &c. Nearly all had been prosperous, and a few had so judiciously invested that they were in receipt of from £10 to £40 a month from rents. They are industrious, economical, and intend to make the colony their permanent home; the outskirts of the town are well sprinkled with their humble but neat dwellings, and their land is yearly increasing in value. By this showing they are a quiet, industrious, and law-abiding people; but there is a drawback, taking them altogether as citizens, which arises from their earnest desire to be on a perfect social equality **with the** whites **at** church, the theatre, concerts, and other public places of **assembly.** When you consider the strong disinclination for their **company, not** only of **our** large American population, but also of Englishmen, who very quickly imbibe **the** American prejudice, you **can** readily conceive that **a** number of disagreeable scenes occur.'

American soil, are the net results of slavery. In truth, to Watt, Hargreaves, Crompton, and Whitney—free **citizens of England and the Northern States**—the **southern planters** owed the whole **value** of their cotton. What slavery may **really** claim as its **own** work is that, by exhausting the soil it occupies by a barbarous agriculture, which sets the laws of chemistry as **well** as of political economy at defiance, it hastens its own extinction from the day that **its** area is once definitely and narrowly circumscribed. This its own advocates admit, but with a singular inference: 'Slavery has, by giving to the laws of nature **free scope,** moved over a thousand miles of territory, leaving not a slave behind. Why should good men attempt to check **it in** its progress? If the laws of nature pass slavery farther **and** farther south, why not let it go, even though, in **process** of time it should, by the operation of natural laws, pass **away** altogether from the territory where it now exists?' Why, we may ask, should devastation be suffered to spread? Should fires in a city be suffered **to burn themselves out** by advancing from street to street until not a house remains to feed the conflagration? The slaveholder, as he moves southward **or westward,** not only carries moral and material destruction with **him,** but leaves it behind for those who come after him. The **rich** slavebreeder follows **him** with his **abominable** trade, and the poor white sinks back into barbarism in the wilderness the slaveholder has made. The order of European progress has been reversed. In Europe, justice, liberty, **industry,** and opulence grew together as Adam Smith described. **In** the Slave **States** of America, as Mr. **Cairnes** has shown, **the Slave** Power constitutes 'the most **formidable** antagonist to civilized progress which has appeared **for many** centuries, representing a system of society at once retrograde and aggressive—a system which, containing within it no germ **from which improvement can** spring, gravitates inevitably towards barbarism, while it is impelled by **exigencies** inherent in its position and circumstances to **a** constant extension of its territorial domain.'

ἄνω ποταμῶν ἱερῶν χωροῦσι παγαί
καὶ δίκα καὶ πάντα πάλιν στρέφεται.

For **the** perpetuation and extension of the system to which is owing this retrogressive movement of the English race in a region endowed with every natural help to progress, the slaveholders are in arms. They have not been slow to point, indeed, at General Butler's misrule in a southern city, and to ask if the cause of their adversaries is the cause of liberty? But such men as General Butler are living arguments against a Slave Power. General Butler was absolute master at New Orleans; and, even in the words of an ardent apologist for slavery, 'that cruelties may be inflicted by the master upon the slave, that instances of inhumanity have occurred and will occur, are necessary incidents of the relation which subsists between master and slave, power and weakness.'* There was never a more striking example of the ease with which men are cheated by words, than the generous sympathy given in England to the cause of the slaveholders, as the cause of independence, and therefore of liberty! It is the cause of independence, such as absolute power enjoys, of every restraint of justice upon pride and selfish passions. The power of England is in a great measure a moral power, founded on the respect of the civilized world for the courageous opposition of her people for centuries to such independence both at home and abroad. And, if the public opinion of England and the leaning of her policy be found ultimately upon the side of the maintenance and extension of the Slave Power in America, she will sustain in the end as great a loss of actual power, as well as of moral dignity, as if she entered into a league with the despots of Europe, and closed her cities of refuge against their victims. The Slave Power fights against all the principles of civil and religious liberty on which England rests her glory, and all the principles of political economy to which she ascribes her wealth. In policy, as well as in justice, England must refuse her countenance to that Power, as the enemy of the liberty as well as of the wealth of nations.

* The South Vindicated, p. 82.

VI.

THE QUESTION OF THE AGE—IS IT PEACE?[*]

(*Macmillan's Magazine*, May, 1860.)

Has **Europe,** at the point of civilization which **it has** reached, passed **beyond** the **military** stage of social progress, so that a disappearance of war is already before us in political prospect? **This question** raises, as will be seen, some collateral inquiries **of practical** and immediate moment; but, apart from **the** temporary interest and **light which they may** afford, the investigation is, at bottom, one **of** a philosophical **character.**

There is a matter of fact to be decided at the beginning. For an obvious, if not altogether conclusive, indication of the exorcism of the **ancient** combative spirit, **and** of the pacific structure **and temper of** modern civilization, **would be a** comparative infrequency in our own **times of** international quarrels and intestine conflicts and **disquietude.** A great predominance of peaceful interests and **tendencies** might naturally be expected **to bear** fruit and witness **both** in the foreign relations, and in **the internal** condition of the states of Europe. **And it** is in fact **asserted that** there has been, beyond all controversy, a steady **decline in** the frequency **of** war in each successive century of modern history; a signal example of which is, as it is alleged, afforded by the repose of Europe, and of this country in particular,[†] during the interval between 1815 and the commence-

---

[*] The reader is requested to bear in mind that this Essay was written nineteen years ago, being the author's first published Essay. Its main principles and conclusions he however **still adheres to,** though not **to** every sentence or expression.

[†] 'That this barbarous pursuit **is in the** progress **of** society steadily declining, must **be** evident even **to the** most superficial reader of European

ment of the Russian war in 1853. With a view to enable the reader to judge for himself of the accuracy of this statement, and to collect such indications of the future as are possible from the observation of proximate antecedents, the following table has been prepared, exhibiting the wars and quarrels in which Great Britain has been involved from 1815 to the present time, as well as the wars and principal insurrections and revolutions which have disturbed the peace of the Continent within the same period.

Wars, &c. of Great Britain.	*Wars, &c. of Continental States of Europe.*
1816.	
War with Algiers.	War between Spain and her revolted American colonies.
Commencement of the Pindaree War.	Army of occupation in France.
British troops continue to occupy France.	Revolutionary movements in several Continental States.
Ships equipped to assist the revolted colonies of Spain.	
1817.	
War in India.	War between Spain and her American colonies.
British troops continue to occupy France.	Invasion of Monte Video by Portugal.
Assistance to the revolted colonies of Spain.	Insurrections in Spain.
	Revolutionary movements in Germany and Sweden.
	Army of occupation in France.

history. If we compare one century with another, we shall find that wars have been becoming less frequent; and now so clearly is the movement marked, that until the late commencement of hostilities (with Russia) we had remained at peace for nearly forty years; a circumstance unparalleled not only in the history of our own country, but also in the history of every other country which has been important enough to play a leading part in the history of the world. In the middle ages there was never a week without war. At the present moment war is deemed a rare and singular occurrence.'—Buckle's History of Civilization, vol. i. p. 173.

Wars, &c. of Great Britain.	Wars, &c. of Continental States of Europe.
1818.	
War in India. British troops continue in France. Assistance to the revolted colonies of Spain; Lord Cochrane takes command of the navy of the patriots.	War between Spain and her American colonies. War in Turkey with the Wahabies. Disturbances at Constantinople. Quarrel between Bavaria and Baden.
1819.	
War in India at the commencement of the year. Assistance to the revolted colonies of Spain.	War between Spain and her American colonies. Serious disturbances in Spain. Insurrections in Turkey.
1820.	
Lord Cochrane and a body of British seamen capture Valdivia, and make an expedition against Lima.	War between Spain and her American colonies. War between the Dutch and Sumatra. Revolutions in Spain and Portugal. Insurrections in Piedmont and Naples. Revolt of Moldavia and Wallachia.
1821.	
Conflicts in India. Policy of Great Britain adverse to the Holy Alliance. Assistance to the revolted colonies of Spain.	War between Spain and her American colonies. War between Turkey and Persia; also between Turkey and Greece. Revolutionary movements in Spain and Italy. Austrian military operations in Italy.
1822.	
Assistance to the revolted colonies of Spain. Quarrel with China.	Turkey at war with Persia and Greece. Spain at war with her colonies. French army marches to the Pyrenees.

The Question of the Age—Is it Peace?

Wars, &c. of Great Britain.	**Wars, &c.** of Continental States of Europe.
1823.	
Burmese War.	War between Spain and her colonies.
Imminent danger of **war with** France.	War between Turkey and Greece.
Lord Byron's expedition to Greece.	Invasion of Spain by a French army.
	Russia makes **war in** Circassia.
1824.	
Burmese **War.**	War between Turkey and Greece.
Ashantee **War.**	War between Spain and the South American **Republics.**
Lord Byron's expedition against Lepanto.	War between the Dutch and Celebes and Sumatra.
Recognition of the independence **of the** revolted colonies **of Spain.**	
1825.	
Burmese War	War between Turkey and Greece.
Ashantee War	Dutch War with Java.
Siege of Bhurtpore	Insurrections in Spain.
1826.	
Burmese **War.**	**War between Turkey and Greece.**
Ashantee **War.**	**War between Russia** and Persia.
War **in** India.	Spain **prepares** for **war** with Portugal; insurrections **in** both countries.
Expedition of British fleet and troops to Portugal.	
1827.	
Rupture **with** Turkey.	War between Russia **and** Turkey.
Operations **of British** army **in** Portugal.	**War between** Turkey and Greece (assisted by the Great Powers)
Dispute with Runjeet Singh.	**Civil** War in Spain.
1828.	
War with Turkey.	**War** between Russia and **Turkey.**
British army in Portugal.	Expedition of French **troops to** Greece.
	Civil War in Spain and Portugal.
	War between Naples and Tripoli.

Wars, &c. of Great Britain.	Wars, &c. of Continental States of Europe.
	1829.
Dispute with China.	War between Russia and Turkey.
	Russian invasion of Circassia.
	Civil War in Portugal.
	1830.
Dispute with China.	War between Holland and Belgium.
	War in Poland.
	Russian War in the Caucasus.
	French War in Algeria.
	Revolution in France.
	Civil War in Spain and Portugal.
	Insurrection in Albania.
	Convulsions in Germany, Italy, and Switzerland.
	1831.
War in India.	War between Holland and Belgium.
Expedition to the Scheldt.	Hostilities between France and Portugal.
Dispute with China.	French expedition against Holland.
	War in Poland.
	Russian War in the Caucasus.
	French War in Algeria.
	Revolt of Mehemet Ali.
	Civil War in Portugal.
	Insurrections in France, Germany, and Italy.
	1832.
War with Holland.	War between Holland and Belguim (assisted by Great Britain and France).
	War between Turkey and Egypt.
	French War in Algeria.
	Russian War in the Caucasus.
	Insurrections in Italy; Austrian troops occupy Bologna.
	Civil War in Portugal.

Wars, &c. of Great Britain.	Wars, &c. of Continental States of Europe.
	1833.
Dispute with France.	**War** between Turkey and Egypt.
English protest against **Treaty** of Constantinople between Russia and **Turkey.**	**Cracow** occupied by Russia and Austria.
Dispute with the Caffres.	**French War in Algeria.**
	Russian **War in the** Caucasus.
	Civil War in Spain and Portugal.
	Insurrections in Germany and Italy.
	1834.
War in **India.**	French War in **Algeria.**
Hostilities **with the** Caffres.	Russian War in **the Caucasus.**
Affray with **the Chinese.**	Civil War in Portugal.
Disturbances in Canada.	Occupation of Ancona by Austria.
Treaty for expulsion of Don Carlos and Don Miguel.	
	1835.
British troops arrive **in Spain.**	French War in Algeria.
Dispute with China.	Russian War in the Caucasus.
	Civil War in Spain.
	Insurrection in Albania.
	1836.
Battle between **British troops and** the Carlists.	Civil **War in Spain.**
Rebellion **in Canada.**	**French War in Algeria.**
British merchants expelled from Canton.	Russian **War in the Caucasus.**
	Revolt **of Cracow,** crushed by Russia and Austria.
	1837.
War in Canada with rebels and American sympathizers.	Civil **War in** Spain.
British troops in Spain.	**French War in** Algeria.
	Russian War in the Caucasus.
	1838.
War in India.	War between France and Mexico.
War in Canada.	War of the French in Algeria.
British troops in Spain.	Russian War in the Caucasus.
	Civil War in Spain.

The Question of the Age—Is it Peace?

Wars, &c. of Great Britain.	Wars, &c. of Continental States of Europe.
1839.	
War with India.	War between France and Mexico.
War with China.	Revolt of Pacha of Egypt.
British troops in Spain.	Civil War in Spain.
	French War in Algeria.
	Russian War in the Caucasus.
1840.	
Affghan War.	War between Turkey and Egypt.
War with Egypt.	Civil War in Spain.
War with China.	French War in Algeria.
Expedition of British fleet to Naples.	Russian War in the Caucasus.
British troops in Spain.	
Disputes with France and with the United States.	
1841.	
War in India.	Civil War in Spain.
War with China.	Civil War in part of the Turkish Empire.
Dispute with the United States.	French War in Algeria.
	Russian War in the Caucasus.
1842.	
War in India.	Civil War in Spain.
Hostilities with the Boers at the Cape.	War between Turkey and Persia.
War with China.	French War in Algeria.
	Russian War in the Caucasus.
1843.	
War in India.	Otaheite occupied by the French.
Annexation of Natal to the Cape.	Insurrections in the Turkish Empire.
	Russian War in the Caucasus.
	French Wars in Algeria and Senegal.
1844.	
Insurrections in India.	War between France and Morocco.
Quarrel with the Sikhs.	Insurrection in Spain.
Arrest by the French of the English Consul at Tahite.	Russian War in the Caucasus.
	French Wars in Algeria and Senegal.

Wars, &c. of Great Britain.	Wars, &c. of Continental States of Europe.
	1845.
Sikh War.	Insurrections in Italy.
Attack on the pirates of Borneo.	French War in Algeria.
Labuan occupied by the British.	Russian War in the Caucasus.
Dispute with the United States.	
	1846.
Sikh War.	Civil War in Portugal.
Engagement with New Zealanders.	Annexation of and insurrection in Cracow.
Expedition to the Tagus.	Agitation in Hungary.
Dissensions with France in consequence of the Spanish marriages and the affairs of Greece.	French War in Algeria.
	Russian War in the Caucasus.
	Revolt of Sleswig and Holstein (encouraged by Prussia) from Denmark.
Revolt of Boers at the Cape.	Revolution in Switzerland.
	Quarrel between Greece and Turkey.
	1847.
War with Caffres and Boers.	Civil War in Spain, Portugal, and Switzerland.
War with China.	Disturbances in Italy; Austria occupies Ferrara.
Insurrections in India.	Insurrection in Poland.
	French War in Algeria, and with Cochin China.
	Russian War in the Caucasus.
	1848.
War in India.	War between Denmark and the Duchies (aided by Prussia).
Caffre War.	War between Austria and Sardinia.
English Ambassador commanded to leave Madrid.	War in Hungary.
	War in the Duchy of Posen.
	Revolutions in France, Austria, Prussia, Italy, and several German States.
	Insurrections in Spain and Italy.
	Russian War in the Caucasus.
	French War in Algeria.

Wars, &c. of Great Britain.	Wars, &c. of Continental States of Europe.
	1849.
War in **India**.	French occupy Civita Vecchia, and besiege **and** storm Rome.
Disturbances in Canada.	War in Hungary.
Admiral Parker enters Besika Bay.	War in the Duchies **of** Sleswig and Holstein.
	Russian War in the Caucasus.
	French War in Algeria.
	1850.
Blockade **of the Piræus** by the British fleet.	**War** in the Danish Duchies.
	Insurrection in Germany and Italy.
Caffre War.	**Prussia on the brink of war with** Austria concerning **Hesse** Cassel.
War in India.	
Destruction of Chinese junks.	
Dispute with France; French Ambassador recalled.	**Russian War in** the Caucasus.
Angry despatch addressed **to Great** Britain by Russia.	French **War in** Algeria.
	French troops occupy Rome.
	1851.
Caffre **War**.	Insurrection in Portugal.
Insurrection of **Hottentots**.	Coup d'état of Louis Napoleon.
Expedition **to Rangoon**.	French **War in** Algeria.
	Russian **War in the** Caucasus.
	French troops occupy Rome.
	1852.
Second Burmese War.	French War in Algeria.
Caffre War.	Russian War in the Caucasus.
	French troops in Rome.
	1853.
Preparations for **War** with Russia.	War between Russia and Turkey.
	French War in Algeria.
Insult **to** British subjects **at** Madrid.	French troops in **Rome**.
	1854.
War with Russia.	Russia at **War** with Turkey, France, **and** Great Britain.
	Austrian army enters the Principalities.

Wars, &c. of Great Britain.	Wars, &c. of Continental States of Europe.
	Insurrections in Italy and Spain.
	Rupture between Turkey and Greece.
	French War in Algeria.
	French troops in Rome.

1855.

War with Russia.	Russia at War with Turkey, France, Sardinia, and Great Britain.
Insurrection of Santals in Bengal.	
Disturbances at the Cape.	French War in Algeria.
	French troops in Rome.

1856.

Peace with Russia in March, against the wishes of the British nation.	Russian War in the Caucasus.
	Insurrections in Spain.
	Insurrectionary movements in Italy.
War with Persia.	
War with China.	Rupture between Prussia and Neufchâtel.
Rupture with Naples.	
Oude annexed.	French troops in Rome.

1857.

War with China.	Russian War in the Caucasus.
Indian Mutiny.	French troops in Rome.
War, in the early part of the year, with Persia.	
Insurrection at Sarawak.	

1858.

Serious differences with France.	Dispute between France and Portugal.
War with the Sepoys.	
War with China.	French fleet despatched to Lisbon.
Bombardment of Jeddah.	
	Russian War in the Caucasus.
	French troops in Rome.

1859.

Preparations by sea and land against invasion; organization of Volunteer Rifle Corps.	France and Sardinia at war with Austria.
	Revolts in Central Italy.
Rebel army in Nepaul.	France and Spain at war with Cochin China.
Hostilities with the Chinese.	

Wars, &c. of Great Britain.	Wars, &c. of Continental States of Europe.
Island of San Juan occupied by American troops.	Russian War in the Caucasus. War between Spain and Morocco. French bombard Tetuan. French troops in Rome.

1860.

Expedition to China. Distrust of the designs of France. Defensive preparations continue.	War between Spain and Morocco. French expedition to China. French troops in Lombardy and Rome. Annexation of Savoy and Nice by France. Carlist rising in Spain. Insurrection in Sicily.

Comparing these statistics with antecedent periods of history, it does not appear that there is evidence of a gradual cessation of warfare and other serious violations of the peace of nations. The table does not exhibit one year from 1815 to the present date in which our own country has not been either engaged in actual hostilities in some part of the world, or in some quarrel or proceeding likely to end in war. Much less does it show a single year in which all Europe was at peace. Nor is the significance of recent wars to be estimated by reference solely to the amount of blood and treasure they have cost; for the struggles of Russia with Turkey, the campaigns of the French in Algeria, Senegal and Lombardy, the conflicts of Great Britain in India and with China, and the aggressions of Spain upon Morocco, are of moment rather as prophetical than as historical facts. Besides, it should be remembered that the period from 1815 to 1854, which has been so erroneously referred to as giving proof of the peacefulness of the modern spirit, began at the termination of the greatest war in the history of mankind; one which by its very severity necessitated a long forbearance from hostilities on a great scale, adding as it did, for example, more than £600,000.000 to the debt of Great Britain, and exhausting France of all her soldiers.

Contrasting one age with another, Great Britain seems never to have been so free from war in this century as in Sir Robert Walpole's time; and Walpole's administration is commonly regarded as crowned by almost unbroken peace. But the nineteenth bears in this respect a still less favourable comparison with the seventeenth century. From the accession of James I. until the civil wars, England may be said to have enjoyed continued peace, for such operations as the expedition to Rochelle scarcely deserve a place in the history of war. Going farther back to the hundred years between the battle of Bosworth and the commencement of the struggle with Spain in Elizabeth's time, considering too the bloodless and theatrical character of Henry the Eighth's campaigns, and the unimportance of the military annals of the two next reigns, there is little exaggeration in saying that England was free from war from the union of the Roses until the equipment of the Spanish Armada. Confining ourselves to English history, it would thus appear that the portion of the nineteenth century already elapsed has been less peaceful than the corresponding period of each of the two preceding ones. And, indeed, it may be doubted whether any prior hundred and twenty years since the Conquest produced so many battles as were fought between 1740 and 1860.

A writer, already referred to, remarks that, 'in the middle ages, there was never a week without war.' But if we are to reckon all the feuds of barons and squires in comparing the frequency of mediæval with modern hostilities, we must weight the scale of the latter with all the bloody revolutions, rebellions, and insurrections of modern times, and with greater justice in consequence of the tendency of these elements of disorder, peculiar to our era, to produce international strife or war in a wider sphere.

It is not an impertinent fact that from 1273 until 1339 England remained throughout at peace with the Continent, if at least the years 1293 and 1297 be excepted; in the former of which there was a collision between the French and English fleets, although their respective countries were not otherwise at war; and in the latter, Edward I. conducted an expedition to Flanders, which ended without a battle. It is true that in this period there were intermittent hostilities with Wales and Scotland. In a military **sense the Welsh wars** of England hardly deserve more notice than **those** of the Heptarchy. But there is a point of view from which the conflicts with Wales and **Scotland,** and those of the Heptarchy, **alike** possess political importance, and have a bearing upon the question **now under** consideration, because of their analogy to a process which is still going on **in Europe,** and still giving rise to problems of which no peaceful **solution** has yet been found possible **for the** most part—knots, as it were, which must be cut with the sword.

The efforts **of** the English sovereigns in **the** middle ages for the annexation of Wales, and the reduction of Scotland to the position **of** a dependency, were **the natural antecedents of a** political unity of Great Britain, corresponding **with its** natural **or** geographical unity, and conducive both to the internal peace **of the island,** and to its security from foreign aggression. **It was** absolutely indispensable for the civilization of England that **the** Heptarchy should be consolidated, and it **was** equally so that Ireland, Wales, and Scotland, should become integral parts of a united kingdom. It is obvious that the causes and chances of war would be infinitely multiplied were these three countries still separate and independent States, and that their union with their more powerful neighbour was requisite for the tranquillity and improvement of all, while it was preceded by struggles which, so far from being peculiar to barbarian or the middle ages, find almost exact parallels in the latest annals of human progress. **Nor is it** unworthy of remark that Edward I., the ablest prince **since** the Conquest, applied himself with equal zeal and ambition **to the** reduction of Wales and Scotland, and to the establishment **of law and order** throughout England. In like manner the **complex** movement which in one word, fruitful of mistakes, we call civilization, while bearing over the globe the seeds of future peace, has entailed all the maritime, colonial, and commercial wars of modern Europe. The art of navigation discovered upon the ocean a **new** element for the practice of hostilities. It was certainly not in a barbarous age, or by barbarous weapons, that the Colonial Empire of **Great** Britain was established. And what but the commercial spirit of the nineteenth century has carried the cannon of Great Britain into China? Surely **it was** not the genius of barbarism that urged the American colonists to win their independence with the sword, nor can that well be called an uncivilized impulse which has flushed so **high** the encroaching pride of the United States at the present hour.

We are thus driven to admit that we cannot with truth assert that a diminution of war is a characteristic of our epoch, or that, if some ancient causes of quarrel have disappeared before the progress of **civilization, it** has imported no new germs of discord into the bosom of nations. Our survey of the past is far from warranting the prediction that all **the ends** which are **for the** ultimate benefit of mankind will be henceforward accomplished without bloodshed. Nor does it seem to entitle **the** warmest advocate of peace to stigmatize a martial spirit as barbarous in every form, and for whatever purpose it is animated. On the other hand, we may **glean** some reason for the general reflection, that it is often by war itself that future wars are made impossible or improbable, while peace is not unfrequently **but** the gathering time for hostile elements.* And the particular observation in reference to our own island lies upon the surface, that, since it has been by the improvements of civilization brought into closer contact **with** the Continent, the chances of collision with Continental States are multiplied, and military institutions and ideas seem to **have** arisen among us pari passu with increased proximity to our military neighbours. Again, the extension of our empire far beyond the confines of Europe has given us enemies and wars in lands of which our mediæval ancestors never heard, and which uncivilized **men** would have never reached.

These inferences are, however, drawn confessedly from partial premises, since we have up to this point regarded only one of the many sides which the modern world presents to the

---

* 'Ah, we are far from Waterloo! We are not now exhausted and ruined by twenty years of heroic war. We have taken advantage of the twenty **years of** peace which Providence has given us, to recruit our forces, and **stimulate** our patriotism. We have **an** army of 600,000 men; we can also fight at sea. We have built gigantic ships, cased with iron; we have gun-boats; in short, we have a powerful **navy**, which formerly we had not.'—La Coalition. **Paris,** April, 16, **1860.**

eye of the statesman and political **philosopher,** and especially omitted one of the most **conspicuous and** important phases **of** European civilization. Industry **and commerce** have revolutionized western society, and established an economical alliance, **as it were,** between its members. One of **the firmest** bases of the feeling of nationality or fellow-citizenship may be traced **at** bottom, says an **eminent** traveller, to the 'need and aid **of each** other in their daily life,'* felt by inhabitants of the same country. Each district, each house, each man has a demand for what another district, house, **or man** supplies ; people are in habitual intercourse or contact of an amicable, or at least pacific character, and reciprocal obligations and conveniences make up the sum and business of existence. But this mutual interdependence now exists, **as it** is urged, between nation and nation, and all **Christendom** feels itself to be literally one commonwealth. **And,** besides the powerful interests altogether opposed to war, **which** have arisen in every state, men's **minds** are habitually swayed by commonplace **and** unromantic ideas ; and the presiding idea of modern communities, we **are** told, is **the** altogether unwarlike one of the acquisition of wealth.

Even France is said to afford a conspicuous example of this; and there are **several** reasons why that country may, with particular propriety, be referred to in connexion with our present topic of inquiry. At this moment the peace of Europe depends mainly upon French policy. France, moreover, boasts, and with reason, of being, **as** regards the continent of Europe, a representative and missionary country in institutions and ideas. What **is of** importance here, moreover—in France and over **most of the** Continent there are wanting some peculiar physical **and historical conditions** which contribute to make pacific interests and **sentiments** unquestionably predominant in Great Britain, the **absence of** which peculiarities would render any estimate of the prospects of Europe, that might be founded upon a mere extension **of** the elements of our own social condition, altogether fallacious. On the other hand there are facts, which have grown up with the present generation, 'depriving former

---

* **Notes on** the Social and Political State of Denmark, by Mr. S. Laing.

times of analogy with our own,' and obliging us to dispute the logic that infers the character of future international relations from their past type.

Eight years before his arguments were sanctioned by a Treaty of Commerce, Mr. Cobden drew public attention to new features of the industrial economy of the world, surely calculated, in his opinion, to render a military policy uncongenial to the great mass of the French people, and a rupture with Great Britain particularly improbable. Those arguments are of course now entitled to additional weight, but they could hardly be more forcibly expressed by Mr. Cobden himself at the present moment than they were in a remarkable pamphlet which he published the year before the Russian War, from which we reproduce the following passage :—

'I come to the really solid guarantee which France has given for a desire to preserve peace with England. As a manufacturing country France stands second only to England in the amount of her productions and the value of her exports; but the most important fact in its bearings on the question before us is that she is more dependent than England upon the importation of the raw materials of her industry; and it is obvious how much this must place her at the mercy of a Power having the command over her at sea. This dependence upon foreigners extends even to those right **arms of peace,** as well as of war, coal and iron. The coal imported into France in 1792, the year before the war, amounted to 80,000 tons **only.** In 1851, her importation of coal and coke reached the prodigious quantity of 2,841,900 tons.

In the article of iron we have another illustration to the same effect. **In 1792 pig iron does** not figure in the French tariff. In 1851 the importation of pig iron amounted to 33,700 tons. The point to which **I wish to** draw attention is that so large a quantity of this prime necessary of life of every industry is imported from abroad; and in proportion as the quantity for which she is thus dependent upon foreigners has increased since 1792, in the same ratio has France given a security to **keep the** peace.

Whilst governments are preparing **for war,** all the tendencies of the age **are** in the opposite direction; **but** that which most loudly and constantly thunders in the **ears of emperors, kings,** and parliaments, the stern command, 'You shall not break the peace,' is the multitude which in every country subsists upon the produce of labour applied to materials brought from abroad. **It is** the gigantic growth which this manufacturing system has attained that deprives former times of any analogy with our own, and is fast depriving of all reality those pedantic displays of diplomacy, and those traditional demonstrations of armed force, upon which peace or war formerly depended.'*

We **have** quoted Mr. Cobden's principal argument, that a war with **a state possessing,** as Great Britain does, a superior navy, would ruin the staple manufactures of **France**; but he has also contended that a great military expenditure would entail **burdens** intolerable to the French people. If it be replied **to this** latter argument that Government loans produce no immediate or sensible pressure, and are rather popular measures, good authority is not wanting **for the** rejoinder that this State mine has been so **freely worked by** French financiers **that** it must be pretty nearly exhausted—the public debt of France having grown from £134,184,176, in 1818, to £301,662,148 in 1858.† To this it is added, that, while the Government has become yearly more embarrassed, the nation has become richer, more comfortable, and less ready **for** military life and pay; and that the very investments which have been so largely made by all classes in the French funds have **arrayed** interests proportionately strong against any course of public action calculated to depreciate **greatly** the value of their securities. In short, we are told **that the** French Emperor is too poor, and that the French people **are too** rich, for war.

These **are** considerations which deserve much attention; but they are, it seems to us, insufficient to prove that France has passed out **of** the military into the industrial stage of national development, or that its economical condition is such as to render war very distasteful to the French nation, as a nation; especially as one which endures in time of peace, with the utmost

---

* '1793 and 1853.' By Richard Cobden, M.P. Ridgway.
† Economist, November 26, 1859.

cheerfulness, one of the heaviest inflictions of a great and protracted war. For if we reflect upon the amount of wealth and industrial power withdrawn from production to sustain an army of 600,000 soldiers, besides an enormous fleet, we cannot but admit that this wonderful people bears, not only with constancy, but with pride, one of the chief economical evils of hostilities on a gigantic scale, and that this conspicuous feature of French society suffices to characterize it as warlike and wasteful, rather than as prudent and pacific. The immense increase of the national debt of France in the last forty years, if it shows that the fund of loanable capital has been largely trenched on, shows also the facility with which this financial engine has been worked hitherto; while the admitted augmentation of the general wealth of the people appears to contain an implicit answer to any conjecture that their capacity to lend has been nearly exhausted. Nor is it immaterial to observe, that the debt of France has been contracted mainly for military purposes,* that it has been considerably added to by the Emperor for actual war, and that his popularity appears to be now much greater than at his accession, in a large measure in consequence of the manner in which he has employed the loans he has raised. We have, indeed, only to recollect the amount of debt incurred by our own Government in the last war with France, and the opinion entertained by the highest authorities of its overwhelming magnitude when it was but a seventh of the sum it afterwards reached, to see the fallacy of prophecies of peace based upon the supposition of the impossibility of a country in the condition of France plunging into a great contest, and emerging from it without ruin. Moscow and Waterloo have been followed by Sebastopol and Solferino; and of disasters befalling his country from a foreign enemy the Frenchman is, we fear, inclined to repeat :—

> 'Merses profundo, pulchrior evenit:
> Luctere, multa proruet integrum
> Cum laude victorem, geretque
> Prœlia conjugibus loquenda.'

Neither can we put unreserved confidence in the pledges

* Tooke's History of Prices, vi. pp. 7 and 13.

of peace afforded by the trade **and manufactures** of France, on the value of which the following figures throw a light which has probably escaped Mr. Cobden's **notice** :—

Exports from France.*
(Expressed in millions sterling and tenths.)

	Mill. sterl.	
To England	11	2
,, United States	7	3
,, Belgium	5	0
,, Sardinia	2	7
,, Switzerland	2	0
,, Zollverein	1	9
,, Turkey	1	0
,, Russia	—	
,, 46 other countries and places	12	5

Imports into France.
(Expressed in millions sterling and tenths.)

	Mill. sterl.	
From England	5	3
,, United States	7	7
,, **Belgium**	5	3
,, **Sardinia**	4	1
,, **Switzerland**	1	4
,, **Zollverein**	2	3
,, Turkey	1	7
,, Russia	1	8
,, 46 other countries and places	13	5

We may observe, that the European trade of France with Belgium ranks next in importance to that with England. Now, **when** it is suggested that France depends upon importation for those **prime** necessaries of both war and peace, iron and coal, and that **this** fact, **above** all others, affords security against French aggression, the reminiscence can hardly fail to excite some inauspicious recollections. Belgium **is** almost traversed from west to east by beds **of** coal, from which, in 1850, nearly six million tons were extracted; and in **the** same year the Belgian mines yielded 472,883 tons of iron. Give Belgium

* Tooke's History of Prices, vi, 652-3.

then to France, or rather let France take Belgium, and she does not want English coal and iron in time of war for her steam navy and ordnance. Is it towards commercial or warlike enterprise—towards the annexation of the adjoining land of coal and iron, or peace with **all** her neighbours—that the mind of the French is likely to be tempted by this consideration? Which policy would **best** consort with some of their longest treasured aspirations, and some of their latest anticipations? Last year a pamphlet, entitled 'L'Avenir de l'Europe,' passed through several editions in Paris. The future sketched for his country by the writer may be conjectured from the following **passage** :—
'De même que nous déclarons la Hollande puissance germanique, de même aussi n'hésitons-nous pas à regarder la Belgique comme française. Elle vit par nous, et sans la pusillanimité **du** dernier roi des Français, l'assimilation serait complète depuis **1830.**' Perhaps **this** allusion **to the** year 1830 may derive illustration from the inspirations of a more celebrated politician. Among the works of Napoleon III. there is a fragment, entitled 'Peace or War,' which expresses a decided opinion upon the policy which became the Sovereign of France in 1830, and by implication upon the policy which becomes its Sovereign in 1860, or 'whenever moral force is in its favour.' It is in these terms:—'All upright men, all firm and just minds agree, that after 1830 only two courses were open to France—a proud and lofty **one,** the result of which might be war ; **or** a humble one, but which would reward humility by **granting to France** all **the** advantages **which** peace engenders and **brings forth.** Our opinion has always been, that in spite of all its dangers, a grand and **bold policy was** the only one which became our country: and **in 1830,** when moral force was **in** our favour, France might easily have regained the rank which is hers by right.'

It is not out **of place, perhaps, to** remark here that the hope of **a** meek and **quiet, but** remunerative, policy on the part of France—rather than one grand and bold but perilous—which Mr. Cobden had some reason to form in 1853 from the nature and extent of the maritime commerce of France, has since lost its foundation by a change in the maritime laws of war brought about by Napoleon III. To have crippled by hostilities with a superior naval power **the sale** of manufactures to the value of £50,000,000 and interrupted the importation **of** more than £40,000,000 worth of the materials of French industry, might well have seemed a risk too prodigious even **for a** sovereign with magnificent ideas to encounter. But—not to speak of the efforts **made by** that Sovereign to place France without a superior on the seas—there is, since the Russian War and the Treaty of Paris, nothing that France imports from foreign shores which she could not continue to receive during a war with England in neutral vessels. Even a blockade of the whole French coast would only send the cargoes round by the Scheldt and the Gulf of Genoa; and to whatever extent **it were** really successful in obstructing neutral **trade, it would tend, on peace** principles themselves, to make America, Sardinia, Spain, Russia, and **Turkey** the enemies of the blockading power, in the ratio of the **intercept of** imports.

It is by no means intended by these observations to attenuate the truism that **the material** interests of France counsel a pacific policy on the part of its Government, but only to show that they do not present an insuperable obstacle to a warlike one, even against ourselves, and therefore do not relieve us of the barbarous onus **of** defensive preparations, or afford us much security that no temptation to achieve distinction by the sword could be strong enough **to divert our powerful** neighbours from the loom and the spade.

In truth, it is no original **discovery of** our era that the commercial demands of France and England make them natural allies. It was seen with perfect clearness **by** that statesman **who** led them into a conflict during which, on each side of the Channel, infants grew to manhood, seldom hearing **of an** overture for peace, and personally unacquainted with any human world but **one of war.**

When laying before Parliament the Treaty **of** Commerce of 1786, Mr. Pitt expressed a confident **hope** that the time was now come **when** those two countries which had hitherto acted as if intended for the **destruction of** each other would ' justify the order **of** the universe, **and show** that they were better calculated for friendly intercourse and mutual benevolence.'

That generous confidence was so soon and signally frustrated, not because of the blindness of both nations to the advantages of trade, but because men are sometimes disposed to exchange blows rather than benefits, and because they have passions, affections, and aspirations both higher and lower than the love of gold or goods. Still, in 1860, the fiery element of war burns ardently in France, because the desire of wealth is not the one ruling thought which moulds the currents of the national will. There, at least, the economical impulse is not paramount over every other, and the social world does not take all its laws from the industrial; of which in politics we find an example in the insignificance of the bourgeoisie, and, in common life, in the preference of the public taste for the ornamental rather than the useful.

There are thinkers who not only speculate upon the future of our own country from a purely English point of view, and take into account in their predictions of its destinies no forces save those visibly in action in ordinary times inside our island shores, but who measure the prospects of the whole human race according to principles which would be valid only if every people had an English history, climate, geographical position, and physical and moral constitution. Yet, in fact, some of the proximate dangers of war arise from the fact that England is the active centre of principles which, were all other countries similarly conditioned, would indeed be favourable to the maintenance of international amity, but which, being dominant in Britain almost alone, come sometimes into violent collision with the elements of national life that are combined elsewhere

The mechanical and commercial conditions common to the modern civilized world have, in many respects, operated but little below the surface to modify diversities betrayed even in the ordinary round of life. The likeness between the Anglo-Saxon and the Gaul of the nineteenth century lies on the outside; but in sympathies and ideas, in heart and soul, in the inner moral life, they are beings representing two distinct phases of European civilization.

The seas kept the inhabitants of the British Islands for centuries aloof from most of those cruel wars which have left deep marks upon the institutions and temper of Continental Europe, and protected that energetic pursuit of material wealth and commercial pre-eminence to be expected from the first maritime position in the world, from customs at once free and aristocratic, and not least from a climate which demands the labour which it renders easy, while precluding foreign modes of existence and amusement.

Five and twenty Continental summers might work some change in the social economy of Britain. They might leave us a gayer and pleasanter, but a vainer people. They might slacken our steps, and quicken our eyes and tongues, thin the city and crowd the park; give a holiday air to English life, and improve manners and the art of conversation amazingly. We might lose something of the cold and sedate reserve, the concentration of the mind on serious business, and of that earnest, patient, and practical character which our history, our Puritan ancestry, and our clouds, have formed for us. We might become less fond of domestic life, less engrossed with personal and family interests, living more in the open air, and abandoning ourselves much to subjects and feelings in which passers-by could share and sympathize. It might become more agreeable to spend than to get; people might love most to shine in society or to see splendid spectacles. In the end perhaps London might be so like Paris, we should find so many of the ways of our lively neighbours worthy of our imitation, that we might gladly wear red ribbons in our button-holes. Our susceptibilities and sense of honour might have grown more refined; the press and the courts of law might fail to arrange many of our differences in a becoming manner, and we might find it imperative to recur to the chivalrous arbitrament of the duel.

This may appear a grotesquely exaggerated picture; yet in America the force of climate and circumstances is seen to excite an eager restlessness of temperament foreign to the ancestral type. And we have glanced at but a few of the influences which tend in France to enervate the industrial spirit, and to give an undue force and direction to other impulses and motives of action. It **is not only** that the Frenchman naturally seeks éclat more than **the sober** Englishman, but **that** his country affords fewer avenues for advancement and enterprise in civil life, **and scarcely one** safe pacific theme of politics. Here the love **of** change and excitement, the public spirit of the citizen, and **the** romantic impulse **of** the man to transcend the narrow boundary of home, **and** to become an actor on a greater stage than the market and **the mill**, find **vent** and exercise, not only in the discussions of a free press, but **in the** possession of a world-wide empire, familiar to the imagination and yet full **of the** unknown—a consideration the more operative on the side of **peace,** that the magnitude of this empire is felt to be largely due to the conquests of industry, not of arms, and that, by universal consent, the nation may have equals in war, but has **no** European rival in the renown and blessings of wealth. The Frenchman, on the other hand, has but a soldier's tent abroad; **he has** no sphere of cosmopolitan action save the campaign, nor anything besides his famous sword to assure him of a conspicuous figure in Europe and **a place in history.**

Nor let **us suppose entirely spent** the original forces of the Revolution of 1789. The **despot** said, 'L'État, c'est moi;' the emancipated **serf awoke to the intoxicating** reflection, 'L'État, c'est moi.' Seldom, since, has an idea of **the dignity and glory** of the State been presented to the popular **mind of France** in any other shape **than** that of victory and military precedence.

Mr. Buckle has been led far astray **when he** maintains that every **great step in** national progress, and every considerable increase **of mental activity,** must be **at the expense** of the warlike spirit; **nor could he have happened on a more** unfortunate reference than to the '**military** predilections of Russia'[*] for an illustration of his theory **that a dislike of** war is peculiar **to** a people whose intellect **has received an** extraordinary **impulse** from the advancement **and general** diffusion of knowledge and civilization. 'It is clear,' he says, 'that Russia **is a** warlike country, not because the inhabitants are immoral, but because

---

[*] Buckle's History of Civilization, vol. i. **p.** 178.

they are unintellectual.' **But, in fact, what** is clear is, that Russia is at present **not a** warlike country. Its situation, climate, history, and institutions, have contributed to make its inhabitants, in the opinion of the best authorities, 'the most pacific people on the face of the earth.'*

Never in Moscow or St. Petersburg would you hear the cry **of War for ever!—Viv**e la guerre!—uttered often unrebuked by the writer's side, as the army of Italy defiled through the streets of Paris on the 14th August, 1859.† Never during the Crimean War would you have seen a Russian manufacturer join the army as a volunteer, confessing with pride, Moi, je n'aime pas la paix.‡

There is, in truth, a natural relationship between the economic impulse, or the desire of a higher and better condition, and those national sentiments to which, in France, an unfortunate course of circumstances has given a military direction. Patriotic pride and emulation are personal ambition purified and exalted by the alliance of some disinterested motives and affections. Nor can that feeling ordinarily fail to have an elevating influence on the character of a people which raises the aspirations of the multitude above selfish ends and material gain, and infuses some measure of enthusiasm and public spirit into the most vulgar minds. Hence political economists of high

---

*' Upon this point, I believe, no difference of opinion exists among all observers. Having lived for several years in a position which enabled me to mix much with the officers and men of the Russian army, such is my strong opinion of the Russian character. M. Haxthausen mentions, as a point admitting of no doubt, ' the **absence of all** warlike tendency amongst the Russian people, and their excessive **fear of the** profession of a soldier.' The Russian people have no pleasure in wearing arms; even in their quarrels among themselves, which are rare, they **hardly ever fight,** and the duel, which now often takes place among the Russian officers, **is contrary to the** national manners, and is a custom imported from the West.'—**Russia on the Black** Sea, by Henry **Danby** Seymour, p. 97.

† This **was among persons who** were able **to pay** twenty francs a-piece for their seats.

‡ The writer **met returning from** Solferino a French manufacturer, who, deserting his business for the campaign, had attached himself to the army of Italy. He had served in like manner in the Crimea, **at** the siege of Rome, and in Algeria. This individual made the above declaration of his disrelish for peace; yet, upon the truce, he quietly resumed **his** business until another war, which he anticipated the following spring, should relieve him of the inglorious **occupation.**

philosophic genius, such as Adam Smith and William Humboldt, have been far from reprobating a martial temper in a people as barbarous in every form and under all conditions. To France, unhappily, we might apply Lord Bacon's lamentation on the improper culture of the seeds of patriotic virtue: 'But the misery is that the most effectual means are applied to the ends least to be desired.' It is not only that the structure of the French polity is such that the ruling classes are those least fit to rule, and most liable to be swayed by passion and caprice, while there is no percolation through successive grades, as in England, of the cooler views and habits of educated thought, but that a morbid intolerance of superiority has been left by the remembrance of the tyranny of the feudal nobility. As Mr. Mill has observed, 'When a class, formerly ascendant, has lost its ascendancy, the prevailing sentiments frequently bear the impress of an impatient dislike of superiority.'* Among the French democracy this hatred of superior eminence, being carried into every direction of the popular thought, often assumes the form of an envious and hostile attitude towards Great Britain. A nation prone to jealousy is placed by the side of another, at the head of all peaceful enterprise. Whatever envy of English fortune might thus arise, is aggravated by traditions of defeat and injury.

France has now no colonies save a few military stations. But a century ago it was otherwise, and her sons might have found themselves in their own country from Quebec to Pondicherry, and from the Strait of Dover to the Strait of Magellan. Why are they now bounded by the Bay of Biscay and the Gulf of Lyons? How is it that Canada, Nova Scotia, Cape Breton and Prince Edward's Island, the Bahamas, Tobago, Grenada and Dominica, St. Lucia and St. Vincent, the Falkland Isles,† Malta, the Ionian Islands, the Mauritius, Rodrique and the Seychelles, and India from the Kistna to Cape Comorin, once held or claimed by France, are now undisputed fragments of the British Empire? It is a question that calls up the names

---

* Essay on Liberty.

† The French were driven from the Falkland Isles in 1766 by the Spaniards, who in 1771 gave place to the British.

of Chatham and his son, of Wolfe and Clive, of Nelson and Wellesley, and other memories retained with different emotions at each side of the Channel. And the answer might throw some light upon the source of the popularity at one side of the theory of natural boundaries, and the eagerness of our rivals to push their frontiers to the Scheldt, the Rhine, and the Alps, and to live in a larger world of their own.

Let us not be too severe in our censure of an ambition, which we must at the same time manfully resist. Suppose the conditions of the two empires to be suddenly reversed. Suppose England to be rankling under a successful invasion, and a long occupation by a foreign army. Suppose the British flag to have been swept from every sea, and almost every distant settlement and ancient dependency transferred to the domain of France. Suppose at the same time that we felt or imagined our ability to restore the balance and resume our former place upon the globe; and who shall say that, less sensitive and less combative as we are, we should not be eager to refer the issue to the trial of the stronger battalions once more? Or who shall say that the ideas of glory throughout the civilized world are not such at this hour that the defeat of England by sea and land would add immensely to the prestige of France, to the personal status of all her citizens in the maxima civitas of nations, and make the meanest of them feel himself conspicuous in the eyes of every people from America to China? When, after such reflections, we imagine the many roads to national distinction upon which the French might occupy the foremost place, but to which they give little heed; when we find among them such an intense appreciation, and such prodigious sacrifices for military fame; when the accumulation of capital among them, and the consequent growth of a pacific political power, is prevented by the fundamental conditions of their polity, it would seem impossible to deny that the latent force of the warlike element in France is at all times prodigious; that so far as it is latent it occupies the place of the deep general attachment to peace which is felt in England; and that its actual ebullition in war depends partly upon the temper and life of a single individual, and partly on the occasions offered by the state of Europe, and the weakness of neighbouring powers. But these are the conditions of a military age and society. And thus it is that De Tocqueville has described his countrymen: 'Apt for all things, but excelling only in war; adoring chance, force, success, splendour, and noise more than true glory; more capable of heroism than of virtue, of genius than of good sense; the most brilliant and the most dangerous of the nations of Europe; and that best fitted to become by turns an object of admiration, of hatred, of pity, of terror, but never of indifference.'

It is this people which has elected an absolute monarch, and that monarch is Napoleon III. But it is an obvious inference from this fact alone, that a community, which, however advanced in some of the arts of civilization, has not outgrown the superintendence of despotic government, nor learned to govern itself or to trust itself with liberty, has not arrived at that stage of progress in which the claims of industry and peace can be steadily and consistently paramount in the councils of the state. The traditions of old, and still more the exigencies and ambitions of new imperial dynasties, are incompatible with the conditions of the greatest economic prosperity. Neither are the independence and robustness of thought educated by free industrial life favourable to the permanence of an unlimited monarchy. Let us, indeed, ask if it be auspicious of the entry of Europe upon the industrial and pacific stage, and the millennium of merchants, that the trade of the world has hung since the truce of Villafranca upon the tokens of peace, few and far between, that have fallen from the lips of a military chief?

Yet that chief has deeply studied history, and gathered the lesson that monarchs must march at the head of the ideas of their age.[*] And there are indications that the vision of a holy alliance of the sovereigns of Europe for the maintenance of the peace and brotherhood of nations rose before his youthful mind as one of such ideas. In 1832, he mused as follows:[†]—

'We hear talk of eternal wars, of interminable struggles, and yet it would be an easy matter for the sovereigns of the

---

[*] Historical Fragments. Works of Napoleon III.
[†] Political Reveries. Works of Napoleon III.

world to consolidate an everlasting peace. Let them consult the mutual relations, the habits of the nations among themselves; let them **grant** the nationality, **the** institutions which they demand, and they will have arrived at the secret of a true political balance. Then will all nations be brothers, and they will embrace each other in the presence of tyranny dethroned, of a world **refreshed** and consolidated, and of a contented humanity.'

But experience has not increased the confidence of the wise in princes **or holy alliances. One** has indeed but to glance at the conditions essential, in the mind of so subtle a politician as Napoleon III., to the peace of Europe, and their inevitable consequence, to rest assured that its present sovereigns could hardly **grant** them if they would, and would not concur to yield them **if they** could. For what are these conditions? The nationality **and the** institutions which the **nations demand.** And what is to be the consequence? **Tyranny** dethroned.

Such really are, **if not the only requisites** to 'consolidate the world and content humanity,' the indispensable supports of 'a true political balance.' And let the history of the last twelve years—let the **war** in Hungary in 1849, and the war in Italy in 1859—let the dungeons of Naples, the people of Venetia, the Romagna, Sicily, and Hungary **in 1860 (should** we not add Nice and Savoy?) say if the sovereigns of Europe are ready to concede without a struggle the nationality **and the** institutions for which the nations cry.

Let us not, however, ungratefully regret that the year 1860 **opened with** an assurance from the chief of the sovereigns of **Europe, of** his desire, ' so far as depends on him, to re-establish **peace and confidence.' Yet this is** but personal security for our confidence. Should Napoleon III. in truth be anxious and resolute for peace, yet a few **years,** and the firmness of the hand which controls an impetuous and warlike democracy must relax, and afterwards the floods of national passion may come and beat against a house of **peace** built upon the sand of an Emperor's words. Gibbon has **remarked** upon the instability of the happiness of the Roman **Empire** in the era of the Antonines, **because** ' depending on the character of a single man.' The son and successor of Marcus Aurelius was the brutal tyrant Commodus. Besides, we cannot forget that he who 'dreamed not of the Empire and of war,'* in 1848, had, 'at the end of four years,' re-established the Empire; that the third year of that Empire was the beginning of strife with Russia, and that its last was a year of unfinished war with Austria. Moreover, under the second Empire, all France is assuming the appearance of a camp in the centre of Europe, and this phenomenon becomes more portentous if we take in connexion with it the Emperor's opinion respecting the precautions necessary to preserve the honour and assert the rightful claims of France. In 1843, he wrote: 'At the present time it is not sufficient for a nation to have a few hundred cavaliers, or some thousand mercenaries, in order to uphold its rank and support its independence; it needs millions of armed men. . . . The terrible example of Waterloo has not taught us. . . . The problem to be resolved is this—to resist a coalition France needs an immense army; nay more, it needs a reserve of trained men, in case of a reverse.'

We must infer, either that in 1843 Louis Napoleon foresaw that France was destined to pursue a policy which would, to a moral certainty, bring her into conflict with the other powers; or that in his deliberate judgment no great European state is secure without millions of disciplined soldiers, against a coalition of other states for its destruction. If this be a true judgment, in what an age do we live! But, at least, the armaments of France prove that its sovereign has not hesitated to employ its utmost resources for the purpose of enabling it to 'resist a coalition;' and a late despatch of Lord John Russell supplies the fitting comment. 'M. Thouvenel conceives that Sardinia might be a member of a confederacy arrayed against France. Now, on this Her Majesty's Government would observe, that there never can be a confederacy organized against France, unless it be for common defence against aggressions on the part of France.'† Another natural reflection presents itself, that if

* 'Je ne suis pas un ambitieux qui rêve l'Empire et la guerre. Si j'étais nommé Président je mettrais mon honneur à laisser au but de quatre ans à mon successeur le pouvoir affermi, la liberté intacte.' Proclamation of Louis Napoleon, December 10, 1848.

† Further Correspondence relative to the Affairs of Italy, Part IV. No. 2.

Napoleon III. can solve 'the **problem,**' and make France powerful enough to defy a confederacy, he has but to divide, in order to tyrannize over Europe. An apology which has been made for the great military, and more especially the great naval, preparations of France—that they indicate no new or Napoleonic idea, but are simply the realization of plans conceived under a former government—may be well founded. But then the question recurs—are these preparations necessary, or are they not? Does France really need 'millions of armed men,' or does she not? If she does, what conclusions must we form respecting the character of the age, and the theory of the extinction of the military element in modern Europe? Shall we say that it is an economical, industrious, and pacific age, or one of restlessness, danger, alarm and war? On the other hand, if there is nothing in surrounding Europe to justify the armaments of France, what must we think of the deliberate schemes of the French Government and the probabilities of peace? There is, too, another consideration—namely, that whatever be the reason and meaning of these facts, they are facts which must be accepted with their natural consequences. You cannot pile barrels of gunpowder round your neighbour's house without danger of a spark falling from your own chimney or his, or from the torch of some fool or incendiary. In the presence then of these phenomena, indicating what they do of the reciprocal relations and attitude of the most civilized states, can we say that the political aspect of the world and the condition of international morality would be unaptly described in the language applied to them two hundred years ago by Hobbes: 'Every nation has a right to do what it pleases to other commonwealths. And withal they live in the condition of perpetual war, with their frontiers armed and cannons planted against their neighbours round about?'

There are, notwithstanding, sanguine politicians, who look upon these things as transitional and well-nigh past, who view the darkest prospects of the hour as the passing clouds of the morning of peace, and the immediate heralds of that day when nation shall not lift up sword against nation, neither shall they learn war any more. Of the advent of that period not one doubt is meant to be suggested here. But the measures of time which history and philosophy put into our hands are different from those which the statesman **must employ.** An age is but as a day to the eye to which the **condition of the globe** when **it was first** trodden by savage men **is present.** But those whose vision is confined to the **fleeting moments so** important to themselves, that cover their **own lifetime and that of their** children, will deem the reign of peace **far distant if** removed to a third generation.

What, then, is the interpretation of the signs of the times on **which a** practical people should fix **its scrutiny?** To this **question, the** question of the **age—whether it means peace or** war—it **is believed** that the **preceding** pages supply **a partial** answer, which we have not here room to make more full and definite; or it could be shown that the form and **spirit of the** age, the imperfection of the mechanism for the adjustment of international rights, the ill organization of continental polities, the **impending** repartition of Europe, and the aspect of remoter portions of the **globe compose a** political horizon charged **with** the elements of war.

VII.

THE FUTURE OF EUROPE FORETOLD IN HISTORY.[*]

(Macmillan's Magazine, September, 1860.)

THE events of the last year and a half, and the character of the agitation over many parts of the continent, must have banished from the most conservative and peaceable minds in this country all confidence in the stability of the present political and territorial divisions of Europe. Whatever there may be in the numerous omens of departure from the status quo to alarm or to interest Englishmen, there is at least no occasion for surprise at the prospect. Europe is not now for the first time occupied about the removal of ancient landmarks. Its history is a chronicle of continual repartitions of its territory. Experience therefore would warrant no other expectation than that of further re-arrangements, but it may not be so obvious that experience can help us to foresee the consummation towards which all such changes converge.

It is the object of this essay to show that all the alterations of the political map, since the dissolution of the Roman Empire, have proceeded upon a uniform principle and in one direction; and that, from a comparison of accomplished facts with the tendency of existing movements, we may gather instruction of a practical kind respecting our prospects and duties, considered as both Englishmen and Europeans,—or as citizens not only of the British Empire, but of the great commonwealth of civilized states.

[*] The reader will remember that this Essay was written nearly nineteen years ago. As in the case of the preceding Essay, the author adheres to its main principles and conclusions, but not to every sentence.

For the most part, nations are not more slow to anticipate the revolutions of time, than they are quick to forget the order of things which those revolutions supersede. Thus French historians of all systems, and politicians of all parties, are accustomed to assume that their nation and government have some ancient, natural, and immutable title to their present, and even more extensive boundaries;* although, in truth, France has very lately reached her existing limits—by nine hundred years of war and usurpation—and has no other right to them than the power to hold what she has seized, the gradual acquiescence of many vanquished peoples, and the final assent of the rest of Europe.

Whatever unity Gaul possessed as a province of the empire of the Cæsars—as a single fraction of that vast imperial unit—was a matter of Roman administration entirely; there was nothing national, much less modern or French in it. Nay, during the integrity of the province, as such, those bands of German warriors (through whom, by a singular fortune, the Frank name came by degrees to be imposed upon several distinct nationalities and independent states) had not crossed the Somme, and they never finally occupied or governed more than a small portion of the land between the Rhine, the Alps, and the Pyrenees. The army of Clovis had but a momentary and partial success south of the Loire, and made no conquest of Brittany. Charles the Great had no better title to the sovereignty of the various nations then in Gaul than to the rest of his evanescent empire, which was but an incident of the German invasions, and scarcely belongs to the history and settlement of modern Europe.

By the treaty of Verdun in 843, the Meuse and the Rhone

* This idea is more deeply rooted in the French mind than is commonly believed in England, and would be dangerous to the peace of Europe even if there were no Bonapartists living.

'La nature ne voulut que le maintien de nos limites naturelles. L'idée de les reprendre ne se perdra jamais : elle est profondément nationale et profondément historique.'—Thierry, Récits des Temps Mérov. i. 194.

'C'est seulement au traité de Verdun, en 843, que la France a reculé du Rhin et des Alpes. Elle n'a cessé de reclamer son antique heritage.'—Duruy, Hist. de France, i. 2.

Jusqu'où allait la Gaule, disait Richelieu, jusque là doit aller là France.' —Id. ii. 224. Compare Thiers, Hist. du Consulat et de l'Empire, vol. xvii. p. 124, and passim.

became the boundaries of Charles the Bald's nominal kingdom of France or Gaul. But so broken is the succession between ancient and Roman Gaul, this Carlovingian France, and the **modern country of** that name, that, towards the end of the tenth century, while the genuine Romans **and** primitive Celts **were** slaves, **the** Bretons, Normans, Burgundians, Visigoths, **and** Gascons maintained against the Franks their separate territories, their distinct nationality, names, and political independence. About **this time it** was that the duke of a small district north **of the Loire,** insulated by natural boundaries, **and long** afterwards called the Isle of France, assumed, with the consent of some **of the chieftains** of **northern Gaul, the title** of King; **thereby** effacing the last vestige of the Carlovingian sovereignty, **while** laying the foundation of the modern realm **of** France. For more than two centuries after Hugh Capet was crowned, **the** people south of the Loire were distinguished by the general name of Romans from the **people above** that river, who were called (though **not invariably or** without dispute) Franks or French. During this period the only monarch who reigned by legitimate right on both sides of this natural boundary of France was the King of England. Until the crusade of Simon de Montfort, followed by the annexation to the crown of France of Languedoc and Provence, 'the French of the north had vainly endeavoured to extend their rule over the Gallo-Roman or Gothic population of the south. The language divided and defined the two yet unmingled races. Throughout the war the Crusaders are described as **the** Franks, as a foreign nation **invading** a separate territory.'* The annexation of Belgium **or** Switzerland at this day would not be a more cruel violation **of national rights** and feelings than that which is thus described by a French historian:—'Thus were annexed to the kingdom of France **the** provinces **of ancient** Gaul situated right and left of the Rhone, except Guienne and the valleys at the foot of the Pyrenees. **The** most disastrous period in the history of the people of southern **France is** that at which **they** became French; when the king, **whom their** ancestors used **to** call the King of Paris, began to term **them his** subjects **of** the langue d'oc, in

* **Milman's** Latin Christianity, iv. 204.

contra-distinction to the French of the Outre Loire, who spoke the langue d'oui. Hatred of the French name was the national passion of the new subjects of the King of France; and, even after more than two hundred years had elapsed, to fall under his immediate government, by the extinction of the counts of Anjou, appeared to the people of Provence a new national calamity.'*

Guienne, likewise, it is well known, formed no part of the original dominions of the Capetian dynasty, and was not annexed until some time after the expulsion of the English in the fifteenth century, whose departure was long lamented by many of the inhabitants of the duchy.

When, finally, the last English town had been captured, in 1558, Francis II. was crowned King of France from Calais to the Pyrenees, by no better title than that which had led to the coronation of Henry VI. of England upon the same throne, that is to say, the fortune of war.

In another sense the war with England may be said to have created the French monarchy and nation; for, as every French historian confesses, it was in the course of that long struggle that the different races began to forget the natural, or primitive and uncivilized divisions of locality and descent, and by making common cause against a common enemy, to regard each other as fellow countrymen. Yet even at the beginning of the seventeenth century the territory of France was far short of its present boundaries; the policy of Richelieu, the merciless encroachments of Louis XIV., and after his death a century and a half of war and annexation followed, before Alsace, la Franche Comté, Roussillon, Lorraine, Nice, and Savoy, could be included under a single government, or inhabited by a united nation.†

Thus the history of France, and of the consolidation of the different races, languages, laws, and governments which once flourished between the Mediterranean, the Alps, and the

* Thierry's Norman Conquest.

† 'La revolution et les guerres de la revolution ont plus fait pour l'unité de la France que n'auraient fait dix siècles.'—Revue des Deux Mondes, 1 Juillet, 1860. Nice and Savoy cannot, even now, be regarded as irrevocably annexed to France.

Atlantic, is identical in its main features with that of the growth of the empire of all the Russias out of the dukedom of Moscow. It is one series of conquests, annexations, and usurpations; one continuous repudiation of geographical, or fixed natural limits; one unsparing denial of claims to national independence and unity founded on race, history, language, institutions, and locality. The genuine traditions of French policy no more recognise the Rhine, the Alps, and the Pyrenees as the natural boundaries of France than the Oise, the Marne, and the Cevennes, the Rhone, the Loire, and the Garonne, or the Vosges and the Saone, which have been successively crossed. The Elbe and the Carpathians, the Ebro, and the Mediterranean,* are beyond. So long as earth and water remain for her heralds to demand, France will not want popular doctrines, 'which may reach forth just occasions (as may be pretended) of war.'† The conscience of the nation is in this respect more easily satisfied than even that of the ancient Romans, who, as Lord Bacon notices in his remarks on the advantage to an empire of habits and ideas suggestive of military enterprise, 'though they esteemed the extending of the limits of their empire to be great honour to their generals when it was accomplished, yet never rested upon that alone to begin a war.'‡ Indeed, the Romans modestly held their public festival in honour of the god of boundaries, 'on the sixth milestone towards Laurentum, because this was originally the extent of the Roman territory in that direction.'§ Upon the same principle the French should celebrate their Terminalia, not at Utrecht, Coblentz, or Genoa, but near the fourth milestone on the road from Paris to St. Denis, along which Louis VI. so often rode, lance in hand, to the abbey of which he was a vassal, at the end of his royal domains; and along which Louis XIV. may have passed on his way to invade the United Provinces in 1672.‖

* The Mediterranean has already been not indistinctly spoken of as a French lake by natural position.
† Bacon. Essay XXIX. Of the True Greatness of Kingdoms.
‡ Ib.
§ Smith's Greek and Roman Antiquities.
‖ In 1671 Sir William Temple predicted this war in terms which an English Statesman might use almost without variation in 1860:—'In regard there are several conquests remaining upon record (though all of them the mere result of our own divisions and invitations),—when trade is grown the design of all

But although the greatness of France has been accomplished by an unswerving policy of aggression, as threatening now **as in the** days of Louis XIV., it would be a blind study of history to overlook the immense acquisitions to the domain of civilization from the substitution of one powerful monarchy for many independent and hostile states. The successors of Hugh Capet might hold the language of the Roman conqueror to the subjugated Gauls: 'Regna bellaque per Gallias semper fuere donec in nostrum jus concederetis.'* It should console us even for the surviving jealousy of the English name, that so many other rancorous national antipathies are **buried for ever; and that a** numerous and illustrious people now dwell together as brethren in unity, and, however high and martial their spirit, will draw the sword against each other as aliens no more. Nay, even this is some compensation for past aggression, that Europe has now the warning of so many centuries that France will, sooner or later, bear down the opposition of all unequal and divided force, acknowledging no frontiers short of the most convenient positions to support the extension of her territory; and that, between it and Russia, only brave, united, and powerful nations can permanently preserve their independence. It is still more pertinent to our argument to observe that the history of France, as of every other great modern **state,** establishes one central

nations in Europe; when, instead of a king of France surrounded and bearded by the dukes of Brittany and Burgundy, as well as our own possessions **of** Normandy and Guienne, we now behold in France the greatest forces that perhaps have ever been known under the command of any Christian Prince, it may import us in this calm we enjoy to hearken to the storms that are now rising abroad, and by the best perspectives that we have, to discover from what coast they break. . . If there were any certain height where the flights of power and ambition use to end, we might imagine that the interest of France were but to conserve its present greatness, so feared by its neighbours, and so glorious **in** the world; but, besides that the motions and desires **of** human minds are endless, it may be necessary for France to have some **war or** other **in** pursuit **abroad** which may amuse the nation, and keep them **from reflecting on** their condition at home, hard and uneasy to all but such as are in pay from the Court. . . . Besides the personal dispositions of the king, active and aspiring, and many circumstances in the Government, the continual increase of their forces in time of peace, and their fresh invasion of Lorraine, are enough to persuade most men that the design of the crown is a war whenever they can open it with a prospect of succeeding to purpose.'—Survey of the Constitutions, &c. in 1671.

* Tacit. **Hist.** lib. iv. cap. 73.

truth, that political unity, and the consequent supremacy of law over all quarrel, can alone supersede the jurisdiction of force,* and that all Europe has been steadily extending the areas of fellow-citizenship and patriotism, and steadily enclosing international feud and the war of independent sovereigns and societies within legal barriers, ever since the anarchy and independence (as it is called) of savage life took shelter under the feudal system.

In that primitive settlement and organization, in fixed localities and homes, of wandering barbarians, we discover the germ and archetype of the state and the nucleus of the modern nation, that is to say, of a society which has fused ancient differences of descent and blood, and is united by a larger and nobler tie than that of the family or tribe. Conquerors and conquered, companions in arms, often of different origins, settled upon the same spot, formed one defensive compact, fixed and fortified their site, choosing where it was possible such frontiers as had natural advantages for defence and war, and which in this sense nature indicated and ordained. Every hill and stream afforded at once a landmark and a natural fortification. Within these narrow and precarious boundaries industry and society might take root at last; for, although there was war —incessant war—without, there was peace within. There was war without, not (as M. Guizot observes) because of the brutality of feudal manners, but on account of the absence of any central authority to make binding general rules, enforce their observance, and settle disputed rights. There is not always in war anything necessarily and essentially barbarous. It is often the only final process by which independent powers can conclude angry differences about subjects to which they attach vital importance. It does not of necessity arise from wilful or conscious injustice on either side; when it does, it implies spirited resistance to injustice on the other side, which civilized men are the most apt to make. The feudal wars were in this respect quite analogous to those of modern states, which, by reason of their independence, have often no means of legislating conclusively

---

* In societate civili aut lex, aut vis valet. Bacon, De Fontibus Juris. Aphorismus I.

for Europe and other parts of the world except by arms, or 'armed opinions.'

But interdependence and peace, not independence and war, seem the ultimate destiny of mankind. And thus we find throughout the middle ages a perpetual consolidation of petty sovereignties and republics, produced by that tendency of human society to unity, which, beginning with the composition of innumerable fiefs in the ninth century, has issued in a few great states and nations in the nineteenth. The poor freeman exchanged his liberty for the protection of the neighbouring lord; the lord became the vassal of the greater count or duke, compelled in his turn to acknowledge the supremacy of some more powerful suzerain; until monarchy rose upon the ruins of their common independence;* and although it rose for the most part cruelly, oppressively, and treacherously, men hailed its appearance because they could fly from petty tyrants to the throne, and only an army capable of invading a great state could annoy a poor man's dwelling.

The decline of feudalism not only proves the essentially transitory character of political divisions and boundaries, and the constant tendency of those forces, which impel the movements of European society, to sweep larger circles of civil union, but also throws a light on the chief cause of the essentially military structure of modern civilization. Petty independent states make war because of their independence, and petty wars because their powers are petty. Great states, too, make war because of their independence, and their wars are great in proportion to their own magnitude. And withal, 'they live,' as Hobbes has said, 'in the condition of perpetual war, with their frontiers armed, and cannons planted against their neighbours round about.' When Richelieu destroyed the fortifications of the

---

* 'The tendency to centralization, towards the formation of a power superior to local powers, was rapid. Long before general royalty—French royalty—appeared, upon all parts of the territory there were formed under the names of duchy, county, viscounty, &c., many petty royalties invested with central government, and under the rule of which the rights of the possessors of fiefs, that is to say, local sovereignties, gradually disappeared. Such were the natural and necessary results of the vices of the feudal system, and especially of the excessive predominance of individual independence.'—GUIZOT, Civilization in France.

feudal engineers. Vauban fortified the frontiers of the kingdom. Powerful countries have powerful adversaries, but they close in a common patriotism a thousand local enmities.

We have seen that this was so in France; so it was in Spain. 'For several hundred years after the Saracenic invasion at the beginning of the eighth century, Spain was broken up into a number of small but independent states, divided in their interests, and often **in deadly** hostility with one another. It was inhabited by races the **most** dissimilar in their origin, religion, and government. . . . By the middle of the fifteenth century the number **of states** into which the country had been divided was reduced **to four, Castile,** Arragon, and Navarre, and the Moorish kingdom **of** Granada. At the close of that century these various races were blended into one great nation under one common **rule. The** war of Granada subjected all the sections of the country to one common action, under the influence of common motives of the most exciting kind; **while** it brought them in conflict with a race, **the** extreme repugnance of whose institutions and character to their own served greatly to nourish the sentiment of nationality. In this way the spark of patriotism was kindled throughout the whole nation, and the most distant provinces of the Peninsula were knit together by a bond of union which has remained indissoluble. The petty states which had before swarmed over the country, neutralizing each other's operations, and preventing any effective movement abroad, were now amalgamated into one whole. Sectional jealousies and antipathies, indeed, were too sturdily rooted to be wholly extinguished, but they gradually subsided under the influence **of a** common government and community of interests. A more enlarged sentiment was infused into the people, who, in their foreign relations at least, assumed the attitude of one great nation. The **names of** Castilian and Arragonese were merged in the comprehensive one of Spaniard.'*

In like manner the comprehensive name of Englishman denotes a fusion of **races which once** hated each other with a hatred passing that of the Breton or Provençal for the Frenchman; and the United Kingdom has grown great by the fall of

* Prescott's Life and Times of Ferdinand and Isabella.

as many independent princes as now divide and harass Germany. The Saxon heptarchy, itself originally far more subdivided, was first compressed into an English monarchy; Wales, Ireland, and Scotland were then included. And this consolidated insular state became the nucleus of a maritime empire, whose outposts in Europe are Heligoland, Gibraltar,* Malta, and those floating fortifications demanded by commerce at an epoch when art has effaced the boundaries of nature, and placed in immediate juxtaposition all the conflicting traditions and interests of the old and new worlds; when in fact civilization itself is militant, as well as conscious that it must perish, if ever it meets with superior force on the side of barbarism. The British isles, in Virgil's days, 'divided from the whole world,' are, in our days, closely united to a larger world than the Roman poet knew.

For three centuries the breadth of the Rhine sufficed to protect the Roman province of Gaul from invasion by the Franks, and was accordingly regarded as the natural boundary of the Empire in that direction. Now the English Channel is not a sufficient boundary, and we are side by side with those same Franks, who have fought their way from the Rhine to the Atlantic, seizing as they came some considerable Gallo-Roman possessions of the English Crown.

Our insular history ceased when our American and Asiatic history began; and we are called on to defend our trade and citizens not only by the British shores, but along the St. Lawrence, the Red Sea, and the Indian Ocean. These are become the natural boundaries of our Empire. But the boundaries of empires are inconstant things; the earth acknowledges the permanent dominion only of powerful and united nations. The laws of nature have decreed that the strong must increase and the feeble decrease, and have set a bounty on the firm conjunction of numerous patriotic hearts.

* The title of Great Britain to Gibraltar is infinitely better than that under which France garrisons Strasburg. Strasburg was treacherously seized, as well as several other towns, by Louis XIV. in time of peace, without the least pretence of justifiable hostilities. Gibraltar was taken by the British in lawful war, and its ownership is confirmed to them not only by the Treaty of Utrecht, but by a possession of nearly the same length as that during which it was previously held by the Spaniards, after having captured it from the Moors. The Spaniards, a very modern nation, have not a better right to their dominion over the greater part of the peninsula.

Where now are the boundaries of Poland, whose internal divisions scattered a dominion which, stretching from the Baltic to the Euxine, and from the Danube to the Dnieper, threatened to defeat the destinies of Brandenburg and Moscow?

Russian patriots and statesman have reason to rejoice that the cruel yoke of the Tartars rescued their country from being lost in Poland, by creating a national unity paramount over the local differences of many petty principalities.* That mighty empire, which has crossed the Urals and broken down the middle wall of partition between Europe and Asia; which has conquered the most stubborn barriers of race and distance; swallowed up Finland, Poland, Siberia, Circassia, and great part of Tartary, and which now threatens at once China and Turkey—first emerged from the union of many feeble independent tribes, which a thousand years ago were spread over the plains of the Volga, and from the gradual subjection to a common government of numerous chiefs, once the equals of the dukes of Moscow.

In the history of the Netherlands our theory finds another melancholy confirmation. Had the Germans and Celts of Holland and Belgium been capable of spontaneous combination, or been consolidated by a line of politic princes, they would not at this moment be regarded as a sort of natural prey by that mixture of German and Celt, the Frenchman. A division of races has made Belgium the battle-field of Europe, and exposed Holland to the peril of ultimate submersion beneath a mightier and more indefatigable power than the ocean. Yet there might have been reared on the opposite shore of the North Sea a polity as grand as that which in these islands has arisen from the union of elements more opposed than any that have divided the Netherlands into two small and precarious kingdoms. In his 'History of the Dutch Republic,' Mr. Motley has well observed—

'Had so many valuable and contrasted characteristics been early fused into a whole, it would be difficult to show a race more richly endowed by nature for dominion and progress than the Belgo-Germanic people. The prominent characteristics, by which the two great races of the land were distinguished, time

† La Verité sur la Russie, par le Prince Dolgoroukow.

has rather hardened than effaced. In their contrast and separation lies the key to much of their history. Had Providence permitted a fusion of the two races, it is possible, from their position, and from the geographical and historical link which they would have afforded to the dominant tribes of people, that a world-empire might have been the result, different in many respects from any which has yet arisen.'

King Leopold said lately to his people, ' Let us never forget the motto which our country has chosen for its own, " It is union that constitutes strength ;" ' and well would it have been if their proper fellow-countrymen, the Dutch, could have adopted and acted on such a motto long ago. But the tide in the affairs of men must be taken at the flood. The narrow sympathies and selfish arrogance of the Dutch have bound them to their native shallows.

Yet some gleam of hope is reflected northwards on Belgium and Holland from the prospects of two other countries by the side of France. It seems to be the destiny of the French to promote the unity of nations both when they fail and when they prosper in their designs on neighbouring states; in one case by identifying with a marvellous faculty the feelings and interests of their new compatriots with their own, and in the other by compelling the communities, whose independence they threaten, to close their differences in the presence of a common danger. Austria, too, seems doomed to forward those amalgamations of mankind which are most opposed to her cherished policy. Thus, although the divisions of Germany and the feuds of Italy are as ancient as the breach between Holland and Belgium, their termination in a broad and generous patriotism is at hand; adding fresh proof that it will not be the fate of Europe to be for ever subdivided by barbarian origin or situation, and that old maps and canons of descent do not fix irrevocably the terms of nationality. Prussia, the hope of Germany, has no frontiers in nature; and her capital is built on a river which once ran between natural enemies—between pitiless Dutchmen and obstinate Wends.* And Piedmont has crept from a transalpine seignory into an Italian kingdom.

* Carlyle's History of Frederick the Great.

There never was a great state or nation which did not combine in one country and people a diversity of territories and races. Affinities of blood may produce congenial manners in contiguous communities, may touch the imagination, and arouse the sympathies of the human heart, and so facilitate the formation of larger and more coherent unions than our ancestors in Europe were able to contrive. Latin, Teutonic, Slavonic, or Scandinavian genealogies may help to conjoin, but they cannot keep for ever apart the people of Christendom. They have failed to put asunder the Frank, the Roman, the Goth, and the Breton in France, and the Dane, the Saxon, the Norman, and the Celt in the British islands. The truth at the bottom of current theories of 'the nationalities' is that there is a tendency of the people of the continent to assemble in great solid masses round a centre. The dissolution of imperfect political formations is but the antecedent of recomposition into more consistent unities. Thus Normandy, Brittany, Anjou, and Guienne parted from England (with which close association was then impossible) to combine inseparably with a nearer neighbour.

Though all the repartitions which Europe has undergone since the fall of the empire of the Romans, which fell because it was unable to unite the men of the north with the men of the south, the operation of one centripetal law is visible in a perpetual effort towards the establishment of wider and firmer bases of civil society, and the composition of fewer and greater states and nations. Everywhere we now find names which are the genuine historical vestiges of the earlier groupings of mankind under petty independent or unconnected governments. Many English counties once were separate kingdoms. The eighty-six departments of France are, as it were, the hatchments of so many departed feudal sovereignties. Germany, which once counted its princes and republics by hundreds, now counts them by tens, and may soon count them by twos. And, in Italy, the same generation, which has tolerated ten nominally independent states, seems no longer able to tolerate more than one. Nationality has so widened its borders that what once was patriotism and fidelity, is now disloyalty and treason; what was the language of a separate people is faintly heard in a

provincial accent; and that which was the general **law of a
kingdom** is with difficulty detected by an antiquary in the usages
of a few quaint and secluded peasants. Europe has already
almost concentrated itself into a heptarchy or **octarchy, or into**
fewer independent states than there were a few years ago in
Italy alone. **But if, in place** of—for example say—seven
hundred **states, there** be only seven, it follows that only the
difference of seven instead of seven hundred nations or governments can lead to war, and that all smaller feuds are brought
under the cognisance of an impartial judge.

Let **us not,** however, **mistake the consequence.** The substitution of civil union for the hostilities incident to a state **of**
natural isolation has neither extinguished warfare, nor has **it**
been for the most part peacefully accomplished. Sword in hand
the sovereigns of Europe have extended their dominions, and
cut off the belligerent right of independence from their conquered
neighbours. And when the supremacy of law has thus been
established over wider areas, ousting therein the jurisdiction of
force and the original trial by battle, the magnitude of external
war bears proportion to the dimensions of the aggrandized states.
Hitherto civilization has led, **not** so much to the extinction **of**
hostilities, **as to** their disappearance on a small scale, and
resumption on **a vast one. When** the battles of the Saxon
heptarchy were finished, England began her battles with Wales,
Ireland, and Scotland, followed by **her greater struggle** with
France. Now a duel between two great **states calls all** the
others into the field. And it may **be that Asia will** one day
rise in arms against the intrusion of western **civilization,** and
that a war of hemispheres may precede **the** submission by
mankind **of all** their differences to legal arbitration.

In societate civili aut **lex aut vis valet.** The existence of
law in civilized society is based upon experience that the natural
state of independent human beings is mistrust, violence, and
warfare; that they covet the same objects, are not, nor can be
just to each other in their competition; and that they are prone
to employ the tyranny of force to obtain submission to their
partial wills. It **is** singular that the very politicians who deride
the **necessity of** precautions against foreign **aggression** are

peculiarly apprehensive of an abuse of the power of the sword by their own government. They admit readily that life and property require protection against the licence of their countrymen; they appear doubtful of the sufficiency of the rigid checks with which the British constitution surrounds the prerogative of their own sovereign; and yet they affirm that we have nothing to apprehend in the most defenceless condition from foreign armies and potentates, over whose movements we have no control of law. They think their fellow-citizens partial, prejudiced, and liable to be swayed by passions and caprice; sometimes even dishonest, and often overbearing. They are urgent against allowing those in high places at home to enforce their own pretensions; yet they ask us to trust implicitly to the fairness and goodwill of people who have, comparatively, few interests and associations in common with us, and some ancient grudges against us. If the chief of another state is capable of shedding the blood of his own subjects for his personal aggrandizement —if he taxes, confiscates, banishes, and imprisons at his arbitrary pleasure in his native territory—if he suffers no voice to be raised against his despotic will among those who have given him all his greatness, is it possible that our wealth, our liberty, our defiant press should never tempt aggression? If it be his manifest policy that all the splendid genius of his nation should be concealed, and only one head figure above the crowd in the eyes of Europe, can he look without jealousy at the celebrity and power of numerous foreigners who thwart his projects and wound his ambition? It is not supposed that we ourselves are just in all our international dealings; that we have done no wrong in Europe, America, or Asia; that we have never invaded a weaker power, and that the most defenceless people are safe from our dictation; and yet we are told that, so far as other nations are concerned, the age of conquest and warfare is gone by. Are Venice, Constantinople, Alexandria, Jerusalem, and Pekin, not prizes which civilized states are eager to grasp, and for which they are likely to contend? 'What would men have?' says Lord Bacon. 'Do they think that those they employ and deal with are saints? Do they not think they will

have their own ends, and be truer to themselves than to them?"*
The course which civilization has pursued is, in truth, so far
from having divested society of a military garb, that it has
animated the most forward communities with an ambition of
aggrandizement, such as the ancient Romans scarcely knew; that
passions and principles, new in the world's history, are in
tumultuous conflict in the bosom of nations; that the boasted
annihilation of distance has brought the armies of Europe so
close, that it is but a word, and then a blow; and that we can
only hope to avoid war by casting the sharpest **sword** into the
scale of peace.

Is this condition, then, the perpetual destiny of Europe?
Shall the sword devour for ever? History, rightly understood,
seems to answer, not. For why should the progress of human
confederation, and of the rule of law, cease so soon as seven or
eight states shall have been compounded of more than as many
hundred? There is **not, as** we have some reason to know,
anything sacred or eternal in the numerical proportions of a
heptarchy or an octarchy,—nor anything to arrest the action of
those natural forces which have extended civic union already
from the hamlet to the vast empire. Φύσει πολιτικὸν ζῶον
ἄνθρωπος. By his whole nature, by his worst and most selfish
passions as well as by his best affections, by his weakness as
well as by his strength, man is driven into political association
with his fellows. Hunger, ambition, avarice, and fear, as well
as public spirit, generosity, and genius, have **been** the architects
of civilized society; and war, alike by its conquests, **its** enthusiasms, and **its** terrors, has been the greatest peacemaker among
mankind. There is, then, in the aggravated perils of Europe,
no **ground for** alarm about its final destinies. Law is not the
child of natural justice in **men. It is** compulsory justice.
Violence, quarrel, and the general danger are its parents; as
pain and disease have called into existence the physician's art.
The more frequent the occasions of international dispute, and
the more awful **their** consequence, the more speedily **does** legal
arbitration naturally, necessarily arise. Already we may discern

---

* Essay on Suspicion.

in the womb of time an infant European senate, **and the rudiments of European law. And as the plot thickens,** as nations **come closer** together in order of **battle, as they confederate for conquest and defence,** European unity gains ground. The fear of France unites Germany; the hatred of Austria consolidates **Italy; and the** question of the East, even if it must be answered **by the sword,** promotes the final settlement of the great question **of** the West—the frame of the future polity of Europe.

Already is Europe more obviously and essentially one country, one state, than France was a few hundred years ago, and more is done for **the** growth of **nations in** a generation now than in a century **then.** 'The inhabitants of Provence,' **says** M. Guizot, **' of Languedoc,** Aquitaine, **Normandy, Maine,** &c., had, it is true, special names, laws, destinies of their **own;** they were, under **the various** appellations **of** Angevins, Manceaux, Normands, Provinçaux, &c., so many nations, so many states, distinct from **each** other, often at war with **each other.** Yet above all these various territories, above **all these** petty nations, there hovered a **sole and** single name, a general idea, **the idea of** a nation called the French, of a common country called France.' It may in like manner be said of Great Britain, France, Germany, Italy, Russia, &c., **that above all** these various territories, above all these **nations, distinct** from each other, **often** at war with each other, there hovers **a sole and single name, a** general idea, the idea of a nation called **the Europeans, of** a common country called Europe.

The people of **that great country** are even now unconsciously debating about its future institutions. It is for us to provide **that** Europe shall finally be something nobler than a great shop, something less miserable than a great prison. The citizens of the future Europe will owe the measure of liberty they may enjoy, and the **degree of** public spirit and generosity with which they may be endowed, partly to the exertions and example of the citizens **of Great Britain.**

VIII.

NATIONS AND INTERNATIONAL LAW.[*]

(*Fortnightly Review*, July 1, 1868.)

'It is easy,' a French publicist announces, in an essay of remarkable interest, 'to see that the perplexities of modern diplomacy—these still-born congresses dissolved before they are assembled, these treaties torn as soon as concluded, all the disorder, in short, to which international relations are given over—have their ultimate source in the difficulty of bending the new principles of government introduced by the French Revolution into conformity with the rules of the old law of nations. Diplomacy, accustomed to maintain the intercourse of kings, masters of their people, knows not how to bring peoples

---

[*] In this Essay, written in 1868, the author, having discussed other aspects of the subject in the two preceding Essays, sought to show that the existence of autocratic government in some of the most powerful Continental States is incompatible with the constant maintenance of peace. He is, however, far from supposing that even the universal establishment of constitutional or republican forms of government would extirpate war. Industry, commerce, morality, and intelligence would not keep the peace between man and man in our own country without an effective system of coercive law, neither can they do so between nation and nation. The Essay had at the same time another object, contemplated also in other Essays in the volume; namely, to show that law has its stages of development, that in its earlier stages it does not conform to Austin's definition, and that in respect alike of the sources from which it proceeds, and the character of its institutions at different stages, it is subject to law in the scientific sense of natural growth or evolution, and discoverable order and sequence. In part, International Law, so-called, is really inchoate or embryo law, analogous to the customary law existing in countries in which a fully organized sovereign government has not yet been developed.

together determined to remain masters of themselves.'* Fully, for our own part, admitting that international relations are in a state of perilous uncertainty, that the old system of regulating them is no longer a rule or a guide, and that the decline of its authority adds to the confusion and danger of Europe, we hold, on the other hand, that it is the old principle of despotism, not the new principle of self-government, which divides Europe into so many camps; that not the introduction of popular sovereignty, but the persistence of an opposite species of sovereignty is the main cause of the critical position of European affairs, and the main obstacle to the formation of a true commonwealth of nations; and that the general establishment, throughout the civilized world, of really representative and national governments and armies is an essential condition precedent of a true international law. We conceive it demonstrable that the so-called international law of the past is a misnomer, not in one only, but in both of its terms, being neither law nor international in the true sense of the words; being a code of kings, not of nations, an interregal, not an international, system—one avowedly based on the lawless and barbarous process of adjudication by battle, and taking account solely of powers not only too lofty to recognise any law for their conduct, but so constituted as to be incompatible with international confidence and concert.

At the root of a host of international antipathies and quarrels lies a confusion for centuries under a common name of nations with governments—of France, Russia, Austria, and Spain, for example, in their political dealings and relations, with the French, the Russians, the Austrians, and the Spaniards; and one result of this confusion—which, like many mischievous errors in both the philosophy and the practical notions of mankind, has its stronghold in language—is to hide even from some of the most learned and accurate writers the real character of the code which takes the name of the law of nations, or international law. With Mr. Austin, they tell us truly enough that it is not law in the jural sense, but only a law of opinion

---

* La Diplomatie et les Principes de la Révolution Française, par M. Albert de Broglie, de l'Académie Française : Revue Des Deux Mondes, 1 Fév., 1868.

emanating from no common legislature, and enforced by no common magistracy. But they fail, apparently, to perceive that it has no more rightful claim to the title of international than of law; that 'taking account of sovereigns only,' and sovereigns being what they have been since the age of Grotius in most powerful States, it has taken no account of nations; that the matters to which it chiefly relates are what they are, because it is really an interregal, not an international, code; that not only the subjects it is most concerned with, but also the rules concerning them, are deeply coloured by the springs from which the whole has been drawn, it being such as monarchs could admit in its form, as well as such as their policy and conduct have made it in its subject-matter. International relations, in other words, would have come to rest on an entirely different footing, and have given rise to a perfectly different system of jurisprudence, had nations themselves, instead of despots, determined their relations towards each other. We hope to show, indeed, that the germs of international law, in the true sense, are discernible; but this, at least, remains certain, that the rude procedure of trial by battle must continue to determine the differences of States, and differences will be created and kept alive for the purpose, until nations determine their own career and position alike in national and international politics.

The first of the foregoing propositions, namely, that what has hitherto been called international law is not law in the jural sense of the term, but only a law of opinion, is proveable out of the mouths of those of its very professors who most stoutly maintain the contrary doctrine, by the position which they claim for themselves, and the lofty moral authority with which they clothe their conclusions. 'The international jurist,' Dr. Travers Twiss, for example, declares, 'is by his vocation placed sentinel upon the outworks of this system; and no nobler end can be proposed to his ambition or sense of duty than to keep vigilant watch, ready to defend the weaker State against the aggressions of the more powerful, and to control the spirit of war and conquest when it attempts to overthrow the established doctrines of public law; and when war has commenced, his province is to restrain the combatants within just limits, and to stay the arm of the belligerent when it would encroach upon the liberties of the neutral.'* It is the language of the prophet, not of the lawyer, 'Cry aloud, spare not; lift up thy voice like a trumpet.' We do not find Mr. Williams on Real Property, or Mr. Chitty on Contracts, proclaiming it as their office to uphold the authority of their jurisprudence, to defend the weak from the strong, the poor from the rich, and to preserve the rights of third parties inviolate when litigation arises. Again, that international politics and the theoretical jurisprudence relating to them have hitherto been what monarchs rather than nations have made them, may be seen on a glance at the history and character of the system which passes by the name of international law. Two prominent characteristics can scarcely fail to strike the student of the chief treatises on the subject, namely, that at first he seems to enter a world of lofty morality, of principles appealing to the best interests and feelings of mankind—of equity, reciprocity, humanity, and piety; but crossing the threshold he finds himself in reality in a world where might is right—a world of war, spoliation, and conquest. From the Prolegomena of the 'De Jure Belli ac Pacis' of Grotius, claiming the acquiescence of Christendom in a moral code sanctioned by the common voice of ancient and modern wisdom, virtue, and religion, he passes to the first chapter, at the head of which is the ominous title—' Quid Bellum ;' and it must soon become evident to him that peace has occupied but a secondary place in the author's mind, as it does in the name of his treatise. 'Upon nearer investigation,' says one of the most learned of his successors, Baron von Ompteda, 'it will be found that it was never the intention of Grotius to make the law of nature in its whole range his study, and that he originally restricted himself to that department of law which establishes the relations of nations and their governments to each other, or, rather, solely to that branch which treats of the laws of war.' Grotius himself wrote to his friends, 'Ego, absoluto Stobæo, do operam commenta-

---

* Introductory Lectures on the Science of International Law. By Travers Twiss, D.C.L., Regius Professor of Civil Law in the University of Oxford.

tioni de jure belli;' and in his Prolegomena he states that the causes which led to the composition of the work were the shameful frequency and licence of wars. Why is it, then, that war forms the staple subject of the prime treatise on what purports to be international justice—the subject to which all others are merely convergent or consequent?

The answer will be found in the political conditions of the epoch of which the 'De Jure Belli ac Pacis' was one of the natural fruits—in the establishment of great military kingdoms, on the one hand, and the decline of even the precarious restraint of the Papal authority on the other, leaving irresponsible monarchs at the head of monarchical armies to determine the relations of nations as their personal caprice or ambition suggested. In the sixteenth century, says M. Guizot, the elements of society had gathered into two cardinal facts—the defeat of absolute power in spiritual affairs and its triumph in temporal; and the external relations of states in particular having no direct domestic interest for the people, fell entirely into the hands of their kings. But 'exterior relations,' he adds, 'form for nearly three centuries the most important portion of history: thus the principal part of the destinies of nations has been abandoned to the prerogative of kings.' In other words, monarchy, standing armies, and wars are three cognate facts. Grotius sought, it is true, to discover a moral authority that might fill the place previously assumed by the Papacy as the arbiter and moderator of the relations of secular Powers; but his principal topic was war, because his treatise grew out of the actual conduct of monarchs, and was meant as a code for their conduct; and it owed its rapid acceptance by monarchs and monarchical statesmen to its uncompromising assertion of the absolute and indefeasible right of sovereignty in rulers and the correlative duty of non-resistance on the part of their subjects. That the character and customs of despotic power had swayed the opinions and enslaved, as one may say, the conscience of its author is but too evident in many of his doctrines. 'A man,' he argues, 'may by his own act make himself the slave of any one; why then may not a people do the same? The right of sovereignty,' he adds, 'may be acquired by war, and it is an error to think governments exist only for the good of the governed; for kingdoms may be established for the good of kings—as are those which are won by conquest, and these are not to be called tyrannies, since tyranny implies injustice.'

The contemporary thoughts of a greater than Grotius throw a yet more vivid light on the connexion between monarchy and war. The last edition of Lord Bacon's essays, with his final corrections, was published in the same year with the De Jure Belli ac Pacis (1625), and the reader may judge of the place which the peace of nations then occupied in the policy of statesmen concerned for the true greatness of kingdoms from some of his maxims. 'Above all for empire and greatness it importeth most that a nation do profess arms as their principal honour, study, and occupation. Incident to this point it is for a State to have those laws or customs which may reach forth unto them just occasion, as may be pretended, of war. For there is that justice imprinted in the nature of men that they enter not upon wars, whereof so many calamities do ensue, but upon some, at the least, specious grounds and quarrels. Nobody can be healthful without exercise, neither natural body nor politic; and certainly, to a kingdom or state, a just and honourable war is the true exercise. But, howsoever it be for happiness, without all question for greatness it maketh most to be still for the most part in arms; and the strength of a veteran army, though it be a chargeable business, is that which commonly giveth the law, or at least the reputation, among neighbour states, as may be seen in Spain. To conclude, no man can, as the Scripture saith, add a cubit to his stature; but in the great frame of kingdoms and commonwealths it is in the power of princes to add amplitude and greatness to their kingdoms. For by introducing such ordinances, constitutions, and customs as we have touched, they may sow greatness to their posterity and succession.'* Of the cruel confusion of

---

* Essay XXIX. In like manner, in his Dissertation, 'Of the True Greatness of the Kingdom of Britain,' Bacon pronounces:—'And let no man so much forget the subject propounded as to find it strange that here is no mention of religion, laws, or policy. For we speak of that which is proper to the

nations with kings, which Lord Bacon thus deliberately fostered, the phrase 'international law' exhibits an unconscious form, as does language such as the following, of a political economist of the present day, on a subject closely related to war.

Speaking of the national debt contracted in the war of the Spanish succession with Louis XIV.—one of the chief real authors of international law, and whose maxim, 'L'Etat c'est moi,' indicates the place nations have occupied in monarchical policy—Mr. Sargant states ' that, in the eyes of the nation, the money spent on the war was well spent; for though the Peace of Utrecht was believed to have given up the advantages we had gained, yet the effect of the whole war was to reduce the French nation to the utmost distress, and to so quell its restless spirit, that for eighty subsequent years Europe was free from French dictation.'* Quidquid delirant reges, plectuntur Achivi. Undoubtedly, the effect of the war was to reduce the French nation to the utmost distress ; but the only 'restless spirit' that unfortunate nation had shown was in resistance to the burdens imposed by the warlike policy of a monarch who sought to make his power of dictating to France a means of dictating to Europe. 'La seule remarque à faire en terminant,' says one of 'the French nation,' writing on the insurrections in his reign, 'c'est ce contraste de gloire publique et de calamités privées ; de grands évènements, de villes conquises, d'agrandissement du territoire, de palais de marbre, de chefs-d'œuvre de toute sorte s'épanouissant comme par enchantement à la voix d'un homme, tandis qu'au-dessous de lui d'autres hommes, mais ceux-là par millions, concourent sans gloire et sans profit, par leur sueurs, leurs souffrances et leur mort, au but poursuivi par un seul.'†

Mr. Wheaton divides the history of ' modern international

amplitude and growth of States, and not of that which is common to their preservation, happiness, and all other points of well-being. For except there be a spur in the State that shall excite and prick them on to wars, they will but keep their own, and seek no further. And in all experience you shall find but three things that prepare and dispose for war—the ambition of governors, a State of soldiers professed, and the hard means to live of many subjects.'

* Apology for Sinking Funds. By William Lucas Sargant. 1868, p. 29.
† Les Émeutes sous Louis XIV. Par Pierre Clément, de l'Institut. Revue des Deux Mondes, 1 Août, 1866.

law' into four periods, the first of which extends from the Peace of Westphalia, in 1648, to that of Utrecht, in 1713, and this is his general description of the state of international relations during it:—' First Period. The intermediate period between the Peace of Westphalia and that of Utrecht was filled with a series of wars growing out of the ambitious projects of Louis XIV. seeking to extend the frontiers of France, and to secure his dynasty the rich inheritance of Spain and the Indies.' It is true, in his other standard treatise on the 'Elements of International Law,' the same author says:—' The international law of Christendom began to be fixed about the time of Grotius, when the combined influence of religion, chivalry, the feudal system, and commercial intercourse had blended together the nations of Europe;' but the subsequent contents of this very treatise bear the same testimony as the passage previously quoted from the author's history, that in place of being blended into one family, the nations of Europe had in reality become divided into a number of separate kingdoms, 'living,' in the strong language of Hobbes, 'in the condition of perpetual war, with their frontiers armed, and cannons planted against their neighbours round about.' Of seventy pages of the first volume of Mr. Wheaton's 'Elements,' nominally devoted to the 'international rights of States in their peaceful relations,' half relate rather to war than to peace; while the whole of the other volume, except a few pages at the end about a treaty of peace, is occupied with the 'international rights of States in their hostile relations.' And returning to the author's History, we find abundant explanation of the preponderance of war over peace as the subject of so-called international law. For example, we are told that the author of the famous 'Projet de Paix Perpetuelle,' the Abbé St. Pierre, having been present at the Conferences of Utrecht, and witnessed the difficulties attending the settlement of terms of peace, drew the plan of a treaty to render it perpetual; but Fleury, to whom the Abbé communicated it, replied, ' Vous avez oublié un article essentiel, celui d'envoyer des missionaires pour toucher les cœurs des princes et leur persuader d'entrer dans vos vues.' Again, Mr. Wheaton relates that Frederick the Great, in his ' Anti-Machiavel,' expressed himself as follows on the subject of war:—' War in general brings with it so many calamities, its aim is so uncertain, and its consequences are so ruinous to a country, that princes cannot sufficiently reflect before they resort to this extremity. The ravages committed by their troops in the enemy's country ar nothing in comparison with the calamities war entails upon the State by which it is undertaken. It is therefore the more extraordinary that so many sovereigns adopt rashly this dreadful alternative. If monarchs could present to themselves a true and faithful picture of the calamities inflicted upon a nation by a single declaration of war, I am persuaded they could not be insensible to the impression. It is, indeed, hardly possible that they should form an adequate conception of evils from which their lot exempts them. How can they feel the weight of taxation by which the people are oppressed?—the loss of youth inflicted by the recruiting system?—the contagious diseases by which whole armies are swept away?—the horrors of battles, and sieges still more horrible?—the desolation of the wounded, deprived of their limbs, on which their means of subsistence depend?—of the widows and orphans who have lost, by the death of their husbands and fathers, their sole support?—the destruction of so many citizens prematurely mowed down by the scythe of death in the flower of their age?'

The royal writer who thus confessed the inability of monarchs to feel as nations feel about war, had afterwards an opportunity of displaying the motives which really actuate them. 'His real motives,' says Mr. Wheaton of his invasion of Silesia, 'are avowed in his private correspondence, which discloses the love of glory, ambition, the desire of employing the army and treasure his father had bequeathed to him, as the secret springs by which he was moved.' It is not merely because monarchs feel none of the sufferings of nations from war that international relations are unsafe in their hands; it is because the interests of nations and monarchs are opposite in the matter. Apart from the ambition of conquest and personal pride, it is often the interest of monarchs to make war, for the very sake of arresting national progress and the spirit of independence which springs from it; it is for the same reason

always their interest to **foster** traditions of military glory and aggrandisement—always their interest, **for** the sake of power to defy **the will** of the nations they govern, to maintain great armies **ready** and desirous for war. Monarchical institutions thus both involve constant preparation for **war,** and make it the personal interest of the most powerful section of society to engage in it; **while** popular **or** national institutions render those who control the decision both indisposed for aggressive war and unprepared for it. Disputes may occur between popular governments, **but** they can have no systematic and deliberate policy of war; they **have** no institutions interesting large and powerful **classes in it**; they are not in constant readiness for it; and, all their deliberations being public, they **cannot plot** it in secret. It is **not too** much to say **that** there has been no national war **in Europe** since it was even partially civilized,—that is to say, **since the** Crusades. The wars attributed **to** the French Revolution—**a** revolution the excesses **of which** sprang from long monarchical tyranny **and** misgovernment—were begun by monarchs abroad and continued by a military despotism at home, the foundations of which were laid by the despotism that preceded it. The so-called democracies of ancient history, with whose wars modern democracy **is** reproached, were, in **fact,** despotisms, being oligarchies **based** upon slavery, and thereby diverted from the occupations **of peace and** the natural interests of industry. It was an oligarchy based **upon** slavery which began the late **war** in America; and can any one dream that had the Northern States been under the rule **of an** emperor, his victorious army **would** have been disbanded, or that Canada would not have been **invaded** immediately? 'Il y a une intime solidarité entre la **politique** intérieure d'un pays et sa politique extérieure,' as a French writer lately remarked, adding, 'La Russie poursuit encore aujourd'hui ce qu'elle poursuivit il y a trente ans, il y a un siècle; elle a les mêmes ambitions et les mêmes vues du côté de l'Europe occidentale, aussi bien que du côté de l'Orient.'*
But will any one **say** that the 'Russia,' in whom this policy

---

* Le Russie sous l'Empereur Alexandre II. Par M. Charles de Mazade **Revue des** Deux Mondes, 15 Mai.

originated, and by which it has been perpetuated, is the Russian nation, the most peaceful people by nature under the sun?

It may then be affirmed that international relations would have come to rest on a perfectly different footing had nations controlled them; that the traditions of conquest and territorial aggrandisement, which disturb the concord of nations, are of monarchical, not of popular, origin; and that the hope of peace in the future lies in the new principle of popular sovereignty or self-government, in the establishment of national, in the room of monarchical, armies, and in the effective predominance of national interests and instincts over the external policy of States. In a volume of Essays on International Policy, which attracted attention two years ago, Mr. Congreve, after remarking that ' the decline of the power of Catholicism and the consequent disunion of mediæval Europe were first evidenced by disorder in the international relations of its constituent States,' has pronounced that 'it is in international relations that the restoration of order must begin, as the first step to the reorganization of modern Europe on a sound basis.' We arrive, on the contrary, at the converse proposition that it is in the internal organization of States and in national institutions that the reconstruction of international relations must begin; and that the first step to a true international law is to make sovereignty really representative and national—the arms which it wields such as cannot be wielded against either the nation itself or its will. We therefore are unable to concur with a learned and useful writer, that the mere institution of an international tribunal would considerably diminish the frequency or the danger of war.[*] Private war between the feudal barons was doubtless, as he argues, put an end to by the intervention of courts of justice; but it was so because kings became strong enough to compel the inferior lords of the soil to submit to their courts, and until they became so the barons did not give up war, and maintaining men of war for the purpose. How can kings, in their turn, be compelled to submit to legal arbitration, and to dismiss their men of war, so long as their power is supreme? Nations may, as they do,

---

[*] On an International High Court. By David Ross, Esq. A Paper read before the Social Science Association at Belfast, September, 1867.

regard war with increasing aversion and dread, and may repine more and more at the increasing burden of armies; but those armies are maintained not to carry out the will of nations, but to conquer it when it conflicts with the will of monarchs. The difference between municipal and international justice is that supreme power, the power of the sword, is on the side of the former, but on the side opposed to the latter.

Nor can the steady improvement in the public opinion and the commercial relations of nations, on which some very eminent writers both in this country and on the Continent rely, be depended upon to remove the causes of war. Means of commerce and communication may move either armies or merchandize, and there is not one powerful State on the Continent in which public opinion decides which the movement shall be. The first step which nations must take to make public opinion an effectual obstacle to war, is to establish governments representing public opinion—the opinion of those who suffer by war and prosper by peace. But this, though the first step, must not be the last. Mere opinion, without the authority and procedure of law, can never supersede altogether the barbarous alternative of trial by combat. We find ourselves at this point at variance with an admirable essay on international law in a former number of this Review, by a writer who never fails to instruct his readers even when he fails to convince them, and whom, on that account, we quote at some length:—

'When we ask what are the sanctions of international law, it is plain that they can only be such as opinion has at its disposal, and may therefore best be gathered by observing the force of social opinion in the sphere in which we are most familiar with its operations—the sphere of private life. Opinion, it is obvious, may enforce its behests by either of two means—by physical coercion or by moral suasion. In the early stages of social progress, opinion makes its energy felt chiefly or, at all events, largely through the former means. But as society advances, a recourse to violence seems to be less needed, as the moral elements in the human character grow in power. Praise and blame are gradually substituted for the coarser sanctions of the earlier state. Already this process has been carried so far in the more advanced nations that these, the moral sanctions of opinion, are now found adequate in the main to all the ends of social intercourse. This being the history of the sanctions of opinion in the social life of individuals, the question occurs how far we are justified in anticipating a like development in the social life of **nations**. And it is at the first glance obvious that up to the present time, mankind has nowhere, even in the most advanced nations, reached the stage at which the sanctions of opinion can in international affairs be **safely** dispensed with. But the mere fact that opinion in international affairs is not yet sufficiently powerful to serve **as its** own sanction, by **no means** proves that it may not become so; and the question for the philosophical publicist is not simply what is the efficacy of public opinion **in the** affairs of nations, but what in the advance of civilization is public opinion capable of becoming. Is a state of mutual distrust and suspended hostility destined to be the normal and inevitable condition of independent States? or may we reasonably look forward to a time when in **the** intercourse of nations, as has already happened in the intercourse of individual men, submission to opinion may supersede the necessity of violent expedients, and 'the kindly earth may slumber, lapt in universal law'? . . . **There** seems reason for believing that all the leading currents of modern **civilization are** setting steadily and rapidly towards the formation of a body of international opinion which, judging from the efficacy that opinion has already developed in analogous departments of **human life,** there is ground **for** hoping may ultimately, **and at no** remote date, **become an** effective check on the **conduct of** nations. International **law must** have **its sanctions, and** for these the alternative lies between fleets and armies and the moral restraints of opinion. **If the** enormous armaments which now weigh upon the physical and mental energies of Europe are ever to be largely and permanently reduced, this will be when, and no sooner than when, international opinion is felt **to have** become strong enough to perform their part.'*

One line quoted in the foregoing carries in itself the com-

---

* International Law. By Professor Cairnes. Nov. 1, 1865.

ment we are desirous of making, namely, that 'universal law' alone can supersede altogether the arbitrament of war between nations. It is law, and not the mere force of opinion, powerful as it has become, which still supersedes physical force as the arbiter in the last resort within nations, both of private and political quarrel. The bare distinctions between meum and tuum owe their establishment and authority entirely to the supremacy of law. There is no social relation whatever,—partner and partner, principal and agent, landlord and tenant, employer and labourer, railway company and passenger, creditor and debtor, husband and wife,—which can dispense with legal command and enforcement. The succession to property would carry war into every family, but for the law and tribunals. Without an arena for debate and legislative decisions, and a powerful executive to enforce the public decisions so arrived at, individuals would by no means submit as they do to the control of public opinion, nor would it be always easy even to ascertain what it is. If civil war were the only mode of measuring their relative strength, political parties would assuredly resort to it; and it is probable that public opinion would be still on the side of the duel, or at least of personal chastisement, were outrage and insult without legal redress. We hold, therefore, that only a law of nations, in the strict sense of the term, can terminate war; and the question follows, Is there a possibility of such a law? We answer that the germ of a true international law, in the proper sense of both terms, 'international' and 'law,' is already discernible: of the first, because, in spite of some sinister indications, sovereignty is steadily becoming more national; of the second, because the political relations of States do in fact exhibit the features of law in its inchoate or rudimentary stage. The first steps of municipal justice in private disputes consist, on the one hand, in subjecting rude strife to some conventional regulations, and investing the appeal to force in this regulated form with the solemn aim and ideal of trial by combat, thus introducing the conception of legal process; on the other hand, by the occasional intervention of neutral parties or bystanders as arbiters. With respect to the latter, the history of Roman law furnishes an instructive and interesting parallel. ' Very far the most ancient judicial proceeding known to us is the Legis Actio Sacramenti of the Romans, out of which all the later Roman law of actions may be proved to have grown. It is impossible to refuse assent to those who see in it a dramatisation of the origin of justice. Two armed men are wrangling about some disputed property. The prætor, vir pietate gravis, happens to be going by, and interferes to stop the contest. The disputants state their case to him, and agree that he shall arbitrate between them.' Thus 'in the original administration of justice the proceedings were a close imitation of the series of acts which were likely to be gone through in private life by persons who were disputing, but who afterwards suffered the quarrel to be appeased. The magistrate carefully simulates the demeanour of a private arbitrator casually called in.'* Trial by combat, on the other hand, was the martial judicial procedure of the barbarian nations to whom the Romans succumbed. Paterculus remarked that all those questions which were decided by process of law among the Romans were settled among the Germans by arms; and this primitive method of adjudication we find but tardily eliminated by gradual steps from English jurisprudence, first by excluding its application in cases of trivial importance, next by subjecting it to rules and solemnities, and finally by substituting for it an appeal to the verdict of equals; and we know that a growing conviction of the extreme injustice of adjudication by arms was one principal cause of the introduction of the institution which ultimately, under various transformations, superseded it altogether. 'The grand assize,' wrote the earliest commentator upon English law, 'is a certain royal benefit bestowed upon the people, and emanating from the clemency of the prince, with the advice of his nobles. So effectually does this proceeding preserve the lives and civil condition of men, that every one may now possess his right in safety, at the same time that he avoids the doubtful event of the duel. This legal institution flows from the most profound equity. For that justice which, after many and long delays, is scarcely elicited by the duel, is more advantageously and expeditiously attained through the benefit of this institution.'†

* Ancient Law. By H. S. Maine, ch. x.
† Beames's Glanville, pp. 54-55.

The subjection of international warfare to regulations and forms, and the growing disposition to resort to arbitration of the differences of States, are thus precisely analogous to the early steps of municipal justice; and to this may be confidently added the tendency to establish popular governments, as clearly facilitating the recognition of a true international law. For nations are not, like monarchs, indisposed and unaccustomed to submit to legal control; the popularity of legal institutions, on the contrary, shows itself among them with the first traces of civilization. Readers of our early chronicles cannot fail to perceive how acceptable to the bulk of the nation was the prerogative which the Crown gradually arrogated of being the common arbiter of disputes and the dispenser of general justice. The previous judicial functions of the allodial and feudal owners of land had a similar origin in the social necessity for some system of magisterial arbitrament to supersede perpetual anarchy and warfare. The constant extension of the boundaries of law is one of the most striking facts in the history of mankind, and the reason is easily discovered in the imperious general need for peace and security. 'The history of mankind,' as Mr. Maine has observed, 'begins with the assumption that kinship in blood is the sole possible ground of community in political functions; nor is there any of those subversions of feeling we term emphatically revolutions so startling and complete as the change accepted when some other principle, such as that, for instance, of local contiguity, establishes itself for the first time as the basis of common political action.' The same eminent jurist remarks, that it is by means of legal fictions that municipal law makes its earliest advances; and it seems to us evident that the fiction of international law, as a real code of legal obligation, has owed its success in a great measure to a deep, universal feeling of necessity for the existence of such a code. Law is a natural and necessary growth of more numerous and closer human relations, and the extension of industry and wealth. As nations come closer together, as their commercial relations multiply, on the one hand, and the danger of sudden destruction, on the other, becomes more instant and appalling, it is inconceivable that, as they become their own lawgivers, they should fail to institute a true law of nations. 'Here then,' even so cold a friend to political liberty as Hume is compelled to conclude, 'are the advantages of free states. Though a republic should be barbarous, it necessarily, by an infallible operation, gives rise to law, even before mankind have made any considerable advances in the other sciences. On the contrary, in a monarchy law arises not necessarily from the forms of government. Monarchy, when absolute, contains even something repugnant to law.'* This reasoning relates, it is true, to the growth of municipal law; but if, even in a barbarous republic, law necessarily arises 'in order to preserve liberty, to secure the persons and the properties of the citizens, to exempt one man from the dominion of another, and to protect every one against the violence and tyranny of his fellow-citizens,'† may we not foretell the growth, for similar reasons, of law in a republic of nations far advanced beyond barbarism?‡

* Essay XIV., 'Of the Rise and Progress of the Arts and Sciences.'
† Id.
‡ It will be objected, we are well aware, that an effective international law involves a universal empire, and the purchase of peace at the cost of the independence of nations. This objection rests on the assumption that sovereignty is of necessity indivisible and unlimited, and that a legislature for international affairs must consequently be either nugatory, or supreme likewise over the domestic affairs of nations; an assumption which we hope upon a future occasion to prove fallacious, but the proof requires a discussion of too much length to be added to the present pages.

IX.

THE MILITARY SYSTEMS OF EUROPE IN 1867.*

(*North British Review, December,* 1867.)

'We have arrived,' observes General Trochu, in one of the ablest and most interesting of the many essays on Military Organization which the war of last year has produced, 'at one of those periods of transition in the existence of armies, which mark the end of certain systems employed in the wars of the past for the inauguration of others to be employed in the wars of the present. It is the merit and the fortune of Prussia in 1866, as formerly in the time of the great Frederick, to have foreseen this evolution of the art of war, to have studied its conditions attentively during a long peace, to have discovered them for the most part, and to have opportunely and resolutely applied them.'† We cite the observation, not merely for the importance in itself of the double conviction of high military authority in France, that military systems have arrived at a period of transition, and that Prussia has correctly apprehended its conditions, but because the passage raises inquiries respecting the causes, objects, and tendencies of the vast armies of the Continent, which it did not fall within the purpose of General

---

* This Essay was written at the suggestion of the late Mr. Herman Merivale, after study on the Continent, not in books alone, of the Continental Military Systems. The author was led by observation and inquiry abroad to change considerably the views put forth by him in a previously published lecture on the military systems of Europe. Some pages relating to promotion by purchase have been omitted.

† L'Armée Française en 1867.

Trochu to treat of, though they are inquiries of the first importance to the people of this country, to many of whom the 'period of transition in the existence of armies' in prospect, has long been a period of general disarmament. The questions which General Trochu discusses, are, indeed, far from being military questions only. To his credit as a man and a citizen, as well as a soldier, he looks at an army not as a mere instrument of victory, but as a powerful social agent for the improvement or the corruption of a nation. Every year, he urges, an army withdraws from different parts of the body of society, and every year it returns to it a number of citizens,—'Une redoubtable question se présente, sont-ils dans l'ordre moral, sont-ils dans l'ordre physique, améliorés ou dénaturés?' 'Public spirit, public morality, public health, the power of the race to increase, the gradual elevation or degradation of the life of the nation in some of its most important conditions,—such is the immense theme which, for fifty years, has agitated legislation on recruiting for the army.' We too, in this country, are deeply interested in the moral and social effects of different military systems, as well as in their efficiency for war, and they raise other questions. Why do these mighty armaments exist? Do they threaten war? Are they all aggressive or defensive alike? Is England safe in her present military system? Even an unreformed Parliament, full of promotion by purchase, could it have realized 'the period of transition in the existence of armies,' at which we have arrived, might have been moved to repentance by the powerful voices which have but preached in the wilderness Army Reform. Nor will the return of a reformed Parliament suffice of itself to insure the sort of army reform that is needed. The sort which eminent Parliamentary Reformers have advocated before now has been army extinction.

So many indeed are the reasons for believing that war must finally disappear before commerce and civilization, that not only is the question of the probability of war always discussed by practical men in this country with reference to some passing cloud in the political sky, but powerful speculative thinkers, both here and on the Continent, have found in the very institution of the standing armies of modern Europe an evidence of the cessation of warfare. Montesquieu, it is true, in a passage cited by M. Jules Simon, lamented, a century and a quarter ago, that a new plague was spreading over Europe, disordering its sovereigns so as to lead to the maintenance of inordinate numbers of troops. 'As soon as one State increases its forces, the others at once increase theirs, so that nothing is got by it but general ruin. Every monarch keeps upon foot all the armies he could if nations were in danger of extermination; and the name of peace is given to an effort of all against all. We are thus poor amid the riches and commerce of the whole world.' Yet Montesquieu reckoned the proportion of soldiers to the population of Europe at one in a hundred; and Adam Smith, nearly half a century later, said it was commonly computed that no greater proportion of men could be employed as soldiers by any civilized State without ruin, while now the Government of France is endeavouring to raise an army of more than 1,200,000, out of a nation of 38,000,000, that is, to make available as soldiers nearly a thirtieth of the whole population. This one fact might stagger those who believe with M. Comte (of whom the late Mr. Buckle was on this point an eminent disciple), that the tendency of the economy of modern Europe to put an end to war was shown in the establishment of permanent armies, as feudalism declined; whereby they argue (and argue with a truth which, in our opinion, militates against the conclusion drawn from the argument), that the majority of the inhabitants of each State were weaned from the practice of arms. We are of those who think, on the one hand, that the tendency of modern civilization is to substitute armed nations, as in Germany and Switzerland, for standing armies such as those of Russia and France; and, on the other hand, that the institution of standing armies, so far from tending to abolish war, created it—created it, that is to say, in the sense of hostilities on a vast scale, waged by immense forces, and protracted often for several years. The feudal militia was a defensive institution, by its structure wholly incapacitated for other than petty hostilities, by its interests at home indisposed for long or distant campaigns, and under no obligation to undertake them in the interests of a monarch. It is a remarkable example of the error of looking at only one side of the shield, that powerful reasoners could regard as pacific institutions, the rise at the same time of military monarchies, and of a special class devoted to warfare, by their interests bound to it, placed at the disposal of a single chief who wielded the resources of a whole nation, and who was enabled by the very existence of such a class, monopolizing all military knowledge and discipline, to defy the wishes of the great body of his subjects for peace. The men of peace were disarmed, while the men of war were armed with the deadliest weapons. The mere establishment of permanent armies placed forces adequate and disposed to great wars upon foot, but they did much more to create such wars by placing at their head the very person who suffers least by the interruption of peace, who feels none of the privations of a campaign, and need incur none of its dangers, even if he takes the field in person; who can stop the war if he tires of it, who has all the pride and ambition generated by immense power and supreme rank—a rank, moreover, which, among his few equals in other nations, is proportionate not to the wealth and prosperity of the nations under his own control, disposing them to peace, but to his own military power and success. Lord Bacon, no mean authority in matters of kingcraft, treating of 'the true greatness of kingdoms,' and meaning literally the greatness of kingdoms as contradistinguished from nations, has authoritatively pronounced: 'In all experience you shall find but three things that prepare and dispose a State for war: the ambition of governors, a state of soldiers prepared, and the hard means to live of many subjects.' Nor is it an immaterial consideration that the establishment of the great military monarchies of modern Europe, with professional armies at their command, involved the cessation of the only attempt that has ever been made towards a general tribunal for the pacific adjustment of international disputes—one beneficent use of the stupendous spiritual tyranny of the Papacy. There are, we believe, two preliminary steps requisite to terminate war—in the establishment of free institutions, and the substitution of national militias for standing armies; but the danger of war can never disappear altogether until the civilized world has a common

legislature, and a common **tribunal for** international affairs;*
and the autocrat who wields the **whole** power of one nation
cannot enter a congress **on** equal terms **with** the mere deputy of
another nation; **he** cannot legislate for either national or international **interests on** purely national or international grounds,
apart **from both** personal **and** dynastic concerns. So opposite to
national **interests for** peace are the interests of personal government, **that after showing** how popular institutions disincline for
war by **the prosperity they** create, and the intelligence they
arouse, M. de **Tocqueville lays** it down as the first maxim in **the**
science **of tyranny,** that the shortest and **surest** method of
destroying political liberty **in** a nation is **to make** war. For
that **is the way** to establish **a** standing army.

From **the** foregoing considerations **alone, it may be** asserted
to follow that Europe is not **done** with armies or with war; **but
there are** other conditions **of** its present situation which tend to
make the dangers of war **more** imminent and alarming, **and
armies** larger than ever, **even in the most** peacefully disposed
States that mean **to maintain** their independence. M. de
Tocqueville points **out** as two of those conditions—first, that
nations are becoming more alike, more equally armed, and versed
in the **same** military practices, so that particular troops, like the
Swiss, **lose their old** national superiority; **the force** of numbers
prevails; **and 'la raison déterminante de la** victoire étant le
nombre, il en **résulte que chaque peuple doit tendre** de tous ses
efforts à amener le **plus d'hommes** possible sur le champ de
bataille.' Another reason **given** by this political prophet is, in
effect, **that the** centralization **of** power has centralized national
life; the enemy who strikes **at the** capital of a country now
strikes at its heart, rendering prolonged struggles on the part
of its other members impossible; **whence it** becomes indispensable **to have a vast** organized force at hand to resist attack from
the **first.** To these circumstances **may be** added another very

---

* We must take **leave, without** entering upon an irrelevant discussion, to enter a protest against the doctrine that the domestic independence of nations is incompatible, under any form of government, with an effective international legislature or tribunal,—a doctrine which rests upon reasoning supported by authority which we highly respect, but rests nevertheless, we presume to assert, **upon a** juridical fallacy.

obvious one, that the increased proximity of States, and the power of concentrating large forces suddenly upon a **given** point, together with the tremendous weapons invented by modern art, make the danger of swift destruction to an unprepared nation such as can scarce be exaggerated. Those eminent writers who, like Mr. Buckle, have seen in improvements **of** the means of locomotion and of arms only persuasives of peace, have looked again only at the white side of the shield.

In days when such dangers as have just been referred **to** were less imminent and less formidable, M. de Tocqueville concluded **as an** indubitable **proposition,** that **the days** of the independence of all small States, that is to say, States unable **to** bring vast forces into the field, were numbered. **But if** States are measured **by** their military forces, if their independence depends upon **such** a condition, in what condition **is** England? **It** is indisputable that we find ourselves, with the largest surface **of** empire open to attack **at** the greatest number **of** points, approaching closer each year to the vast and increasing armies of the great Continental Powers, with not only small but diminishing and deteriorating forces on our side. Cries have been consequently heard **from our** Press from time to time **for** disarmament, especially **on the** part of the two great States nearest to us; **but** apart from the fact that great armies **are** rather the effects than **the** causes of the situation of Europe, we could ill spare the very two armies chiefly complained of, notwithstanding the uneasiness they occasion, and the reforms we may wish to introduce especially into **one of them.** Were both those armies annihilated to-morrow, a **Czar** would reign from Behring **Strait to the** English Channel, **and** England could hardly preserve her independence by decoupling her forces. We have reason to regard **the troops of** Prussia, and even of France, as police who protect us unpaid; at the same time that we must also regard them as evidences of the imminent danger **of general** war, for the chances of **which we are,** in the eyes **of other** nations, ludicrously, and by our own almost unanimous confession, lamentably unprepared. It is true that there are some who trust to non-intervention to keep England out of all future conflicts; but would Switzerland, Belgium, Holland, Denmark, Sweden,

Italy, or Turkey, be secured by crying non-intervention? And why England more so, save in so far as she is more powerful to enforce non-intervention in her affairs on the part of other States? The desire of the citizens of a peaceful commercial nation to enter a regular army is not stimulated by the prospect of danger; and students of De Tocqueville will remember his confident prediction that, in the face of the growing necessity on the one hand for larger armies to maintain national independence, and of the increasing dislike of commercial populations for military life on the other, all nations must abandon the system of voluntary enlistment for that of compulsory service in arms. He was speaking, however, of the bare conditions of self-preservation, strictly considered; and we entertain little doubt that he would have answered that a double military system, retaining the voluntary element, is necessary for Great Britain, so long as she has an Indian and a Colonial Empire, in addition to her own insular territory, to defend. The point which demands our immediate attention is that there are very different systems of compulsory military service in Europe, differing in their cost, their moral and social effects, their efficiency for national preservation and aggressive war respectively, and their tendency to foster a free and patriotic spirit, or a spirit of tame submission to tyranny at home and of domination over neighbours abroad. The present system of conscription for the regular army in France, with a long period of service, has been sometimes erroneously ascribed to the French Revolution. It is, on the contrary, significant that the inventor of conscription in its modern shape (for compulsory service of some sort, for instance, impressment in England, is an old institution or practice in most countries) was the autocrat Peter the Great, the founder of a policy of territorial aggrandizement which, unless Russia emerges, with unparalleled rapidity, from the condition of a military empire, must inevitably drown the world in blood once more. The French Revolution, on the other hand, was a national revolt against the whole system, of which a standing army is the body, and tyranny the soul; the leaders of the Revolution vehemently proclaimed that standing armies are the weapons of despotism, and that there is no obstacle to both tyranny and aggressive wars like placing the sword in the hands of those whose urgent interest it is never to draw it save in the defence of their country.* Assailed from without, however, a country without training either in arms or in political liberty, became the recruiting ground of a military chief; and that military system was founded, which military authorities, such as General Trochu, condemn almost as emphatically as social economists, such as M. Jules Simon.† The distinctive characteristics of the French system hitherto followed, in contrast with the Prussian, are, first, that only a proportion, a very large proportion indeed, of the able-bodied youths of the French population attaining the military age is drawn for the army by ballot; secondly, that substitution is allowed in the case of those who can pay for a substitute; and, thirdly, that the conscript's period of service in the active army in France is twice as long as in Prussia. These distinctive characteristics make the French soldiery a separate class, and military service a special trade; whereas in Prussia there is a national army in which every man's service is rendered as a duty to his country. The number of conscripts drawn yearly in France has hitherto varied from 60,000 to 100,000, the legal period of service being seven years. General Trochu, who throughout his pages speaks as the exponent not only of his own convictions, but also of the principles of Marshal Bugeaud, pronounces, without qualification, against those conditions which make a professional soldiery of the French army, and separate it morally and socially from the nation. The efficiency of any army has, he says, two main conditions, a motive power and a mechanism, a soul and a body. The one is the spirit which animates the individual members; the other, its organization as a whole; and of these he attaches most importance to

---

* 'Les armées perpétuelles n'ont été, ne sont, et ne seront pas bonnes,' was Mirabeau's cry, 'qu'à établir l'autorité arbitraire, et la maintenir. La corruption, la vénalité préparent les chaines d'un peuple libre, mais c'est, et c'est seulement la puissance légionnaire qui les rive. Le peuple a droit d'avoir et de porter les armes pour la défense commune. Quand il en perd l'habitude, il se trouve bientôt quelque ambitieux qui met tout en œuvre pour en profiter. Une milice bien réglée est la défense convenable, naturelle et sûre d'un gouvernement libre. Point de mercenaires.'

† The reader will bear in mind that this essay was written in 1867.

the former. But what are the feelings in which he finds the true motive power or soul of an army?—Not in the habits of discipline, the supposed esprit de corps, the self-interest of a veteran soldiery, but in the fresh patriotism of the citizen, the natural sentiments of the man, and the élan of youth. The passages in which he speaks on this subject are a study not only in military art, but in mental philosophy. In popular estimation, both in England and France, the true soldier is the 'old soldier,' whose heart, such as it is, is supposed to be in his profession. Far different is General Trochu's estimate of the worth of such soldiers, considered even merely as soldiers. From the day, he maintains, that the soldier looks on his regiment as his home, and military life as his career, the best ingredients in the true soldierly spirit begin to forsake him,—patriotic devotion, chivalrous ardour, and the natural affections of the human heart. 'Non, mon vieux soldat est un jeune homme. Il a dans l'ordre moral comme dans l'ordre physique, tous les ressorts de la jeunesse, et il en a les croyances et les illusions. Il est plein de force, et il est plein d'honneur. Il n'entend pas donner au pays un jour au delà des années qu'il lui doit aux termes de la loi, car des devoirs antérieurs le rappellent dans la famille. Mais ces années, il les lui donne sans restriction ni calcul.'

Adam Smith traces the successive fall of Carthage and Rome to the irrestible superiority of a standing army, constantly disciplined in arms, over a militia in which 'the civil predominated over the military character.' General Trochu, on the contrary, refers to the military history of Carthage and Rome, as exemplifying one invariable truth—the superiority of a national over a mere professional army. In this he has the testimony of good historians on his side; and so opposite is his theory to that of Adam Smith, who attributed the victories of Hannibal to long discipline in the school of actual war, that he ventures the maxim, that 'it is peace, properly turned to account, that makes good armies; it is war, especially prolonged war, that disorganizes them.'

But if on the mere ground of military efficiency, the long service in the French army is open to such question, what is the judgment we must pronounce when its consequences, economic, moral, physical, and political, are added to the scale? Looking, indeed, at the mere pecuniary cost at which the French troops figure in the accounts of the State, it might be pronounced a cheap system. M. Jules Simon estimates the cost of an army of 400,000 men, for example, at 360,000,000 francs (£14,400,000), and the Count de Casabianca, in a later estimate, places the cost of nearly half a million of French troops at very little more; whereas we can hardly maintain more than quarter of the latter number of soldiers for such a sum. But the French ballot (while it lets the class of idle youth whom military service might utilise escape by substitution) falls indiscriminately on the whole mass whose means are unequal to purchase their ransom, and so hammers into mere soldiers a multitude which must include much of the highest industrial genius and intellectual power in the country. To the real cost of the French army we must add, then, not only every shilling above a soldier's pay which each actual soldier could have earned in a civil occupation, but also the lost value of all the indirect and distant results of invention and special productive capacity. Had Watt been forced to spend seven years as a soldier in barracks, what would the cost of that one soldier have been to his country, and to mankind? Nor does the cost of the French conscription stop when we have added to it the loss of all the men of superior industrial or intellectual power it spoils for their natural pursuits. It spoils, more or less, the greater number of the men it lays hold of. Taking every year from 60,000 to 100,000 of the flower of the youth of the population, it returns them at the end of six or seven years, if at all, unfitted for the occupation from which they were torn, with barrack habits of idleness and dissipation, and probably an impaired constitution. They may now at length marry; and 'old soldiers' of this sort, along with the part of the male civil population which was exempted from the ballot for infirmity or other physical defects—in other words, drunkenness and disease, along with debility and deformity—become in large measure the parents of the next generation. Put a young peasant or mechanic into the army, says General Trochu, for a short time, and he returns home a better man and a better citizen, stronger, smarter, with more enthusiasm for his country, still in the suppleness of youth, and able to bend over the plough, or to resume the tools of the artisan. Keep him in the army for double the time, and he becomes both too rusty and too lazy for his old trade. General Lamoricière has pronounced, in an official report, a similar opinion with respect to the inaptitude for civil occupations resulting from a septennial military service, and its tendency to swell the population of the towns with an unproductive class, of whom many were born to be hardy and industrious peasants.* Curran translated in jest the saying, Nemo repente fuit turpissimus, into 'It takes seven years to make an attorney;' but a faithful paraphrase in earnest might be, 'It takes seven years to make a vieux soldat.' And the artificial concentration of the French population in towns is demonstrably traceable, in part, to this vice in the military system.* When we add that the French army, while less efficient for defence than a truly national force, is far more easily employed in aggressive war, for which it is by its constitution disposed, we have, we believe, said enough to establish the urgent necessity in the interests of both Europe at large and France itself, of that change in its military system, which M. Jules Simon so strenuously invokes.

If a further example of the true character and objects of a vast standing army were needed, we have but to glance at the military system of Russia. The period of service for which the conscript is drawn there, twenty years, is the longest in Europe; and the army is thus more totally separated from the nation than any other in Europe. This military system, it is instructive to remember, was instituted as the principal machinery of a despotic usurpation, which not only deprived the nobles of their ancient independence, but reduced the bulk of the population to servitude, establishing at the same time the study of foreign aggrandizement as a permanent and principal element in the policy of the empire. 'Whoever,' says Adam Smith (probably in unconscious admiration of his own doctrine of the

---

* L'Ouvrier de Huit Ans. Par Jules Simon, p. 53.

separation of occupations, which has however really **no** application to compulsory occupations), 'examines with attention the improvements which Peter the Great introduced into the Russian empire, will find that they almost all resolve themselves into the establishment of a well-regulated standing army. It is' (he very truly **adds**) 'this instrument which executes and maintains all his other regulations.' It is the instrument of a purely autocratic as opposed to national policy. No other country in Europe has a population so pacific, or a foreign policy so aggressive. In no other country is military service so detested; the peasantry regard it as **penal servitude for life.** And it is **in** perfect harmony with the fundamental principle of a system **in** which the soldier has in him **nothing** of the citizen, the **army** nothing national, that criminals **under thirty** years are condemned to the army, and wear its uniform as a badge of disgrace; while in Prussia the forfeiture of civil rights **by** crime entails the dishonour of exclusion from the military service due from the citizen.

Between France and Russia, with their vast standing armies, lies Prussia or North Germany, with a mixed military system, combining a standing army with a national militia. Under the present arrangements, every youth physically equal to the standard, **with unimportant exceptions,** is bound by law to enter the ranks of the regular or active army on attaining his twentieth year. For **the mass** of recruits the legal period of service is three years (in practice shortened to two **and a half), but** those who can pass an examination, or present sufficient academic certificates of education, are allowed to enter as volunteers, defraying all their own expenses (unless for arms and ammunition), and serving but **for one year. With** the qualifications just stated, every able-bodied Prussian serves in the ranks of the active army from his twentieth to his twenty-third year, then passing into the reserve for four years, liable to be called on to rejoin his regiment on emergency, or for a short period of **annual** exercise. From twenty-seven to thirty-two he **belongs to the** first ban of the Landwehr, in which he is still liable to foreign service in time of war, and to periodical exercises in peace; from thirty-two to thirty-eight his place is in the **2nd** ban of Landwehr, only called out when the country is in extreme danger. From thirty-eight to fifty he belongs to the Landsturm or levy en masse of the population in case of invasion. Thus of all military systems in Europe which have any standing army, the Prussian is that in which the period of service in the standing army is shortest—so short that the civil necessarily predominates in it over the military character, while the remainder of the able-bodied population forms a true citizen army. The extension of this system throughout North Germany contemporaneously with rapid progress in the arts of both industry and war, presents a remarkable contradiction to the doctrine of Adam Smith, that two causes, namely, the progress of manufactures and improvement in the art of war, combine, as society advances, to make the soldier's a separate trade. We believe that, even in the Prussian army, the original period of service is excessive; but it is at any rate long enough in the opinions of such authorities as Marshal Bugeaud and General Trochu, and the late war has established the character of the Prussian army as second to none, if not foremost in point of efficiency. Prior to its late victories, even those military authorities in France who thought most lightly of it as an engine of war, placed it in the first rank as regards the spirit that animates it. Colonel Reilly, in his memorandum on the Prussian army,* establishes by striking facts, it is true, that 'the Prussians overthrew a disaffected army.'† This circumstance, however, only adds important negative evidence of the military value of the patriotism of a national army, and of the weakness of a standing army without it.

An army composed of such materials as the Prussian certainly cannot be employed in war without immense loss and suffering both to the soldiers and the whole nation, the nature of which may be illustrated by reference to some actual instances within our knowledge. The chief cashier of a principal bank at Berlin was called out for active service in the late war, at the risk of losing his post, which must, indeed, have happened had the

---

* Report on the Medical and Sanitary Services of the Prussian Army during the Campaign in Bohemia, 1866. Published in the last volume of the Reports of the Army Medical Department.

† The Austrian Army.

war been prolonged; in which event, moreover, the banker himself would probably have been ordered to join the army. From a town in Rhenish Prussia a young physician was called out, to find on his return that another physician, exempt on account of age or less vigorous constitution, had taken up his practice. A small shopkeeper, again, in Pomerania had his two assistants taken in the first instance, then a substitute he had managed to procure, and lastly was called out himself, to find on his return that a rival had taken up his business, or that it had gone into the hands of the pedlars. The losses arising in this way are sometimes of such magnitude that special exemptions are granted by the Government; but these very exemptions illustrate the losses that must be sustained in the cases where they are not granted, as of course they very rarely are. A manufacturer of locomotive engines at Berlin, who employs 3000 hands, and had just completed his 2000th engine, was required to join the army. 'I am quite ready to go,' was his response, 'but I manage all my business myself, having neither partner nor manager. If I go, my works must therefore be closed, and all the hands thrown out of employment.' In the foregoing case, and also in that of an eminent sculptor, much employed by the Government, exemption was granted. A late able critic of the Prussian system, foreseeing such results as have just been exemplified, has objected to it:—'A Prussian army may be assembled on the frontiers, but however brilliant, expert, and well-disciplined, it is so constituted that it is scarcely available as a political machine. The life, the property, the industry, the intelligence, the influence of the country are in its ranks. An army composed of such materials cannot be risked unless national existence is at stake.'*

That an army composed of such materials can be risked when national existence or national objects are at stake, the Prussian army has given recent proof; but that it is scarcely available as a mere political machine in the hands of a Government is, we presume to assert, an advantage to Germany of the first order, more than compensating, even economically speaking, for the cost of such an army when contending for national exist-

* Notes of a Traveller. By Samuel Laing.

ence. Giving, on the one hand, to every valid citizen the training and spirit of a true soldier, it is a pure national gain that, on the other hand, this system makes aggressive war unpopular with the bulk of both army and nation, and goes far to make it impossible. 'War,' in the words of M. de Laveleye, 'unless undertaken in the defence of German soil, will never be popular in Prussia, because it affects every family; and the soldier who merely passes through a period of regimental duty does not make a trade or career of the service. Even after the astounding successes of last year, people said to me, "We don't like war; look at our cities all in mourning." In France, on the contrary, the sad consequences of battle scarcely affect any class, save one whose sorrow passes unseen.'

We have, however, to consider whether the advantages of the Prussian system are not attained at excessive cost; and whether, by establishing a more purely national force, such as the Swiss, an army might not be constituted at much less expense, equally efficient for national defence, while even less available for aggressive war in the interests of a dynasty or a government than the Prussian. Estimated in the figures of a budget, the cost of the Prussian or German system doubtless appears very low. Colonel Reilly, in a table compiled from authentic sources, puts the cost of the active army of 212,172 Prussian soldiers, in 1866, at £6,545,944. Under the new federal budget, a regular army of 360,000 in time of peace (raisable to at least 900,000 in case of war), is estimated at a cost of less than £10,000,000. And against the loss incurred by the three years' military service of the strength and skill of the industrial population, must be set off the benefit of increased strength and expertness which the men undoubtedly derive from many occupations. The young peasant, the servant, the hotel waiter, the future railway employé, the artisan, comes out of the ranks a smarter, more orderly, stronger, and in many other respects, better workman. But the military service postpones to a relatively very late period the productive use of the productive power of the country. The professional and wealthier classes, who can afford to serve as volunteers, are, indeed, we fully believe, all the better and nothing the worse of a year's service as soldiers; the more so, as they can generally secure being quartered during it in a town where they can pursue their studies to advantage. But the waste of skilled labour in the case of the classes below them is enormous. The future artisan or mechanic has not learned his business when he enters the army in his twentieth year, nor (unless in the case of a very few trades, such as shoemakers and tailors, who can work for the army), can he practise it until he leaves the regiment for the reserve; he has then still almost everything to learn, and the consequence is that he seldom actually begins business before twenty-five. But twenty-five years, or half the lifetime of the flower of the population, is thus unproductively spent. Even in the case of unskilled labourers and peasants, who can go to work from the day they leave barracks, a considerable loss is sustained. The withdrawal of the male peasantry forces women to labour in the fields; and it not unfrequently happens in various localities that the harvest is ill saved for want of hands. If all this cost must unavoidably be incurred to secure both a citizen army and national preservation, no more could be said than that no loss is too great to incur for such objects. But the truth is, that the army might be made much more national at much less cost, while retaining all its efficiency for the defence of the country.

Does it, in fact, take three years' drill to teach a man the art of a soldier? That one year is found enough for the volunteers in Prussia, is a practical admission on the part of the Government that so much time is not required to train educated men. But is even one year necessary to discipline even an ordinary man? Speaking of British recruits, so experienced a General as Lord Hardinge declared,—'The thoughtless boy enlists, the grown-up man will not. Give us a good stout man, and let us have him for sixty days to train, and he will be as good a soldier as you can have.' The length of the soldier's service in the army in Prussia is not, in fact, determined solely by considerations of military efficiency.

The examples and traditions of long military service in the armies of the two great monarchies lying on the borders of the young kingdom, had their natural effect upon the mind of General

Scharnhorst, when designing the present military system of his country, after its humiliation by **Napoleon,** and the limitation of the **numbers of** its army by that **insolent** conqueror to 40,000 soldiers; but Scharnhorst's main **reason** for fixing upon the period of three **years** for the military training of all the able-bodied **youths was to** enable the Government to **have a** large and **unexpected army ready at** a moment's notice against a future **invader.** The same **motive** has necessarily remained **in the** mind of **the Government** ever since, **in** the presence **of** the standing armies of Austria, Russia, and France, but **the Prussian Government has** also another motive. As **already said, the Prussian** army is not purely a national **one;** it represents in its constitution the conflicting elements **in** the **political** constitution **of monarchy** on one **hand, and** political liberty or national self-government on the other. It is no part **of a** monarch's policy **that his** soldiers should be available only **for the** accomplishment of national objects; it **is, on** the contrary, expedient for him to have always at command, **at** whatever **cost to** the nation, a mass **of** soldiers who have **nothing** else to **do but** to obey military orders. The danger **to** national liberty and peace created by a great standing army **is,** indeed, such that M. de Tocqueville, after demonstrating **that** popular institutions necessarily incline a nation **to peace,** observes that **in the** army there must always remain an element **of despotism and** aggression, against which he despairs of guarding.

Yet against this **danger, at** least, the Swiss military system makes ample provision, while **it** saves the huge **cost** of a long **deduction** from the productive **life** of the manhood of the country **in barracks.** Every male citizen **of** Switzerland is bound to **serve in** the army in defence of his country, from the age of nineteen to forty-four. But the actual service in time of peace, during the recruit's first year, is but twenty-eight days for the infantry, and forty-two **for the** cavalry and artillery. During the subsequent period of military obligation, three days a year (or six days in each alternate year) of military exercises, with one day's rifle-shooting annually, and a few days in camp at some part of **the** whole period, from nineteen to forty-four, make up the entire deduction from peaceful pursuits for military purposes of the army of Switzerland. The infantry soldier's whole service makes from 100 to 110 days, the cavalry soldier's about 170.

We have already quoted the statement of Lord Hardinge, that sixty days' drill will make of a good stout man as good a soldier for a regular army as can be had; but the Swiss system demands only twenty-eight days in the first year, and subsequently the small number mentioned. Lord Hardinge doubtless meant to keep his nine weeks' soldier,—not to let him go back to civil business as soon as he had learned the business of a soldier. But the Swiss system, in the first place, is only intended to produce a defensive militia for a small territory; and, in the second, it has for its base a preliminary military training at school, which, if carried out in the manner Mr. Chadwick proposes for Great Britain, throws back from the productive to the unproductive period of life the acquisition of military discipline and art, and at the same time affords the amplest time, even if years instead of months be requisite to acquire them.

For the defence of a vast empire, such as that of Great Britain, a standing army, in addition to a national militia, is an obvious necessity, and, moreover, a standing army recruited by voluntary enlistment. The immense distance of several of the regions the British soldier must serve in, and the bare cost of moving troops backwards and forwards, render the service necessarily both one of some length, and one which the citizens of a free country could not be compelled to perform. A sufficient army indeed for any great country, even if its territory lay together and compact, in place of being dispersed over both hemispheres, would require a permanent nucleus and support. Nevertheless, Adam Smith (his conviction of the superiority of a standing army over a militia notwithstanding) considered national training in military exercises not only an important part of national education, which it is the duty of the State to supervise and enforce, but also an important addition to the means of national defence. 'Even,' he argued, 'though the martial spirit of the people were of no use towards the defence of the society, yet to prevent that sort of mental mutilation, deformity, and wretchedness which cowardice necessarily involves in it, from spreading through the great body of the people, would still deserve the most serious attention of Government. . . . But the security of every society must always depend, more or less, upon the martial spirit of the people. In the present times, indeed, that martial spirit, alone and unsupported by a well-disciplined standing army, could not perhaps be sufficient for the defence and security of any society. But where every citizen had the spirit of a soldier, a smaller standing army would surely be requisite.' It is as constituting in itself the materials of a powerful national force for the defence of the country, auxiliary to the standing army, and lightening the demands on it, and again, as elevating and strengthening the nation itself, that we think a general military training desirable. Mr. Chadwick has the great merit of having proposed a system by which this general training may be begun and carried to a considerable extent, in the simplest manner, almost without cost, and free from the practical difficulties that might seem to oppose the introduction of compulsory military discipline and duties into a country with a migratory population, unaccustomed to Government interference in the disposal of their time. 'The principle,' he says, 'of the chief measure which I have to propose is an old one, involved in the old practice of the kingdom, when every local community, every parish and burgh, was required to exercise the whole male population, beginning with the very young, in military exercises and the use of the bow. I propose to change the commencement of military exercises from the productive adult to the non-productive juvenile, or to the earliest of the school stages; and to provide that in all elementary schools throughout the kingdom aided by the State, the boys shall be trained in the military exercises and appropriate gymnastics.'

We are confident that every member of the present Volunteer force can attest the truth of all that Mr. Chadwick advances with respect to the tendency of military exercise in the company of numbers, and under command, to correct peculiar physical, intellectual, and moral defects of individuals, to communicate readiness, sharpness, presence of mind, temper, public spirit, and the power both to obey **and to command** in proper place. To diffuse and maintain a general **spirit** of high patriotism through **the people in the times** that **are coming, requires, however, more** than mere military **measures and reforms.** The system which General Scharnhorst introduced into **Prussia** would have had **little success, if** unaccompanied by the measures by which **Stein and** Hardenberg **elevated** the condition of the great body **of the** people, and bound their affection to their country.

Great Britain **ought, in like manner, to be able to say to** every class **of** her citizens, Spartam sortitus es, hanc orna. **To the** measures **necessary to** that end, no less than to military **reforms,** the maxim **of General** Trochu applies: 'C'est la paix, utilisée **comme** il convient, **qui fait** des bonnes armées.' Great Britain **has at** this **moment** only too many citizens who in war would **be a** formidable enemy within **her gates.**

THE POLITICAL ECONOMY OF ADAM SMITH.

(*Fortnightly Review, November* 1, 1870.)

'POLITICAL ECONOMY belongs to no nation; it is of no country. It is the science of the rules for the production, the accumulation, the distribution, and the consumption of wealth. It will assert itself whether you wish it or not. It is founded on the attributes of the human mind, and no power can change it.'* In these words—accompanying an admission that the Irish Land Bill, which he nevertheless defended on other grounds, 'offended against the principles of political economy'—Mr. Lowe gave expression last session to the conception of one school of the followers of Adam Smith that Political Economy is, not what Adam Smith called his own treatise, 'An Inquiry into the Nature and Causes of the Wealth of Nations,' but a final answer to the inquiry—a body of necessary and universal truth, founded on invariable laws of nature, and deduced from the constitution of the human mind.

I venture to maintain, to the contrary, that Political Economy is not a body of natural laws in the true sense, or of universal and immutable truths, but an assemblage of speculations and doctrines which are the result of a particular history, coloured even by the history and character of its chief writers; that, so far from being of no country, and unchangeable from age to age, it has varied much in different ages and countries, and even with different expositors in the same age and country; that, in fact, its expositors, since the time of Adam Smith, are substantially divisible into two schools, following opposite methods; and that the method of one of them, of which the fundamental

* Speech on the Irish Land Bill, April 4th, 1870.

conception is, that their political economy is an ascertained body of laws of nature, is an offshoot of the ancient fiction of a Code of Nature, and a natural order of things, in a form given to that fiction in modern times, by theology on one hand, and a revolt against the tyranny of the folly and inequality of such human codes as the world had known on the other.

No branch of philosophical doctrine, indeed, can be fairly investigated or apprehended apart from its history. All our systems of politics, morals, and metaphysics, would be different if we knew exactly how they grew up, and what transformations they have undergone; if we knew, in short, the true history of human ideas. And the history of Political Economy, at any rate, is not lost. It would not be difficult to trace the connection between every extant treatise prior to the Wealth of Nations, and conditions of thought at the epoch at which it appeared. But there is the less occasion, for the purpose of these pages, or of ascertaining the origin and foundation of the economic doctrines of our own day, to go behind the epoch of Adam Smith, that he has himself traced the systems of political economy antecedent to his own to a particular course of history, to 'the different progress of opulence in different ages and nations,' and 'the private interests and prejudices of particular orders of men.' What he did not see was, that his own system, in its turn, was the product of a particular history; that what he regarded as the system of nature was a descendant of the System of Nature as conceived by the ancients, in a form fashioned by the ideas and circumstances of his own time, and coloured by his own disposition and course of life. Still less could he see how, after his time, 'the progress of opulence' would govern the interpretation of his doctrines, or how the system he promulgated as the system of liberty, justice, and divine benevolence, would be moulded into a system of selfishness by 'the private interests and prejudices of particular orders of men.'

'The Wealth of Nations,' says Mr. Buckle, 'is entirely deductive. Smith generalises the laws of wealth, not from the phenomena of wealth, but from the phenomena of selfishness. He makes men naturally selfish; he represents them as pursuing wealth for sordid objects, and for the narrowest personal pleasures.'* This description is not misapplied to a political economy of later days, which has guided Mr. Buckle's interpretation of the system of Adam Smith; but with respect to that system itself, it involves two fundamental misconceptions. Selfishness was not the fundamental principle of Adam Smith's theory; and his method, though combining throughout a vein of unsound à priori speculation, was in a large measure inductive. The investigation which establishes this will be found also to exhibit the connection between his economic system and the chief problems pressing for solution in his time; the methods which the philosophy of the age provided for their solution; and the history and phenomena of the economic world in which he lived, and from which his ideas, his inductions, and his verifications were drawn.

One consideration to be carried in mind in the interpretation of the Wealth of Nations, is that its author's system of philosophy ought to be studied as a whole; his economic system was part of a complete system of social, or, as he called it, moral philosophy. Mr. Buckle, who on other points has much misconceived the Wealth of Nations, properly says of it, and the 'Theory of Moral Sentiments,' that the two must be taken together and considered as one, both forming parts of the scheme embraced in his course of moral philosophy at Glasgow—a course which, it is important to observe, began with Natural Theology, and included, along with Ethics and Political Economy, the Philosophy of Law. Again, as his social philosophy should be considered as a whole, so the whole should be considered in connection with the philosophical systems or methods of investigation of his time. Two essentially opposite systems of reasoning respecting the fundamental laws of human society were before the world at that epoch, which may be respectively designated as the theory of a Code of Nature, and the inductive system of Montesquieu—the former speculating à priori about 'Nature,' and seeking to develop from a particular hypothesis the 'Natural' order of things; the latter investigating in history and the phenomena of the actual world the different states of

---

* 'History of Civilization in England,' i. 228; ii. 419.

society and their antecedents or causes—or, in short, the real, as contrasted with an ideal, order of things. The peculiarity of Adam Smith's philosophy is, that it combines these two opposite methods, and hence it is that we have two systems of political economy claiming descent from him—one, of which Mr. Ricardo was the founder, reasoning entirely from hypothetical laws or principles of nature, and discarding induction not only for the ascertainment of its premises, but even for the verification of its deductive conclusions; the other—of which Malthus in the generation after Adam Smith, and Mr. Mill in our own, may be taken as the representatives—combining, like Adam Smith himself, the à priori and the inductive methods, reasoning sometimes, it is true, from pure hypotheses, but also from experience, and shrinking from no corrections which the test of experience may require in deductions. Of the two schools, distinguished by their methods, the first finds in assumptions respecting the nature of man, and the course of conduct it prompts, a complete 'natural' organization of the economic world, and aims at the discovery of 'natural prices,' 'natural wages,' and 'natural profits.'

An examination of Adam Smith's philosophy enables us to trace to its foundation the theory upon which the school in question has built its whole superstructure. We shall see that the original foundation is in fact no other than that theory of Nature which, descending through Roman jural philosophy from the speculations of Greece, taught that there is a simple Code of Nature which human institutions have disturbed, though its principles are distinctly visible through them, and a beneficial and harmonious natural order of things which appears wherever Nature is left to itself. In the last century this theory assumed a variety of forms and disguises, all of them, however, involving one fundamental fallacy of reasoning à priori from assumptions obtained, not by the interrogation but by the anticipation of nature; what is assumed as Nature being at bottom a mere conjecture respecting its constitution and arrangements. The political philosophy flowing from this ideal source presents to us sometimes an assumed state of nature or of society in its natural simplicity; sometimes an assumed natural tendency or order of events, and sometimes a law or principle of human nature; and these different aspects greatly thicken the confusion perpetually arising between the real and the ideal, between that which by the assumption ought to be, and that which actually is. The philosophy of Adam Smith, though combining an inductive investigation of the real order of things, is pervaded throughout by this theory of Nature, in a form given to it by theology, by political history, and by the cast of his own mind. 'The great and leading object of his speculations,' says Dugald Stewart, by no means intending a criticism, for Mr. Maine had not then explored the fallacies lurking in the terms Nature and Natural Law, 'is to illustrate the provisions made by Nature in the principles of the human mind, and in the circumstances of man's external situation, for a gradual and progressive augmentation in the means of national wealth, and to demonstrate that the most effectual means of advancing a people to greatness is to maintain that order of things which Nature has pointed out.' At the end of Book IV. of the Wealth of Nations we find the Code of Nature and its institutions definitely marked out: 'All systems either of preference or restraint being completely taken away, the obvious and simple system of natural liberty establishes itself of its own accord. According to the system of natural liberty, the State has only three duties to attend to:' namely, to protect the nation from foreign aggressions, to administer justice, and to maintain certain great institutions beyond the reach of individual enterprise; a supposed natural limitation of the province of law and government which has been the cause of infinite error in both theoretical political economy and practical legislation.

The same fundamental conception pervades both Smith's system of ethics and his philosophy of law. Investigating the character of virtue, he treats first of 'the order in which Nature recommends objects to the care of individuals' for their own personal happiness; next, of 'the order which Nature has traced out for the direction of our powers of beneficence: first, towards other individuals; and, secondly, towards societies.' So, in the description given by himself of his proposed history of jurisprudence, he states that 'every system of positive law may be regarded as a more or less imperfect attempt towards a system of natural jurisprudence;' and that the main end of jural inquiry is to ascertain 'what were the natural rules of justice, independent of all positive institutions'—a description, perfectly coinciding with Mr. Maine's, of the place which the law of Nature filled in the conception of the Roman jurist. 'After Nature had become a household word, the belief gradually prevailed among the Roman lawyers that the old Jus Gentium was in fact the lost Code of Nature. The Roman conceived that by careful observation of existing institutions, parts of them could be singled out which either exhibited already, or could by judicious purification be made to exhibit, the vestiges of the reign of Nature.'*

But abstraction would never have played so great a part in Adam Smith's philosophy, would never have resulted in such sweeping generalizations respecting the beneficent and equitable economy resulting from the play of the natural inclinations and individual interests of men, had not the classical conception of nature's harmonious code become blended with the theological conception of 'that great, benevolent, and all-wise Being, who directs all the movements of nature, and who is determined to maintain in it at all times the greatest possible quantity of happiness.' Ideas thus derived from early philosophy became converted into the plans of Providence. Mr. Buckle displays less than his customary erudition when he states that theology had been finally separated from morals in the seventeenth century, from politics before the middle of the eighteenth.

Natural theology makes the first part of Adam Smith's course of moral philosophy, and its principles pervade every other part. The law of Nature becomes with him an article of religious belief; the principles of human nature, in accordance with the nature of their divine Author, necessarily tend to the most beneficial employments of man's faculties and resources. And as the classical conception of Nature supposed simplicity, harmony, order, and equality in the moral as in the physical world, in Adam Smith's philosophy it becomes associated with

---

* 'Ancient Law,' pp. 56, 88.

divine equity and equal benevolence towards all mankind, and by consequence with a substantially equal distribution of wealth, as the means of material happiness. Nothing, therefore, is needed from human legislation—and this conclusion was powerfully fortified, as we shall afterwards see, by the political ideas of the age—beyond the maintenance of equal justice and security for every man to pursue his own interest in his own way. In the Wealth of Nations, after laying it down that every individual endeavours as much as he can both to employ his capital in the support of domestic industry and so to direct that industry that its produce may be of the greatest value, and therefore necessarily labours to render the annual revenue of his own nation as great as he can, Adam Smith adds: 'He generally, indeed, neither intends to promote the public interest, nor knows how much he is promoting it. By preferring the support of domestic to that of foreign industry, he intends only his own security; and by directing that industry that its freedom may be of the greatest value, he intends only his own gain, and he is in this, as in many other cases, led by an invisible hand to promote an end which was no part of his intention.'

So in the Theory of Moral Sentiments :* 'The produce of the soil maintains at all times nearly that number of inhabitants which it is capable of maintaining. The rich only select from the heap what is most precious and agreeable. They consume little more than the poor, and, in spite of their natural selfishness and rapacity, though they mean only their own conveniency, though the sole end which they propose from the labours of all the thousands whom they employ be the gratification of their own vain and insatiable desires, they divide with the poor the produce of all their improvements. They are led by an invisible hand to make nearly the same distribution of the necessaries of life which would have been made had the earth been divided into equal portions among all its inhabitants; and thus without intending it, without knowing it, advance the interest of the society, and afford means to the multiplication

---

* Theory of Moral Sentiments. Part VI. sec. II. chap. iii.

of the species. **When** Providence divided the earth among a few lordly masters, it neither forgot nor abandoned those who seemed to have been left out in the partition.'

The mischief done in political economy by this assumption respecting the beneficent constitution of nature, and therefore of all human inclinations and desires, has been incalculable. It became **an axiom of science with** many economists, and with all English statesmen, that by a natural law the interests of individuals harmonise with the interests **of the** public; and one pernicious consequence is that the important department of the consumption of wealth has—though Mr. Lowe properly includes it in his definition of political economy—been in **reality either** altogether **set** aside, as lying beyond the pale **of economic** investigation, or passed over with a general **assumption**, after the manner of Mandeville, that private vices are public benefits. The **real** interests which determine the production, and subsequently, **in the course of** consumption, in a great degree the distribution of wealth, are the interests of consumers; although **the** truth is veiled by **the** division of labour, the process of exchange, and the **intervention of** money, which makes wealth in the abstract, or pecuniary interest, seem the motive of producers. If every man produced for himself what he desires to consume or use, it would be patent how diverse are the interests summed up in one vague general **term**, self-interest—interests which **vary in** different individuals, different classes, different nations, and different **states** of civilization. And economic investigation would long since have penetrated beneath the surface **of** pecuniary interest to the widely different character of the real **aims,** determining **the** nature and uses of wealth, but for **that assumption of** an identity between public and private interest which Adam Smith's authority converted into an axiom. Under its influence we find him assuming that the great landowners of the sixteenth century, in enclosing their manors and dismissing tenants, retainers, and labourers, to purchase luxuries for themselves, employed no less national labour than before; although the land fed sheep instead of men, and the wool of the sheep, **in place of** clothing labourers at home, **went** from the country to foreigners in exchange for wines, silks, velvets and trinkets, for the personal consumption of the lord of the manor. When William the Conqueror afforested at once some three-score parishes, he did only what landowners have done from the fifteenth century to the present time. To take the children's food and give it unto dogs is, by this reasoning, to give it back to the children!

The Nature hypothesis had, however, with Adam Smith another powerful ally besides theology in the idea of liberty. The idea of civil and religious liberty, of resistance to arbitrary government and unequal laws, of confidence in individual reason and private judgment as opposed to the dictates of external authority, had begun even in the seventeenth century to spread from the world of religion and politics to the daily business of life. At the beginning of the second half of the eighteenth century the predominant form which this idea took was the liberation of individual effort in the world of industry and trade from oppressive restrictions and arbitrary and unequal imposts; and it found in the code of nature a quasi-philosophical basis on which to build a complete economic 'system of natural liberty.' The French Revolution, of which the seeds were then being sown by the Économistes (or Physiocrates, as they were afterwards called, from the name they gave to their system, a name denoting the government of society by nature or natural laws), was, in its origin, an economic revolution, a 'rebellion of the belly,' stirred up ab initio by the Économistes, who saw in the fetters and insecurity of industry the cause of the poverty of France, and in the superior freedom and security of its cultivators and tradespeople the secret of the superior prosperity of Great Britain. Living in such a world of human misgovernment and suffering toil, beholding, as the Physiocrates did, all the natural sources of wealth locked up by human laws, it is not surprising that the doctrine of a code of nature, of natural rights of liberty and property, of a natural organization of society for the increase of human prosperity, and a just distribution of the fruits of the earth and of industry, came upon them like a new revelation, and carried the authority of one. Thus, like Adam Smith, on whom their doctrines had no small influence, the Physiocrates invested the ideal code of nature, which had come to them through the lawyers of their country from the jurisprudence of Rome, with a divine origin, and found in it a complete circumscription and definition of the province of human sovereignty. The three same fundamental conceptions derived from the three same sources—from Græco-Roman speculation, from Christian theology, and from the revolt of the age against arbitrary interference with private industry and unequal imposts on the fruits of labour, formed the groundwork of the political economy of Adam Smith and the Physiocrates; the sole difference in this respect is that the latter gave the name political economy to the whole of social philosophy, while Adam Smith limits the particular name to a department of social philosophy relating to wealth, and that they enunciated these doctrines as laws of nature and God with more passionate emphasis. Adam Smith had not derived any of the three fundamental ideas of his political economy from the Physiocrates—for those ideas came to both from the history and philosophy of the past, and from the circumstances of the age—but he was strongly confirmed in them by his visits to France, his personal intercourse with them, and his study of their writings; he caught from them, moreover, not only particular propositions and expressions, but something of the form which his doctrine of natural distribution has taken, and also the precise limitation which he gives to the functions of the State.

Smith was himself so sensible of his debt to the Physiocrates, that he not only speaks of Quesnay's system as 'the nearest approximation to the truth that had been published upon the subject of political economy,' but was prevented only by Quesnay's death from dedicating to him his own great treatise. He was, however, under a much more solid obligation to a much greater Frenchman, the illustrious Montesquieu. Mr. Buckle, who in his excellent chapters on the Intellectual History of France justly traces to England the origination of the spirit of liberty which in the eighteenth century took possession of French philosophy, nevertheless does injustice at once to France and to Great Britain in overlooking the influence of Montesquieu over Scotch philosophy in Adam Smith's age. And the same oversight, coupled with a view of political economy which

Mr. Buckle himself adopted from Ricardo and his school, leads him to describe Adam Smith's method as entirely deductive. The philosophy of Great Britain, Mr. Buckle affirms, owes nothing to France; and he represents the intellect of Scotland as having, under clerical guidance, become wholly deductive, referring as a crucial example to Adam Smith, Scotland's most eminent political philosopher. The clerical system of deductive reasoning certainly runs through and warps the whole philosophy of Adam Smith. Nevertheless, his philosophical love of truth, and of interrogating nature itself in its real phenomena, and the inductive method of doing so which Scotch philosophy in his age had adopted from Montesquieu, preserved him from many errors into which the method of deduction from assumptions respecting nature and its laws has led one school of his followers, which at the present day is not backward in claiming the clerical prerogative of orthodoxy. It has already been observed that two opposite systems of reasoning were before the world in Adam Smith's age, and that he combined them both—the system of reasoning from a theoretical law of Nature, and the historical inductive method of Montesquieu, which traces the real order of things, and seeks in the circumstances and history of society the explanation of its different states in different ages and countries. The latter method had a powerful attraction for a new school of political and jural philosophy in Scotland to which Adam Smith belonged. Lord Kaimes, his literary patron, and Millar, his own pupil, alike followed Montesquieu's method. Dalrymple, also a disciple of Lord Kaimes, states in the dedication of his 'History of Feudal Property'—a work which seems to have afforded Adam Smith not a few important suggestions—that much of his manuscript had actually been 'revised by the greatest genius of the age, President Montesquieu.' And Millar expressly states that in his lectures on the Philosophy of Law, his great master 'followed the plan which seems to have been suggested by Montesquieu; endeavouring to trace the gradual progress of jurisprudence from the earliest to the most refined ages, and to point out the effects of those arts which contribute to subsistence and to the accumulation of property in producing corresponding improvements in law and government.' But, as Mr. Buckle himself says, Adam **Smith's** political economy and the rest of his philosophy were ' **part** of a single scheme.' And a comparison of books iii., iv., and v. (chapter i.) of the ' Wealth of Nations,' with Adam Smith's own description, on the one hand, of the work he had previously contemplated on the History of Law, **and** Millar's account **of** his lectures, on the other, shows how closely connected were his economic and **his jural researches.** So closely indeed were they so, that internal evidence confirms the statement of Dugald Stewart, that he actually published in **the ' Wealth of** Nations ' a valuable part of the work he had **long** before announced on the jural history of mankind; **and** we have in **this fact** a probable explanation of the story that he destroyed a few days before his death the manuscript of his lectures on jurisprudence. He preserved in the ' Wealth **of** Nations ' what he probably thought their most valuable results.*

The problem which Adam Smith proposed to himself was by no means only the illusive one, What is à priori the **order** of Nature, or ' the natural progress of opulence ? ' He inquired further, ' What had been the actual order of things, the actual progress of opulence, and its causes ? ' What had occasioned the slow progress of Europe from the time of the barbarian conquests down to modern times? What **the** more rapid advance of Great Britain than of France and other parts of the continent ? To answer these inquiries he subjected **the phenomena of** history and the existing state of the world to a searching investigation, traced the actual economic progress of different countries, the influences of laws of succession, and of the political distribution of property, the action and reaction of legal and industrial changes, and **the real movements of** wages and profits so far as they could be ascertained. Nor was he content with the induc-

---

* An eminent Scotch philosopher of the present day, Mr. Alexander Bain, has expressed to me a doubt that Adam Smith destroyed anything which he considered valuable; adding, that he was little disposed to consider anything to which he had given research and thought of small value. The preservation of the chief results of his jural studies in the ' Wealth of Nations ' reconciles Mr. Bain's opinion on this point with the destruction of the manuscripts, of which there seems **to** me conclusive evidence.

tions of the closet from written evidence—though necessarily the most important field of inductive investigation in social philosophy —he compared all the phenomena which careful personal observation, both in his own country and in France, had brought under his view. In short, he added to the experience of mankind a large personal experience for inductive investigation. Even the Physiocrates, although their study of actual phenomena was much less comprehensive and minute, though they were far more given to accepting at once their own unverified ideas as laws of nature, yet by no means neglected experience entirely. They had studied the economic condition of their own country, and compared it with what they knew of Great Britain; and they believed their theories of the natural order of things founded on the evidence of the results of interference with industry and spoliation of its fruits on the one hand, and of individual liberty and security of property on the other. The extent to which observation guided their doctrines is remarkably illustrated by their division substantially into two schools, whose conclusions, though converging in the main, were reached by different paths of personal experience, and moulded by it. Quesnay, the son of a small farmer, reared in the country amid the sufferings of the peasantry and the stagnation of agriculture under despotic restriction and ruinous imposts, and knowing of what imprisoned riches the soil was possessed, taught that land was the sole original source of wealth, agriculture the sole really productive employment, to whose fruits other industries gave only changes of form or place. Gournay, on the other hand, a merchant himself, and of a line of merchants, made the freedom of trade his staple doctrine, and summed up in the maxim, Laissez faire et passer, the duties of government.* The distinction exemplifies, moreover, that influence of personal history on the forms of political economy to which reference has been made.

There run thus through the political economy of both Adam Smith and the Physiocrates, though much more extensively and systematically in the former, a combination of the experience philosophy, of inductive investigation, with à priori speculation

---

* Les Économistes Français du XVIIIme Siècle, by M. Léonce de Lavergne, pp. 173-5.

derived from the Nature hypothesis. Hence, while on one hand the inductive method preserved the great Scotchman from grave errors into which not a few of his English followers in the mother-country of inductive philosophy have been led by the à priori method, on the other hand the bias given by preconceived ideas was so strong in the case of Smith himself, as to cause him to see in all his inductions proofs of a complete code of nature—of a beneficent order of nature flowing from individual liberty and the natural desires and dispositions of men. Like the Physiocrates, he blended the so-called 'evidence,' or self-evidence, of the law of nature in itself, with the evidence of phenomena carefully collated and sifted. The truth is, that Smith wrote before the physical sciences had developed canons of induction, and he thought an induction complete when he had obtained an immense number of instances, and a theory proved when it seemed to fit every observed case. Throughout history, and over Europe, he saw nothing but disorder and misery from such human legislation as the world had known, wherever it went beyond protecting personal liberty and property; he saw on all sides a mass of poverty traceable to State interference; the only sources of whatever wealth and prosperity existed were the natural motives to industry, and the natural powers of production of individual men, and he leaped to the conclusion that nothing was requisite but to leave Nature to itself, that complete harmony existed between individual and public interests, and that the natural conduct of mankind secured not only the greatest abundance, but an equal distribution of wealth. He thought he found in phenomena positive proof of the Law of Nature, and of the character of its enactments. We find here the explanation of the seeming contradiction which Adam Smith's combination of the theory of Natural Law with the inductive historical method gives to Mr. Maine's proposition 'that the book of Montesquieu, with all its defects, still proceeded on that Historical Method, before which the Law of Nature has never maintained its footing for an instant.' It is incontrovertible that historical investigation convicts the Nature hypothesis of reproducing a mere fiction of ancient philosophy; nevertheless Adam Smith, partly under the bias given by the theory itself, partly because the method of interrogating nature itself was new, and the canons of induction unsettled, conceived that the method of Montesquieu proved the truth of the theory of nature ; in short, that nature, when interrogated, confirmed his anticipations of nature.

One cause of the misconception that Adam Smith's economic method was one of mere à priori deduction is the arrangement he has adopted in the order of the five books of the Wealth of Nations. In the order of logic the third and fourth books come before the first and second. They contain the induction on which is based the conclusion that the State has only to protect individual liberty and the natural effort of every individual to better his own condition—or, in one word (with which his first book begins), labour—will supply in the most ample manner all the necessaries and conveniences of life, will divide its functions spontaneously in the best manner, and will distribute its produce in a natural order, and with the utmost equality. It has already been suggested that no such complete organization for the distribution of wealth is made by individual action, or what Adam Smith called Nature. Mr. Mill has shown the fallacy of defining political economy as the science of exchanges; a definition which, besides omitting some of the most important conditions determining the production of wealth, overlooks the truth that human institutions, laws of property and succession, are necessarily chief agencies determining its distribution. And it affords an instructive exemplification of the two methods which Adam Smith combined, à priori deduction from supposed principles of nature, and inductive investigation of facts, that when the order of nature is present to his mind, he finds a complete natural organization for the distribution of wealth, and no function for the State in the matter; but when he traces the actual progress of opulence, his readers are confronted at once with laws of succession, to which he traces the slow and irregular course of European progress after the barbarian conquests; laws founded on those conquests, and designed to perpetuate the unequal distribution of wealth they effected; laws which are potent agencies in the distribution of wealth in England to this day, and in the determination of its whole social and industrial economy.

But even while tracing in his first book the 'natural' distribution of wealth by exchange, or as he expresses it, 'the order according to which the produce of labour is naturally distributed among the different ranks of the people,' Adam Smith has been preserved by the inductive method which he combined with à priori deduction from enormous fallacies into which the school of Ricardo has since been betrayed by their method of pure deduction. The ancient theory of natural law involved the idea of uniformity **and equality**; and this idea **in Adam** Smith's case was powerfully reinforced both by that of an ideal order deducible from the equity and equal benevolence towards mankind of the **Author** of Nature, and by the love of **system**, symmetry, and harmonious arrangement which plays a conspicuous part in **the** Theory of Moral Sentiments, because it did so in the author's own mind. With all these conceptions the theory of a complete equality of the advantages and disadvantages of different human occupations, and an equality, in that sense, of wages and profits, had obviously a powerful attraction for Smith. It affords surprising evidence of his true philosophical spirit of inquiry into facts that he should nevertheless have denied the actual equality of wages and profits, traced the great actual inequalities to their causes, and defined the conditions of equality and inequality, and the actual effect of industrial progress on these movements, in such a manner as to indicate the very progressive divergence which can be shown to have since taken place, and which a school of modern economists not only ignores, but sometimes angrily denies as inconsistent **with** its à priori deductions. Adam Smith, for his **own part, not** only limited ab initio the tendency to equality to what was practically the **same neighbourhood,** but pointed out that the kingdom was in fact divided into a number of different neighbourhoods with very different rates. **Secondly, he traced** many of the actual inequalities to pernicious institutions, a class of causes of inequality which later economists have done much to perpetuate by affirming a substantial equality. Thirdly, in place of insisting that competition alone determines the rate of **wages**, and gives the labourer the utmost value of what he produces, Adam Smith maintained that combination on one hand, tacit or open, on the part of employers, was the normal condition of things, while, on the other, the **necessitous** position of the labourer exposed him to the exaction of **very** unequal terms. Fourthly, he expressly confined the tendency to equality in the case of both wages and profits, even where competition was in full and free activity, to a stationary and simple condition of **the industrial world.** Fifthly, he showed that in place of equal**izing wages, industrial** progress had already produced great inequalities in England, **and was** beginning to do so in Scotland.

After observing that the price of labour varied much more in England than in Scotland, he adds: 'In the last century the **most usual** day wages **of common** labour through the greater **part of** Scotland were **sixpence in** summer and fivepence in **winter.** Three shillings a week, the same price very nearly, still continues to be paid in some parts of the Highlands. **Through** the greater part of the low country the most usual wages **of** common labour are now eightpence a day; tenpence, and sometimes a **shilling** about Edinburgh, in the counties which border upon England, and in a few other places where there has lately been a considerable rise in the demand for labour, about Glasgow, Carron, Ayrshire, &c. In England the improvements **of** agriculture, manufactures, and commerce began much earlier than **in** Scotland. The demand for labour, and consequently its **price, must necessarily** have increased with those improvements.'

Manufactures and trade on **a** great scale were only beginning in Scotland; the steam-engine had not yet been brought to bear **on the** mine or the loom when the Wealth of Nations was **composed**; and the great inequalities in the local demand for **labour** throughout the kingdom, which have followed in the wake of steam, were yet to appear. Adam Smith, in truth, lived **in a very** early industrial world; the only steam-engine he refers **to is** Newcomen's; the word 'manufacture' had not lost its true **meaning** and become as inappropriate as hideous. In the clothing manufacture, he expressly says, the division of labour was nearly the same **as** it had been for a century, and the machines employed **were** the same; adding that only three improvements in **them** of any importance had taken place since the **reign** of Edward IV. **In** place of the infinite diversities of complexity and difficulty in the different employments of capital which have followed the progress of mechanics and chemistry, all modes of employing capital were, he says, about equally easy. The foreign trade of the kingdom was so small, that he computed the annual importation of corn at only 23,000 quarters; and concluded that the freest importation never could sensibly affect prices in the home market.

In short, he applied the doctrine of equality only to a simple and almost stationary condition of industry and neighbourhood trade, in which few changes in the mode of production or the channels of trade took place from one century to another, and in which the inhabitants of each neighbourhood might comparatively easily estimate the profits and prospects of each different employment; and even to such a world, only with many modifications and exceptions. To such a world, in positive terms, he limited the tendency to equality which has been made by his successors, not only an unconditional assumption, but the basis of finance. The truth is, that the doctrine of a tendency to equality is a mere theorem in political economy; and a theorem which imports the tendency only under special conditions well enunciated by Adam Smith—conditions the opposites of those which prevail in the present industrial world.

A state of the industrial world which was exceptional in Adam Smith's time is the normal state in our own; and it is certain, both from his positive doctrine and from his close attention to the realities of life, that had he lived even two generations later, his general theory of the organization of the economic world and the results of the competition for economic life would have been cast in a very different mould. Alike in the theory of Nature which pervades his entire philosophy of society, and in his general conceptions of the industrial world, we trace the influence of the early world in which he lived. One striking example of this is that one-half of society has been almost entirely overlooked in his philosophy. His language appears at first sight to point to unrestricted liberty as the unconditional principle of a true political economy, and the indispensable requisite of the full development of the economic resources of nature; but on closer inspection it will be found that where he speaks of 'the natural effort of every individual to better his own condition, when suffered to exert itself with freedom and security,' as the cause of national wealth and prosperity, he had only the half of the nation denoted by the masculine pronoun in his mind; he meant only what he elsewhere says, 'the natural effort of every man.' He seems to have been perfectly content—though it involves an inconsistency which is fatal to his whole theory—with the existing restraints on the energies of women; and the only effort on the part of a woman to better her own condition which he has in view is 'to become the mistress of a family.' In the only passage in the Wealth of Nations in which women are referred to, we discover at once how far was he from having developed universal laws of industry and wealth, how far he was from escaping from the ideas of a primitive world. 'There are,' he said, ' no public institutions for the education of women, and there is accordingly nothing useless, absurd, or fantastical, in the common course of their education. They are taught what their parents or guardians judge it necessary or useful for them to learn, and they are taught nothing else. Every part of their education tends evidently to some useful purpose,—either to improve the natural attractions of their person, or to form their minds to reserve, to modesty, to chastity, and to economy; to render them both likely to become the mistresses of a family, and to behave properly when they have become such. In every part of her life a woman feels some convenience or advantage from every part of her education.'

Although ' the obvious and simple system of natural liberty' is the foundation of Smith's whole system, though he regarded it as the law of the beneficent Author of Nature, it turns out that he applied it only to one-half of mankind. The reason is that the law and the exception alike came to him from the age in which he lived, and the ideas of a yet earlier state of society. The insurrection against the oppressive and unequal economic régime of the past was as yet only on the part of men, and the very theory of the Law of Nature which men invoked for their own emancipation, as it was the offspring of the speculation of the ancient world, so it bore the impress of its narrowness and injustice.

THE HISTORY OF GERMAN POLITICAL ECONOMY.

(*Fortnightly Review, July* 1, 1875.)

Two different conceptions of political economy now divide economists throughout Europe; of which, looking to their origin, one may be called English, the other German, though neither meets with universal acceptance in either England or Germany. English writers in general have treated political economy as a body of universal truths or natural laws; or at least as a science whose fundamental principles are all fully ascertained and indisputable, and which has nearly reached perfection. The view, on the other hand, now almost unanimously received at the universities, and gaining ground among practical politicians, in Germany, is that it is a branch of philosophy which has received various forms in different times and places from antecedent and surrounding conditions of thought, and is still at a stage of very imperfect development. Each of these conceptions has its appropriate method; the first proceeding by deduction from certain postulates or assumptions, the second by investigation of the actual course of history, or the historical method. In England it is usual to speak of induction as the method opposed to à priori deduction, but the inductive and historical methods are identical. Both aim at discovering the laws of succession and co-existence which have produced the present economic structure and condition of society. A subsidiary branch of historical investigation traces the progress of thought and philosophical theory, but this branch has the closest relation to the main body of economic history, since one of the chief conditions determining the subjects and forms of thought at each period has been the actual **state of** society; and ideas and theories, again, have powerfully influenced the actual phenomena and movement of the economic world. Dr. Wilhelm Roscher's History of Political Economy in Germany (Geschichte Der National-Oekonomik in Deutschland) is by far the most considerable contribution that has yet been made to this subsidiary branch **of enquiry.** It would be impossible in a few pages **to review a book which ranges** over several centuries, and **discusses the doctrines of** several hundred authors, besides drawing **from** numerous unnamed works. What is sought here is to indicate **some of** the leading features in the history of this department of **German** thought, with some observations suggested by Roscher's **book, or** by its subject.

An English historian **cited** by Roscher, speaks as if the history **of** political economy had begun and almost ended with Adam Smith. Roscher himself begins with the Middle Ages, and ends with the conflicting doctrines of different schools and **parties** in Germany **at the present day.** The structure and phenomena of mediæval society in Germany as elsewhere were far from suggesting an economic theory based on individual interest and exchange. Common property in land, common rights over land held in severalty; scanty wealth of any kind, and no inconsiderable part of it in mortmain, or otherwise intransferable; labour almost as immovable as the soil; production mainly for home consumption, not for the market; the division of labour in its infancy, and little circulation of money; **the** family, the commune, the corporation, the class, not individuals, the component units of society; such are some of the **leading** features of mediæval economy. In the intellectual world, **the** division of labour was even less advanced than in material **production;** philosophy was in the hands of an ecclesiastical order, **antagonistic to** both **the** individual liberty and the engrossing pursuit of wealth **which modern** political economy assumes. Roscher points **to the Canon Law** as embodying the earliest economic **theory, and** it is deeply tinctured with both communism and asceticism; poverty is the state pleasing to God, superfluous wealth should be given to the church and the poor, **interest** on money is unlawful, to buy in the cheapest and sell in the dearest market is a twofold wrong. Nor did the secular law harmonize better with modern economic assumptions. Every system of positive law, as Roscher observes, has a corresponding economic system as its background; and the economic system at the back of the secular law was based on status, not on contract, on duty and loyalty, not on individual interest. Thus whether we look to the actual economy of mediæval Germany, to its moral philosophy, or to its positive law, we find a condition of things incompatible with the economic doctrines of modern times.

A new era opened with the Reformation, and Roscher divides the history of modern political economy in Germany into **three periods,** the first of which he calls a theological and **humanistic** one (das theologisch-humanistische Zeitalter), on account of the influence of both the doctrines of the Reformers, and the literature of **classical** antiquity. But the economic movement of society itself tended to awaken new ideas. The Reformation not only created considerable economic changes of a material kind, but was in fact the result of general social progress, one aspect of the economic side of which shows itself in the discovery of the new world, and the consequent revolution in prices. In Germany too, though to a less extent than in England, something doubtless was visible of that change from status to contract, and from service for duty to service for personal gain, which struck the great English poet, who was himself among the productions of the new age.* We may take Erasmus and Luther as representatives of the economic influences of the new theology and classical literature in Germany. The saying of the mendicant friars with respect to theology is true also, Roscher observes, in the region of economics, that Erasmus laid the egg which Luther **hatched.** 'Erasmus, going back to the best age of classical antiquity as well as to pure Christianity,

---

* ' O good old man! how **well** in thee appears
    The constant service of the antique world,
    When service sweat for duty, not for meed!
    Thou art not for the fashion of these times,
    When none will sweat but for promotion.'
                                    As You Like It, act ii., sc. 3.

proclaimed that labour was honourable.' Luther preached the same doctrine, and moreover anticipated Adam Smith's proposition, that labour is the measure of value. Luther's enthusiasm for the increase of population illustrates the connexion of the economic ideas of the age with both its theology and its material condition, since it sprang on the one hand from antagonism to monastic celibacy, and on the other hand from the rapid increase in the means of subsistence. The chief economic influences of classical antiquity are classed by Roscher under five heads. Its literature, being that of a high state of civilization, furthered the rise of Germany to a higher social stage. The states from which this literature emanated were cities, whose example fostered the development of town life and economy. They were also highly centralized states, with the liveliest national spirit; and their history and ideas could not but promote the development of the modern State and of national unity, as opposed to the mediæval division of each nation into innumerable petty groups and governments. They were also either monarchical or democratic States, the study of which tended to accelerate the decline of the feudal aristocracy. Lastly, types of life and thought so unlike those which the mediæval world had bequeathed, could not but nurture a critical and inquiring spirit, which made itself felt in the economic, as in other directions of the German mind. The only indications, however, of an independent economic literature in this period seem to have been the writings of Camerarius and Agricola on currency. Germany seems to have produced nothing so remarkable as the famous tract by W. S., once attributed to Shakespeare, which the revolution in prices and the contemporary economic changes gave birth to in England.* The period closes with the Thirty Years' War, in connexion with which Roscher adverts to the influence on Germany, both for good and for evil, of its geographical position; including among its beneficial effects a disposition to learn from all sides, which is visible in the subsequent history of its economic ideas and literature.

The second period in the history of German political economy,

* See an Essay by the present writer on the Distribution of the Precious Metals in the Sixteenth and Nineteenth Centuries, reprinted in this volume.

The History of German Political Economy.

which covers more than a century from the Thirty Years' War to the period of Frederick the Great, is called by Roscher das polizeilichcameralistiche Zeitalter, as being one of State regulation and fiscal science. The term 'cameralistic,' which makes a great figure in early German economics, originated (as Roscher mentions in another work) in the office or chamber (cammer), which in each German state was charged with the supervision and administration of the Crown revenues. Hence the science called cameralistische wissenschaft, which is perhaps best explained by reference to one of the two objects which Adam Smith, at the beginning of his account of the Mercantile system, says political economy, 'considered as a branch of the science of the statesman or legislator,' has in view. It proposes, he says, to provide a plentiful revenue both for the state and the people. Cameralistic science aimed at augmenting the revenue of the State or the sovereign, rather than the people. Roscher's second period might, more intelligibly to English readers, be distinguished as the Mercantile period, since one of its chief features was the Mercantile system, interwoven with the system of State regulation and finance. It is a modern error, which, as Roscher remarks, is not attributable to Adam Smith, to ascribe to the Mercantile school the notion that money is the only wealth. What that school really taught was that money, in Locke's words, was the most solid and substantial part of the movable wealth of a country; that it had more extensive utility than any other kind of wealth, on account of its universal exchangeability abroad as well as at home; and that a considerable stock of the precious metals in the treasury of the State, or within its reach, was requisite as a provision for foreign wars. Money had really acquired great additional usefulness and importance by the change from the mediæval to the modern economy, with the substitution of payments in coin for payments in kind, and the great increase in the division of labour, and in trade both internal and foreign. And as the Mercantile system was thus connected on the economic side with the actual movement of society, so on the political side it was connected with the growth of monarchical states, increased activity and interference on the part of the central governments, and the maintenance of monarchical armies, and increased need for money in State finance. A circumstance not adverted to by Roscher, which doubtless contributed to the growth of the Mercantile system, was the revolution in prices, and in international trade, consequent on the influx of American gold and silver, which really placed the countries with a small stock of money and a low range of prices at a disadvantage. They bought dear and sold cheap in the foreign market. The system was thus not so irrational in its objects as many modern writers have supposed; but its history is chiefly important, in the point of view with which we are concerned, as illustrative of the connexion between economic theories and surrounding phenomena and conditions of thought.

The first period in Roscher's division, is, as already said, classed by him as theological and humanistic. In the second period German political economy in his view disengaged itself finally from both theology and jurisprudence, and became an independent science. It is, however, a fact of no small importance to a right understanding of economic history, and to a due appreciation of the authority of some of the economic doctrines of our own day, that economic philosophy was so far from emancipating itself in the seventeenth century completely and finally from theological and juridical theories, that the system not only of the French Physiocrates, but also of Adam Smith, whose Wealth of Nations had a prodigious influence over Germany, was in great part built on an ancient juridical theory in a modern theological form, and penetrated by a theological spirit. Roscher's third period, which reaches down to the present day, begins with the introduction of the system of the Physiocrates into Germany, where he says it influenced only some individual minds, adding that in England it could gain almost no ground. But the influence of the Wealth of Nations both in Germany and elsewhere was so great that 'the whole of political economy might be divided into two parts—before and since Adam Smith; the first part being a prelude, and the second a sequel (in the way either of continuation or opposition) to him.' The system of the Physiocrates had doubtless some peculiar features, traceable to its country and parentage, the study of which throws much light on the causes which have shaped economic ideas, and forms an instructive chapter in the general history of philosophy. Nevertheless its main foundation was essentially the same as that on which Adam Smith's political economy rested. Roscher himself, along with other eminent German economists, has drawn attention to the connexion between both systems and the idea of a Law of Nature, which eighteenth century philosophy had derived from Roman jurisprudence. What they seem to have overlooked is that both with the Physiocrates, and with Adam Smith, the Law of Nature distinctly assumed a theological form. The simple, harmonious, and beneficent order of nature which human laws should leave undisturbed and only protect, became of divine institution, and Nature in short became Providence. Dupont de Nemours, who invented the name Physiocratie, to signify the reign of natural law, says in the dedication of the system to the sovereigns of the world, ' Vous y reconnaîtrez la source de vos droits, la base et l'étendue de votre autorité, qui n'a et ne peut avoir de borne que celle imposée par Dieu même.' In Adam Smith's lectures on moral philosophy, political economy formed one part of a course of which natural theology was another part, and the real ground of his confidence in the beneficial economy resulting from the undisturbed play of individual interest, is expressly stated in the Wealth of Nations, as well as in his Theory of Moral Sentiments, to be the guidance of Providence. 'Every individual necessarily labours to render the annual revenue of the society as great as he can. He generally, indeed, neither intends to promote the public interest, nor knows how much he is promoting it. He intends only his own gain, and he is in this as in many other cases led by an invisible hand to promote an end which was no part of his intention.'* The process of specialization which has differentiated one branch of secular knowledge after another from theology had not reached political economy in Adam Smith's age, nor with many of his successors. Scientifically regarded, the theory of Malthus was fatal to the assumption of a beneficent tendency of the natural desires of mankind, but it did not prevent Archbishop Whately from

* Wealth of Nations, Book iv. chap. ii.

finding in political economy the strongest evidences of natural theology; and the harmony of a beneficent economy of nature with the theism of modern times unquestionably contributed, though often by an unperceived connexion, to the success which the political economy of Adam Smith and the system of laissez faire met with in Germany as well as England.* The principal merit of Adam Smith's economic philosophy has been generally overlooked. He combines the historical method of Montesquieu with the theory of Natural Law, and although that theory together with his theological system gave a bias to his inductive study of the real order of social progress, he has a true title to be regarded as the founder of the historical method in political economy, in the sense at least of having been the first to apply it. In Germany, it is true, this method has been of indigenous and more recent growth, having been transferred from other branches of German historical science, especially in relation to law. And as Adam Smith's system has been generally associated only with that portion of it which is based on natural law, the historical school of German economists have for the most part assumed an attitude of antagonism to what they call Smithianismus.

The last chapter of Roscher's history describes the tenets and methods of the different schools and parties which the economic and political condition of Germany on the one hand, and the progress of science on the other, have evolved during the last thirty years. Dr. Roscher does not exclude even socialism from a place in his history, his object being to portray all the principal phases of German thought on the subject of the production and distribution of wealth. Two conditions concurred to stimulate economic inquiry and discussion in Germany in recent years: the material progress of the country in population, production, trade, and means of communication, presenting new economic phenomena and raising new problems, especially in relation to the working classes; and the great contemporary progress of the sciences of observation, especially history. Political causes, too, have had a

---

* American political economy to this day is theistical, and its principles drawn in great measure from assumptions respecting the method of divine government.

share in producing a diversity of economical creed. Roscher distinguishes five different groups, designated as the free traders, socialists, reactionary conservative economists, officials, and the historical or 'realistic' school. Of these five groups, two, however (the 'reactionary' and the 'official' economists), may be left out of consideration here—the former as insignificant in number, and the latter as distinguishable only in reference to the subjects on which they write, and the special knowledge they bring to bear on them. We need concern ourselves only with the free-trade school—sometimes called, by way of reproach, the Manchester party,—the socialists, or socialist-democrats (socialdemokraten), and the realistic or historical school. The free traders, under the leadership of Prince Smith, Michaelis, and Julius Faucher, formed some years ago an association, called the German Economic Congress (Volkswirthschaftlicher Congress), and all German economists are agreed that they rendered great service to Germany by their strenuous exertions for industrial and commercial liberty. Roscher, too, refuses to stigmatise them with the name, 'Manchester party,' on account of their patriotism; but he objects to their economic theory, which was that of Bastiat and the old English laissez-faire school, as too abstract, too optimist, and too regardless of history and reality. But many of the younger members are broader in their creed, and by no means opposed to the historical or realistic method of economic inquiry. The socialists or social-democrats, of whom Karl Marx and the late Ferdinand Lassalle may be taken as the exponents, aim both at political revolution and at the abolition of private property in land and capital; and Roscher points out that they are even more unhistorical in their method, and more given to misleading abstractions—for example, the argument that capital is accumulated labour, and labour therefore should have all its produce—than the extremest of the elder free traders. Signor Pozzoni signally errs in classing, in a recent article in this Review, the realistic German school with the socialists. The realistic school, which has its chief strength in the universities, is no other than the historical school, which Signor Pozzoni classes apart; and the Association for Social Politics (Verein für Social-politik) which its members have formed, and which, by a play on words, led to the nickname of Katheder-Socialisten, now includes some of the Economic Congress, or free-trade party, along with Government officials, merchants, and manufacturers, as well as professors and working men. The true meaning of the term 'realistic' is sufficiently explained by Roscher's words:—'The direction of the political economy now prevailing at our universities is with reason called realistic. It aims at taking men as they really are, influenced by various and withal other than economic motives, and belonging to a particular nation, State, and period of history.' Man, in the eyes of the historical or realistic school, is not merely 'an exchanging animal,' as Archbishop Whately defined him, with a single unvarying interest, removed from all the real conditions of time and place —a personification of an abstraction; he is the actual human being such as history and surrounding circumstances have made him, with all his wants, passions, and infirmities. The economists of this school investigate the actual economy of society and its causes, and are not content to infer the distribution of wealth from the possible tendencies of undisturbed pecuniary interest. Such a practical investigation cannot be without practical fruit, but its chief aim is light. And it is needless to say what a boundless field of instruction the study of the economic progress and condition of society on this method opens up. Among the works which it has recently produced in Germany may be mentioned Roscher's Nationalökonomik des Ackerbaues, Schmoller's Geschichte der deutschen Kleingewerbe, Brentano's Arbeitergilden der Gegenwart, and Nasse's well-known Essay on the Agricultural Community of the Middle Ages in England. Nor has the historical method been unproductive in England. A great part of the Wealth of Nations belongs to it; and to it we owe Malthus's treatise on Population, Tooke's History of Prices, and Thorold Rogers's History of Agriculture and Prices. Sir Henry Maine's works on Ancient Law, Village Communities in the East and West, and the Early History of Institutions, not only afford models of the historical method, but actually belong to economic as well as to legal history, and exemplify the nature and extent of the region of investigation which those English economists who are not content with barren abstraction have before them.

Nothing can be more unfounded than the imputation of socialist or destructive tendencies which the nickname of Katheder-Socialisten has linked with the historical school of German economists. Historical philosophy has assuredly no revolutionary tendencies; it has been with more justice accused of tending to make its disciples distrustful of reforms which do not seem to be evolved by historical sequence, and the spontaneous births of time. But, as a matter of fact, a great diversity of opinion is to be found among the economists of this school in Germany; some being Conservative, and others Liberal in their politics, but no revolutionary or socialist schemes have emanated from its most advanced Liberal rank. Their principal practical aims would excite little terror in England. Some legislation after the model of the English Factory Laws, some system of arbitration for the adjustment of disputes about wages, and the legalization of trade-unions under certain conditions, are the main points in their practical programme; and they are supported by some of the warmest friends of the German throne and aristocracy.

It is impossible to praise too highly the extraordinary erudition, the immense industry, and the manysidedness of intellectual sympathy which distinguish Roscher's history of German political economy; but we venture to suggest to him a revision of the brief notice which it includes of the history of English political economy in the last thirty years. Generous in the extreme in his estimate of the earlier economic literature of this country, he is less than just in his criticism of it in recent years —an injustice of which the present writer may speak without prejudice, being excepted along with Thornton and Thorold Rogers from Dr. Roscher's unfavourable judgment; one for which no other reasons are assigned than some defects in Mr. Mill's system, on the one hand, which are really attributable to Mr. Mill's predecessors, and the doctrines of a writer,* on the other hand, who represents no English school, and has no sup-

---

* Mr. H. D. Macleod.

porter among authors of economic works or professors of political economy in this country. In this single instance Dr. Roscher has deviated from the impartiality which is one of the great merits of his History. Readers interested in the historical study of political economy, will find an excellent companion to Dr. Roscher's History in Dr. Karl Knies's highly philosophical treatise, Die Politische Oekonomie vom Standpunkte der Geschichtlichen Methode.

XII.

'SOME LEADING PRINCIPLES OF POLITICAL ECONOMY NEWLY EXPOUNDED,' BY PROFESSOR CAIRNES.

(The Academy, June 27, 1874.)

Any new work by Mr. Cairnes would be sure of a succès d'estime, but the present is one, the importance of which the economist most opposed to some of the principles it expounds with so much force, clearness, and skill, will not call in question. Its very importance, on the other hand, the high reputation of its author, and the consummate literary art it displays, impose on a reviewer the duty of sifting it closely. Mr. Cairnes himself sets an example of independent criticism. Thus he speaks of Mr. Mill's doctrine of cost of production as 'radically unsound, confounding things in their own nature distinct and even antithetical, setting in an essentially false light the incidents of production and exchange, and leading to practical errors of a serious kind, not merely with regard to value, but also with regard to some other important doctrines of the science.'

As we, for our own part, think not a few of Mr. Cairnes's own positions, including his doctrine of the relation of cost of production to value, untenable, we must claim for ourselves like independence of judgment and freedom of speech. Mr. Cairnes, we may observe, overestimates sometimes the amount of authority opposed to his own views, sometimes the amount on their side. In the case just referred to, he too hastily assumes that the view he dissents from 'has the general concurrence of economists.' The English market for economic publications is extremely limited, the works on the subject are necessarily few, but it is notorious that various doctrines to be met with in the

English text-books have often been questioned in lectures, articles, discussions, and private conversation; and that the general concurrence even of English economists—of whom alone English economists are apt to take account—ought not to be assumed from the agreement of those books. In the second place, the definition of cost of production which Mr. Cairnes puts forward, had, in fact, been set forth in very similar terms in a treatise which has gone through many editions. Mr. Senior, criticising Malthus for terming profit a part of the cost of production, says, 'Want of the term abstinence has led Mr. Malthus into inaccuracy . . . an inaccuracy precisely similar to that committed by those who term wages a part of the cost of production.' Mr. Senior proceeds to define cost of production as 'the sum of the labour and abstinence necessary to production.' Mr. Senior's analysis is, indeed, defective in omitting the element of risk, but that defect is beside the question, and in respect to it we may observe that Mr. Cairnes too narrowly limits it, in the case of the labourer, to risk to mental and bodily faculties. The labourer often shares the pecuniary risks of the capitalist's enterprise; he runs the risk of being thrown out of work and wages at a critical time; and this is only one of a number of facts inconsistent with the assumption of an equality of wages, even within the limits which Mr. Cairnes sets to it.

The doctrine of cost of production involves the whole theory of wages and profit; and an immense superstructure which has been built on what Mr. Cairnes would call the orthodox theory, must stand or fall with that theory. The subject may be conveniently approached by an examination of the doctrine of 'the Wages Fund' and an 'average rate of wages,' for which Mr. Cairnes contends. An instance has just been noticed of an over-estimate, on his part, of the amount of difference between his own views and those of other economists: we here meet with one of an over-estimate of the amount of support from authority which Mr. Cairnes is entitled to claim for his own view. He terms his own side of the question with respect to the Wages Fund 'the orthodox side.' If orthodoxy in economics is to be determined by authority, some weight surely is to be attached to continental authority. And in Germany, as **Dr. Gustav** Cohn has lately pointed out, the doctrine of a Wages Fund was controverted more than fifty years ago, and has been repeatedly assailed since; nor does it now form, we may believe **we may** affirm, an article of the creed of any scientific school of German economists. **It is condemned** by M. Emile de Laveleye, **of** Belgium, **to whom** Mr. Cairnes will not **deny** a place in the front rank of European economists. French economists have never been polled on the question, but **it is at** least certain **that** the notion that there **is** an aggregate national wages fund, the proportion of which to the entire number of labourers determines the general rate of wages, is incompatible with **the** exposition **which** M. Léonce de Lavergne—who, it is needless to say, combines **the** highest theoretical attainments **with** the most extensive knowledge of the actual economic phenomena of his own country—has given of the diversity of the rates of wages and the causes determining them, in different parts of France. In England the doctrine was, after mature consideration, abandoned by Mr. Mill; it has been vigorously assailed by Mr. Thornton; it is repudiated by Mr. Jevons; and among other economists in this country, **the** present reviewer long ago combated it. On the whole, we believe that the chief weight of European **authority is against the doctrine**, and that it is **a** heresy, if that constitutes one. **But the terms orthodoxy** and heresy are singularly inappropriate in philosophical discussions. What philosophy seeks is reason and truth, not authority; **and** we will briefly state some of the grounds of reason and fact on which we take our stand in maintaining that an aggregate wages fund and an average rate of wages are mere fictions— fictions which have done much harm, both theoretically and practically, by hiding the real rates of wages, the real causes which govern them, and the real sources from which wages proceed. In every country in Europe, the rates of wages even in the same occupation vary from place to place; in other words, the **same** amount of labour **and** sacrifice of the same kind is **differently** remunerated in different localities. The Devonshire, **Somerset**shire, or Dorsetshire labourer has been earning **for the last** fifty years less than half what the same man might have earned in Northumberland; the pay of Belgian farm labour is three times higher in the valley of the Meuse than in the Campine, and twice as high as in Flanders; it varies likewise prodigiously in Germany, even in adjoining districts. Whence these diversities? The **reason**, obviously, is that **distinct** and dissimilar conditions determine wages in different parts of each country. Mr. Cairnes urges: 'A rise of wages, let us suppose, occurs in the coal trade—does any one suppose that this could continue without affecting wages, not merely in other mining industries **in full competition with coal mining**, but in industries the **most remote** from coal **mining, industries** alike higher **and lower** in the **industrial** scale? Most undoubtedly **it could not.'**

We answer, most undoubtedly it could, **and** actually did. **Wages** rose continuously **for a century in** mining **and other industries** in some counties in England, while in others the **earnings of** the agricultural labourer remained stationary **throughout** the whole period. In 1850, Mr. Caird found the **rate of** agricultural wages **in one northern parish** 16s. a week, in another parish **in the south only** 6s. a week. In the former parish, mines and manufactures competed with farming for labour; in the latter, **the** one employer was a farmer holding 5,000 **acres.** Would it be reasonable to say there was an average **rate in the two** parishes of 11s. a week, resulting from the ratio of the aggregate **wages fund to the** number of labourers in both? What **share had the** southern labourer in the funds from which his fellow in **the** north earned his 16s. a week? In like manner, the funds expended in wages **in** the Rhine Province **no** more govern **the** price of labour in Pomerania and Posen than in Cornwall or Kent. A farm labourer in Flanders **earns 1 fr. 50 c.** a day, an inferior labourer **in** another part of Belgium may earn 3 fr. 50 c. and upwards. Why? Because the Fleming no **more** shares in the funds which afford such high wages around Charleroi and Liége, than a provincial journalist does in the funds **from** which the writers of the Times are remunerated. Moreover, **to speak of** the **ratio** of an aggregate wages fund to the number **of** labourers as determining wages in each country surely implies that **the sum** expendible in wages at any **given** time is **a** fixed quantity; and, accordingly, M. de Laveleye remarks that one of many facts which give a practical refutation to the doctrine is that wages have recently risen in some parts of Belgium at the expense of rent. The demand for labour in manufactures on the one hand, and the novel attitude of the Belgian farm labourer on the other, have compelled farmers in certain districts to raise wages to a point at which farming has become a losing business; rents, therefore, are falling. It was seriously urged against trade-unions and combinations of labourers in England a few years ago by some advocates of the doctrine of the wages fund, that wages could not be raised by combination in one trade or locality without a proportionate fall of wages elsewhere, there being only a certain aggregate fund to be distributed. Mr. Heath's statement, however, is incontrovertible that the mere report of the formation of an agricultural labourers' union in Warwickshire raised wages immediately in several neighbouring counties, and it will hardly be contended that there was a corresponding fall in other counties.

It is evident that the result has been mistaken for the cause; that the aggregate amount of wages is nothing but the sum of the particular amounts in all particular cases taken together; and that it would be as rational to say that the income of each individual in the United Kingdom depends on the proportion of the total national income to the number of individuals, as to say that the wages of each labourer in every place and in every occupation depend on the ratio of the sum total of wages to the total number of labourers. The statistician may find some interest in calculating the average rate resulting from the ratio of the aggregate amount of wages, if it could be ascertained, to the number of labourers in the kingdom; but the economist deludes himself and misleads others by representing this as the problem of wages. If farm wages be 10s. a week in Devonshire, and 20s. in Northumberland, to say that the average rate is 15s. a week is to speak of a rate which has no existence in either, and to withdraw attention from the causes of the real rates in both. In every country, instead of an average or common rate of wages, there is a great number of different rates, and the real problem is, what are the causes which produce these different rates? Hence we are driven to conclude that Mr. Cairnes is not 'justified,' to use his own words, 'in generalizing the various facts of wages into a single conception, and in discussing "general" or "average wages."'

At this point we are brought to enquire whether there is any better reason for maintaining the existence of an average rate of profit. The doctrine of average profit is closely connected in Mr. Cairnes's exposition with that of average wages. While contending, erroneously as we have shown, for an equality of wages throughout all similar occupations in the same country, he admits that working classes of very different degrees of skill do not compete, and may be paid at different rates for equal sacrifice and exertion. But, he adds, 'though labourers in certain departments of industry are practically cut off from competition with labourers in other departments, the competition of capitalists is effective over the whole field. The communication between the different sections of industrial life, which is not kept open by the movements of labour, is effectually maintained by the action of capital constantly moving towards the more profitable employments. In this way our entire industrial organization becomes a connected system, any change occurring in any part of which will extend itself to others, and entail complementary changes.'

In Mr. Cairnes's view, if wages were below par in any trade or locality, although the labourers there might not be able to migrate, a movement of capital seeking cheap labour would at once set in. It might almost be a sufficient refutation of this doctrine, in relation both to wages and to profit, to point out that no migration of capital has equalized the wages of agricultural labourers in any country in Europe. What migration there has been—and it has been altogether inadequate to produce an approach to equality of wages—has been almost altogether a migration of labour. Moreover, if in a single occupation so simple as that of agricultural labour there has been no such effective competition as Mr. Cairnes assumes, there seems some antecedent reason for suspecting error in the assumption of such an effective competition among capitalists as to equalize the rates of profit in all the countless employments of capital. There is something like a circular movement in Mr. Cairnes's reasoning on this subject. He first argues—'Each competitor, aiming at the largest reward in return for his sacrifices, will be drawn towards the occupations which happen at the time to be the best remunerated; while he will equally be repelled from those in which the remuneration is below the actual level. The supply of products proceeding from the better paid employments will thus be increased, and that from the less remunerative reduced, until supply, acting on price, corrects the inequality, and brings remuneration into proportion with the sacrifices undergone.'

But afterwards we read—'The one and sufficient test of the existence of an effective industrial competition, is the correspondence of remuneration with the sacrifices undergone—a substantial equality, that is to say, making allowance for the different circumstances of different industries, of profits and wages. Such a test applied to domestic transactions shows the existence of a very large amount of effective industrial competition throughout the various industries carried on within the limits of a single country. The competition of different capitals within such limits may be said to be universally effective.'

Is not this very like arguing that the equality of profits is proved by the fact that there is an effective competition of capital, and that the equality of profits proves the fact of an effective competition? Nor is this the only seeming flaw in Mr. Cairnes's logic. In proof of the equalization of profits, he urges that capital deserts or avoids occupations which are known to be comparatively unremunerative; while if large profits are known to be realized in any investment, there is a flow of capital towards it. Hence it is inferred that capital finds its level like water. But surely the movement of capital from losing to highly profitable trades proves only a great inequality of profits. There is, in like manner, a considerable emigration of labourers from Europe to America; does that prove that wages are equalized over the two continents? Let Mr. Cairnes himself answer—'Great as has been the emigration from Europe to the United States, it may be doubted if any appreciable effect has been produced on the rates of wages in the latter country. Throughout the Union, wages remain in all occupations very considerably higher than in the corresponding occupations in this country.'

Elsewhere he estimates American wages at twice the English, and four times the German rate. The emigration of labour, **thus, is** neither sign nor cause of an equality of wages; it is, on the contrary, consequence and proof of their **inequality; and the** migration of capital from losing or unprofitable to promising businesses, in like manner, only lands those who refer to it in evidence of the equalization of profits in an ignoratio elenchi. Mr. Cairnes, it seems clear, has not taken into consideration the main objections to **the** doctrine he **espouses.** The only objections he notices are the difficulty of transferring buildings, **plant,** and material from one use to another, and of learning a new branch of business. The fact **is, that** there are, in the first place, no means whatever of knowing the profits and prospects of all the occupations and investments of capital. No capitalist knows so much as the names, or even the **number of** the trades in the London Directory, only a **part of the** trades of the kingdom; and their number and names are yearly increasing. If, again, there were any statistics showing the actual gains of the different trades, **they would show** that the profits of the individual members **of each trade** vary immensely.

The business of insurance used to be thought one in which there was a certain general rate **of profit. But a** few years ago the subject was investigated **by** Mr. Black, and also in the Economist, and the result arrived at was the fact of 'extremes of success and disaster in the experience of companies still underwriting.' Mr. Cairnes's reasoning assumes that the profits of every business are well known; but as they vary greatly with different companies and different individuals, the assumption implies that individual profits are known. If they were, it would be seen that to speak of the average profits, even of a single business, is idle. Moreover, even if the past profits of every individual in every trade were known, it would be a serious error on the part of capitalists, though one which they often commit, **to judge of** the future from the past. The changes in production **and the** conditions **of** trades, in international competition, and in prices, the effects of speculation, fluctuations of credit, and commercial crises, of scarce and abundant seasons, wars and other political events, new discoveries and inventions, would upset all these calculations. Curiously enough, Mr. Cairnes himself has maintained that the new gold mines introduced a disturbing element which will probably affect profits for thirty or forty years. Ricardo admitted **that** at the very time he was building a pile of theory on the assumption of **an** equality of profits, the return of peace had made them in fact very unequal. Had he looked back for a quarter of a century, he would have found abundant proof that they had been very unequal throughout the long **war;** and had **he** been able to foresee the immediate future, he would have learned from the crisis of 1825, which Mr. Tooke so well described, how blindly mercantile men often reason, how far they are from possessing the knowledge, sagacity, and prescience his theory supposed. So far, indeed, are men in business from knowing the conditions on which future prices and profits depend, that they are often ignorant, after the event, of the causes of their own past profits and losses. Not a single farmer or corn merchant, no witness whatever before the parliamentary committees save himself, Mr. Tooke states, dreamt of referring the high prices of corn in the early part of this century to the succession of bad harvests. It is not even true that losing **businesses** are always abandoned. Hope springs eternal in the human breast, and it is an old saying that all the mines in Cornwall **are worked at a** loss— that is to say, the average result is a balance on the wrong side. Mr. Mill, indeed, has reduced the supposed equality to one not of actual profits, but of expectations of profit. There is not, however, even this: no capitalist ever attempts to survey the whole field, or to estimate the probable relative gains of every investment.

The doctrine of average profit, like that of average wages, thus falls to the ground, and with it falls the superstructure built on it, including Mr. Cairnes's doctrine of value. 'The indispensable condition,' he states, 'to the action of cost of production is the existence of an effective competition amongst those engaged in industrial pursuits'—that is to say, a competition which equalizes profits; and we have seen that no such competition is possible. If we are, in economic theory, to exhaust space and time of their contents, and to suppose a vacuum in which no obstacles to the movements of labour and capital in pursuit of gain exist within the limits of each country, so that wages and profits are equalized, why not apply the same supposition to international trade and international values? We might, in like manner, theorise about wages, profit, prices, and rent at the bottom of the ocean on the supposition of the absence of water. The truth is—and it is a truth which Mr. Cairnes has missed, though he has made an important step towards it—that the principle regulating domestic as well as international values is not cost of production, but 'the equation of demand,' or 'demand and supply;' though the formula is one which requires much interpretation, and by no means contains in its very terms the full explanation of values and prices which many people suppose.

But more than the superstructure of economic theory built on the doctrine of cost of production falls to the ground along with it. The method of deduction from assumption, conjecture, and premature generalization falls too. Mr. Cairnes speaks in his preface of certain 'assumptions respecting human character and the physical conditions of external nature,' as constituting 'the ultimate premisses of economic science;' and of 'the method of combined deduction and verification by comparison with facts,' as 'the only fruitful or, indeed, possible method of economic inquiry.' But is a theorist likely to be very searching in his verification of assumptions on which he has built his whole science and his own reputation? Have the economists of the deductive school ever verified their doctrines respecting the equality of profits and of wages? If they are at liberty to set aside as 'disturbing causes,' all the obstacles to the pursuit of gain resulting from other principles of human nature, and from external circumstances, and to theorise respecting wages profits, and prices in vacuo, what right have they to assume the existence of the love of gain itself in such an imaginary world? The only facts in human nature, we may add, which abstract political economy takes account of are far indeed from being ultimate facts, or from being susceptible of treatment in economic reasoning as simple, universal, and invariable principles. Self-interest and the desire of wealth are both names for a **multitude** of different passions, ideas, and aims, varying in different ages and countries, and with different classes and different individuals; and each having its own peculiar effects on the nature, production, and distribution of wealth.

The 'principle of population,' again, so far from being an ultimate fact in human nature from which general conclusions can be drawn, is a highly artificial and widely varying principle, inseparably interwoven with religious **and moral** ideas and historical causes. Its force in Bengal is the result mainly of a particular superstition; and, owing to causes which have never been probed to the bottom, its force varies greatly not only in neighbouring countries like England and France, **but** in different parts of the same country, Normandy and Britanny for example.

Our limits prevent our even alluding to many special questions of great interest raised by Mr. Cairnes, but we will take two or three examples from the chapter 'On some Derivative Laws of Value.' **In** the early stages of a nation's growth, tillage for the production of **corn** steadily gains ground on pasture; but Mr. Cairnes **treats it** as a '**law** of industrial progress' that **in** the later stages this process is reversed, and pasture constantly encroaches on tillage. We think **we** find here an instance of the economic error resulting from inattention to both continental phenomena and continental literature. Save in exceptional situations, the increasing supply of meat in Europe is obtained by stall-feeding and tillage, not by the extension **of pasture. As** Professor Nasse states, the aridity of the climate and the character of the soil preclude pasture throughout the greater part of Germany. M. de Laveleye maintains that, by means of stall-feeding, Flanders, in spite of the poverty of its soil, supports more cattle to the acre than England. It is noticeable that both these distinguished economists point to one condition unnoticed by Mr. Cairnes, which may in future, to some extent, counteract the causes hitherto operating so decisively in favour of tillage for the production of meat over most of the continent—namely, the rise in the price of labour. How far mechanical art, on the other hand, may neutralize this condition it is useless here to enquire; but M. de Laveleye makes the important observation, that even where a country like England, with exceptional advantages for pasture, imports a great part of its corn, the importing and exporting countries become virtually one economic region in which tillage is constantly advancing. Hence an enormous extension of tillage in the United States, for the supply both of its own population and that of Europe, is as certain as any fact in the economic future can be. Connected with the foregoing question is one respecting the price of corn, which, according to Mr. Cairnes, 'at length, in the progress of society, reaches a point beyond which (unless so far as it is affected by changes in the value of money) it manifests no tendency to advance further.' This point, in Mr. Cairnes's judgment, was already reached in England three centuries ago, if not, as he has no doubt, some centuries earlier; the reason he assigns being that, after a certain point, an advance in the price of corn reacts on population and checks the demand. There are, however, several methods by which a nation may meet an advancing cost of corn—by a diminished consumption of animal food, for instance, or a diminished cost of manufactures. As a matter of fact, the labouring population of England has much diminished its use of animal food since the fifteenth century, while it clothes itself cheaper. The enormous prices of corn towards the close of the last, and during the early part of the present century, again, show how an advance in the price of bread may be met by privation. The whole population of the United States is now a meat-consuming one; but if Macaulay's prediction should be fulfilled, at no very distant future an increased cost of corn would be met by relinquishing meat; and a part of the nation might possibly even fall back on potatoes, or some other cheap vegetable; so that the future price of corn can only be matter of speculation. The price of timber, it may be observed, has followed a different course on the Continent from that which Mr. Cairnes lays down for it. Its value, he says, 'rises in general slowly, but never attains a very great elevation, reckoning from its height at starting.' Professor Rau, however, has given the following prices of a given measure of the same wood in Würtemberg, in florins and kreuzers:—1690-1730, 57 **kr.**; 1748-1780, 2 fl. **14 kr.**; 1790-1830, 8 fl. 22 kr. And **Dr. Engel's statistics** show that the price of wood in another part **of Germany nearly quadrupled** itself between 1830 and 1865.

While **we** dissent altogether from most **of the** fundamental propositions of **Mr.** Cairnes's book, from the economic method it follows, and **from not a few of** its inferences and speculations, we see much to admire in it. It abounds in valuable criticisms, such as that of Mr. Brassey's proposition that dear labour is **the** great obstacle to British trade, **and of the** argument of American protectionists that the States with their high-priced **labour** cannot compete with the cheap labour of Europe.

XIII.

THE INCIDENCE OF IMPERIAL AND LOCAL TAXATION ON THE WORKING CLASSES.

(Fortnightly Review, February 1, 1874.)

The working classes comprehend in this article all grades of working people, skilled and unskilled, in both town and country, domestic servants, and also that numerous body of small dealers whose earnings are derived more from their labour than from their little stock in trade. It is not very important whether foremen are included or not, but they are so here as receiving wages. To measure the burden imposed on this vast section of society by both imperial and local taxation is a problem of much complexity and difficulty, admitting of no exact solution, but the grounds for a rational judgment may be found. Two questions are involved: How much do the working classes contribute to the revenue of the State? and—How much do they actually lose by the system of taxation? The first may possibly be answered with some approximation to accuracy; but the second is really the principal inquiry, and it is one as impossible to answer in arithmetical terms, as it would have been to estimate in precise figures the pecuniary loss inflicted on the working classes by the corn duties. The theoretical canons commonly applied to determine the incidence of taxes afford but moderate assistance, and are often misleading. They furnish us amply with inferences from ideal 'average' or 'natural' rates of wages and profit, respecting the 'tendencies' of taxes 'in the long run,' and ' in the absence of disturbing causes.' But taxes are paid immediately, under the real conditions of life, and out of the actual wages and profits or other funds of individuals, not out of hypotheses or abstractions in the minds of economists. The working classes have had especial reason to complain of the acceptance of such abstractions as realities, and of inferences from them as rules of practical finance. The doctrine of the equality of wages has done much to perpetuate the low wages of agricultural labour in the southern counties, that of the equality of profits has injured the labouring classes generally, alike as recipients of wages, as consumers, and as taxpayers; and the doctrine of a 'natural' rate of wages was the chief cause of the passing of the Corn Laws, the least mischief of which to the classes who live by labour, **was the rise in the price** of bread. It was inferred that the labourer's pay must rise with **the** price of his food, and that taxes on wages are really taxes on profits,* and accordingly members of Parliament, on both sides of the House, discussed **the** duty on corn under the conviction that it could not **fall** on **the** labourer.† **Mr.** Ricardo himself **opposed** the duty **in** Parliament, simply on the ground that it would lower **the profits of** capitalists. In **place of** raising wages, it really lowered them, in a manner highly important to remember in an inquiry into the effects of existing taxation. 'Take the great change in the Corn Laws,' said Mr. Gladstone, in a celebrated Budget speech. '**You have created** a trade in corn; by that trade you have **created a** corresponding demand for the commodities of which **they** (the working classes) are the producers, **their labour being an** essential **element** in their production, and **it is** the enhanced price their labour brings, even more than the cheaper **price of** commodities, that forms the main benefit they receive.' One **of the** chief causes of **the impossibility of** ascertaining with exactness the amount of **the burden** of existing taxation **on the** classes in question, is that the **effect** on wages must be **taken into account**. But, although **I** cannot pretend to furnish an accurate estimate, I think **the** following investigation, brief as it necessarily is, will be **found** to establish at least: (1.) That the real burden imposed on the working classes by the present system of taxation, imperial and local, is incalculably greater than is generally supposed. (2.) That taxes

---

* Ricardo's 'Principles of Political Economy and Taxation,' **chap xvi.**
† See, on **this** point, the 'Speeches of Mr. Cobden,' vol. **i.** p. 16-17.

which admittedly fall on **them, seriously** affect them in various ways besides those ordinarily taken **account of.** (3.) That they **are contributors to a** number **of taxes generally believed not** to **touch them at all.**

Take first imperial taxation. **Of the** grievous inequality of **the contribution** levied from the working classes by the customs and excise duties, which produced nearly forty-seven millions of **the sixty-five and a** half millions raised by imperial taxation in the last financial year (exclusive of the revenue from the post-office, telegraphs, crown lands, and miscellaneous receipts), there can be no **question.** The duty, for instance, on all qualities of **tea is** the same; the duty on a pound of the finest cigars is little heavier than on a pound of common unmanufactured tobacco; **the duties** on beer, spirits, and wine **make** no distinction between **rich and** poor. It is indeed sometimes asserted that the wealthier classes pay, in addition to their own, their servants' taxes on tea, sugar,* and beer; but the very language in which one well-known **writer defends** this assumption, affords **proof of** its error: 'A gamekeeper,' **says** Mr. Dudley Baxter, '**is** employed by a country gentleman at weekly wages, **but lives in** his own cottage, and pays his own taxes on beer and sugar. If the taxes are **taken off,** he reaps the benefit, **and** is therefore the true **taxpayer.** But a house-servant, **if his provisions** are paid for him, would **not receive any benefit, so that** his master is the taxpayer.'† Were the taxes referred to removed, the result would be that outdoor servants would have more money to spend, **while** indoor servants in **the** very same establishments would **have no** more than before, unless their wages were raised, as **they could** be in proportion **to the** reduced cost **of** their board, **without any** loss to their masters. It is, indeed, a mere fiction, that competition equalizes wages in all occupations and all over the kingdom; but such an inequality as the foregoing obviously could not continue. It is not, however, **by** the cost to them as consumers, even adding the charges for the advance of the duties by the producers and dealers, that the sums of which customs

---

* The duty on sugar has been **abolished since the first publication** of this Essay.

† 'The Taxation of the United Kingdom,' **p.** 48.

and excise duties deprive the working classes can be measured. Not to mention that the forty to fifty millions advanced, would otherwise be productively employed, yielding wages as well as profit on each turn of the capital, the system by which they are raised is a network of obstructions and restrictions to trade, production, and the employment of labour. For evidence in detail of the mass of impediments which customs and excise regulations oppose to the growth of commerce, manufactures, agriculture, capital, and wages, I must refer to a former essay.*
But I may instance one fact not particularized there. Conservatives and Liberals are now agreed that protective and discriminative duties impede the development of our resources, and diminish the demand for labour. Yet we still maintain four protective and discriminative duties, on sugar, spirits, wines, and tobacco. The sugar duties are framed for the protection of the British refiners, and the protection afforded appears to be disastrous, even to many of them.† The duty on foreign spirits protects the British against the German distiller, in ordinary years. The wine duties place all wine-producing countries other than France, and our trade with them, under a heavy disadvantage. The licensed British cigar-maker pays little more than the importer of raw tobacco, and the duty becomes virtually protective. These four duties, accordingly, by obstructing the natural course of commerce and industry, diminish the earnings of the working classes, besides taxing them on their expenditure. Just as the duty on foreign corn was a tax not only on the bread, but also on the wages of working classes, so the sugar duties mulct them, not only as buyers of sugar, but also as sellers of labour; and the duties on wine, spirits and tobacco are taxes

---

* Financial Reform. Cobden Club Essays, 2nd Series, 1871-2.

† 'Since 1840 they had had no less than twenty-seven changes in the sugar duties, and since 1863 they had had four or five conventions with Foreign Powers for the purpose of protecting the refining trade, and also the revenue. The result had been this, that while there were twenty-three sugar refiners existing in London in 1862, only three or four were left in existence now. He had the curiosity to ascertain what proportion of foreign sugar and English sugar was sold in this town (Bradford). He went to one of the leading grocers and asked him the question, and was astonished to hear that he did not sell a single ounce of English-made sugar, and that he found it more profitable to buy it from France.'—Speech of Mr. Jacob Behrens at Bradford, November 29.

on the wages of men and women who never drink a glass of strong liquor, or smoke a pipe in the year. It may, on account of the difficulty of levying the imperial revenue by direct taxation, be absolutely necessary, it may, for moral and sanitary reasons, be desirable to tax the consumption of stimulants; but in estimating the actual incidence and pressure of our system of taxation, we are bound to take account of the fact that the duties levied on commodities are not only taxes, and most unequal ones, on the working classes as consumers, but also taxes on their earnings as producers.

Another incidence of a number of taxes on the working classes as producers, has been concealed by the doctrine that taxes on particular commodities and particular employments fall on consumers only, not on producers. The theory of taxation abounds in examples of the danger of the abstract and hypothetical method of reasoning in economics. The economist sets out with an assumption surrounded with conditions and qualifications, and perhaps itself open to question, such as that in the long run, and on the average, the profits of different occupations tend to equality, and presently forgetting all his qualifications and conditions, concludes that the profits of individuals must be equal; and therefore all special taxes advanced by producers must come back to them with equal or average profit. Individual profits really, in almost every business, vary from enormous gain to absolute loss. Profit depends, as Mr. Mill says, not only on the skill of the capitalist himself, and the conduct and honesty of those he deals with, but also 'on the accidents of personal connexion, and even on chance. That equal capitals give equal profits, as a general maxim of trade, would be as false as that equal age and size give equal bodily strength.'* Nevertheless, it is taken for granted that every special tax on a business is recovered 'with average profit,' though the net result of all a trader's advances is not unfrequently ruin; though all such taxes give an advantage to the larger capitalists; and though our customs and excise duties have been steadily driving small producers and dealers from

---

* 'Principles of Political Economy,' Book ii. chap. xv.

one business after another. There is a numerous working class (as, from the small proportion of their capital to their work, they are properly considered) who are frequently losers by the taxes they advance. A petty retailer, to give real examples, takes out licences to sell spirits, beer and tobacco, he advances the customs and excise duties on tea, sugar, and the rest of his stock, he pays perhaps sixpence in the pound on his shop, and after all these duties have been advanced, his shop is burned to the ground, or he falls sick and loses his business, or he is defrauded and becomes bankrupt; or a large dealer, to whom the taxes are 'a fleabite,' takes away his customers; or from one of twenty other causes the return to all his outgoings is ruin. Take another actual case. A cab driver saves a little money and sets up a cab for himself; soon afterwards his cab is smashed in a street collision, and his horse is so seriously injured that it has to be shot. A large cab proprietor would feel the loss of one horse almost as little as the cost of his licence, but to the poor cabman I speak of his licence itself was a considerable outlay, and he will never recover it. There are thousands of poor men who every year embark their little savings or borrowed money, in losing ventures of this sort on which they pay taxes; and not unfrequently one cause of their failure is the advantage which wealthier rivals find in those very taxes. Thus excise and customs duties on commodities, trade licences, licences to keep horses and public carriages, &c. —though treated not only by theorists but even by chancellors of the exchequer, as taxes on consumers alone—are often heavy direct taxes on a working class of producers, over and above the general diminution of wages which the whole system of so-called indirect taxation occasions.

Again, it is commonly assumed in estimates of the incidence of taxation, that the working classes are entirely unaffected by a number of imperial taxes which really fall on them. Thus probate and legacy duties, and stamp duties in general, the income-tax, the house-tax, the wine duties, the railway duty, and the duty on dogs, are usually supposed never to fall on working men or women, directly or indirectly. Now, in fact, the succession duty, in the first place, really falls upon many of

them. Numbers of **working men and** women in towns and **man**ufacturing districts **have become** owners of houses—originally in most cases through **building** societies—and succession duty is often **paid** on them. At Bradford, for instance, a high local authority answers as follows the questions given:—
'Do any **of the working** classes own **the houses they occupy?**'
'A large **number.'—' Do** cases occur **in which** they pay **probate and** legacy, **or succession** duties?' 'Yes, frequently, as **large** numbers **own house** property.' Another good authority states with **respect to the** same town: 'Very many workmen **own the** cottages **they live in. A** smaller but still fair number **own two, and some even** four cottages. The cottages are **worth from £100 to £150** each.' A London workman's house **is sometimes worth from £400** to £500, **and, if** a leasehold, **pays the higher succession** duty on personalty. It does **not** so often **happen that working** men leave to **their** families other property of sufficient **value to** become liable to probate **and** legacy duty; yet **it does** sometimes happen, **in the case alike of workmen,** servants, and small dealers belonging **to the working** class. Servants, too, sometimes receive **legacies, subject to duty, from their masters;** and working people of all classes sometimes succeed **to per**sonalty, or receive legacies from relatives who have made money as emigrants **or** otherwise. The house-**tax,** again, sometimes falls **on the highest** class of skilled **workmen, and** sometimes on workmen of a **poorer** class, either **as lodgers or** letters of lodgings. The income-tax, **though directly incident** on but a small **num**ber of the **highest paid** workmen **or** foremen, has an **incidence on the working** classes which **one of the** current **canons of** taxation conceals. **It is** laid down that taxes on the **profits of** all employments fall **on** capitalists only, **and** cannot **be shifted on any other class. But** there is in reality a perpetual **migration along the borders between** capital and labour, as there **is also an** intermediate class who individually may be regarded **either** as capitalists or workmen, according as capital or labour **forms the main** element **in their** earnings. To instance actual examples of the migration referred to: I have **known** the same man **successively a** butler, a grocer, and a court-crier; the same **man an upper** servant, a small trader,

and a railway-platform inspector; the same man a groom, a cab proprietor, and the conductor of an omnibus; the same man a waiter, a tavern-keeper, and a waiter again; the same man a private servant, a servant in a hotel, and the proprietor of the hotel; the same woman a housekeeper, a shopkeeper, and the matron of a workhouse. It is quite a common thing for servants to set up shops with their savings; and the inducements to do so, as also their success in doing so, depend a good deal on the taxes on profits. Few, indeed, of the working classes are sufficiently versed in the real incidence of taxation to estimate the pressure of indirect imposts; but they are quite alive to the pressure of such a tax as the income-tax, and to the vexatious and often oppressive manner in which it has latterly, with grievous impolicy, been levied. So long as the exemptions of small incomes are not carried considerably further, Schedule D must fall indirectly on servants and other working classes, by diminishing the migration from their ranks to those of employers, and so lowering wages. Other commonly overlooked taxes on working people, as above said, are stamps on receipts, bills, &c.; the railway duty, the duty on dogs, and the wine duties. Small retailers and other dealers, carpenters, smiths, and other workmen, have often occasion to use stamps; besides which, stamp duties reach the labouring classes generally as consumers. The railway duty falls on them both as regular passengers and as excursionists; and the duty on dogs, though sometimes regarded by country gentlemen, in relation to the working classes, as a duty on poaching, is really often a duty on the sentinel who guards the poor man's or poor woman's cottage from tramps and peculating neighbours. Even the wine duties fall sometimes on working people in sickness, 'for the poor are sometimes sick,' as Mr. Gladstone once said on the subject; and the heaviest duties are imposed on the kinds of wine they use. The wine duties in such cases have, too, like several other taxes, another incidence on the poor, in the shape of privation. Law taxes have been said to fall heaviest on a class who, at first sight, seem not to be subject to them at all—namely, those who are too poor to go to law on account of its cost, and thereby forfeit their rights. Stamp duties on deeds are of this character; they constitute also part of the system which makes land—the common and favourite investment for the savings of working men on the continent—an impossible investment for them in England.

Thus the pressure of imperial taxation in the mass on the working classes is enormous, though it cannot be accurately measured, and is not distributed equally over the entire body. In the financial year ending March 31, 1873, its different branches* yielded :—

Customs.	Excise, Licences, &c.	Stamps (including Probate, Legacy, and Succession Duties).	Land Tax and House Duty.	Property and Income Tax.
£ 21,033,000	£ 25,785,000	£ 9,947,000	£ 2,337,000	£ 7,500,000

To the two first of these branches, which yielded more than two-thirds of the whole, the working classes contributed out of all proportion to their incomes; and the other branches, in place of compensating for that inequality, added heavily to the burden sustained by many working people. But this statement affords no adequate measure of the relative pressure of taxation, since it omits the incalculable losses in wages which the system of raising it occasions.

Bearing these considerations in mind, let us glance at an arithmetical estimate by one of our most distinguished economists, of the relative contributions of different classes to both imperial and local taxation; one which seems to estimate as accurately as is possible the chief taxes on expenditure, save that it adds to the burden on the wealthier class the duties on the consumption of their servants; the objection to which has been stated already. Summing up the results of an investigation into the taxes falling on three typical families—the first, a common labourer's, with an income of £40 a year; the second, an artisan's, with £85 a year; and the third, a middle class

---

* Exclusive of the Post Office, Telegraph Service, Crown Lands, and Miscellaneous Receipts. See Statistical Abstract, 1873.

family, with £500 a year—Mr. Jevons arrives at the following table :*—

Description of Tax.	Percentage of Income paid in Taxes by Families expending in the Year, respectively—		
	£40	£85	£500
On necessaries	2·1	1·7	·8
On stimulants	5·5	4·1	1·8
Direct taxes	—	—	2·7
Legacy and Probate duties	—	—	·8
Rates and Tolls	2·5	2·4	1·8
Total Taxation	10·1	8·2	8·0

It will be seen that, according to this estimate, the weight of taxation decreases as the income increases, being 10·1 per cent. on the common labourer's income, and only 8·0 per cent. on a income of £500 a year; and it seems clear that if the estimate had been carried up to the higher incomes, the burden would be seen to bear an inverse proportion to the ability to bear it. Yet the estimate omits a number of items which, as we have seen, must be included in the real pressure, direct and indirect, of taxation on the working classes. To Mr. Jevons' estimate ought to be added the incidence, direct or indirect, or both, of the income tax, the house tax, the probate, legacy, succession, and other stamp duties, trade licences, taxes on shops, and on public carriages, railways, horses and dogs, and sundry taxes paid by a number of small dealers. Above all, I submit, with unfeigned respect, to Mr. Jevons, that a large addition ought to be made for the losses in wages arising from the system of indirect taxation.

Another estimate, by Mr. Leone Levi, reckons the taxes paid by the working classes out of their total taxable income, at twelve-and-a-half per cent., and the taxation of the upper and middle classes at twelve per cent. This estimate includes some of the taxes on labour omitted by Mr. Jevons, but omits a number of others which it has been shown ought to be included. And so far is Mr. Levi's estimate from taking any

* The Match Tax. By W. Stanley Jevons, p. 64. As the estimate occurs only incidentally in the able essay referred to, it could not well be exhaustive, but it furnishes a good basis for calculation.

account of the loss of wages, or even allowing for the additional cost of taxation occasioned by the advance of duties by dealers (which Mr. Jevons puts at twenty per cent.) that he strangely assumes that the advance causes an addition to wages.* Nevertheless he concludes that the whole burden of taxation on the upper and middle classes is 'rather less than that which falls on the income of the working classes.'

Both the estimates just referred to include the important element of local taxation. The question now follows, whether local taxation redresses or aggravates the very unequal burden which, it has been shown, imperial taxation casts on the working classes?

Some recent writers on local taxation set out with the assumption that local rates in England are always levied on the occupier, but the proposition does not hold good in the case of the occupiers of premises of small rateable value;† the greatest diversity of practice exists in different towns and parishes with respect to the levy of rates on owners and small occupiers. But the real incidence of rates does not depend on their levy from owner or occupier, and the subject is one of great complexity, though some economists find a simple key to its solution in the doctrine of an equality of the profits of different occupations and investments. Neither farmers, house builders, nor people in trade, they argue, will take less or can get more than 'average,' 'ordinary,' or 'natural profits;' none of them, therefore, will bear special taxation, and the rates in the case of farmers will fall on land-rent; in the case of houses (unless in special situations, where the ground owner is affected), on the occupiers; in the case of the premises of traders, on consumers. Respecting the profits of farmers, I will only say, so far are they from being determined by a knowledge of the profits of other occupations, that a farmer seldom knows the profits of any other business in the nearest market town, and never knows the profits of farming itself in the different parts of the kingdom.

---

* 'Estimate,' &c. By Leone Levi, Esq., p. 10.

† See with respect to the levy of poor-rates, in the case of small occupiers, the 'Poor Rate Assessment and Collection Act, 1869.' The levy of other rates is affected by a number of Acts, and the powers given to authorities.

Farming is a speculative business, depending very much on the seasons and other local conditions, and its profit varies in different localities, under different landlords, with different farmers, at different periods. We can only make sure that farmers in general will shift the burden of rates from their own to other shoulders if they can. And the question follows, are there no shoulders but the landlord's to which they may shift it? Are there not two other possible sources besides rent, from which they may recoup themselves for special local taxation, namely, wages and prices? As regards prices, foreign competition has hitherto presented no insurmountable obstacle to a rise in the price of a great part of farming produce, such as fresh meat, milk, butter, eggs, and sundry vegetables; the price of corn itself depends a good deal on the domestic supply. Then as to wages, the truth is, that while economists have been assuming, contrary to Adam Smith, a free competition and an equal rate of wages throughout the kingdom, farmers have had all along the price of labour very much under their own control in a number of places. 'The wages of labour on Salisbury Plain,' Mr. Caird wrote, in his famous 'Letters on English Agriculture in 1851,' in which he showed that agricultural wages varied from six to sixteen shillings a week, 'are lower than in Dorsetshire. An explanation of this may partly be found in the fact that the command of wages is altogether under the control of the large farmers, some of whom employ the whole labour of a parish. Six shillings a week was the amount given for ordinary labourers by the most extensive farmer in South Wilts, who holds nearly five thousand acres of land, great part of which is his own property. Seven shillings, however, is the more common rate; out of that the labourer has to pay one shilling a week for the rent of his cottage.' Twenty years later, wages in Dorsetshire were generally from seven to eight shillings a week;* and if we look to the low wages of labour in many parts of the country on the one hand, and the high price of farm produce on the other, it is impossible not

---

* On the different rates of wages of agricultural labour in England and their causes, see the present writer's 'Land Systems of Ireland, England, and the Continent,' pp. 353-4, 357-79.

to see that farmers in many places have been able to put the burden of rates on labourers as well as consumers, and have exercised the power; so that in fact labourers have been mulcted in both wages and prices. We find here the explanation of a difficulty which seems to have puzzled both members of the committee of the House of Commons on Local Taxation (1870) and witnesses. It was argued, on the one hand, that the great increase of rates must have come out of the pocket of the farmer, since rents had not fallen; and, on the other hand, that it must have come out of the landlord's pocket, since agricultural profits had not fallen. It seems not to have occurred to either landlord or farmer that a rise in the price of farm produce, without a corresponding rise in farm wages, reconciles the two statements respecting profits and rent, and proves at the same time the incidence of the rates on consumers and labourers:—

'2,373. Are you an owner of land in Somersetshire?—I am.

'2,374. Do you farm your own land?—I do.

'2,375. Have you given attention to the subject of rating? —I have.

* * * * *

'2,432. Is this a fair way to state your opinion, that the owner does not reduce the rent in consequence of the rise in the rates? —Certainly he does not; I believe that during the last thirty years, when the rate has nearly doubled, nearly the whole of the increase has been paid by the occupier.

'2,433. Because there has been no readjustment of the rent? —Exactly; rents are not readjusted very often. Farming is one of those fluctuating businesses that an owner does not readjust his rent very often, perhaps not even for one or more lives.

'2,435. Then you have this curious result, that though a farmer's profits must be enormously affected by a rise in the rates, which you have described as 100 per cent., nevertheless it has had no influence on the rent?—Very little indeed.

'2,445. Have the farmer's profits diminished generally in your neighbourhood?—No; I think not.'

But more general incidences of the rates, both in country and town, have to be considered. In the first place, on whom do the rates on the houses occupied by working people, both in country and town, fall? Secondly, what is the effect of the poor-rate on wages? It would save a world of trouble to follow, in respect to the first question, the formula that the builders of houses and investors in house property must get the average rate of profit, and therefore the rates must fall on the occupiers, whether working people or not. It gives, too, an air of complete command over the subject, and of rigorous logic, to argue strictly from assumptions such as the equality of profits. But there are really no such short cuts to the end of economic inquiries. In one of the excellent articles on finance which M. Leroy-Beaulieu, an economist of very high reputation, and editor of the Economiste Français, has recently contributed to that useful journal, it is shown that there are no external characteristics by which the State can measure, for the purpose of an income-tax, the profits of business. 'The system is in its very nature defective. One of its principal faults is, that it can throw no light on the individual profits of each trader; it has, in fact, for its base, the supposed average profit which each class of traders may reasonably obtain. In this system, therefore, individual injustices must always be numerous.'—(Economiste Français, Dec. 20, 1873.) Nevertheless, the State has a thousand times better means of ascertaining the actual profits of every business than any private person in business can have, inasmuch as it can make it the business of a large staff to collect information on the subject in every locality, while each man in business must mind his own business, instead of the business of other people all over the country. What would be thought of a project to assess the taxpayers under Schedule D to the income-tax, on an assumption that every man actually makes the same percentage of profit on his capital? Such, verily, is the assumption on which the common theory of the incidence, alike of local rates, of customs, and excise duties, is based; a theory which suits large and successful capitalists, no doubt; it justifies both low wages and high prices; and it serves as a screen for enormous profits from the competition of 'low men'—to borrow the language of a high authority in such matters—who would 'cut in' if they knew the real state of affairs. A flagrant ignoratio elenchi in economics has arisen from this readiness to 'cut in;'

it is put forward as proving that profits are, by consequence, equalized. The fact that capital deserts losing businesses for others in which extraordinary profits are made, proves only that profits are actually very unequal. The new capital, moreover, often comes in only for a loss at the turn of the tide, after the earlier men in the trade have doubled their capitals, and a fresh inequality is the real consequence. Take the common case of building-ground to be let for ninety-nine years, and consider for one moment the nature of the assumption that the profit on houses is determined by the knowledge which capitalists have of the profits of all investments, and the consequent equalization of building with other profits. The profits of each occupation vary, as we have seen, with different individuals, from immense gain to utter ruin, and vary at different times in the case of the same individual. We are told by Mr. Brassey's biographer that there were times when he would have died a poor man; and he might have died a poor man, had the economic assumption been well founded, and had other people known the real state of his business. The same capitalist, in several cases known to myself, is making profits on different investments under his own management, varying from upwards of 100 per cent. to a balance on the wrong side. Adam Smith, writing at a time when the number of employments for capital was comparatively insignificant, when the modes of carrying on business were almost stationary, when speculation was a much less active element than now, and when all the conditions of an estimate of the profits of different businesses were comparatively simple, said:—' It is not easy to ascertain what are the average wages of labour even in a particular place, and at a particular time. We can, even in this case, seldom determine more than what are the most usual wages; but even this can seldom be done with regard to the profits of stock. Profit is so fluctuating that the person who carries on a particular trade cannot always tell you himself what is the average of his annual profit. It is affected not only by every variation of price in the commodities he deals in, but by the good or bad fortune both of his rivals and of his customers, and by a thousand other accidents to which goods, when carried either by sea or land, or even when stored in a warehouse, are liable. It varies, therefore, not only from year to year, but from day to day, and even from hour to hour. To ascertain what is the average profit of all the different trades carried on in a great kingdom must be much more difficult: and to judge of what it may have been formerly, or in remote periods of time, must be altogether impossible.'

The doctrine by which eminent economists of our own day affect to determine the incidence of rates assumes much more than the knowledge of which Adam Smith demonstrated the impossibility. It assumes that capitalists not only know the past and present profits of all occupations and investments, but foreknow them at remote periods—to the end of a long building-lease, for example. Yet it is clearly impossible for persons contemplating the building or buying of new houses to foretell, even for twenty years, the profits that single investment will yield. The movements of business and population, the demand for houses and other buildings, the increase of wealth and money, and the general range of incomes and prices, the supply of new houses on the spot, the means of locomotion bringing other districts within reach, all defy calculation. The underground railway defeated the expectations of many house-owners in London. There are indeed house-agents who will affect to tell you the rate of profit on houses, just as there are actuaries who profess to be able to capitalize and assess to the income tax the profits of every man in every business, though of two men assessed at the same rate, one will be bankrupt within the year, and the other will make money for half a century, and die richer than Mr. Brassey. The truth is that the profits of house property, the rents that can be exacted from occupiers, and the incidence of rates, depend on no such fiction as 'the average rate of profit,' but on the demand for and the supply of houses, and these conditions vary from time to time, and from place to place. The house-builder, having cast in his lot with house and ground, and covenanted to pay a ground-rent, determined, not by any knowledge of the profits of all occupations, but simply by the local demand for and supply of building-ground, afterwards makes such terms as he can with his tenants. And the constant increase of population, the narrow limits of distance from their business within which it is convenient to most people to live, and the cost and trouble to existing occupiers of removal, give the owner, in most cases, the stronger position, and enable him to throw any increase in the rates on the occupier. But, on the other hand, if rates were abolished, house-owners in most places might exact some addition to their rent, and to that extent they may be said to pay a part of the present rates in reduced rents; their power of raising the rent on the abolition of rates being limited, not by any 'average rate of profit,' but by the supply and demand for houses, and the encouragement to building which the prospect of higher rents might occasion. No universal or strict rule, therefore, can be laid down on the subject; but generally speaking the occupier is the weaker party, and the chief burden of the rates can be laid upon him.

In the case of occupiers of the working class, the inquiries I have been able to make, lead to the conclusion that, generally speaking, the bulk of the rates falls either directly, or indirectly in rent, upon them; but as rent usually could and would be somewhat raised, were rates to be done away with, a part may be said to fall on the house-owner. It would be unfair, at the same time, to take no account of the fact that on some large estates, owing to the liberality of the landlords, the payment of the rates on the cottages of labourers falls altogether on the former. So differently, indeed, are labourers circumstanced in respect of both house-rents and rates, as well as of wages, in different places, that in one parish I know of, belonging to a large proprietor, the labourer pays only £2 12s. for a decent cottage and garden, and nothing for rates; while in neighbouring parishes, in which the rate of wages is the same, he pays £6 for a worse house without garden, and the rates in addition. The estate of the great landlord is, to speak fairly, in most cases, the best estate for the labourer to live on. Where great landlords and great estates injure the working classes, is as buttresses of a system which keeps land out of the market, obstructs agriculture, manufactures, and trade, and causes the very notion of little farms to appear a chimera to the untravelled Englishman.

The only conclusion we can come to with respect to the

incidence of rates, as between owner and occupier, is that generally the working man, as occupier of a house in country or town, pays (sometimes to a man as poor as himself), all the rent that can be screwed out of him. A little more could be screwed out of him were there no rates, and to that extent the rates may be said to fall on the owner, the remainder being borne by the workman. Even where the local authorities exempt the occupier from the payment of rates on the score of poverty, the rent is often raised in proportion. But it must not be forgotten that, whatever may be the incidence of the rates, as between owner and occupier, working men are now, in a considerable number of cases, the owners of the houses they occupy, and bear the whole burden of the rates, even where their houses are mortgaged. In not a few cases, moreover, the owners of the cottages occupied by workmen, are themselves working men; and here, too, whatever the incidence of the rates, as between owner and occupier, working men pay the entire amount. It is estimated that there are 2,000 building societies in England, and although the English building societies do not build, they advance money to working people both to build and to buy houses, and the number of houses consequently owned by men and women of those classes in some places is truly prodigious.* 'We have,' says a witness connected with some of the chief building societies in Birmingham, in evidence before the Friendly and Building Societies' Commission, '13,000 houses in Birmingham belonging to our working men. We have streets more than a mile long, in which absolutely every house belongs to the working classes.' The value of a working man's house, and the amount of the rates on it, are sometimes considerable. 'To-morrow,' says another witness before the Commission, 'I have to settle an advance to a workman on the Metropolitan Railway; we are to lend him £360; he has bought a house for £420.' The amount of local taxation on a town

---

* A useful essay on English Building Societies has been published by Mr. Ernst von Plener (lately First Secretary to the Austrian Embassy in London, now a Member of the Austrian Parliament), the author of a 'History of English Factory Legislation,' of which an English translation was procured by Mr. Mundella.

workman's house is, in short, sometimes actually not far below the amount paid by a millionaire, who keeps only an office in town, and lives in a parish where rates are low. But it is not town workmen only who pay rates as owners of houses. The famous Mr. Joseph Arch, for example, has long been a village ratepayer, as owner of a house left to him by his mother.

Two other classes of working people ought not to be left unnoticed, who are neither owners nor occupiers of whole houses, but letters of lodgings and lodgers. The vestry clerk of St. Leonard's, Shoreditch, gave the following evidence before the Poor-rates Assessment Committee of 1868, with respect to inhabitants of houses of £10 a year rateable value in that parish :—

'2,543. Do you know in what way those people are employed who live in those houses?—A great many of them have stalls in the streets, and they go out with hearthstones, and there are a great many birdcatchers and brickmakers.

'2,544. Are there many bricklayers and masons' labourers in your parish?—Yes, there are a good many bricklayers, and a good many cabinet-makers.

'2,546. Do those people chiefly take in lodgers in their houses?—A great many of them take a house—for instance, widows and those sort of people—and let it out to lodgers.'

The vestry clerk of Bethnal Green also gave evidence :—

'2,707. Are the people who occupy a £10 house, even though they pay a weekly rent, unable to pay their rates?—In many instances they take in lodgers, and with that they are scarcely able to get along.'

It may be assumed, for the reasons given above respecting occupiers, that in such cases the letter of the lodging in the first instance generally pays at least the greater part of the rates in rent, but the question follows,—Is it finally paid by the lodging-letter or by the lodgers? The stoutest advocate of 'the average rate of profit,' as the key to the incidence of taxation, will hardly contend that costermongers, sellers of hearthstones, birdcatchers, bricklayers, and poor widows in Shoreditch are accurately informed respecting the rates of profit to be made in every trade and investment. The case, indeed, falls within one of the exceptions which Adam Smith emphatically made to the doctrine of a tendency of the gains of different occupations in the same neighbourhood to equality— exceptions which deprive the doctrine of all application to the profits of English trade at the present day. There is no general principle to determine the incidence of rates in the case of the lodgings of poor workpeople. We can only assume that the letters of such lodgings get as much rent as they can, but its payment is precarious, and even if they succeed in shifting both their own rent and the rates on their lodgers, they pay themselves for the exemption in discomfort and injury to health. And whether they or the lodgers are the real ratepayers, the rate falls on a working class. Nor does the incidence of local taxation on the working classes end there. Both as consumers and as producers, they are likewise contributors to local rates levied on shops and other trade premises, and to tolls and dues for roads, bridges, canals, ferries, fairs, markets and harbours. They contribute as consumers, like other classes, when the price of the commodities they use is enhanced by such local taxation. And they pay much more heavily as small producers and dealers, when their business is unremunerative, and they fail to recover their outgoings. It has been demonstrated already that so-called indirect imperial taxes are often crushing direct taxes on poor working men and women with a small stock in trade; and local taxation, too, is sometimes the last straw that breaks the back of the petty trader. It is, therefore, certain that, on the whole, the working classes bear out of their scanty incomes an amount of local taxation in rates which forms a heavy addition to their imperial taxation. What, then, if nearly one-half of the whole amount levied in rates is applied in a manner which makes it, in fact, to a great extent a deduction from wages? What if, in addition, a great part of the remainder of the local revenue is applied to purposes from which the owners of property derive the chief, and in some cases, the whole advantage, as in the case of various permanent local improvements, and other objects of local expenditure which raise the value of land and buildings?

Out of nearly twenty-two millions of local taxation in

England and Wales, between seventeen and eighteen millions are raised directly by rates, and of this amount about eight millions are applied, directly or indirectly, to the relief of the poor. But that the relief of the poor cheapens labour, and is to a considerable extent taken out of wages, as Mr. Purdy and Mr. Thorold Rogers have argued, appears incontrovertible. I by no means go the length of saying that its operation in that respect can be nicely calculated, or that the whole of the fund raised for the relief of the poor—who must not in that sense be confounded with the working classes, many of whom never get any relief, and who are not the only classes relieved—is practically a deduction from wages. But it is certain that, were it not for the poor-rate, there would be a smaller supply of labour, and a higher rate of wages. Both the preventive and the positive checks to population would act in increased force. There would be fewer improvident marriages and more emigration, on the one hand; and more deaths from sickness and want, more vagrancy and mendicancy, on the other hand. If the poor-rate were abolished, the difference would not all go into the pockets either of landlords or farmers in the country, or of owners or occupiers in towns; for wages would certainly rise in both country and town. And it follows that many members of the working classes contribute in poor-rates to a fund from which they not only derive no advantage, but which is so applied that it diminishes their own earnings. They are taxed, therefore, twice to the poor-rate; and they are taxed further for local improvements, from which a wealthier class derives the chief benefit. It is not, indeed, possible to measure exactly the amount of benefit derived by different classes from the objects of either imperial or local taxation. And few falser maxims of finance have ever been propounded than that of the great French economist, M. Say, which Sir William Harcourt appears to follow, that 'the best system of finance is to spend little, and the best taxation is that which is least in amount.' On the contrary, as Mr. Wells observes in a Report on the local taxation of New York, 'probably there is no act which can be performed by a community, which brings in so large a return to the credit of civilization and general happiness, as the judicious expenditure, for public purposes, of a percentage of the general wealth raised by an equitable system of taxation. It will be found to be a general rule that no high degree of civilization can be maintained in a community, and indeed no highly civilized community can exist, without comparatively large taxation.' Mr. Wells cites, in the same Report, the wise remark of Mr. Jevons:—' There is sure to be a continuous increase of local taxation. We may hope for a reduction of the general expenditure, and we shall expect rather to reduce than raise the weight of duties; but all the more immediate needs of society—boards of health, medical officers, public schools, reformatories, free libraries, highway boards, main-drainage schemes, water supplies, purgation of rivers, improved police, better poor laws—these, and a score of other costly reforms, must be supported mainly out of local rates.' The working classes undoubtedly share the benefits of such institutions, but a much larger share often accrues to a wealthier class, whose contribution, in proportion to their ability, is immeasurably smaller. Local improvements in towns, for example, whether made by municipal authority or by great companies, often raise prodigiously the value of the property of the rich, while causing only loss and distress to working people, whom they disturb from their dwellings, whose rents they raise, and who do not remain long enough to participate in the ultimate advantages.

As in the case of imperial, so in the case of local taxation, I make no pretence to offer an exact estimate of the relative burdens imposed on the working and other classes. But the candid reader who has followed the investigation which my limits have narrowly circumscribed, must, I think, be convinced that, on the one hand, imperial taxation falls with enormously disproportionate weight on the working classes; and, on the other hand, local taxation, in place of redressing, greatly aggravates the inequality. I will venture only to add that, under these circumstances, to abolish the income-tax on Schedule D (which includes many of the wealthiest and least taxed men in the world), instead of repealing the duties on sugar and tea, would be a monstrous injustice. In a debate in the House of Commons on local taxation, in 1872, Mr. Rathbone, M.P. for Liverpool, said: 'Local taxation, as at present levied, pressed heavily on labour as compared with capital, and the wealthiest classes were allowed to escape from paying anything like their fair share of the rates. In the case of London, or any other seaport where merchants were the wealthy class, and their visible personal estate consisted mainly of ships and stock in trade of great value, the anomaly became apparent. It was this class who directly or indirectly derived benefit from the labouring classes, so long as they were earning wages, and escaped almost entirely when they became chargeable. From inquiry into a number of cases he had ascertained that many large merchants and brokers were only paying one-half to two per cent. (in rates), while the labouring men in their employ were paying twice to seven times as much in proportion to their income. In a word, a merchant or shipowner, deriving an income of £15,000 a year from a capital of £150,000, paid £62 in rates on his country-house and warehouses, and £65 on his suburban residence assessed at £450 a year. The young doctor or solicitor paid £14 out of his income of £600 a year on his £60 house; and the labourer £2 8s. 9d. out of his £1 4s. a week on his 4s. cottage. Thus an income of £15,000 a year paid less than 1 per cent.; an income of £600 a year paid 2½ per cent.; and an income of £1 4s. a week paid 4 per cent.'

Take also the evidence of a witness before the Select Committee on Local Taxation:—

'2,792. You are a Justice of the Peace at Liverpool?—I am.

'2,793. Have you been a member of the Town Council at Liverpool?—Yes, for many years.

'2,938. . . . A gentleman comes and hires an office in Liverpool, and he makes his £50,000 a year in it; but he goes and lives in Cheshire, and pays nothing to the rates of Liverpool beyond the rates that are levied on his office.'

The Chairman of the Middlesex Quarter Sessions, again, stated with respect to the metropolitan county in which so many millionaires live:—

'Unfortunately the rates do not keep pace with a man's wealth; there is many an individual that has £10,000 a year, whose rates are perhaps no more than upon a house of £500 a year, and there is the injustice, I think, of the poor rate.'

The levy of a large portion of the revenue by indirect taxation gives, however, the smaller incomes included in Schedule D a claim to exemption, and the argument for it is fortified by the fact that otherwise the income-tax must, for reasons given above, fall indirectly on the working classes. Those classes are, moreover, virtually subjected to a heavy income-tax (though one which brings nothing into the treasury of the State) in the diminution of wages resulting from customs and excise duties and regulations. A remodelled succession duty, equalizing the duties on real and personal property, and raising both in the case of remote successions, but reducing both in case of successions to property of small value, seems the best remedy for the inequalities of the income-tax as regards permanent and temporary incomes—inequalities which are not peculiar to the income-tax, being incident also to all duties on articles of common consumption. To substitute a naked property-tax for the income-tax is to tax the houses and savings of poor working people in order to exempt the income of the Rothschilds from taxation.

XIV.

ON THE PHILOSOPHICAL METHOD OF POLITICAL ECONOMY.

(*Hermathena*, iv., 1876.)

Adam Smith called his famous treatise an inquiry into the nature and causes of the wealth of nations. Mr. Senior defines political economy as the science which treats of the nature, the production, and the distribution of wealth. The definition in Mr. Mill's Principles of Political Economy is similar, though broader: 'Writers on political economy profess to teach or to investigate the nature of wealth, and the laws of its production and distribution; including, directly or remotely, the operation of all the causes by which the condition of mankind, or of any society of human beings in respect to this universal object of desire, is made prosperous or the reverse.'

These definitions sufficiently indicate the character of the problem of political economy—namely, to investigate the nature, the amount, and the distribution of wealth in human society, and the laws of coexistence and sequence discoverable in this class of social phenomena. The solution offered by the method hitherto chiefly followed by English economists—known as the abstract, à priori, and deductive method—may be briefly stated as follows. The nature of wealth is explained by defining it as comprising all things which are objects of human desire, limited in supply, and valuable in exchange. Of the causes governing its amount and distribution the chief exposition is, that the desire of wealth naturally leads, where security and liberty exist, to labour, accumulation of capital, appropriation of land, separation of employments, commerce, and the use of money; whence a continual increase in the total stock of wealth, and its distribution in wages, profit, rent, and the prices of products, in proportion to the labour, sacrifice, amount of capital, and quantity and quality of land, contributed by each individual to production. It is added that, inasmuch as human fecundity tends to augment population in a geometrical ratio, while the productiveness of the soil is limited, the proportion of rent to wages and profit tends to increase in the progress of society.

This theory, it is here submitted, is illusory, as a solution of the problem. It throws, in the first place, hardly any light on the nature of wealth. There is a multitude of different kinds of wealth, differing widely in their economic effects. Land, houses, furniture, clothing, implements, arms, ornaments, animals, corn, wine, money, pictures, statues, books, are but a few of the different kinds of wealth; and of each kind there are various species. No inconsiderable part of the present wealth of the United Kingdom consists of intoxicating drink. Wealth, moreover, undergoes great changes in kind in different states of society, and one of the most important features of economical history is the evolution of new kinds, profoundly affecting the material as well as the moral condition of nations. The wealth of Rome under the Cæsars differed from its wealth in the first age of the Republic, in quality as well as quantity; and there are essential differences, as well as resemblances and historical relations, between the constituents of mediæval and modern wealth. Some of the fundamental distinctions between Oriental and European wealth have been vividly brought before us in the last few months. One of these is that the moveable wealth of rich men in the East consists chiefly of precious stones, gold and silver ornaments, and splendid apparel. An English writer long ago described a religious ceremony in Turkey, at which a prince of eleven years old 'was so overloaded with jewels, both on himself and his horse, that one might say that he carried the value of an empire about him.' That is to say, the wealth that might have made a territory prosperous, and been distributed in wages through many hundreds of families, was concentrated on the bodies of a child and a horse. The correspondent of the Times recently remarked on the appearance of the officers of an Indian municipality: 'It would have rather astonished the members of an English Town Council to have seen these Punjabees in turbans of the finest tissue, gold-brocaded gowns and robes, with coils of emeralds, rubies, and pearls round their necks finer than any Lord Mayor's chain.' This allusion to the surviving finery of English official dress illustrates a change which has taken place since the French Revolution in the ordinary dress of men in Western Europe. Another description of a reception of native chiefs at Calcutta a few months ago seems to give indication of the beginning of a similar change in India. While one Maharajah 'dressed in black satin and silver lace, wore a cap which was literally covered with diamonds, said to be worth £100,000,' and another was 'resplendent in a dress of mauve embroidered with gold,' Holkar and Sir Salar Jung 'presented a striking contrast from the extreme simplicity of their attire.' It is no unimportant example of the mutation in the nature of wealth, in the progress of society, that diversities exist in Western Europe, in respect of splendour and costliness of apparel, between masculine and feminine wealth, which did not manifest themselves conspicuously before the present century. The accounts of the dresses of the princes and nobles of India during the Prince's visit read like one of the dresses of a number of great ladies at a London ball; but even in England the fashion of wearing silks, satins, velvets, diamonds, and jewels, was formerly not confined to one sex. There was a time when men 'wore a manor on their backs.' The remark of Addison in the Spectator that 'one may observe that women in all ages have taken more pains than men to adorn the outside of their heads' is inaccurate. An Eastern Prince still sometimes wears precious stones on his turban to the value of half a million; and probably no lady ever wore such a weight of diamonds as the Shah of Persia displayed in London. It is at least conceivable that the attire of an English lady may one day rival in simplicity and inexpensiveness that of a gentleman. The wealth of all but the stationary part of mankind of both sexes undergoes various changes in the nature as well as in the number of its constituents; and the differences and changes in the character of Eastern and Western, mediæval and modern, masculine and feminine wealth, of which some indications have been given, ought surely to meet with investigation, as regards both cause and effect, in a true Science of Wealth. The definition already referred to, that wealth comprehends all things which possess exchangeable value, is a mere abstraction throwing no light on these differences and mutations, or on the laws of society and social evolution by which they are governed. It originated in opposition to the Mercantile theory, and amounts in fact to little more than a negation of the doctrine, erroneously imputed to the Mercantile School, that money only is wealth. What that school really taught was that money is the most durable and generally useful kind of moveable wealth, and their chief error lay in the measures by which they sought artificially to increase its amount. Money really had acquired great additional usefulness by its substitution for barter and payments in kind, and by the extension of international trade; and money is one of the kinds of wealth the invention and variations of which form a most instructive chapter in economical history. Adam Smith, it should be observed, did not fall into the error of later antagonists to the Mercantile theory. His doctrine was that wealth consists chiefly, not in money, but in consumable commodities; in the necessaries, conveniences, and luxuries of life. Although he did not systematically investigate the subject, he has in several passages indicated important differences in the economic effects of different sorts of wealth, and pointed out some essential changes which have taken place in its component elements, in the progress of society.

Closely connected with the illusory exposition of the nature of wealth to which attention has been drawn is the doctrine of abstract political economy, that the mental principle which leads to its production and accumulation 'is the desire of wealth.' No other branch of philosophy is still so deeply tinctured with the realism of the schools as economic science. A host of different things resemble each other in a single aspect, and a common name is given to them in reference to the single feature which they have in common. It is, properly speaking, only an indication of this common feature, but it puts their

essential differences out of mind, and they come to be thought of in the lump as one sort of thing. The desire of wealth is a general name for a great variety of wants, desires, and sentiments, widely differing in their economical character and effect, undergoing fundamental changes in some respects, while preserving an historical continuity in others. Moralists have fallen into a similar error, though from an opposite point of view, and, in their horror of an abstraction, have denounced under the common name of love of wealth, the love of life, health, cleanliness, decency, knowledge and art, along with sensuality, avarice, and vanity. So all the needs, appetites, passions, tastes, aims, and ideas which the various things comprehended in the word wealth satisfy, are lumped together in political economy as a principle of human nature which is the source of industry and the moving principle of the economic world.*
'That every man desires to obtain additional wealth, with as little sacrifice as possible, is in political economy,' says Mr. Senior, ' what gravitation is in Physics, or the dictum de omni et nullo in Logic, the ultimate fact beyond which reasoning cannot go, and of which almost every other proposition is merely an illustration.' The division of labour, the process of exchange, and the intervention of money, have made abstract wealth or money appear to be the motive to production, and veiled the truth that the real motives are the wants and desires of consumers; the demands of consumers determining the commodities supplied by producers. After all the reproach cast on the Mercantile School, modern economists have themselves lapsed into the error they have imputed to it. If every man produced for himself what he desires to use or possess, it would be patent and palpable how diverse are the motives summed up in the phrase 'desire for wealth,' motives which vary in different individuals, different classes, different nations, different sexes, and different states of society. Hunger and thirst were the first forms of the desire of wealth. A desire for cattle is its principal form at the next social stage. A desire

---

* Many years ago I endeavoured to draw attention to the error of both economists and moralists on this subject, in an Essay on the Love of Money. [This Essay is reprinted at the beginning of the present volume.]

for land comes into existence with agriculture, but the desire for land is itself a name for different feelings, aims, and associations in different ages, countries, classes, and individuals; producing at this day widely different effects in two countries so close to each other as England and France. Adam Smith's historical and inductive mind here again preserved him from the realistic error. He has even attempted to indicate the actual order in which the desires of wealth succeed one another in the progress of history, and although his generalizations on this point are scanty and inaccurate, they ought to have suggested a fruitful line of investigation to his followers, and doubtless would have done so but for the dominion over their minds which the abstract method acquired. His illustrious successor, John Stuart Mill, has indeed made some instructive observations on the point in the Preliminary Remarks of his Principles of Political Economy, but he had been brought up in the straitest sect of the abstract economists, and his method was formed before his mind was matured; so that there is no systematic application of historical and inductive investigation in his treatise, although it abounds in luminous suggestions, and corrections of the crude generalizations of the school in which he was taught. An investigation of the diverse and varying desires confounded in the phrase 'desire of wealth' would be requisite, were we even, with some of that school, to regard political economy as a mere theory of exchanges and value. For the value of commodities rises and falls with changes in the degree and direction of these desires. Both in England and France, the love of land, for example, raises its price out of proportion to the income it yields, but this may not always be, as it has not always been, the case; or, on the contrary, it may display itself hereafter in increased price. At this day it is a national passion in France, but felt only by a limited number in England. Works of art, again, undergo extraordinary variations in value with the currents of fashion and taste; and diamonds would lose almost all their value, were the indifference towards them, already felt by one sex in this country, to extend to the other, and to become general throughout the world.

It is true that a love of accumulation or of property, an acquisitive propensity, a desire for wealth apart from its immediate or particular uses, is a principle of social growth of which the economist must take account. But this principle opens up another neglected chapter in the science of wealth, for the love of property, or of accumulation, takes very different concrete forms in different states of society. Were there no division of labour, it would take forms—land, cattle, houses, furniture, clothing, jewels, &c.,—determined by the existing or anticipated wants of the accumulator himself, or his family. In the actual commercial world in which we live, its forms are determined, either by the wants and demands of other consumers, or the accumulator's own desires, anticipations and associations. The holder of a share in a mine may never see his investment, and may have no desire for the coal, iron or silver it contains, yet the form of his accumulation is determined by the demand for these particular kinds of wealth on the part of surrounding society.

The questions we have been discussing are immediately connected with the conditions which govern the amount of wealth. The abstract theory on this subject is of the most fragmentary character. It exists only in the form of a few propositions and doctrines, such as that under the influence of the desire of wealth, human energy and effort are constantly devoted to its acquisition; that its amount is largely augmented by the division of labour; that of the three great instruments of production, the supply of two, labour and capital, tends to increase, but that of the third, land, remains stationary, while its productiveness tends to decrease with the growth of population; that wealth is increased by productive and diminished by unproductive expenditure and consumption. The first of these propositions really throws as little light on the amount, as on the nature, of wealth. The desire for it is by no means necessarily an incentive to industry, and still less to abstinence. War, conquest, plunder, piracy, theft, fraud, are all modes of acquisition to which it leads. The robber baron in the reign of Stephen, and the merchant and the Jew whom he tortured, may have been influenced by the same motives. The prodigal son who wastes his substance in riotous living is influenced by the same motives—the love of sport, sensual pleasure, luxury, and ostentatious display—which impel many other men to strenuous exertion in business. Good cheer, meat, beer, and tobacco, are the chief inducements to labour with the majority of working men, and to beggary and crime with another part of the population. Unproductive expenditure and consumption, on the other hand, do not necessarily tend to diminish wealth. They are the ultimate incentives to all production, and without habits of considerable superfluous expenditure, as Mr. Senior himself has observed, a nation would be reduced to destitution. Moreover, the effect of expenditure on the amount of wealth depends on the direction which it takes, for example, whether of services and perishable commodities, or on the contrary, of durable articles. Here, once more, Adam Smith opened the way to a line of investigation which abstract political economy afterwards closed. He observed that a man of fortune may spend his revenue, either in a profuse and sumptuous table, or in maintaining a great number of menial servants and a multitude of dogs and horses, or in fine clothes, or in jewels and baubles; or, again, in useful and ornamental buildings, furniture, books, statues, pictures. 'Were two men of equal fortune to spend their revenue, the **one** chiefly in the one way, the other in the other, the former would, at the end of the period, be the richer man of the two: he would have a stock of goods of some kind or other. As the one mode of expense is more favourable than the other to the opulence of an individual, so is it likewise to that of a nation. The houses, the furniture, the clothing of the rich become useful to the inferior and middling **ranks of the people.'** Consumption and expenditure in abstract political economy have become misleading terms. Both have come to denote the using up and destruction of things, whereas expenditure properly denotes simply the purchase, and consumption simply the use, of the article in question. If the things purchased be of a durable kind, unproductive consumption so called may amount in reality **to** a form of accumulation. It was, in fact, one of the chief forms down to recent times. In the fifteenth century, and long afterwards, one of the chief modes of laying by for a man's wife and family was the purchase of plate, furniture, household stuff, and even clothing. Some modes of expenditure, although intended simply as such, may be actually productive, as in the case of articles which, like rare works of art, or lands for purposes of enjoyment and amusement, acquire increased value with time and the growth of surrounding wealth. Even a stock of wine in a private cellar may, on the death of the owner, prove to have been a good investment for his family. The main questions respecting the influence alike of the 'desire of wealth,' and of expenditure and consumption are—to what kinds of wealth, what modes of acquisition, and what actual uses do they lead in different states of society, and under different institutions, and other surrounding conditions? To what laws of social evolution are they subject in the foregoing respects? On these points we learn nothing from abstract political economy. A distinguished English economist and man of science, has lately admitted, in the following passage, the absolute necessity for a true theory of consumption: 'We, first of all, need a theory of the consumption of wealth.' Mr. J. S. Mill, indeed, has given an opinion inconsistent with this. 'Political economy,' he says, 'has nothing to do with the consumption of wealth, further than as the consideration of it is inseparable from that of production, as from that of distribution. We know not of any laws of the consumption of wealth, as the subject of a distinct science of wealth; they can be no other than the laws of human enjoyment.' But it is surely obvious that political economy does rest upon the laws of human enjoyment. We labour to produce with the object of consuming, and the kinds and amounts of wealth must be governed entirely by our requirements. Every manufacturer knows and feels how closely he must anticipate the tastes and needs of his customers, his whole success depends upon it, and in like manner the whole theory of Economy depends upon a correct theory of consumption.'* No such theory, however, respecting the effect of consumption on either the nature or the amount of wealth can

---

* The Theory of Political Economy. By William Stanley Jevons. Pp. 46-7.

be forthcoming without a study of the history and the entire structure of society, and the laws which they disclose.

But further, in order to form any approach to an adequate estimate of the influence of human desires on the amount of wealth, it must surely be evident that we need an investigation, not only of the motives and impulses which prompt to the acquisition of wealth, but also of those which withdraw men from its pursuit, or give other directions to their energies. What abstract political economy has to teach on this subject is stated by Mr. Mill in his Essay on the Definition and Method of Political Economy, and also in his Logic, as follows:

'Political economy is concerned with man solely as a being who desires to possess wealth. It makes entire abstraction of every other human passion or motive; except those which may be regarded as perpetually antagonizing principles to the desire of wealth, namely, aversion to labour, and desire of the present enjoyment of earthly indulgences. These it takes to a certain extent into its calculation, because these do not merely, like other desires, occasionally conflict with the pursuit of wealth, but accompany it always as a drag or impediment, and are therefore inseparably mixed up in the consideration of it.'

Abstraction has here clouded the reasoning of the most celebrated logician of the century. Had Mr. Mill looked to actual life, he must have at once perceived that among the strongest desires confounded in the abstract 'desire of wealth,' are desires for the present enjoyment of luxuries; and that the aversion to labour itself has been one of the principal causes of inventions and improvements which abridge it. Frugality, as Adam Smith has observed, has never been a characteristic virtue of the inhabitants of England; commodities for immediate consumption and luxuries have always been the chief motives to exertion on the part of the bulk of the English population. The love of ease is the motive which has led to the production of a great part of household furniture, and is one of the chief sources of architecture.

'A great part of the machines,' says Adam Smith, 'made use of in those manufactures in which labour is most subdivided were originally the inventions of common workmen who naturally turned their thoughts towards finding out easier and readier methods of performing it. . . . One of the greatest improvements (in the steam engine) was the discovery of a boy who wanted to save his own labour.' By what logical principle, moreover, can economists justify the admission of 'two antagonizing principles' into their theory, while excluding or ignoring others? In fact no economist has ever been able to limit his exposition in this manner. Mr. Mill, in his own Principles of Political Economy, follows Adam Smith in including in his doctrine of the causes which govern the choice of occupations, and the rates of wages and profit, many other motives, such as the love of distinction, of power, of rural life, of certain pursuits for their own sake, of our own country, the consequent indisposition to emigrate, &c.

The real defect of the treatment by economists of these other principles is, that it is superficial and unphilosophical; that no attempt has been made even to enumerate them adequately, much less to measure their relative force in different states of society; and that they are employed simply to prop up rude generalizations for which the authority of 'laws' is claimed. They serve, along with other conditions, to give some sort of support to saving clauses,—such as 'allowing for differences in the nature of different employments,' 'cæteris paribus,' 'in the absence of disturbing causes,' 'making allowance for friction'—by which the 'law' that wages and profits tend to equality eludes scrutiny. Had the actual operation of the motives in question been investigated, it would have been seen to vary widely in different states of society, and under different conditions. The love of distinction or of social position, for example, may either counteract the desires of wealth, or greatly add to their force as a motive to industry and accumulation. It may lead one man to make a fortune, another to spend it. At the head of the inquiry into the causes on which the amount of the wealth of nations depends is the problem—what are the conditions which direct the energies and determine the actual occupations and pursuits of mankind in different ages and countries? A theory surely cannot be said to interpret the laws regulating the amount of wealth, which takes no account, for instance, either of the causes that make arms the occupation of the best part of the male population of Europe at this day, or, on the other hand, of those which determine the employments of women.

Enough has been said in proof that the abstract à priori and deductive method yields no explanation of the causes which regulate either the nature or the amount of wealth. With respect to distribution, it furnishes only a theory of exchange (or of wages, profits, prices, and rent) which will be hereafter examined. The point calling for immediate attention **is,** that such a theory, even if true, must be altogether inadequate to explain the distribution of wealth. One **has** but to think of the different partition of land in England and France, of the different partition of real and personal property in England, of the different partition of both between the two sexes, of the influence of the State, the Church, the Family, of marriage and **succession, to** see its utter inadequacy. Take land, for example. Sir Henry Maine has justly observed that exchange lies historically at the source of its present distribution **in** England to a greater extent than most modern writers on the subject seem aware. The purchase and sale of land was active, both in the Middle Ages and in the age of the Reformation; and the original root of the title of the existing holder, in a vast number of cases, is a purchase either in those ages or since. But **it is** only by historical investigation that we can mount up in this manner to purchase; **and** the present distribution of land, descending from such a source, is none the less the result of another set of causes, among which that great historical institution, the Family, which has never ceased to be **one** of the chief factors in the economy of human society, holds a principal place.

The truth is, that the whole economy of every nation, as regards the occupations and pursuits of both sexes, the nature, amount, distribution and consumption of wealth, is the result of a long evolution in which there has been both continuity **and** change, and of which the economical side is only **a particular** aspect or phase. And the laws of which it is the result must be sought in history and the general laws of society and social evolution.

The succession of the hunting, pastoral, agricultural and commercial states is commonly referred to as an economic development, but it is, in fact, a social evolution, the economical side of which is indissolubly connected with its moral, intellectual, and political sides. To each of these successive states there is a corresponding moral and intellectual condition with a corresponding polity. With the changes from savage hunting life to that of the nomad tribe, thence to fixed habitations, and the cultivation of the soil, and thence to the rise of trade and towns, there are changes in feelings, desires, morals, thought and knowledge, in domestic and civil relations, and in institutions and customs, which show themselves in the economic structure of the community, and the nature, amount, and distribution of its wealth.

The celebrated German economist, Wilhelm Roscher, has remarked that every economical system has a corresponding legal system as its background; but the more general proposition may be advanced that every successive phase of social progress presents inseparably connected phenomena to the observation of the economist, the jurist, the mental, the moral, and the political philosopher. The same institutions—marriage, the Family, landed property, for example—may be regarded from a moral, a legal, a political, or an economical point of view. Both an intellectual and a moral evolution is visible in the successive modes of satisfying human wants,—by hunting and cannibalism; by the domestication of animals, with slavery instead of the slaughter of captured enemies; by agriculture, with serfdom gradually superseding slavery; and by free industry and commerce, instead of conquest and piracy. And it may be affirmed that the means by which wealth is acquired in successive states of society are subject to regular laws of social evolution, as a whole, although only in the earlier stages is their operation easily traced. Slavery would exist in England at this day but for the co-operation of moral and political, with what are specially termed economical, causes. The successive evolution of the hunting, pastoral, agricultural and commercial states is intimately connected with 'the movement from status to contract,' to employ Sir Henry Maine's appropriate formula; one which affords striking evidence of the indissoluble nature of the connexion between the moral, intellectual, legal, political and economical phases of social progress. Sir H. Maine has considered it chiefly in its legal aspects, but it is easily shown to involve the other aspects referred to. To that primitive state in which there are no individual rights, in which the legal position of every one—law then appearing in the embryo form of usage—is determined by blood, birth and sex, there is a corresponding polity, that is to say, a rude tribal organization, not without analogy to that of a herd of wild animals; and there is a correlative economic structure, limiting individual possession to certain articles of personal use, recognising no property in land, making sex and age the sole basis of division of labour, and leading to no exchanges between individuals. The moral condition is of a corresponding type. Communism in women is one of its original features; another is an entire absence of the feeling of individual responsibility. Tribes and groups of kinsfolk collectively are responsible for offences.

The intellectual state is strictly analogous. There is no mental individuality, no originality, or invention; all think as well as act and live alike. The savage is a savage in his intellectual development and ideas, as in his morals, his institutions, and his economy. The movement from status to contract, on the other hand, evolves not only individual property from communal ownership, and rights based on individual agreement from the transactions of whole communities of families, but also individual responsibility and individuality of thought and invention. It is likewise inseparably connected with a political development, with the gradual growth of a central government, and the substitution of the control of the state for that of the family or kindred. Every institution relating to property, occupation and trade, evolved by this movement, is an economic, as much as a legal, phenomenon. Changes in the law of succession, the growth of the testamentary power, the alienability of land, its liability for debt, are economical, as well as juridical, facts; they involve changes in the economical structure of society, and in the amount and distribution of wealth. And every successive intellectual discovery, every new employment of the mental energy, has its part in determining the economical condition of the nation. A priori political economy has sought to deduce the laws which govern the directions of human energies, the division of employments, the modes of production, and the nature, amount and distribution of wealth, from an assumption respecting the course of conduct prompted by individual interest; but the conclusion which the study of society makes every day more irresistible is, that the germ from which the existing economy of every nation has been evolved is not the individual, still less the mere personification of an abstraction, but the primitive community—a community one in blood, property, thought, moral responsibility, and manner of life; and that individual interest itself, and the desires, aims, and pursuits of every man and woman in the nation have been moulded by, and received their direction and form from, the history of that community.

Both the desires of which wealth of different kinds is the object, and those which compete with them, are in every nation the results of its historical career, and state of civilization. What are called economical forces are not only connected, but identical with, forces which are also moral and intellectual. The desires which govern the production, accumulation, distribution and consumption of wealth are passions, appetites, affections, moral and religious sentiments, family feelings, æsthetical tastes, and intellectual wants. The changes which Roman wealth underwent after the conquest of Asia Minor represent moral changes; the new desires of wealth which became dominant were gluttony, sensuality, cruelty, and ostentation. These moral changes, again, were inseparably connected with the political history of Rome, and they had intellectual aspects which the author of the Dialogus de Oratoribus has vividly portrayed. Allusion was made in an earlier page to the passion for jewels which distinguishes the men of the East from the men of the West, and this form of the desire of wealth has sprung mainly from the absence for many ages of the conditions essential to general prosperity. economic progress, and the accumulation of wealth in really useful forms. Where insecurity has long prevailed, not only are those aims and distinctions which take the place, with the growth of civilization, of personal display, prevented from emerging, but a desire is generated for the kinds of wealth which contain great value in a durable and portable form, and are easily hidden, easily removed in flight, and nothing the worse for being buried for months or years. The wealth of England at this day, it should be observed, although dissimilar in some essential respects to that of Asia, ancient Rome, and mediæval Europe, displays also features of resemblance, alike to oriental, to classical, and to mediæval wealth—for example, in architecture, both ecclesiastical and civil, in the structure of landed property and the associations surrounding it, and in the surviving passion in women for jewellery—which are, in fact, historical features. Our wealth is historical wealth, has been made what it is by historical causes, and preserves visible traces of its history. How long a history lies behind the feelings with which land is regarded, and its price in the market, as well as behind its existing distribution! Our whole national economy is a historical structure, and in no other manner to be explained or accounted for.

Recent apologists for the à priori and abstract method of economic reasoning feel themselves constrained to confine its application to the most advanced stage of commercial society; they seem even prepared to concede its inapplicability to every country save England, and to confine it to the latest development of English economy. The position which they take up seems to be, that the social evolution, already referred to as a movement from status to contract, issues in an economy to which the assumptions and deductions of abstract theory respecting the tendencies of individual interest fit. In modern England, they say, there is such a commercial pursuit of gain, and such a consequent choice of occupations, as to effect a distribution of the produce of industry to which the doctrines of Ricardo respecting wages, profits, prices and rents may be fairly applied. They thus abandon at once the claim formerly made on behalf of political economy to the character of a universal science founded on invariable laws of nature. 'Political Economy,' said Mr. Lowe only six years ago, 'belongs to no nation, it is of no country. It is founded on the attributes of the human mind, and no power can change it.' It is now restricted by Mr. Bagehot to 'a single kind of society—a society of competitive commerce, such as we have in England.'* The economic society which we behold in England, and which is the result of the social evolution referred to, is however one which displays on every side the influence of tradition, custom, law, political institution, religion and moral sentiment; it is one in which the State, the Family, and even the Church are powerful elements directly and indirectly, and in which the pursuits of individuals, the nature and value of different kinds of wealth, the structure of trades and professions, are incapable of explanation apart from history. It is one in which, as Mr. Bagehot himself has remarked, 'there are city families, and university and legal families—families where a special kind of taste and knowledge are passed on in each generation by tradition;' and in which the system even of banking and the money market is the product of a peculiar history. Not even looking exclusively to the purely commercial side of the English economical structure; not even as a mere analysis of 'business' or 'commerce,' in the narrowest sense, is the abstract theory which used to claim rank as a Science of Wealth able to hold its ground. It is, in fact, as inapplicable to the most advanced stage of commerce as to that primitive state of nature from which Ricardo deduced it, by a process which deserves a high place in the history of fallacies, and which was not present to Mr. Mill's mind when arguing that 'no political economists pretend that the laws of wages, profits, values, prices, and the like, set down in their treatises would be strictly true, or many of them true at all, in the savage state.'† The principal foundation of Ricardo's theory of value, prices, wages, and profits, is the assumption that 'in the early stage of society the exchangeable value of commodities depends almost exclusively on the comparative quantity of labour expended on each. Among a nation of hunters, for example, it is natural that what is usually the produce of two days', or two hours', labour should be worth

---

* Fortnightly Review, February, 1876.
† Auguste Comte and Positivism. By J. S. Mill, p. 81.

double of what is usually the produce of one day's or one hour's labour.'* The minor premiss in his syllogism is the assumption that it is 'natural' that in a tribe of savages things should exchange in proportion to the labour required to produce them; the major premiss is, that what is natural in the earliest, must be natural in the most advanced, state of society. The minor involves a petitio principii, and one entirely at variance with fact, for savages work only by fits, and have no measures of labour and sacrifice. The produce of the chase is determined largely by chance. Such exchanges as take place are of the special products of different localities, and between groups or communities, not individuals. If any exchanges took place between individuals within the community, they would obviously be governed, not by cost of production, but like the exchange between Esau and Jacob, by the urgency of the respective needs of the parties. The major premiss, on the other hand, involves the fallacy of undistributed middle, the two states of society being entirely dissimilar. Thrown into a form less unfavourable to Ricardo's conclusion than the one he has himself given to it, his argument is, that in a small and stationary community—in which employments are few and simple, and every man knows all his neighbours' affairs, how much they make, how they make it, and can transfer himself to any more gainful employment than his own—the values of commodities and the earnings of individuals depend on labour and sacrifice; and therefore, in a great commercial nation in which there is an infinite subdivision of labour, an immense and ever-increasing variety of occupations, incessant change in the modes of production and in the channels of trade, constant fluctuations in speculation, credit and values, and in which each man has enough to do to mind his own business,—wages, profits, and prices, and the distribution of the gains of production are determined by the same principle, namely, the labour and sacrifice undergone by producers. It is the conclusion thus arrived at by Ricardo which

---

* 'That this is really the foundation of the exchangeable value of all things,' he continues, 'excepting those which cannot be increased by human industry, is a doctrine of the utmost importance in Political Economy.'—Ricardo's Works, Principles of Political Economy, chap. i.

Mr. Bagehot sets forth as the first fundamental assumption of abstract political economy, applied to advanced commercial society, though with an exception with respect to one sex which illustrates its essential weakness. 'The assumption,' he says, 'which I shall take is that which is perhaps oftener made in our economical reasonings than any other, namely, that labour (masculine labour I mean) and capital circulate within the limits of a nation from employment to employment, leaving that in which the remuneration is smaller, and going to that in which it is greater. No assumption can be better founded, as respects such a country as England, in such an economical state as our present one.' It is an assumption equally ill-founded with respect to both the extremes of economical progress, the earliest and the most advanced;—to the former, because there is no regular labour, no calculation of gain, and no exchange between individuals; to the second, because each of a vast multiplicity of occupations needs unremitting attention, and exchanges are infinitely numerous, and subject to perpetual variations in the conditions affecting them. Ricardo ignored both the homogeneousness of primitive, and the heterogeneousness of advanced, society; Mr. Bagehot ignores the infinite heterogeneousness of the latter. The assumption really made its only approach to truth in the intermediate economical stage to which Adam Smith expressly limited it, when he restricted it to well-known and long-established employments, in the same neighbourhood, undisturbed by speculation or other causes of fluctuation, and between which there is perfect facility of migration*—in other words, to a small and stationary world of trade. Consider the complexity of the causes which, in the modern commercial world, affect the price of a single commodity, and judge of the possibility of estimating the relative profit to be made by the manufacture and sale of every article. The

---

* In order that this equality may take place in the whole of the advantages and disadvantages of the different employments of labour and stock, three things are requisite, even where there is the most perfect freedom. First, the employments must be well known and long established in the neighbourhood; secondly, they must be in their ordinary or natural state; and thirdly, they must be the sole or principal employments of those who occupy them.—Wealth of Nations, Book i., c. 10.

following passage, written by one of the most **eminent** living philosophers, **with no** reference to political economy, will enable the reader to form some conception of the demand which the abstract economic assumption makes on his faith:—'The extreme complexity of social actions, and the transcendent difficulty which hence arises, of counting on special results, will **be** still better seen if we enumerate the factors which determine one single phenomenon, the price of a commodity, say cotton. A manufacturer of calicoes has to decide whether he will increase his stock of raw material, at **its current price**. Before doing this, he **must** ascertain, as **well as he can, the following data** :— Whether **the** stocks of calicoes in the hands **of manufacturers** and wholesalers at home are large or small; whether **by recent** prices retailers have been led to lay in stocks **or not**; whether the colonial and foreign markets are glutted or otherwise; and **what is now**, and is likely to be the production of calico by foreign manufacturers. Having formed some idea of the probable demand for calico, he has to ask what other manufacturers have done and are doing as buyers of cotton—whether they have been waiting for the price to fall, or have been buying in anticipation of a rise. From cotton-brokers' circulars he **has** to judge what is the state of speculation at Liverpool—whether the stocks there are large or small, **and** whether many or few cargoes are on their way. **The stocks** and prices **at New** Orleans and other cotton ports have **also to be taken** note of; and then there come questions respecting **forthcoming crops in** the States, in India, in Egypt and elsewhere. **Here** are sufficiently numerous factors, but these are by no **means all.** The **consumption** of calico, and therefore the consumption of cotton, **and the price,** depend in part on the supplies and prices of other textile **products.** . . . Surely the factors are now all enumerated? By no means. There is the estimate of mercantile opinion. The views of buyers and sellers respecting future prices, never more than approximations to the truth, **often** diverge from it widely. . . . Nor has he got to the end of the matter when he has considered all these things. He has still **to ask,** what are the general **mercantile conditions** of the **country,** and what the immediate future of the money market will be; since the course of speculation in every commodity must be affected by the rate of discount. See then the enormous complication of causes which determine so simple a thing as the rise or fall of a farthing per pound in cotton some months hence.'* To admit the assumption on which the abstract doctrine of the equality of profits rests—and on which, again, the doctrine of indirect taxation is based—one must be prepared to admit that men in business are able to make, and do make, similar calculations respecting every other commodity, and thus are enabled to estimate the relative profits of different businesses.

The only verification adduced in support of the assumption is, that capital and labour desert employments known to be comparatively unremunerative for those which are known to yield better returns. Even this proposition is far from being universally true, and, if it proved the conclusion, would prove that the migration of labour from Europe to America must long ago have equalized European and American wages. Mr. Mill in stating the doctrine has granted that individual profits depend, among other things, 'on the accidents of personal connexion and even on chance,' adding, 'that equal capitals give equal profits, as a general maxim of trade, would be as false as that equal age or size gives equal bodily strength, or that equal reading or experience gives equal knowledge.' He supposed, however, that bankers and other dealers in money, by lending it to the more profitable trades, put the various employments of capital 'on such a footing as to hold out, not equal profits, but equal expectations of profit.' In like manner, Mr. Bagehot argues that 'the capital of the country is by the lending capitalists transmitted where it is most wanted.' If individual profits vary to the extent which Mr. Mill admitted, since there are no means of knowing what individual profits really are, it is hard to imagine how bankers and bill brokers can gauge the existing profits of different trades, and still harder to imagine how they can foreknow them. How much they really know of the matter has been recently exemplified by

---

* The Study of Sociology. By Herbert Spencer, pp. 18-19.

the transactions of banks and bill brokers in the cases of Messrs. Overend and Gurney, and Messrs. Collie and Co.* Mr. Bagehot himself, writing on the money market and joint-stock banks, has observed: 'The old private banks in former times used to lend much to private individuals; the banker formed his judgment of the discretion, the sense, and the solvency of those to whom he lent. And when London was by comparison a small city, and when by comparison every one stuck to his proper business, this practice might have been safe. But now that London is enormous, and that no one can watch any one, such a trade would be disastrous; it would hardly be safe in a country town.'†

If there is one lesson which the history of trade and the money market in the last ten years ought to have brought home to us more clearly than another, it is that both the lending and the borrowing capitalists, both bankers and traders, are singularly ill-informed and short-sighted with respect even to the condition and prospects of their own business. The Deputy Governor of the Bank of England told a meeting of Turkish bondholders a few months ago, that he had gone into these bonds largely himself, and had advised others to do so. A man of business of considerable experience had asked my own opinion, as an economist, of that very security, and afterwards complained that I had dissuaded him from a good investment.

Such is the stability of the main proposition of abstract political economy. The nature of the superstructure built on it may be judged from the doctrine that all special taxes on production fall, not on the producer but on consumers, the former receiving the tax with 'average' profit on its advance; although in fact the producer may make no profit, may never sell the articles taxed, may even be driven from the trade and ruined by the impost, as the last load which breaks the back of the camel, for taxation has notoriously contributed to drive the

---

* On the failure of these firms a commercial writer observes: 'The nation entrusted most of its floating capital to the bill brokers, and the public found that they had no check on their indiscretion: . . . Bankers took the bills as security because bill brokers did, and hardly stopped to test the bills or to study their nature.'—The Rationale of Market Fluctuations, pp. 52-3.

† Lombard Street. By Walter Bagehot. 6th ed., p. 251.

smaller capitalists from several branches of business, for example, distilling and brewing. I must leave it to physicists, geologists, and naturalists to judge of the analogy for which Mr. Bagehot contends, of reasoning of this kind to the processes by which their sciences have been built up; nor may I attempt to pass judgment on the sufficiency of the method which Mr. Darwin in particular has followed. But where it is urged that the abstract **economist, like** Mr. Darwin, reasons deductively from 'one **vera causa,**'* the rejoinder is obvious that the 'desire of wealth,' **which** in abstract political economy occupies the place of gravitation in astronomy, and of natural selection in Mr. **Darwin's** theory, so far from being **a vera causa,** is an abstraction, **confounding** a great **variety of** different and heterogeneous **motives,** which have been mistaken for **a single homogeneous force;** and that Mr. Darwin's hypothesis was based on **many previous** inductions, and followed by minute and elaborate verification, for which the **sole** substitute **in** political economy **has** been an ignoratio elenchi. Mr. Cairnes, **indeed,** emphasizes in italics **the** proposition that 'the economist starts with a knowledge of ultimate causes;'† adding: 'He is already, at the outset **of** his enterprise, in the position which the physicist only attains **after ages of** laborious research. If anybody doubts this, he **has only to** consider what the ultimate principles governing **economic phenomena are.' First** among these 'ultimate principles' **he places 'the general desire** for physical well-being, and for **wealth as the means of** obtaining it.' Yet **the** desire for physical well-being is so far from being identical **with** the desire of wealth that they are often in direct antagonism **to each** other. And the **title of** such an abstraction as **the desire** for wealth to rank as an ultimate principle has been, it is hoped, sufficiently refuted.

The abstract à priori method, it ought **not** to be overlooked, has almost **entirely lost credit in** Germany, and has never had undisputed **possession of the field in** either England or France. It is repudiated **by M. de Laveleye,** and by some of the most eminent economists **in Italy.** Malthus and Say, the two most

---

* Fortnightly Review. **February** 1876, p. 223.
† Logical Method, &c., p 75.

eminent contemporaries of Ricardo, emphatically protested against it. Mr. J. S. Mill's treatise on the Principles of Political Economy often departs from it, and in his later writings he showed an increasing tendency to question its generalizations. Nor did the founders of political economy, either in England or France, intend to separate the laws of the economical world from the general laws of society. Their error lay in the assumption of a simple harmonious and beneficent order of nature, in accordance with which human wants and propensities tend to the utmost amount of wealth, happiness, and good. Mercier de la Rivière, whom Adam Smith calls the best expositor of the doctrines of the Economistes, entitled his work L'Ordre Naturel et Essentiel des Sociétés Politiques; and with Adam Smith himself political economy was part of a complete system of social philosophy, comprising also natural theology, moral philosophy, and jurisprudence. He regarded the economical structure of the world as the result of a social evolution, but the dominant idea of a natural order of things disposed him to dwell chiefly on 'the natural progress of opulence;' and led him to regard its actual progress as 'unnatural and retrograde' wherever it diverged from the imaginary natural order, in place of being the result of the real laws of nature at work. He followed nevertheless the historical, as well as the à priori, method, the latter being simply an offshoot of the eighteenth century theory of Natural Law; and the same language may be used in reference to political economy, which Sir H. Maine has employed in describing the influence of that theory on jurisprudence: 'It gave birth or intense stimulus to vices of mental habit all but universal, disdain of positive law, impatience of experience, and the preference of à priori to all other reasoning. . . . There is not much presumption in asserting that what has hitherto stood in the place of a science has, for the most part, been a set of guesses, the very guesses of the Roman lawyers.'*

Ricardo's fundamental assumption is a 'guess' respecting the natural principle regulating value and the distribution of

---

* Ancient Law, pp. 91-113.

wealth in the early stages of society, or in a state of nature; and he proceeds to determine by the same process the 'natural' course of wages, profits, and prices in advanced society. In proof that every improvement in the processes of manufacture which abridges labour is attended with a corresponding fall in the price of the product, his argument is: 'Suppose that, in the early stages of society, the bow and arrows of the hunter were of equal value and of equal durability with the canoe and implements of the fisherman, both being the produce of the same quantity of labour. Under such circumstances, the value of the deer, the produce of the hunter's day's labour, would be exactly equal to the value of the fish, the produce of the fisherman's day's labour. The comparative value of the fish and the game would be entirely regulated by the quantity of labour realized in each, whatever might be the quantity of production, or however high or low general wages or profits might be.' To prove that profits are equalized in the modern world by the flow of capital into the more profitable trades, he resorts, in like manner, to a 'guess:'—'It is perhaps very difficult to trace the steps by which this change is effected: it is probably by a manufacturer not actually changing his employment, but only lessening the quantity of capital he has in that employment.' How far this conjecture was well founded, appears in his own words in the same chapter. 'The present time appears to be one of the exceptions to the justice of this remark. The termination of the war has so deranged the division which before existed of employments in Europe, that every capitalist has not found his place in the new division which has now become necessary.'

Mr. Cairnes defines political economy as 'the science which traces the phenomena of the production and distribution of wealth up to their causes in the principles of human nature and the laws and events, physical, political and social, of the external world.'* This process has been exactly reversed by the à priori and deductive method. The economist 'starts,' according to it, with the assumption of a 'knowledge of ultimate

---

* Logical Method of Political Economy, 2nd ed., p. 57.

causes,' and deduces the phenomena from the causes so assumed. What has still to be done is to investigate the actual phenomena, and discover their ultimate causes in the laws of social evolution and national history. The bane of political economy has been the haste of its students to possess themselves of a complete and symmetrical system, solving all the problems before it with mathematical certainty and exactness. The very attempt shows an entire misconception of the nature of those problems, and of the means available for their solution. The phenomena of wealth may be made the subject of a special inquiry by a special set of inquirers, but the laws of co-existence and sequence by which they are governed must be sought in the great Science of Society, and by the methods which it holds out. And that science itself is still in its infancy. Auguste Comte's System of Positive Philosophy (not his System of Positive Polity) is a work of prodigious genius, yet it did but suggest and illustrate, it did not create the science—that could not be done by a single mind, nor in his time; still less did it work out the connexion between the economic and the other phases of the social evolution. If Political Economy, under that name, be not now bent to the task, it will speedily be taken out of the hands of its teachers by Sociology.

Inadequate as is the exposition contained in this Essay, it is submitted as establishing, on the one hand, that the abstract and à priori method yields no explanation of the laws determining either the nature, the amount, or the distribution of wealth; and on the other hand, that the philosophical method must be historical, and must trace the connexion between the economical and the other phases of national history. As regards the nature of wealth, it has been shown that essential differences in its kinds and constituents, profoundly affecting the economical condition of mankind, manifest themselves at different stages of progress, and that their causes must be sought in the entire state of society, physical, moral, intellectual, and civil. The amount of wealth has been proved to depend on all the conditions determining the direction and employments of human energies, as well as on the state of the arts of production, and the means of supply. And the distribution of wealth has been shown to be the result, not of exchange alone, but also of moral, religious, and family ideas and sentiments, and the whole history of the nation. The distribution effected by exchange itself demonstrably varies at different stages of social progress, and is by no means in accordance with the doctrines of à priori political economy. Every successive stage—the hunting, the pastoral, the agricultural, the commercial stages, for example—has an economy which is indissolubly connected with the physical, intellectual, moral, and civil development; and the economical condition of English society at this day is the outcome of the entire movement which has evolved the political constitution, the structure of the family, the forms of religion, the learned professions, the arts and sciences, the state of agriculture, manufactures and commerce. The philosophical method of political economy must be one which expounds this evolution.

XV.

JOHN STUART MILL.*

(*The Academy*, June 5, 1875.)

THE volume which completes the series of Mr. Mill's Dissertations and Discussions, illustrates a passage in his Autobiography, in which he describes his own as 'a mind which was always pressing forward, equally ready to learn either from his own thoughts or from those of others.' History affords scarcely another example of a philosopher so ready to review his positions, to abandon them if untenable, and to take lessons from his own disciples, as the discussion, for instance, of Mr. Thornton's book on Labour shows Mr. Mill to have been. On the other hand, the volume adds links to a chain of evidence against another judgment pronounced by Mr. Mill on his own intellect, in a passage of his Autobiography which speaks of his natural powers as not above par but rather below it, and of his eminence being due, 'among other fortunate circumstances, to his early training.' His early training had undoubtedly a remarkable effect on his intellectual career—though in our judgment a very different one from that attributed to it by himself; and certainly without reference to it, neither his system of philosophy nor his mental calibre can be properly estimated. It ought to be taken into particular account in connexion with some phases of his economics exhibited in the volume before us; but the question with respect to its influence has a much wider importance. It is a special instance of the great general question concerning not only the causes which produce great minds and direct their energies, but also those which govern the general course of

---

* This article appeared as a review of Volume IV. of Mr. Mill's Dissertations and Discussions.

philosophy and thought, since Mr. Mill's works had no small share in determining the ideas held in his time by a great part of the civilized world on some of the principal subjects of both theoretical speculation and practical opinion. For it will not be disputed that he was looked up to in several countries as the writer of chief authority on logic, political economy, and politics, and one of the first on psychology and morals. Latterly, however—not to speak of the passing influence of a political reaction on his popularity—it has been generally admitted that his methods in mental and social philosophy were inadequate; and his political economy is now censured, especially in Germany, for inconsistency and insufficient breadth of conception. 'His ground-plan,' says Dr. Roscher in his History of German Political Economy, 'is a mere theory of the tendencies of undisturbed individual interest, yet he frequently admits the existence of practical exceptions to the theoretical rules thus arrived at, and the presence of other forces and motives.' Other writers, English, Germans, and Americans, have expressed astonishment that he could ever have adopted the doctrine of the wages-fund, which two of the dissertations in the present volume show that he finally discarded. The inquiry follows, Are the defects of his system to be traced to his own mind, or to his education?

One thing is plain in the matter. Education can nurture, develop, and direct the application of great mental powers; it can also misdirect, and even cramp and distort, but cannot create them. And no man without great and varied powers could have produced such works as Mr. Mill's System of Logic, Principles of Political Economy, Examination of Sir W. Hamilton's Philosophy, and the four volumes of Dissertations and Discussions; not to speak of minor works, such as his essays on Utilitarianism and Liberty. One of his Dissertations shows that even a poetical fibre—one rarely found in the logician or the economist—was not absent from his mental constitution; and more than one of them refutes Dr. Roscher's criticism that 'his was not an historical mind,' if by that is meant that he lacked the genius for historical inquiry; though it must be confessed that the historical method is rarely applied in his philosophy. Add to this, that thirty-six of the best years of his life were spent in a public office in which he displayed administrative powers of the first order, and discharged his official duties not only with efficiency, but such ease and despatch, that he found time to distinguish himself among the foremost writers in several departments of intellectual speculation; and that he afterwards took a considerable place as a debater in Parliament. The man who did all these things also exhibited in private society remarkable conversational powers, quickness of apprehension and reply, a facility of allusion and anecdote, with a vein of gentle humour, and such felicity and force of expression that even when his conversation was grave, the present writer was often reminded of Steele's description of Sir Andrew Freeport that 'the perspicuity of his discourse gave the same pleasure that wit would in another man.'

If, however, Mr. Mill's 'early training' does not account for his intellectual eminence, it assuredly went far to form his philosophy; but a great deal more than the peculiar mental discipline to which his father subjected him must be included in that early training. We must include the fundamental conceptions, and the method of inquiry, of the leading intellects of the age from which he received his education. It was an age in which Bentham was justly regarded as the first social philosopher —Ricardo less justly as the highest authority in political economy, in spite of the protest of Malthus against his abstractions and precipitate generalization; Mr. Mill's father, James Mill, as the most eminent political thinker and writer of the time, and one of its chief lights in psychology; and John Austin as facile princeps in jurisprudence. No leaders of thought ever reposed more unbounded confidence in their own systems than did this famous band. They seemed to themselves to hold in their hands the keys to every problem in the science of man. In psychology the master-key was the association of ideas; in morals it was utility ascertained by a balance of pleasures and pains; in political philosophy it was utility combined with representative government; in political economy it was pecuniary self-interest together with the principle of population; in jurisprudence it was a particular definition of law and classification of rights. All these methods the younger Mill applied with a power never surpassed, and in addition he in good part created a system of logic which may be corrected and improved, but will ever hold a place among the chief works of the human mind. It was the fault of his age and of his education if the doctrine of evolution found no place in his psychology or his social science; if the historical method was taken up in his Political Economy, as it was in the Preliminary Remarks of his treatise, only to be laid aside; and if corrections from observation and fact of the inferences from à priori reasoning appear, both in that treatise and in the present volume of his Dissertations and Discussions, only in the form of practical exceptions to abstract theory, or of 'applications' of economic science, when the fault really lay in the original conception of the science itself. It was not possible to weld the abstractions of Ricardo and the actual forces governing economic phenomena into a consistent and scientific system; or to furnish an adequate theory of the origin and growth of human ideas without investigation of the entire history of human society. But if any one individual is especially to be blamed for the shortcomings of his system, it is not John, but James Mill. No training ever was more carefully adapted at once to crush all originality and to inspire excessive confidence in the methods adopted, than that which the younger Mill received from his father. It should, too, be borne in mind that the à priori political economy had its chief charm for John Mill, not in the simplicity and symmetry which recommended it to narrower and shallower minds, but in the complete individual liberty which it supposes. How far he was from trusting to individual interest to secure the best economy in all cases, is sufficiently shown in the remarks in the first dissertation in the present volume (on Endowments) with respect to free trade in general, and to the doctrine that education should be left to demand and supply, in particular.

The action of demand and supply in another economic aspect, namely on value, is discussed with conspicuous ability in the second dissertation, on Mr. Thornton's book. The theory of a wages-fund, the proportion of which to the number of labourers in the country determines the price of labour, is there rejected; and it should be observed that this doctrine was not originated by Mill, but appeared in its most uncompromising and fallacious forms in the works of his predecessors, MacCulloch and Senior. It is, in fact, a corollary to the doctrines of an average rate of profit and an average rate of wages. If profits could not be higher, nor wages lower in one employment or place than in another, there would really be such a mobility of capital and such a connexion between the funds out of which wages are everywhere paid, that it would not be very inaccurate to speak of them as forming a general fund on which the price of labour depends; though even in that case the combination of labourers might produce a higher general rate of wages and a lower general rate of profit than competition had done. What neither Mr. Mill nor Mr. Thornton seems to us sufficiently to bring out, is that the main power of trades unions to raise wages in particular cases has arisen from the actual inequalities of both profits and wages. Where extraordinary gains have been made in a business, the labourers have been enabled by concerted action to extort a share which competition would not have assigned to them; and again, where wages have been abnormally low, they have been able in like manner to compel a rise. The dissertation on the land question, and the papers on land reform in this volume, show that Mr. Mill, like most people of all political parties when they were written, underrated the strength of the forces on the side of the existing land systems: and the same remark is applicable to some passages in a review of Sir H. Maine's Village Communities, which deserves particular notice for the generous interest and admiration which it shows that Mr. Mill felt for works of genius and learning, even when allied to far more conservative tendencies than his own. The essay on Bishop Berkeley's works, besides its great intrinsic merits as a piece of psychological criticism, is remarkable likewise for the sympathy it evinces with genius allied to religious opinions widely opposed to Mr. Mill's.

The volume contains, besides other instructive essays, a review of Grote's Aristotle by one to whom few will deny the highest claim to be listened to as a critic on such a subject, and to whom many will assign a place beside Bacon among the most illustrious successors of the original founder of logic.

XVI.

PROFESSOR CAIRNES.*

(*The Academy*, July 17, 1875.)

PROFESSOR CAIRNES has been laid to rest with extraordinary honour. No other author's death in our time, save Mr. Mill's, has called forth so strong and general an expression of feeling; and Mr. Mill had been a leader of a philosophical school for a generation, and for several years a distinguished and active member of Parliament, while Mr. Cairnes had resided in England only for a few years, during the greater number of which he was the victim of a cruel malady which secluded him from the world and deprived him latterly even of the use of his pen. It is but thirteen years since Professor Cairnes, then holding a chair of Political Economy in Ireland, and known only to a few of the more studious economists in England, suddenly attained a wide celebrity by the publication, at the most critical moment in the American civil war, of The Slave Power; one of the most masterly essays in the literature of political controversy, and, even now that American slavery is extinct, one of the most instructive and interesting treatises which students either of politics or of economics can find in the English language. The progress of economic science, and the changes in the views of economists, of which there are indications all over Europe, may disturb some of the conclusions of Mr. Cairnes's other works, but The Slave Power will ever defy criticism; and no serious answer was attempted to be made to it, even when the war was at its height, and when the Southern States had the sympathy and support of some of the

---

* This article appeared as an obituary notice immediately after the death of Mr. Cairnes.

most powerful organs of the English press. The practical object for which The Slave Power was published has been triumphantly accomplished, but it had also a philosophical purpose which gives it a permanent value as an economic classic, for its subject was originally selected by Mr. Cairnes for a course of lectures 'to show that the course of history is largely determined by economic causes.' The skill and ability with which this purpose was carried into effect will, we believe, make future economists regret more and more as their science advances that Mr. Cairnes did not in his subsequent works develop another side of the relation between history and political economy, namely, the connexion between the whole social history of a country and its economic condition as one of the phases of the entire movement, and not as the result of a single principle or desire.

Before the publication of The Slave Power, two essays in Fraser's Magazine, 'towards the Solution of the Gold Question,' had attracted the attention of economists in this country, especially Mr. Mill, to Mr. Cairnes's remarkable talent for deductive reasoning and exposition in economics. We think for our own part, and we have reason to believe that such was subsequently Mr. Mill's view, that in his practical conclusion Mr. Cairnes took insufficient account of the influence on prices of the acquisition by France, Germany, and other continental countries of the power of production and communication by steam, contemporaneously with the diffusion of the new gold; but those who dissent from the proposition that prices have risen more since the discovery of the new gold mines in England than in any continental country, will nevertheless find nothing to dispute in the principles which Mr. Cairnes applied with consummate skill to the solution of the problem. The causes which have raised prices on the continent so greatly above their former low level are causes of the same order with those whose operation Mr. Cairnes discussed in relation to England.

Although an invalid, impeded in every physical movement by the malady from which he suffered, Mr. Cairnes took an active, though sometimes an unseen, part in the discussion of all the chief political controversies in this country during the last ten years, especially the Irish land question and Irish University education; and to him more than to any other single person it is due that University education in Ireland is not now under the control of an Ultramontane hierarchy, and that some of the chief subjects of historical and philosophical study have not been banished from the University of Dublin and the Queen's Colleges.

Last year, although then no longer able to write with his own hand, Mr. Cairnes published his Leading Principles of Political Economy newly Expounded, a work which ought to be regarded, even by those who dissent most from some of its principles, as an important contribution to economic science. To state with the greatest possible clearness and force the reasons for espousing one side of a scientific controversy, is to render one of the best services to those who seek to know all that can be said on both sides. And if any position which Mr. Cairnes takes up is unsuccessfully maintained, the student may feel assured that if literary and dialectical skill could have defended it, it would be impregnable. The second edition of Mr. Cairnes's Logical Method of Political Economy, which has recently been published, and which we hope on a future occasion to review, ought in like manner to be welcomed by those economists who incline to the inductive or historical method, not only for the intellectual interest which the reasoning of a powerful mind must always excite, but also as a masterly exposition of the deductive method, and a complete presentation of all that can be said for it or got out it.

We have no words to express our admiration of the heroic fortitude and public spirit without which no amount of intellectual power would have enabled Mr. Cairnes, under sufferings of the most prostrating kind, to maintain so high a place in the philosophical and political history of his time as that which is assigned to him by universal consent. His moral as well as his intellectual qualities won for him the reputation which has now become historical.

XVII.

MR. BAGEHOT.*

(*The Academy, March* 31, 1877.)

Mr. Walter Bagehot, the eminent editor, author, and political economist, died on Saturday last, at the same early age as the late Professor Cairnes, having reached only his fifty-second year. He was educated at University College, and graduated with distinction in the University of London, in which he was lately examiner in Political Economy. He was known to the public chiefly as editor of the Economist, and by his books and essays; but he was also a partner in a bank, and was thus one of four remarkable men of letters in this century who have also been English bankers—Samuel Rogers, the poet; Grote, the historian; and Sir John Lubbock, making the other three. As editor of the Economist, Mr. Bagehot was the successor of its founder, the late Right Honourable James Wilson, whose son-in-law he was. He conducted that journal with consummate ability, and raised it to the first rank, both as a financial and as a political authority. He might, doubtless, have augmented his fortune by lending adroit support from time to time to particular financial and commercial speculations, but no line of the Economist ever showed the smallest favour of that kind, and it did honour to the English press under his management, alike by its absolute integrity and impartiality, and by its intellectual calibre.

As a political economist Mr. Bagehot belonged to the older deductive school, but his recent essays in the Fortnightly Review mark an epoch in the history of English political

---

* This article appeared as an obituary notice.

economy by abandoning the ground hitherto claimed by the leaders of that school for their method and doctrines. It is not many years since Mr. Lowe affirmed that 'political economy belongs to no nation, is of no country, and no power can change it.' Mr. Bagehot, on the contrary, emphatically limited the application of the postulates of the à priori and deductive method to England at its present commercial stage. And within this limit he further circumscribed and qualified what he termed 'the fundamental principle of English political economy,' by assuming only 'that there is a tendency, a tendency limited and contracted, but still a tendency, to an equality of profits through commerce.' Thus circumscribed, the principle can no longer serve as a foundation for the superstructure erected upon it, which is built on the assumption that the tendency is so effectual, and so arithmetically true and exact in its operation, that every shilling of cost to which every producer is put by any special tax or burden is nicely recovered, with neither more nor less than ordinary profit, in the market. Besides the essays referred to, and the numerous articles which he wrote in the Economist, Mr. Bagehot contributed to economic literature an excellent work on banking and the money-market, under the title of 'Lombard Street.' He was the author, also, of a work entitled Physics and Politics, which embodies a series of ingenious, though rather fragmentary, essays on the natural history of political society.

The work which displays in the highest degree both the original powers and some of the peculiar characteristics of Mr. Bagehot's mind is his English Constitution, which is unquestionably entitled to a place among English political classics. It is not without a tinge of cynicism, but it undoubtedly brings to light principles overlooked in all previous works on the Constitution, and which must be admitted by the disciples of Mr. Mill as qualifying to some extent the doctrines of that great writer's Representative Government. One of the curious practical contradictions, which, as Mr. Bagehot has pointed out, the political history of England gives to political theory, is that the £10 householders who, under the Reform Act of 1832, formed the bulk of the constituency were, above all classes, the one most hardly treated in the imposition of taxes; so little did representation secure especial care for their interests.

Although of the Liberal party, Mr. Bagehot was, by disposition and cast of thought, what, for want of a more appropriate word, we must call an aristocrat in political opinion and feeling—a Whig, not a Radical. In his English Constitution he speaks of the order of nobility as useful, not only for what it creates, but for what it prevents, and in particular as preventing the absolute rule of gold, 'the natural idol of the Anglo-Saxon,' who is 'always trying to make money,' and who 'bows down before a great heap, and sneers as he passes a little heap.' If Mr. Bagehot did not himself bow down before the great heap, he was a little disposed to sneer at the little heap. Thus in 'Lombard Street,' speaking of the democratic structure of English commerce as preventing a long duration of families of great merchant princes, he says 'they are pushed out, so to say, by the dirty crowd of little men.' And in the discussions which arose out of the agitation for a reform of the Irish law of landlord and tenant, he could not conceal his scorn for little farms and little properties in land, such as form the main foundation of the prosperity of France.

Mr. Bagehot unsuccessfully sought at one time a seat in Parliament, but with all his political sagacity, knowledge, and talent, he was scarcely qualified to make a considerable figure in the House of Commons; for, although he might have made an administrator of a high order in a public office, he remarkably exemplified the essential difference between the qualifications of a writer and those of a speaker. The position that actually fell to him in life was the one he was best fitted for, and it was one really more honourable and more useful than that of many eminent members of Parliament.

XVIII.

THE RECLAMATION OF WASTE.

(Saturday Review, August 23, 1862.)

Dr. Trench has remarked that among the changes which language undergoes in time, there is a perceptible tendency in words to lose their original moral significance. Words which once conveyed, as a portion of their meaning, the indignation or contempt of society, come to have a very mild tincture of either, or none at all. Dr. Trench traces this to the want of depth and strength in the moral sentiments of mankind, and of constancy and earnestness in their blame of sin and evil. They cease to be shocked at common vices and offences, and lightly take their names in vain until those names lose their reproach. Something of this kind has no doubt taken place in the usages of speech, but the phenomenon appears to have also another and brighter side. Among the causes that lift words out of degradation into an innocent and even a respectable position, there is one which the moralist may regard with satisfaction. The things denoted by words sometimes undergo a change for the better. They are divested of noxious and disagreeable qualities, and become useful members of society, and they are spoken of with different feelings accordingly. If they still bear their old names, these names cease to be hard names. This takes place in cases such as the reclamation of waste substances, the purification of offensive and unwholesome matter, the discovery of uses for hitherto neglected and worthless articles, and the actual improvement of the world and its inhabitants in the progress of civilization. A foreigner ceases to be in fact an enemy; a peasant is not now commonly a pagan, a boor, a churl, or a villain, and the name he retains is no longer one of reproach;

a Scot is **not** thought of in connexion with beggary, **nor** an Italian with treachery and cunning. Wild animals, once regarded with fear and hatred, have been domesticated, and other names are used in fondness. In like manner, if all matter could be put in its right place, or to its right use, a variety of terms for waste and dirt would either disappear from **our** vocabulary altogether, or change their signification. There would **be no** such thing as weeds, rubbish, litter, refuse, offal, and dregs, in their present sense; and these words would either become obsolete, or get blended with **different** associations. Commerce and the useful arts have already accomplished changes of this sort to a considerable extent. **Coal, for** instance, was long in great disgrace as the **name** of a dirty and unwholesome fuel, unfit for household use—which in fact it was, while it filled the room with smoke and gas, for want **of** proper means **of** ventilation. Until rags had obtained a high commercial **value,** and **so** long as they were associated with repulsive forms **of** human misery, their name, like themselves, could have no other than an ignominious position, out of which increased cleanliness and utility have been steadily raising **it.** So among the things of which paper can be made, Mr. Simmonds, in his 'Waste Products and Undeveloped Substances,' enumerates sugar-cane trash, silk, flax, and cotton waste, woollen refuse, beetroot refuse, shavings, **leather scraps,** cabbage stalks, thistles, and **nettles, all** of which **are applicable to** several other uses, and being no longer outlaws, vagabonds, and nuisances in the world, may become citizenized in its language.

Dr. Trench tells us that 'weeds were originally whatever covered **the** earth, or the person; while now, as respects the **earth, those only are** weeds which are noxious or wild; as **regards the person, we speak of no** other weeds but the widow's.' But it is hardly an exaggeration **to say** that the earth was once covered with weeds **in** the modern sense of the word, and that in time there will be **no** such thing as a weed in that sense. Our garden vegetables are all domesticated weeds or wild plants; so it is with our cereals. Darwin, indeed, asserts that neither Australia, the Cape of Good Hope, nor any other region inhabited **by** quite uncivilized **man, has** afforded us a single plant worth cultivation. It is not, he adds, that these countries do not possess the original stocks of very useful plants, but that they have not been improved up to the standard of perfection required in civilized countries. There are, however, numerous wild plants which are at once available for human uses, without the long process of selection and nursing to which we owe our cauliflowers, turnips, potatoes, pears, apples, plums, grapes, and corn plants. We have had unmistakable warnings too, in the last few years, that we cannot afford to be dependent for the staples of our food and industry on any single place or production. The potato disease was one of those warnings. Yet though it should have come home to us more than to any other people, the French, as Mr. Simmonds observes, have been much more zealous in the search for edible roots. The war with Russia forced us to look for substitutes for some of the most important materials of our manufactures, for which we had been nearly dependent on that country. Mexican grass, for example, was forced to supply the place of bristles for many different kinds of brushes, and while equally strong and flexible, is much cheaper.

In dealing with the materials of our most important branches of industry, we seem to have often acted on the principle that a half is more than the whole, and have rejected, accordingly, as refuse, much useful substance. Mr. Simmonds has drawn attention to this in the case of cotton. A new manufacture has recently sprung up on the Continent, which is based on the principle of picking up the fragments that nothing may be lost, and which promises to yield an economical substitute for cotton in some of its uses, besides rendering other services to the world.

Had the Romans been in possession of Mr. Simmonds' book, it would have seemed to them singularly inappropriate to speak of 'inutilis alga,' for sea-weed seems to be convertible to more uses than even that pliant servant of mankind, gutta percha, which has itself been only twenty years in European business, having been first discovered at Singapore in 1842.

Even sources of national poverty are transformed by modern art into sources of national wealth. Mr. Goldwin Smith has remarked that Ireland pays a heavy price for lakes and rivers, in having nearly a seventh of her area covered with bog. Mr. Simmonds, on the other hand, points to this extent of bog as a magazine of future wealth, and thinks it not too much to assume that peat tracts may become to Ireland what coal mines are to England.

It is in agriculture, however, that the metamorphoses of waste, refuse, and filth into useful and respectable substances are most remarkable. The problem of modern agriculture is one of prevention of waste. Until the present century, agriculture was another name for a gradual waste or exhaustion of the soil, and the towns were in fact ruining the country. But we learn from chemistry that none of the materials of the soil need be lost. Indeed, Liebig seems to grudge the phosphate lost by the burial of bones, but we could afford that solemn item in our national expenditure, were we to be guided by Mr. Simmonds' advice respecting the waste products of our fisheries.

There is one reclaimable waste to which Mr. Simmonds has not adverted, and that is the waste of intellect. It was one of Coleridge's sayings, that 'every true science bears in itself the seeds of a cognate profession, and the more trades are elevated into professions the better.' In France this truth has been for many years appreciated. And whoever considers, on the one hand, the overcrowded state of our learned professions, and, on the other, the abundant room for scientific ability in numerous branches of manufacture and production, can hardly deny that a great waste of English intellect might be saved, and that an immense addition to our national resources might be effected by the elevation, on the shoulders of science, of various common occupations into skilful professions.

[*₊*] The discovery of the new gold mines, the colonization of new countries, and the development of their resources, metallic and non-metallic, are examples of the reclamation of waste on a grand scale in the present age. The same process is discernible likewise in the development of hitherto neglected advantages and capabilities in old countries, and the consequent rise in the money value of their labour and produce. The reader will discover many applications of the principle in the six next essays. But as the first of the six essays—on British Columbia—shows, the development of a new country may follow a very different course from what at first sight might be anticipated.]

XIX.

BRITISH COLUMBIA IN 1862.

(Saturday Review, October 25, 1862.)

Our most distant North American colonies, British Columbia and Vancouver Island, move in a course the very reverse of what Adam Smith has called the natural progress of opulence. He argues that as subsistence is necessarily prior to comfort and luxury, the cultivation and improvement of the country must, in the nature of things, precede the growth of towns, and the greater part of the capital of a rising community must be first directed to agriculture, next to manufacture, and last of all to foreign commerce. This necessary order of things is also, he observes, in conformity with the natural inclinations of mankind; agriculture being the pleasantest of all occupations, and being unattended with the risks of trade. From these premisses the philosopher concludes that if human institutions had not thwarted nature, the towns would nowhere have increased beyond what the improvement and cultivation of the territory in which they were situated could support, until the whole of that territory was completely cultivated. But he points out that this natural order of progress was inverted in the growth of all the States of Europe after the dissolution of the Roman Empire. The foreign commerce of these cities introduced all their fine manufactures, and manufactures and commerce together gave birth to the principal improvements of agriculture. The causes which forced the different countries of Europe into 'the unnatural and retrograde order' are investigated in the Third Book of the Wealth of Nations; and the explanation amounts in brief to this, that the mediæval laws and customs affecting the ownership and tenure of land discouraged agriculture, while the inhabitants of towns arrived at independence and liberty much earlier than the occupiers of the soil.

But how are we to account for the phenomenon that the youngest colonies of Great Britain in North America are following the same paths of progress as the feudal States of the Middle Ages? The very first consequence of the rush to the mines of British Columbia in 1858 was to create the flourishing town of Victoria in Vancouver Island, which before was merely a factory of the Hudson Bay Company. On the mainland, the less populous and less prosperous town of New Westminster, the capital of British Columbia, grew up, between which and the mining districts are now several smaller towns. All these towns are purely commercial. In Vancouver Island agriculture is still in its infancy. In British Columbia it can hardly be said to exist as yet. In the latter the colonial population, as distinct from the native Indian tribes, consists almost exclusively of miners, shopkeepers, carriers, or packers, town and road labourers, and military and civil officials—the mining element largely preponderating during the mining season. Some time ago the Victoria 'Daily British Colonist,' a sensibly written but villainously printed paper, observed:—'The town and country begin to swarm with men, most of them inured to labour. The majority are, perhaps, better acquainted with agriculture than with any other art. Yet all profess to be bound for Cariboo. Agriculture seems never to be taken into account.' This is a state of things not only irreconcileable, in appearance at least, with Adam Smith's doctrine, but diametrically opposed to the precepts of a yet more famous philosopher respecting a colonial community. 'The people wherewith you plant,' according to Lord Bacon, 'ought to be gardeners, labourers, smiths, carpenters, joiners, fishermen, fowlers, with some few apothecaries, engineers, cooks and bakers. But,' he adds, 'moil not too much underground, for the hope of mines is uncertain, and useth to make the planters lazy in other things.'

Were there no land fit for either pasture or tillage in British Columbia, it would be needless to say anything more about the cause of the backwardness of agriculture. No one now disputes that Vancouver Island possesses, in addition to a climate closely resembling that of England, several rich tracts of arable and pasture land, which are however only beginning to be settled. But as to the agricultural capabilities of British Columbia, there has been some controversy, which appears to have arisen from a confusion between the coast and inland districts. In the former, mountains and forests predominate, but the mines are all in the interior, and beyond the range of the Cascade Mountains. There is abundant room for a large farming population. In the country of the Thompson, the Bonaparte, and the Pavilion rivers, for example, as well as in that of the Similkameen and of the O'Kanagan Lake, there are great tracts of excellent land. The soil and climate are not the obstacles to the growth of agriculture in British Columbia. The traveller there may indeed be reminded of the gloomy horrors of 'those matted woods where birds forget to sing,' to which the exiles from the Deserted Village were driven; but we have unquestionable evidence that between the Thompson and the Quesnelle rivers there are vast undulating table lands where there is not more than sufficient wood for the settlers' requirements. The traveller, for instance, from Kamloops may canter his horse for days without a check from the nature of the ground, turning him out to grass at night. Such being the capabilities of this country, the British Colonist impresses upon its readers that there is a way in which a fortune can be made in British Columbia without breasting the snow on the hills or packing beans and bacon on their backs from creek to creek in Cariboo:—'That way is simply by taking farms on the road to Cariboo. That way is by raising hay, oats, wheat, potatoes, beans, pork, beef, and mutton. These are the commodities that can be most easily exchanged for gold. There is not a country under the face of heaven that now offers such brilliant inducements to the farmer as British Columbia.'

How is it then that such brilliant inducements have been held out in vain if they exist? Is it simply an instance of the truth of Bacon's observation, that the hope of mines useth to make the planters lazy in other things? Or is there any-

thing peculiar to the economic condition of a **gold country**
tending to the discouragement of agriculture, and to the removal
of the order of industrial development that **Adam** Smith
describes as the natural one? Upon Adam Smith's own principles **it follows that** the industries which supply the prime
necessaries of the miner's life and occupation must be the first to
settle themselves near the gold diggings, and this alone would
account for commerce taking precedence of agriculture, **since**
the miner cannot wait for food until it is grown in his new country,
and he wants many things besides the food that **the most fertile
soil** can supply him with. **He wants,** for instance, first of **all
things,** whisky. 'If **you ask,'** says a Cariboo correspondent
of the British Colonist, '**why** provisions are so high, look at the
nature of the first invoices which invariably follow civilization,
and the predominant **article** will invariably be whisky.' The
miner wants also tools, boots, and other articles, which will **not**
grow out of the ground, and which he **must get from** the merchant,
and not from the farmer. **For this reason alone** we might look
for the appearance of ships before farms **in a mining** colony, and
the growth of **towns** before the **cultivation** of the country.
But this is not the whole of the matter. Another principle,
known **to the student of** modern political economy, is on the
side **of commerce** against agriculture. That is, when a country
has a pre-eminent **advantage** over other countries **in** the production of one or two commodities, it may be more profitable to
import than to produce **at home** commodities for the production
of which it has not so decided a superiority. It may be that
British Columbia has pastures richer than any in the British
Isles; yet it may be cheaper to bring English cheeses and Irish
cattle round Cape Horn than to find them in the colony. The
British Colonist speaks of Cariboo prices as offering a bounty
on farming near Cariboo, but forgets that those prices also
impose an **enormous tax on** the farmer, who has to pay for
labour and every other requisite at an extravagant rate. Gold
is cheap at **Cariboo**, and dear abroad; it flies from the cheap to
the dear market, and the first people to surround the miner are
those who act as his agents and carriers to and from foreign
countries. Packers, storekeepers, merchants, are the people he

deals with, because they fetch what he wants from places where gold is comparatively scarce, and labour comparatively cheap. The metallic riches of British Columbia make agriculture proportionately costly in the colony, since every labourer looks for a miner's earnings, and farm labourers are not to be had unless for enormous wages. It is not then absence of fertile land, nor the presence of Red Indians and mosquitoes that forms the main impediment to farming in British Columbia; it is the presence of mines of still greater fertility for the time than its richest soils. The distance of the mines from the coast, the distance again of the colonial harbours from Oregon and San Francisco may afford protection to the colonial producer of fresh meat and vegetables for the gold diggings; but the growth of cereals to any extent, or anything in the nature of elaborate agriculture is not likely to be seen in British Columbia for years. Its exports of gold for some time will probably be great, and its imports of provisions in exchange will as probably not be small.

XX.

THE DISTRIBUTION AND VALUE OF THE PRECIOUS METALS IN THE SIXTEENTH AND NINETEENTH CENTURIES.

(*Macmillan's Magazine, August,* 1864.)

It seems to be still a matter of doubt with many, whether the new mines have actually diminished the purchasing power of gold, or have only contributed the additional currency required by the increase of the world's commodities and trade. Fortunately for those who care to pursue the inquiry, the very causes which, by their complexity and fluctuating character, make it vain to seek an exact measure of the effect of the new gold on prices, are in themselves subjects of great interest; for the history of prices is interwoven with the history of the progress and fortunes of mankind. Several writers on the gold question have drawn conclusions from the fall in the value of both the precious metals after the discovery of America; but, without a careful comparison of the economical conditions of that epoch and the present, no sort of inference can be rationally made; and the comparison—one might say the contrast—abounds in instruction apart from the light it throws on the monetary problem. The proper region of money is the region of industry, roads, navigation, and trade; and prices tend to approach to equality as these are improved, as men become equally civilized, and as political disorders cease to interrupt human intercourse and prosperity. At this day, in the most civilized countries, the precious metals serve two masters—war and commerce; but in those least civilized they serve none. The currents from the mines may vibrate through a third of the habitable globe, but they have no conductors through more than half of Asia and South America, or through almost the whole of Africa. In the sixteenth century, the bulk of the people of Europe itself could seldom, if ever, have touched a coin from the mines of Mexico or Peru. There was no even distribution through Christendom of the treasure which the Spaniards tore from the New World; and on this and other accounts prices rose unequally in different places, and not at all in some. In the chief towns of Spain they seem to have risen even before the fifteenth century had closed; and in the Netherlands their ascent was much earlier than in England, where the state of the currency before 1560, and the drain consequent on its debasement, together with the foreign expenditure of the Government, both retarded and concealed the first symptoms of the falling value of the precious metals. During the first sixteen years after the mine of Potosi was opened,* although prices measured in base coin rose rapidly in England, they rose in no proportion to the increase of silver and gold in the world. There was, as it were, a hole in the English purse; and the ancient fine coin of the realm ran out into the foreigner's hands as fast as the new base coin was poured in (just as eagles and dollars have been driven from the American States by the issues of paper). Moreover, war with France and Scotland drew much money out of England, and most of the treasure netted upon trade was hoarded or made into plate. But with Elizabeth came peace with France and a reformation of the currency; silver flowed fast into the Royal Mint; old fine coin returned into the market; and prices, instead of falling in proportion to the improvement of the currency, continued to rise, because the new issues exceeded the old, and the increase of commodities, great as it was, did not keep pace with the increase of money and men in the most prosperous parts of the country. Prices depend on the quantity of money in proportion to commodities—not on its quality—whether it be made of

---

* In 1545. The increase of the precious metals before that year was not considerable.

metal or paper. Prices accordingly in England before 1560 rose in proportion to the increase of base money, and not in proportion to its baseness. One Englishman alone, however, down to 1581, seems to have connected the phenomenon of extraordinary dearness in the midst of extraordinary plenty, which was the common complaint, with the mines of the New World.* With others it was a cry of class against class, for covetousness, extortion, extravagance, and luxury; and of all classes against the landlords for exorbitant rents and enclosures. The complaint against enclosures, that they fed sheep instead of men, was no new one; it had been a popular grievance for more than a century, and a subject of legislation before the discovery of America. A recent writer, nevertheless, supposes that at the period of Stafford's Dialogues, 'the foreign demand springing from the increased supply of the precious metals fell principally upon wool. The price of wool accordingly rose more rapidly than that of other industrial products in England; the profits of sheep-farming outran the profits of other occupations, and the result was that extensive conversion of arable land into pasture which the interlocutors in the Dialogues describe, and which was undoubtedly the proximate cause of the prevailing distress.'† But the truth is, that corn was not, as this theory assumes, at once comparatively scarce and comparatively cheap; the real paradox is, that it was, like other articles of food, extraordinarily plentiful in the country, and extraordinarily dear in and near the

---

* William Stafford, the supposed author of the famous 'Dialogues,' published in 1851. He says:—'Another cause I conceive to be the great plenty of treasure which is walking in these parts of the world, far more than our forefathers have seen. Who doth not understand of the infinite sums of gold and silver which are gathered from the Indies and other countries, and so yearly transferred into these coasts?' &c., &c.—See Harl. Misc. vol. ix.

† 'Political Eonomy as a Branch of General Education.' By J. E. Cairnes, Esq. It is immaterial to the point in question above, but not to the monetary history of the period, to observe that unmanufactured wool was then far from being the chief export from England, and that the loom was then as now England's chief mine. But, had the price of wool been disproportionately high, and led to the growth of sheep in place of corn, the price of mutton should have been comparatively low, whereas its price, like that of beef, was extravagantly high in comparison with all former rates.

capital and chief towns.* England had become rich both in money and in commodities, but not in roads and means of carriage; and wool had risen only with all other produce of the realm within reach of the chief markets. The gains of the wool-grower were not greater than those of the clothier, the hatter, the shoemaker, the blacksmith, the butcher, the baker, or the tillage farmer, in most places near the chief centres of increasing population and trade.† Before the New World was discovered, and down to the eve of Elizabeth's reign, the extension of pasture had caused much real distress. But, for a generation before the 'Dialogues,' **tillage** had increased and prospered; and the popular charge against the landlords had become an anachronism. Poverty and suffering, it is true, still existed side by side with rapidly increasing wealth, but not through the scarcity of corn. Food of **all** sorts, though abundant in the country, **was** dear beyond precedent in and around the places **where the** population had multiplied fastest. The old feudal and ecclesiastical economy of society had broken up; monasteries **and** noble houses no longer maintained swarms of serfs, and paupers, and waiting and fighting men; the nobility and gentry were deserting the country for the town; a long peace, while it had swelled the general numbers of the people, had extinguished the calling **of the soldiers; and** labourers seeking bread were

* 'Albeit,' says a historian of that age, 'there be much more ground eared now almost in every place than hath been of late years, yet such a price continueth in **each** town and market that the artificer and poor labouring man is not able to reach unto it, but is driven to content himself with horse corn; I mean beans, peas, oats, tares, and lentils.'—Harrison's Description of Great Britain. And again, 'There are few towns in England that **have** not their weekly markets, whereby no occupier shall have **occasion** to travel far off with his commodities, except it be to seek for the highest prices, which commonly are near unto great cities.' And the knight in the 'Dialogues' says: 'I say it is long of you husbandmen that we are forced to raise our rents, by reason we must buy so dear all **things** we have of you, as corn, cattle, goose, pig, chicken, butter, and eggs. Cannot you, neighbour, remember that I could, in this town buy the best pig for fourpence, which now costeth twelvepence? It is likewise in greater ware, as beef or mutton.'

† One cause of corn being cheap in some places was that the gains of the farmer had stimulated agriculture and produced unusual abundance. Harrison accordingly says: 'Certainly the soil is now grown to be much more fruitful than in times past. The cause is that our countrymen are grown to be much more painful and skilful through recompense of gain than hitherto they have been.'

gathering to the chief centres of employment and wealth. The dearness of provisions in and within reach of the markets where the competition of mouths was thus greatest, was caused not by a decrease of tillage, nor yet by the increase of money alone, but in part by the fact that the increasing supplies which were wanted were drawn at an extravagant cost of carriage from limited districts, pack-horses being the principal means of land transport from the country to the town. For a similar reason food is now extravagantly dear at the mines of British Columbia, and not merely on account of the plenty of gold, for it is cheaper at San Francisco than in London. The price of meat was even more unequal than that of bread in town and country generally, because there were few roads by which cattle could be driven to market. Corn was, as it still is, more portable than fresh meat; but the means of carrying even corn were so scanty and costly that it was often at a famine price in one place and cheap in another not far off. Wool, again, was more portable than corn, and might be sent to market with profit from districts too remote to supply corn or fresh meat. These circumstances explain the inconsistency of statements in the Dialogues and other writings of that period, respecting the prices of corn and meat, and the numbers of the population. Cheapness and dearness, plenty and scarcity, of corn and other food, depopulation and rapidly increasing numbers, really co-existed in the kingdom. There were places from which the husbandman and labourer disappeared, and the beasts of the field grazed where their cottages had stood; and there were places where men were multiplying to the dismay of statesmen. There were places where corn was above the labourer's reach, and places where it had come little or not at all within the waves of the monetary revolution about all the chief centres of traffic. In every locality and with respect to every commodity, the range of prices was determined by the quantity of money circulating there on the one hand, and the quantity of commodities, or their cost of production, on the other; and these proportions varied in different places, in different years, and with respect to different commodities. In the very year after Stafford's tract was published, 'all the commodities of Greece, Syria, Egypt, and India were obtained by England much cheaper than formerly,'* by a direct trade with Turkey, which saved the charges of the Venetian carrier. Nor was the rise of corn or meal general throughout the country, for the cost of carriage cut off the remoter places altogether from the markets in which the new gold and silver abounded. Most writers, from Adam Smith downwards, have taken the price of corn in or near the principal markets of the most opulent and commercial countries as the measure of the effect of the mines in the sixteenth century, and have treated the fall in the value of money as general and uniform over Europe. Mr. Jacob, for example, came to the conclusion that 'in England and the other kingdoms of Europe, within the first century after the discovery of America, the quantity of the precious metals had increased nearly fivefold, and the prices of commodities had advanced nearly in the same proportion.' Most subsequent writers have followed in Mr. Jacob's steps. It generally happens that, when a man gains the position of an authority on a question, all that he says is accepted in a lump, and his errors and oversights take rank with his best-established conclusions. One recent inquirer, however, has pertinently asked whether prices were really trebled or quadrupled (some economists have said more than decupled), even in all the chief cities of Europe? 'And what was the extent in Muscovy and Poland, or in the Highlands of Scotland and the West of Ireland?'†

The inquiry is important apart from the bare question of depreciation to which it refers, for the answer goes far to give a measure of the progress and civilization of the different districts of Europe. Two centuries and a quarter after the mine of Potosi had begun to affect the value of money, Arthur Young compiled a table of the comparative prices of provisions at different distances north of London. Within fifty miles of the capital he found the price of a pound of meat in several places fourpence—at greater distances, in several, only twopence. 'The variations in the prices of butcher's meat,' he observed, 'are so regular, the fall so unbroken, that one cannot but attribute it to

---

* Macpherson's 'Annals of Commerce,' A.D. 1582.
† Letter in the Times, by W. M. J., September 3, 1863.

the distance, nor can any other satisfactory account be given of it.' It was not, however, the mere difference of distance from London, which made prices so unequal; for in the southern counties Arthur Young himself found them more uniform. Distance both north and south operated on prices through the cost of carriage; and, when the distance was short, the result was the same as if it were great, where access to good markets was hindered by the badness of the roads. There were both north and south of London lower prices than any tabled by Arthur Young. About the time of his tours, the price of mutton at Horsham, in Sussex, was only five farthings a pound,* or, allowing for the difference in the standards, little higher than what seems to have been a common price in England before the conquest of Peru.† In Scotland, again, down to the Union, there were, as Adam Smith relates, places where meat, if sold at all, was cheaper than bread made of oatmeal; and he speaks of a village in his own time, in which money was so scarce that nails were carried to the alehouse. At a later period, indeed, in many parts of the Highlands, men were their own butchers and brewers, and no money passed from the right hand to the left. In Ireland, in like manner, until the famine of 1846, there were districts in which not a coin from the American mines was in circulation; the labourer was hired with land or potatoes, and paid his rent in turn, and bought his clothes, with labour. Neither in the British Isles, nor in any continental country, was the money from the mines of the West spread over all localities and commodities alike. Much that was grown and manufactured in every State was both produced and consumed at home, gave money no occupation, and absorbed nothing of its

---

* See Porter's 'Progress of the Nation.' Ed. 1851, p. 296. 'The only means,' says Mr. Porter, 'of reaching the metropolis from Horsham was either by going on foot, or by riding on horseback. The roads were not at any time in such a state as to admit of sheep or cattle being driven to the London market, and for this reason the farmers were prevented from sending thither the produce of their land, the immediate neighbourhood being, in fact, their only market.'

† In 1527 the pound weight of silver was coined into £2; and about that time the price of mutton seems to have been generally three-farthings a pound. At the period referred to above, the pound weight of silver was coined into £3.

power. Had every Englishman in the reign of Elizabeth bought and sold as he does now, the money which the Queen coined could not have raised prices through the kingdom as it actually did in the chief towns. Nor did the new streams of silver penetrate into the remoter and more backward districts of the Continent. The trade of the Low Countries, then the distributors of the precious metals, with Denmark, Sweden, Norway, Russia, and Poland, was almost entirely a barter of Oriental luxuries and Western manufactures for the raw produce of those countries. The price of the bulky merchandise of the north and east of Europe in Western markets was principally freight, which the Western merchant got; what balance there was for the remote producer was usually paid in kind. In Guicciardini's tables of the exports of the Netherlands to the countries named above, the precious metals are not named, and Raleigh, in the 17th century, lamented the small English trade with Russia, because 'it was a cheap country, and the trade very gainful.' Less than a hundred years ago, an English traveller found the price of a pound of meat at Novgorod three-halfpence; but it was much cheaper, or without a price, in the forest and the steppe, and is so in some such places still. Adam Smith, it is true, has asserted that, although Poland was in his time 'as beggarly a country as before the discovery of America, yet the money price of corn had risen, and the value of money had fallen, there as in other parts of Europe.' But this opinion must have been founded on the price of a small part of the produce of Poland, in foreign markets, for the chief part of the produce of the country was not sold for money at all. Down to our own time, the bulk of the people of Eastern Europe have lived for the most part on their own productions, or on a common stock; their few exchanges have commonly been performed in kind; what little money they have gotten from time to time has been hoarded and not circulated; and prices have not risen where there have been no prices at all. Nor did prices rise in all the secluded inland towns and villages of France, as they did in Paris and near the ports of commerce with the Netherlands, England, and Spain. From the prices of corn in Paris, a French economist concludes that prices generally in France were twelve times higher in 1590 than in 1515, owing to the American mines. But the true history of the Paris market itself cannot be learned from naked figures of the prices of a single commodity. The movements of the city and surrounding population, the harvests in the neighbourhood, and the means of carriage from a distance, political and military events, and many other circumstances, besides the bare fact of the increase of silver in Europe, must be taken into account. Prices are the abstract and brief chronicles of the times, but they are often too concise for clear interpretation, and many leaves are missing. And the Paris prices of corn are so far from giving the average of prices generally throughout France, that, as we shall presently see, a great inequality of prices in different parts of the country continued down to the era of railways, and the contemporary influx of gold from the new mines; and the market of the capital exercised, until recent years, little or no influence upon the produce of the remoter rural districts.

Although, then, there is evidence of a great fall in the purchasing power of money in Europe in the 16th century, it was unequal in point of time and place; it was a partial and irregular depreciation, and one which cannot be measured with any approach to arithmetical precision. There were still, when it had reached its lowest point, millions of men, and the cattle on a thousand hills, fetching no more money than before; and the change would have been much less than it actually was at the centres of commerce, had the sums collected there been spread over all the people and produce of this quarter of the globe. The most of the money was expended in a few particular places—those most commercial and advanced—in which other causes besides the fertility of the new mines contributed to raise the price of the very commodity, corn, which has been commonly referred to as an accurate measure of the force of the metallic cause alone. Such rise of prices as really took place was almost confined to the neighbourhood of the chief seats of wealth and traffic; but there, certainly within a few years from the first arrival of silver from Potosi, it was rapid, evident, and in respect of nearly all commodities, raw and manufactured, domestic and foreign.

Is any such phenomenon discernible now in Europe, and in the chief towns of Europe in particular, after the lapse of a similar interval from the first discovery of mines of extraordinary fertility? The same economic laws still govern prices. Different countries, now as then, share unequally in the new treasure according to their produce, situation, and the balance of their trade; and its expenditure must have different effects in different markets and on different articles, according to the local supply of goods as well as money. Now, as then, it is a question not as to the total increase of the stock of gold and silver in the world at large, but as to the addition to, and the local distribution of the currency of each country, compared with the quantity forthcoming of each sort of commodity on which more money is spent than formerly. According as the supply of each sort of thing has increased as fast as, or not so fast as, or, on the contrary, faster than the increase of money expenditure upon it in each place, its price should evidently have remained stationary, risen, or, on the contrary, fallen there. In the 16th century the things on which the new money was poured out were not only comparatively few, but comparatively cheap, even in the dearest markets—so that a small sum made a large addition to their price. Sixpence more doubled the price of a pair of shoes in an English town at the beginning of Elizabeth's reign; another penny doubled the price of a chicken, and a shilling trebled that of a goose or a pig. In the four and forty years of her reign, Elizabeth coined little more than five millions of money, but that was nearly five times as much as was current before; and the things on which the additional money was laid out were, after all, but a scanty assortment. The modes of manufacture were little improved, and the greater supplies of raw produce required in the principal towns were carried to market at increasing expense. The new money of this age, on the contrary, while very much greater in amount, has been spread over a far wider area, and a much larger stock of goods; and it found on its arrival a much higher level of prices in the principal markets than that which the silver from Potosi disturbed. The period of the new gold mines, moreover, is one in which several other new agencies have been at work, tending on the one hand to counteract to a great extent the effect of the circulation of more money in the markets previously dearest, and tending on the other (by contrast to what happened at the earlier epoch), to raise most considerably the price of the produce of some of the more remote and recently backward countries and districts. The bare question of the rise of prices is in itself, and so far as merely relates to the change in the value of money, of comparatively little importance. Its chief interest lies in the test the inquiry may elicit of the pace and direction of industrial and commercial advancement. For, in proportion to improvement in the processes of production and the means of importation, the monetary power of the mines is counteracted at the chief seats of industry and commerce by the contemporary increase of commodities—while, again, in proportion to the improvement of the methods of locomotion and the extension of trade, prices are brought nearer to equality over the world, and the more distant and undeveloped regions gain access at diminished expense to the markets where prices have been hitherto highest. Hence, by a seeming contradiction, it is a sign of great progress in commerce and the arts in the places farthest advanced in civilization, if the prices of commodities are found slowly advancing in the face of an uncommon abundance of money; while it is, on the contrary, usually a sign of the growing importance and economic elevation of the poorer and cheaper and hitherto backward localities, if prices are rising in them. By reason of their previous poverty and remoteness from good markets, and consequent cheapness, the pecuniary value of the produce of the latter sort of places suddenly rises when they are brought into easy communication with the former; and the rise is a mark of improvement in their commercial position and command over distant markets and foreign commodities. The sort of produce in which undeveloped regions are naturally richest—the produce of nature—is the sort for which the population, capital, and skill of the wealthiest and most industrious communities have created the most urgent demand; and it is the sort which, in many cases, derives the greatest additional value from cheap and rapid modes of conveyance. The cheapest land-carriage, less than ninety years ago, of two hundred tons of goods from Edinburgh to London, would, we are told by Adam Smith, have required 100 men, 50 waggons, and 400 horses, for three weeks. A single engine, twenty trucks, and three men, would do it now in a day. All the ships of England, again, would not have sufficed, in Adam Smith's time, he tells us, to carry grain, to the value of £5,000,000, from Portugal to England. In 1862, we imported grain to the value of nearly £38,000,000—most of it from a much greater distance. And the extension in the last fifteen years (the very period of the new gold) of the best means of land and water carriage to many distant and formerly neglected and valueless districts, has brought about, both in international trade, to a great extent, and in the home trade of many countries, the sort of change which Adam Smith perceived in the last century, to some extent, in the home trade of the United Kingdom—a change, however, which, even in the United Kingdom, has only very lately become anything like general and complete. 'Good roads, canals, and navigable rivers,' said the philosopher, 'by diminishing the expense of carriage, put the more remote parts of the country more nearly on a level with the neighbourhood of the towns.' Railways and steam navigation have done more to equalize the conditions of sale through the world, since the new mines were discovered, than all preceding improvements in the means of communication since the fall of the Roman Empire and the ruin of its roads.

Immediately after the Californian discoveries, a Russian economist predicted that, if a fall in the value of gold should ensue, England must be the first country to feel it;* and an English economist more recently argued that a greater rise of prices had, in fact, taken place in England than anywhere else, save in the gold countries themselves and the States of America.† Looking back, however, at the situation of England since the opening of the new mines, it is easy to see several agencies tending to counteract the effect upon prices here, some of which tended, on the contrary, to turn their chief effects upon prices

---

* M. De Tegoborski: 'Commentaries on the Productive Forces of Russia.'

† J. E. Cairnes, Esq.: Dublin Statistical Journal, 1859; Fraser's Magazine, 1859 and 1860; and letters to the Economist and Times, 1863.

abroad. Our vast importations of food and materials, through recent legislation, aided by steam, have, thanks to the gold mines, been easily paid for, but they have made foreigners the recipients of the bulk of the new treasure;* and, while tending to lower the price of the produce of our own soil, they have added to the price of the foreigners' produce sent to our market at diminished expense, owing both to the reduction of duties, and to cheaper and faster means of transportation. Corn was, therefore, less likely to rise in Great Britain than in many other regions; and the improvement in our manufactures generally surpassed the production of gold until the failure of cotton from America. About six-sevenths of the exports of Great Britain are manufactured commodities, and accordingly the productions of this country, which first felt the influence of the new money, generally fell instead of rising in price. Nine-tenths of our imports, on the contrary, are unmanufactured commodities, and the things which have really risen most in our markets are, consequently, to a large extent, foreign com-

---

* Mr. Cairnes reasons that England, in consequence of the greater amount of its trade with the gold countries, must receive much more gold than other countries, and that the gold it receives must act more powerfully upon prices because of the activity of credit in the English system of circulation. But the comparative increase of the precious metals in England, or any other country, depends, as Mr. Mill has pointed out, not on the comparative amount of its trade with the mining regions alone, but on the comparative balance of its whole foreign trade and expenditure. The general course of international demand and transactions may be such that a country may even part with all, or more than all, the bullion it imports. Such, in fact, has been the situation of England in several years past. In the four years, 1859—1862, the exports of specie exceeded the imports according to the returns, and there is reason to think the balance was more against England than appears by the official accounts. What bullion we got in those years went from us at once into foreigners' hands; and much of the money we get for our manufactures abroad is always in reality partly the price of the foreign materials of which they are made, and the articles of foreign production which the makers consume. Again, although speculative credit often raises prices for the moment above their natural level, representative credit, which merely saves the expense of coin, is only a substitute for it, and not an augmentation of the currency, and the prices it fixes are not higher than would prevail under a metallic system. Moreover, a given addition to prices here would make less change than in previously cheaper countries. And there have been, lastly, peculiar circumstances, pointed out in the text, tending to cheapen prices in the English market.

modities; as to which it is important to notice that comparative tables of past and present prices in England do not measure the change in prices abroad. Even a low price of wheat, for example, to the buyer in London may be a high price to the grower in Poland or Spain; and the French peasant may be trebling the price of his eggs and his butter, when the Londoner pays little more for those articles than he did before French railways and free trade. In fact, the chief monetary phenomenon of this epoch is the rise of prices in remote places, put suddenly more nearly on a level with the neighbourhood of the great centres of commerce as regards the market for their produce. And the tables by which Mr. Jevons has attempted to measure the change in the value of money fail on this very account to exhibit the real extent of the change even in the United Kingdom itself, to which his researches have been confined. They give comparative prices in England of several sorts of country produce for some years before and since the opening of the gold mines; but they are the prices of the capital and chief towns, not of the remote places of the kingdom. Beef, mutton, veal, butter, eggs, and poultry, for example, have risen about twenty-five per cent. in the London market; but they have risen a hundred per cent. above their rates a few years ago in the inland parts of Ireland and Scotland on the new lines of railway. The common price of meat in the towns in the interior of Ireland before they were connected with the ports and the English market by railways, was from 3½d. to 4d. a pound, and now is from 7d. to 8d. The rise of wages, again, in the agricultural districts of England falls far short of the rise from a much lower level in the rural districts of Ireland, suddenly brought into easy and cheap communication with both England and America. The complete revolution which has thus taken place in the scale of local prices in the United Kingdom itself renders all arithmetical measures of the change in the value of money, founded on the rates in a few particular markets, altogether fallacious. The truth is, that the change has been unequal in different years and different places, and in respect to different commodities. Measured in corn, the value of money in these islands is much greater now than it was during the Crimean War; measured in cotton, the value of money is much less than before the war in America. Speaking generally, however, the monetary movement of the sixteenth century has been reversed, and the rise of prices has been much greater in Ireland and the north of Scotland than in England, and greater in the remote parts of the country than in the capital. This contrast illustrates the general distinction already pointed out between the commercial and monetary phenomena of the former and the present metallic epochs. At the former period, the change in the worth of money was greatest in the country **receiving** its supplies directly from the mines, and next at or around the chief centres of commerce, such as **Antwerp and** London, and moreover, in what **had been the dearest** markets before, **or** the towns as compared with **the country.** Now, it will be found most conspicuous in many of the ruder and remoter localities, where prices were previously **lowest.**

Not one-tenth of the general produce **of** the mines of the **world,** since the new **gold was discovered, has** been finally allotted by the balance **of trade to Great** Britain, and some signs of the presence of the **remainder** might naturally be looked for in places having little or no direct dealings with the mining countries themselves. The new gold regions have, for example, added a much larger amount to **the** treasure **of** France than of England. From the returns of the French Custom-house, it would appear that bullion **to the** value of nearly £100,000,000 had **been** added, by the end **of** 1862, to **the** metallic stock of France; but the issues of gold coin from the French Mint since 1848 greatly exceed the declared imports of that metal. And **we are** not without evidence **of** perceptible effects of so vast an **addition to the** French currency upon the market of the country. In 1848, the French Government revised the official scale of prices, **based upon a scale of** 1827, **and** found that prices generally (inclusive **of** raw produce) **had** fallen in the interval. Since then, the current and the ancient money values of all commodities, imported **and exported, have** been set down year by year; and it appears **from** their comparison, that in 1852, a change **took** place. Prices, instead of falling, began to rise, and down **to the** end **of 1861, ranged** generally much **above** the old valuation, in spite of an enormous increase of importation and production. But these statistics, like those of Mr. Jevons for Great Britain, **afford** no real measure of the actual changes which the purchasing power of money has undergone throughout France; for, wherever railways have intersected the country, they have carried up prices towards the metropolitan level; and the **advance** upon former rates has been much greater in France **than in** England, because of the previous inferiority of **the** former in the means of locomotion, and the more backward condition of the places farthest from the capital.* In France, as in England, there has been some controversy respecting the influence of **the gold** mines on prices; but there too writers on both sides have overlooked the effect of railways upon the distribution of the national currency and the prices of country productions. **The** writer **on the** Precious Metals, for example, in the 'Dictionnaire Universel du Commerce,' simply pronounces that provisions **and raw** materials are rapidly rising in price, but manufactures tending rather to fall. But in the article on Railways, in the same work, it is remarked that prices have risen enormously in the districts they traverse, and that 'one hears every day, in some place where people lived lately almost for nothing, that the passage of a railway has made everything dear.' The rise **of** prices in the provincial towns and rural districts forms the most prominent subject in most of **the** Reports of the British Consuls in France for several years past.† In each locality, special

---

* See on this subject 'Les Chemins de Fer en 1862 et 1863,' par Eugène Flachat.

† Thus the Consul at Nantes, in his Report **for** 1862, observes : '**The** market prices of goods **have** been greatly increased **by** the railway communication between Nantes and Paris, while house-rent has risen to a price almost equal to **Paris.**' The Consul at Bordeaux, in his Report for 1859, says : 'For a while **the** hope was entertained that the establishment of railways would realize the problem of cheap living; but this has proved a fallacy, for the facility of transport and increased demands of the capital have created a drain in that direction. House-rent has within the last few years doubled, if not trebled.' In his Report **for** 1862, the same Consul says : 'With the exception of bread, the price of every commodity remains excessively high ; and, though wages have risen in proportion, there does not appear to be any marked improvement in the state of the lower classes. It cannot be denied, however, that the progress of civilization has gradually created among them a tendency towards more expensive habits, and that what formerly were esteemed luxuries have now become indispensable wants.' There are similar reports from the Consuls at Havre and Marseilles. Nor is it

causes are commonly assigned by persons on the spot, for 'the dearness of living;' but how is it that the same phenomenon presents itself in so many different localities—in the capital, the provincial town, and the agricultural district? How is it, if railways have raised wages, prices, and rents, that the rise has taken place at both ends of and along their lines? How is it, if labour and produce are rising in the country, because they are carried off to the town, that they are rising also in the town? And how could the prices of things, for the most part increased greatly in quantity, have risen prodigiously throughout France, if there were no more money than formerly circulating through it? Many persons seem to imagine they have accounted for a rise of prices, without reference to the influx of money from the mines, when they have pointed out how the additional money has been actually laid out, and through whose hands it has most recently passed. Unless they see the miner himself, they will not believe that he is the prime agent in the matter, although it is commonly only being brought by other hands than his own, that his gold can raise prices at a distance. An interesting German writer has reproduced one of the popular theories of Elizabeth's reign—that luxury, ostentation, and expensive habits among all classes are the causes of the modern dearness of living, and not the abundance of money.* There cannot, however, be more money spent, if people have no more to spend than before. A mere change in the ideas and desires of society would add nothing to the number of pieces of money, and could not affect the sum-total of prices. If more money were spent upon houses, furniture, and show, less would remain, if pecuniary means were not increased, to be spent upon labour and food, and the substantial necessaries of life; and, if the former became dearer, the latter would at the same time become cheaper. But, when people have really more money than

---

only in the provincial towns that this monetary revolution has taken place. The cultivators of the soil, although they sell their produce at much elevated rates, complain bitterly of the increased cost of rural labour. The rise of house-rent in the towns is, no doubt, due in part to the concentration of the population; but this would not, if there were not more money in general circulation, raise wages and commodities both in town and country.

* 'Der Geld-preis und die Sitte,' in Riehl's 'Culturstudien.'

formerly to spend, they naturally spend more than they formerly did, and their unaccustomed expenditure is considered excessive and extravagant. And, when an increase in the pecuniary incomes of large classes arises from, or accompanies, greater commercial activity and general progress, there commonly is a general taste for a better or more costly style of living than there was at a lower stage of society. There is always, it is true, much folly and vanity in human expenditure; and masses of men do not become philosophers of a sudden because they are making more money, and their state is improving upon the whole. But their state is improving on the whole when **their** trade is increasing, and the value of their produce rising to **a level with that of the** most forward communities, and when the **lowest** classes are breaking **the chains** of barbarous custom, and furnishing life with better accommodation than servile and ignorant boors **could** appreciate. It is better to see German peasants building chimneys **and** embellishing **their** houses than burying their money; **even if** we find them copying their superiors in non-essentials and in finery, as well as in the plain requisites of civilization. The greater expense of ordinary life in North than South Germany has been cited as positive proof that the growing dearness of living on the Continent comes not from the plenty of money, but from the costlier habits of the people; and there may **be much that is wasteful and** silly in modern German fashion, as well as **much that is uncleanly** and unwholesome in what is called ancient German simplicity. But the chief reason why South Germany is comparatively cheap **is that** there is really less money in circulation: partly **because it has** more recently **been** opened up by railways, and still remains farther from the best markets of Europe; and partly because a greater **proportion of the money actually gotten is** hoarded,*—which

---

* The following passage **is taken from the** Revue Germanique for October, 1863, in which it forms part of a translation from an article which appeared in 1857 in a German Quarterly:—' La population des campagnes a été dans les huit dernières années comme une éponge qui s'est gorgée d'argent. Des statisticiens ont calculé que dans un seul canton à blé de l'Allemagne **du** sud, lequel ne compte que quelque milles carrés, on a thésaurisé dans le cours des dix dernières années au moins un million de florins d'argent comptant, qui n'est pas rentré dans le commerce.'

is a sign of comparative backwardness, and illustrates the connexion between progress and ascending prices noticed already. Wherever backwardness is changing into progress, and stagnation into commercial activity, it will be found that cheapness is changing into dearness, and that something like English prices follow hard upon something like English prosperity. Thus the British consul at Bilbao reported lately: 'The increased trade and prosperous condition of the country have drawn numbers of families to Bilbao. As a result of this the cost of living has risen enormously, and Bilbao, long one of the cheapest towns in Europe, has become a comparatively dear place.'* To Spain, which in the sixteenth century robbed the treasures of the New World directly from their source, gold now comes by honest trade, and the miner is hidden behind the merchant. Unaccustomed streams of money are flowing, not only into the towns of Northern Spain, but through all the more fertile districts of the Peninsula near the new lines of railway. And the sums by which prices have been raised in Portugal and Spain could evidently not have been drawn from England and France without a corresponding fall of prices in those countries, had their coffers not been replenished from a new source. It is, too, in regions like the great corn-district of Medina del Campo, poor lately in money, but rich in the wealth of nature, that prices must rise fastest when they are brought into easy communication with the markets where money abounds, since the money is both attracted by their cheapness, and produces the more sensible change on account of it. It is in such places also that the unwonted abundance of such treasure, and the rise in

---

* The Consul gives the following comparative table of prices in 1854 and 1860:—

	1854.			1860.		
	£	s.	d.	£	s.	d.
Houses and apartments	15 to 30 0	0		50 to 80 0	0	
Beef (per lb)	0	0	2½	0	0	4
Mutton ,,	0	0	2½	0	0	4¾
Veal ,,	0	0	3¼	0	0	8
Bread ,,	0	0	1	0	0	2
Potatoes (per stone)	0	2	0	0	3	7½
Eggs (per dozen)	0	0	3¾	0	0	7½
Wine (two quarts)	0	0	7½	0	1	3¼

the pecuniary value of the labour and produce of the people, are to be regarded as signs of rise in the international and economical scale, and of the obstacles being at length overcome which for centuries prevented them from contributing their natural resources and energies to advance the general prosperity and happiness of mankind. Thus the trade of the Swiss, shut out by their own mountains from the principal markets of Europe in the last century, now reaches to the farthest regions of gold; the merchant and the traveller pour the precious metals into their lap; and a country, not long ago scantily furnished with a base native currency, is now flowing with money from the mints of the wealthiest states. In the north and east of Europe we likewise find the range of prices indicating the course of local fortunes, and the share of remote places in the increased currency of the world depending on the improvement of their means of intercourse and trade with the more forward regions and their general progress. In Norway, which, with a population about half of that of London, is, in respect of its commercial marine, the fourth among maritime powers, the wages of seamen rose at a bound to the British level on the repeal of the navigation laws; and no sooner did Australian gold appear in Europe than the Norwegian currency swelled to an unprecedented balance, and prices rose to a pitch unknown before.* In Russia, a commodity which, a few years ago, was worth to the producer in the interior only a fourth of the sum it would sell for in the capital, may now be carried thither at comparatively trifling cost in fewer days than it might formerly have taken months to perform the journey; and the producer gains the difference. Such a burst of traffic ensued upon the new means of locomotion that the receipts of the St. Petersburg and Moscow Railway for the carriage of goods in 1859 are said to have equalled those of the best

---

* British Consul's Report for 1852-3. The Consul at Gottenberg, in Sweden, reports for 1855: 'The year 1855 has been most prosperous. Notwithstanding that most articles are now admitted free of duty, provisions of every kind are excessively dear, many articles having within the last few years advanced to treble and in no instance to less than double in price. This may be attributed to the general prosperity and consequent increased consumption of better food among the working classes.'

railways in England; **and in** the summer of **the** previous year 300 steamers plied the waters of the Volga, where only ten could be counted in **1853.** This rapid growth of trade was accompanied, as the British Secretary **of** Legation reported, by a great improvement in the condition of the people, increased demand for labour, and **higher wages,** better food, and the exchange of the sheepskin for cloth. **The** exports of Riga, again, are of the **very** class which benefited most by the alterations in the English tariff, and which rose the **most in** the English market immediately after the influx of new gold began; and at Riga **the** same monetary revolution has ensued **which** Bilbao and other Western towns have experienced. In his report for 1859, **the British** Consul says:—'A fact which seems rather to weigh **against** Riga is the rapid increase of late years in the cost **of** living in this port. The necessaries of life have doubled in ten **years;** labour has risen **in** proportion.'* It would, however, be an inference wide of the truth, **that the** whole Russian Empire exhibits similar indications **of a rise towards** the Western level. Great part of it is **hardly better furnished** with the paths of traffic than before **the discovery of America; the** carrier in many places leaves the cultivator little or no surplus; and the resources of a teeming soil and the industry of an ingenious people **are imprisoned** and valueless. There is, in fact, still great inequality of prices, as of opportunities **of progress, in** different parts of Europe; **but** there is evidence, nevertheless, **of the** presence **of a new money** power in parts of every European country since the new gold first glittered in the **market, and** the Englishman **has** had, in his **own** quarter of the globe, many successful competitors for a share in the treasure, **some of** whom have been realizing prices much more above the **ancient level** than those which have ruled in the wealthiest towns of this island. Different countries—different localities— by reason not only of the inequality of comparative progress, but also of the vicissitudes of the seasons and political affairs — have participated unequally from time to time

---

* A part of this rise is attributable to the depreciation of the paper rouble, but this was not considerable at the period referred to.

in the general enlargement of the circulating medium of Europe. One prevailing tendency is, however, discernible in the commercial movement of this age — to reverse the monetary order of the 16th century, and to raise most, in relation to money, the produce of places where money was scarcest before. Is it so in Europe only? On the contrary, the most remarkable contrast between the former and the present epoch in the history of the precious metals lies in the share allotted to eastern countries, and the rise of Eastern industry and productions in international value, as measured by the universal standard of money. From 1500 to 1595, the Portuguese monopolised the maritime trade with the East Indies; and the cargoes of Asiatic merchandize which arrived in Europe, few and small in the first half of the century, declined in the latter half; nor does Mr. Jacob estimate at more than fourteen millions the entire amount of treasure which moved to Asia from the West in the first 108 years after America was discovered. In the last fourteen years, India has netted a balance of about a hundred and fifty millions. For upwards of two years the scale has been loaded in favour of India with money lost to the American States by the war—a fact which illustrates the connexion with the fortunes of nations of the movement of the precious metals. This influx into India began, however, with the increase of their quantity in the world,* following the general law of the period of the attraction of money to cheap and fertile places with which communication has been improved, and in favour of which international trade must be redressed. The money has flowed into India, it is true, not only in the immediate purchase of its commodities, but also in loans, public works, and investments of English capital—a fact, however, springing from the same general cause, and tending in the same direction. It is a fact of the same order with the gradual rise of the country to an economic level with the earlier elevated towns, which struck the sagacious mind of Adam Smith. 'Everywhere,' he said, 'the greatest improvements of the

---

* The bullion imports of India in 1852-3 exceeded five millions sterling; in 1855-6 they rose nearly to eleven millions and a-half; in the year 1856-7, the year before the mutiny, they reached £14,413,690.

country have been owing to the overflowing of the stock originally accumulated in the towns.' The ruder and remoter regions are at length, if commerce be allowed its natural course, brought into neighbourhood and fellowship with the regions more advanced, and endowed with the same advantages, especially with that advantage to which the latter mainly owed their earlier progress, the advantage of a good commercial situation—which steam navigation, railways, and roads are giving to many districts in India, rich in the food of mankind and the materials of industry, but until lately unable to dispose of their wealth, unless upon beggarly terms. There are some who view the accession of metallic treasure to such countries as a burden and a loss to them — who maintain that the money exported to India, for example, abstracts a proportionate sum of commodities from the consumption of the natives, and then disappears in useless hoards or frivolous ornaments, adding little or nothing to its industrial spirit and power, or to the pecuniary value and command over foreign markets of its produce. As to the actual use of the new treasure in India, the truth is, that there, as in Egypt, and every continental country in Europe, it has been both hoarded and circulated. Even in England there is always a considerable quantity of money lying temporarily idle in the purse of the people too poor to keep bankers; and we shall see reason to believe that the amount of hoarding in India is by no means so great as some English writers assume. Almost all the gold, however, or rather more than a third of the whole treasure lately imported into India, has certainly been either hoarded or made into ornaments. By reason of gold not being legal tender in India, the gold mines have added only indirectly to its currency—adding not gold but silver money. In the West, the new gold has taken the place of silver; the greater part of the silver set free has been finally carried to India, where it has a purchasing power—which gold—a far more portable, convenient, and economic medium—has unfortunately been denied. Even the hoards and ornaments in India, however, are not to be regarded merely as waste. They are not only as legitimate pleasures and uses of wealth as many of the modes of expenditure common in the West, but they are also **the private banks and** insurance offices of the Indian natives.*

The total coinage at the three Indian Mints, including an insignificant quantity of copper and gold, since the discovery of the gold mines, amounts to about a hundred millions of English money; and, in considering the effects of so great an addition to the coinage, it is material to observe that prices had generally been falling in India for more than five and twenty years previously. During that period the balance of treasure netted by India had not been large, owing to the slow development of its export trade, and **the** considerable remittances of specie **to** England. On the other hand **the production of** commodities increased from internal quiet, **and the work to** be done by the circulating **medium of the country** was multiplied not only by the increase **of** ordinary traffic, **but also** by the adoption under British rule **of payments in** money for taxes and other purposes, **where** payments in kind and barter **had** been customary before. **The amount of** the currency **had** in consequence become

---

* It may not be considered out of place here to notice **a** misconception which seems to exist with respect to the effect on prices of the large portion of the annual supplies of silver and gold made in all countries, not into money, but into articles of use or ornament. Some writers treat this portion as having no effect at all on prices; others make calculations in which the whole additional stock of the precious metals from the new mines is counted as money. But, when the precious metals are converted into articles other than money, and sold and circulated as commodities, they tend not to raise, but to lower, the general level of prices, by absorbing a portion of the currency in their own circulation; for money cannot be in two places or doing two things at the same time, and the quantity engaged in buying plate, watches, ornaments, &c., is withdrawn from the market of other commodities. Hence the whole addition to the stock of the precious metals in England since the discovery of the new mines has not only not tended **to** raise the prices, but **a** portion, and probably a very considerable portion, has **really** acted in the contrary direction, having been made into articles **which** added **to** the stock of commodities to be circulated. The consumption of gold and silver in the useful **and** ornamental arts in England, for watches, plate, jewellery, and **decoration,** must be very great. In Adam Smith's time the value consumed **in** the town of Birmingham in plating and gilding alone was estimated at more than £50,000 ('Wealth of Nations,' Book i. ch. ii.); and last year it was stated, in the Campden House case, that 'a single artist had received from the proprietor of a single house no less a sum than £1,000, not for the work of gilding generally, but for the actual gold to be used in the process.'—Times, **Sept. 5,** 1863.

insufficient; the natives were often inconvenienced, and sometimes even ruined by its scarcity; and the labour and commodities of India were bought cheaper and cheaper by other countries. In fact, the price of labour and of many commodities was lower in India in 1845 than in England when the mine of Potosi was discovered three hundred years before, and we have seen how the previous cheapness of the English market contributed to the monetary revolution which followed the first considerable influx of silver from the New World.

But it would be an error to look for a rise of price in all commodities and localities alike in India, on the augmentation of its currency. The apparent effect of an expanded currency is sure in any country to be magnified in the case of some commodities, and diminished in the case of others, by extrinsic causes. The additional money is, in the first place, not laid out on all things or in all places equally—on some there may be no additional expenditure at all; and it raises more, or less, or not at all, the prices of the things on which it is expended, according to the supply forthcoming in each case to meet the increased pecuniary demand. Thus, for example, the paper price of different commodities at New York had arisen above their level a year before in different degrees from 10 to 220 per cent.* In India prices have varied much in different places, and in different seasons, partly through the unequal distribution of the new money through the different localities, and partly on account of local inequalities in the supply not of money but of commodities. The defect of means of internal communication, more than any other circumstance, has contributed to cause great local inequalities in Indian prices in the last ten years.† It throws some

---

* See a table of prices of fifty-five commodities in the New York Market. Economist, March 28, 1863.

† The effect of the increase of money in India cannot be measured by the rates at which Indian products sell in the English market. Prices are very unequal in different parts of the East, and our imports may come from the cheapest places. Moreover, prices may be actually rising at the place of exportation, while falling at the place of importation, and the very cause of a fall at the latter may produce a rise at the former. Thus, the price of rice has been low of late years in the English market, because of large importations from the cheap Burmese provinces, where, however, the price has risen in consequence. For the same reason, together with the abundance

light upon the English prices in the 16th century to read that, in the North-west Provinces during the famine which followed the Mutiny, 'while in one bazaar prices of 4 Rupees per maund might be ruling, in another not far off the price would be R. 1.8; yet no flow could take place from the full to the exhausted market, because roads were not in existence.'* Before the Mutiny the prosperity of these provinces had steadily increased, and labour bore a price in them from 1854 to 1857 that it had never borne before. Then came destruction and famine; and, while the price of labour fell, that of food increased—just as, in the winter of 1586, food bore an enormous price at Antwerp and Brussels, not because the new mines were prolific—for the plenty of money had disappeared—but because the Spaniards had stopped cultivation.† In the adjoining provinces of Holland,

of the crops on the spot, the price of rice has latterly been low in some districts of Bengal in which prices generally have been high. Thus, at Dacca, the price of rice was not higher in 1862 than in 1854; it was, however, 30 per cent. higher at Berhampore, and 100 per cent. higher at Cuttack. The exports of India—coffee, cotton, grains, hemp, hides, indigo, jute, oils, opium, saltpetre, seeds, shawls, silk, sugar, tea, wood, wool—have almost all risen greatly even in foreign markets. Nevertheless the prices in Mr. Jevons's tables of 'tea, sugar, rice, foreign spirits, spices, seeds,' have been referred to by an able writer as confirming his conclusion that prices have risen less abroad, and especially in India, and Eastern and tropical countries generally, than in England. But English prices are not foreign prices. Of the commodities just named, rice has greatly risen in most parts of India; tea has risen considerably even in the English market, but much more in India; and sugar has risen in India (more than 100 per cent. in some places), but it has fallen in Europe for several years, owing to the enormous increase of the produce of Cuba and Porto Rico, and of Beetroot sugar on the Continent. Foreign spirits (except brandy, which has much risen) have fallen in England in common with British spirits, by reason partly of the immense production of rum in the West Indies, and partly of diminished consumption in England and Ireland. Spices have been falling in the British market ever since the cessation of the Dutch monopoly, owing partly to the immense increase in the sources and amount of supply, partly to the extent of adulteration, and partly to the alteration in our tastes and customs of cookery, through which the demand has not increased with the supply. Oil seeds have risen enormously in India. Opium (to which the writer quoted has not referred) is the only Indian export of importance which has fallen in India itself; the causes of the fall being first, a great increase of production since the Government raised the price to the cultivator, in order to drive rivals from the Chinese market, and secondly, the late monetary crisis at Calcutta.

* Colonel Baird Smith's 'Report.'
† Motley's 'United Netherlands.'

on the contrary, prices at the same period were high, though every commodity abounded in the market, because American silver abounded there too; so likewise in India, while famine prices reigned in the North West, there were other provinces in which things were at once abundant and dear, because the harvest of money as well as of food had been rich; and the same may be said of the North West itself for two years past. During the famine years in the North West, the enormous rise in prices generally in the Lower provinces of Bengal was not attributable exclusively to the operations of the Indian Mints; but in 1862 and 1863 plenty reigned all around, and yet prices ranged far above their level in 1854, with striking inequalities in the rise in different districts in different commodities, varying from above 300 per cent. to less than 20. Sugar, for example, was only 25 per cent. higher at Dacca in 1863, but at Patna and Dinapore it was 130 per cent. higher than in 1854. Rice is almost the only native product in any part of the lower provinces of Bengal which did not sell much higher in 1863 than before the drain of silver to the East, which the gold mines made possible; and the rare exception is accounted for not only by splendid crops upon the spot, but by the diversion of a part of the demand to the Burmese rice-grounds. Corn, in like manner, is as cheap in the London market now as it was a hundred years ago, because the supply of last year has outgrown the money demand. But rice sold in 1863 for double its ancient price in many parts of Madras, although cultivation had extended, and the two last harvests had been good, while the importations of food had increased, and its exportation diminished. In the interior of Bombay such unprecedented prices have been latterly witnessed that the natives (who seem to be equally blamed whether they save or spend) have been accused in an official Report of 'playing with their money like the Californian gold-finders in the first days of the diggings.' In this novel profusion of expenditure, in the new comforts and luxuries with which the natives of India are filling their houses, in the new and more numerous exchanges which money performs in the interior of the country, and the larger sums necessary to perform them at rates enormously higher than formerly, we have the real account of much of the money supposed to have been hoarded because it has not found its way back to the bankers in the chief towns. The peasantry of the poorest districts in Ireland, in the late famine of 1847, were in like manner supposed to be hoarding the silver introduced by the Board of Works, because it did not return to the banks: the true explanation being that barter had ceased, and the coins which had disappeared were busy performing common exchanges, which had never been performed by money before. It is no slight advantage to the Indian natives to have their industry excited, and their traffic facilitated by the unwonted abundance of the currency, and it liberates the ryot from the cruel exactions of the money-lender. It raises the value of Indian commodities in the market of the world, and the Hindoo is no longer forced to sell cheap and buy dear, in international trade.* It is in the rate of wages, perhaps, that the most remarkable proof is afforded of the elevated rank of the Indian people in the scale of nations; for the comparative powers of production and purchase of different nations are measured by the average pecuniary earnings of labour in each. The rise of money-wages in England is seldom computed at so much as 20 per cent.; but the localities are now few in India where the labourer cannot earn more than twice the sum he could have done twelve years ago, and there are many in which he can earn more than three times as much. The railways, and new public works, and the emigration of Coolies to Ceylon, Mauritius, and the West Indies have, along with the European purchases of cotton, contributed largely to this result; but a

---

* The disadvantage to which a country is exposed in international trade from a lower range of prices than obtains in the countries with which it trades is well explained in the following answer of the Doctor to the Knight in the old Dialogues referred to in the early part of this article :—

'Knight.—Yea, but, sir, if the increase of treasure be partly the occasion of this continued dearth, then by likelihood in other our neighbours' nations, unto whom yearly is consigned great store of gold and silver, the prices of victuals and other wares in like sort be raised, according to the increase of their treasure.

'Doctor.—It is even so; and therefore, as I account it a matter hard to revoke all our English wares unto their old prices, so do I not take it to be either profitable or convenient to the realm, except one should wish that our commodities should be uttered cheap to strangers, and on the other side be dear unto us, which could not be without great impoverishment of the commonwealth.'

fact is not explained away by showing how it has come to pass. The better market for the industry of the Hindoo, the expenditure of unprecedented sums upon it, and its extraordinary rise in price, are the very things spoken of. All the silver sent to the East could not add a rupee to the price of its produce and industry unless it were expended; the railways, public works, and the payments for cotton, are among the channels of expenditure; but the true sources of the money, though it be nearly all silver, are the new gold mines, for the silver could not have been spared from the West, had its place not been supplied by new gold.

There is, then, upon the whole, incontrovertible evidence of a great change in the value of the precious metals in the world, far more extensive than occurred in the 16th century, and upon a different ground-plan; but, like that earlier monetary revolution, it has been neither universal, nor equal where it has occurred. It has not been universal, for the Egyptian is almost the only African enriched; China has netted nothing on the balance of its trade for many years, and the cattle wandering in the pampas of La Plata soon leave the golden circle. Nor has it been equal, for the change has been greater in cheap markets than in dear. But the immense rise of prices in many of the former has been balanced by no corresponding fall in any of the latter markets, and a great diminution in the value of money on the whole is therefore clear, though to attempt to measure it with precision is vain, and to talk of it in terms of arithmetic is an abuse of figures. The only reasonable conclusion on the subject is, that money has for the present lost much of its purchasing power in the general world of trade—a conclusion by itself little to be desired. To load the exchanges of men—to alter the terms of agreement, and disappoint just expectations—to make landlords unwilling to grant leases, and all classes doubtful about contracts for time and thrifty investments—were a calamitous result of the enterprise and toils of the miners. And some evil of this kind has undoubtedly been done. The first consequence, too, of the discovery of the new mines was a diminution in the production of commodities. In 1851, half the male population of Victoria deserted their occupations for the diggings. In 1850, when the population of the colony was only 76,000, more than 52,000 acres were under cultivation. In 1854, when the population amounted to nearly 237,000, only 34,657 acres were cultivated. In 1860, this very colony imported from the rest of the world consumable commodities to the value of more than fifteen millions, and gave commodities in exchange to the value of only four millions and a quarter. British Columbia to this day has produced little but gold, and has levied a continual tribute upon the food, clothing, and implements of the rest of the world. Nevertheless, the good and the gain which have accompanied the evil and the loss are infinitely greater. The new gold has not only founded commercial nations of great promise round its sources, and enabled our own nation to work out (not only without a paralysing monetary drain, but with triumphant success) the problem of free trade, and to purchase in most critical times the material of our manufactures; but it has assisted many backward communities to rise rapidly in the scale of civilization, and 'wandered heaven-directed to the poor.' The rapid rise in the pecuniary value of the labour and produce of several such communities, of which evidence has been given, is not merely a sign and effect of their growing prosperity and elevated commercial position; it has also helped to conduce to their progress. The new money has obtained the immediate execution of great works such as a long line of ancient Egyptian tyrants could not have compelled;* it has been a stimulus to the cultivator's

---

* 'An extraordinary revolution is rapidly proceeding in this country (Egypt). Europe has finally understood the immense future of Egypt, and is eager to develop her yet budding resources. Every steamer is pouring a new population and a golden stream on our shores; energy and capital are taking possession of the land, and urging it forward in the path of civilization and wealth. Not only are the cities of Alexandria and Cairo receiving so great an influx of inhabitants that, although whole quarters are rising on every side, house-room is still insufficient, and rents are always increasing; but the inland towns and villages are overrun, and factories with high chimneys and long lines of black smoke cut the sky of our flat landscape through the length and breadth of Lower Egypt. Gradually, but surely, the tide is creeping upwards, and will soon people the shores of the Thebaid. Englishmen, I am glad to say, are not behind in the race, and their numbers must always increase in a corresponding ratio to the amount of machinery employed. The effect of all this is telling on the natives. I lately heard that Halim Pacha, in conversing with his farm

industry and to the merchant's activity; and it has substituted to a considerable extent a civilized medium of exchange for the barbarous and obstructive contrivance of barter.

So much the increase of the precious metals may be said to have accomplished. What more in their future increase they may accomplish it is not in the province of political economy to forecast. They may become a curse instead of a blessing; they may turn the reaping-hook into a sword, and become the sinews of war in Europe, when the sinews of war are exhausted in America. In Asia they may be buried out of the reach of the merchant by rebellion and anarchy, and prices may rise although money is scarce, because food is scarcer still. But, should both hemispheres be blessed with peace, their hoards as well as their mines may pour their contents into the lap of trade, and a new use may be found for all. The emancipation of the Russian serfs affords, in the payment of wages it involves, an example of the useful employment which the progress of civilization may provide for an increase of silver and gold in the world. The history of the last fifteen years bids us believe that, if the sword can be kept in its sheath, the precious metals will become less precious, chiefly in places where they are too precious at present; that prices will rise fastest where they are now lower than they should be, or could be, if commerce had convenient pathways; and that commodities will finally be multiplied as much as pieces of money on the market. Given the fertility of the mines and the total quantity of money in circulation, prices in the aggregate must be lower through the world as a whole, in proportion to the general industry and skill of mankind, and the extent and facility of their trade; but in the same proportion they must also be nearer equality in different markets; and the rise of prices in cheap places to the level of the dearest is a sign of advancing civilization and prosperity. If prices were at a perfect equality in all places, it would prove that even distance as

labourers, had found the intellect of the lads who have grown up since the introduction of the new mechanical appliances was greatly in advance of that of the men who had reached manhood under the former primitive system of cultivation, when the ox was the all in all to the fellah, and when his mind had no stimulus and no cause for thought or inquiry.'—Times, March 28, 1864.

well as war had ceased to separate mankind. Although the literal attainment of a perfect **monetary** level **is,** therefore, manifestly impossible, the history of prices proves that, while many obstacles to human fellowship remain, more has **been done** since the new gold mines were discovered to make the world one neighbourhood than was done in 300 years before.

XXI.

THE NEW GOLD MINES AND PRICES IN EUROPE IN 1865.

(North British Review, June, 1865.)

On the discovery of the new gold mines, under the name of the Gold Question, an economic inquiry, unconnected with party politics, for the first time gained the ear of the public at large. Yet public interest has been languid, in comparison with the real importance of the monetary problems involved. The chief reason for this is perhaps the diffusion of an opinion, that the effect of the increase of money upon prices practically concerns persons alone whose pecuniary incomes are fixed; an opinion which would be sufficiently true if prices were everywhere uniformly affected, and with respect to all things alike. But the fact is, that the scale of relative incomes, and of relative prices, in different places, and with respect to different commodities, has been so altered, that the old level of profits in different employments, and the old rates of expenditure in different situations, have been permanently disturbed, and new elements must be imported into all calculations respecting the best markets to buy and sell in, the cost of living in different localities, the outgoings and returns in different trades, and the rates of interest which different investments will yield. Those who omit to take these new elements into account may find that their expenses, both as producers and consumers, are largely increased, while the prices of their own productions are not higher than formerly; or they may find themselves buyers in markets in which prices have unexpectedly and enormously risen, and sellers where they have risen in no such proportion; or again, they may miss investments which would yield extraordinary gain. The

British farmer complains that while labour and many of the requisites of production are dearer, he gets no more money than formerly for his wheat, and the migration of population from the country to the towns, and the production of animal food instead of corn, are among the results of changes in relative prices at home. Most writers on the effects of the Mines have confined their observations to changes in prices at home. The truth, however, is, that changes in prices abroad are of equal importance even to Englishmen, not for the purpose of theoretical instruction alone, but even with a view to pecuniary saving and gain. Every day people are making speculations and entering into transactions—in emigration, in foreign trade, and in foreign loans and undertakings—the prudence of which depends upon the movements of prices abroad. Great undertakings by Englishmen abroad in fact have been based upon estimates which have proved fallacious, because they made no sufficient allowance for the effects of an extraordinary increase of money in remote places. Chairmen of Indian Railway and Irrigation Companies, for example, have reported in London that the rise of prices in India had falsified all their calculations, and entailed the heaviest losses on contractors. Nor is it in production alone that the unequal alteration of prices has made itself felt, for consumers have been very differently affected, according to the place of their residence and the things they are accustomed to use. The class of British holders of fixed incomes, who have really been the chief sufferers from the increase of money in other hands than their own, are not fundholders and Government servants in Great Britain, who are generally placed first in dissertations on the subject, but military and civil servants of the Crown in India, who are confronted by a rise of prices to which there has been nothing similar in England since the reign of Elizabeth. Even in England itself, consumers are differently affected, according to their class of life and habits, and the localities they live in. To the agricultural labourer the price of grain is the chief matter, and grain is cheap; he suffers comparatively little from the dearness of butter and meat, and nothing from the dearness of service, now pressing so hard on the poorer gentry and tradesmen, especially in the parts of the country where such things used to be cheapest. It depends entirely on the localities men buy and sell in, and the things they buy and sell in them, how they are affected by the greater amount of money in the world; and statistical averages of prices in general are not only fallacious in principle, but misleading in practice. The **additional money has** been unequally distributed by the balance of trade **to different** countries, and very unequally shared by different **classes** in the countries receiving it; again it has been spent by the classes receiving it, **not** upon all commodities alike, but unequally, and the supply of some things upon which there has been **an** additional expenditure has increased very much more than that of others. Moreover, a low range of prices **is** raised more **by a given** addition to money **than a** high one, which **is** one reason why the change has been greatest in places once remarkable for their cheapness.* And from what has been said, it is plain that **a change** in comparative **incomes** and prices would have **been** caused by the new **gold alone, since it** would increase the incomes and expenditure only **of the** classes, beginning with the miners, to whose **hands it successively** came. But the new gold has by no means been the only new agency at work; an altered distribution of money through the world has been brought about **by more** general and permanent causes. And at a time like the present—a time of doubtful markets and hesitating trade—it is peculiarly desirable to lay hold of the fundamental causes at work, because, although the fortunes of individuals here and there may depend on the momentary **condition** of things, to **the** bulk of society the permanent agencies which prevail in the end, and the permanent rates

---

* The greater effect on low prices of an additional sum of money is a matter of considerable practical importance, which may **be** illustrated in this way. Let us suppose that the price of **common** labour was formerly 1s. 6d. a day in England, and **1d. a** day in India, **and** that the increased demand for labour has added a sixpence to the rate **of** daily wages in both countries, raising the rate from 1s. **6d.** to 2s. in England, and from 1d. to 7d. in parts of India. Wages would **then have risen 33** per cent. in England, and 600 per cent. in India; and whereas **a contractor** could only hire three men in England for the sum with which he could formerly have hired four, in India he could only hire **one man** for the sum with which he could formerly have hired six.

they tend to establish, are the objects of greatest importance. Commerce and enterprise may pause and falter for a few weeks or months; a transitory disturbance originating in America may possibly agitate all markets; but such possibilities only make it of greater importance to know what to look forward to afterwards, and to distinguish between permanent and temporary changes of prices, and of the profits of production in each place and with respect to each sort of thing.

The general principle determining the distribution of the precious metals is, that money is spent by those who receive it on the things they want most for production or consumption, and in the places where those things can be procured at the smallest expense. To buy in the cheapest and sell in the dearest market is the policy of trade; and a combination of causes has latterly given, and is continually giving buyers, on the one hand, access to cheaper places of production for many commodities, and the sellers of the produce of such places, on the other hand, easier access to the markets where their value is greatest. But this necessarily leads to a change in the seats of production and in relative prices, the tendency being always towards the production of everything in the places within reach where its cost of production is least, and towards an equality in the prices of portable goods over the area of cheaper and closer commercial intercommunication. Producers in particular occupations and particular places, accordingly, have not only obtained no share in the new treasure, getting no additional custom either from the mining countries or from the countries these deal with, but have even found the demand for their produce decreasing, and transferred to other localities; and capital and industry are in a course of migration, not only because extraordinary profits are offered in new regions and new employments, but also because ordinary profits are no longer to be made in old places and old employments.

The great gold movement itself—that is to say, the production and distribution of the new gold—is only a part of a much larger movement, resulting from the new facilities of producing many things, gold among the number, in cheaper places than formerly, and disposing of them more readily in the places where their value is the highest, and the enterprise with which such facilities are being turned to account. The mines of California and Australia, for which older mines were forsaken,* are only a particular class of new sources of production from which the markets of the world are being supplied, and their rapid development is only a particular instance of the energy with which cheaper and better sources of supply are sought and developed. The bent of the industrial and commercial movement of our times is, above all things, to discover and put to profitable use the special resources, metallic and non-metallic in which each region excels, to seat every industry in the places best adapted for it, and to apply the skill and capital of old countries more productively in remote places with great natural resources. 'The first phenomenon,' Mr. Patterson observes 'attendant upon the gold discoveries, has been the great emigration—the transfer of large masses of population from the old seats to new ones, the vast and sudden spread of civilized mankind over the earth. The countries where these gold beds have been found are in the utmost ends of the earth, regions the most isolated from the seats of civilization. Of all spots on the globe California was the farthest removed from the highways of enterprise. Not a road to it was to be found on the map of the traveller; not a route to it was laid down in the charts of the mariner. Australia was, if possible, a still more isolated quarter of the globe.' This migration to the remote regions of the new gold is not, however, a singular and isolated movement of industry. We shall find, on the contrary, that the key to the principal permanent changes in prices which have followed the path of the new gold through the world, is to be found in the fact that remoteness is no longer the obstacle it was to the best territorial division of labour, and that buried natural riches, and neglected local capabilities, are obtaining, in a thousand directions at once, a value proportionate rather to their actual quality than to their nearness to market, and attracting capital and skill by high profits to their development. For the same reason

* 'The product of gold in the Atlantic States has fallen off since the discoveries of gold in California.'—Preliminary Report on the Eighth Census of the United States, p. 63.

and by the same aids to industrial enterprise which have brought miners and merchants to cheaper places for gold, cheaper places for the production and purchase of many other things have been contemporaneously found, and the distribution of the new gold and its effects upon prices have been very different from what they would have been, had the fertility of the new mines been the only altered condition of international trade. The general principle which regulates the distribution of money through the world is, as we have said, that those who receive it naturally spend it on the things they want most, and in the places where such things can be had cheapest; but they have of late years obtained access to markets not formerly within reach, and much of the new money has been absorbed in new regions, and in the circulation of produce not before in the market. The world may at present be divided into three classes of regions: first, those in which prices were formerly highest; in the second place, those in which the new movements of trade have already raised prices towards the level prevailing in the former regions; and, thirdly, the places not yet within the influence of the new means of commercial intercommunication. The first and second class of regions may be said to be fast merging into one, with pecuniary rates approaching to equality, while the third class is also, in numerous directions, on the point of assimilation. A permanent change is thus taking place in the conditions which govern comparative prices in different markets, and one the more worthy of notice, since, in the earlier years after the discovery of the new mines, there was, both in the gold countries themselves, and in the chief markets of Europe, an abnormal, and in a great measure, temporary elevation of prices, which, although not in reality principally due to the increase of gold, led to mistaken conclusions respecting its real effects.

The first rise of prices in California and Australia, from which M. Chevalier and other eminent writers were led to apprehend a proportionate fall in the value of money throughout Europe, was, in fact, as Mr. Newmarch has shown,[*] both

---

[*] History of Prices, vol. vi., Appendix.

temporary in degree and **partial in** extent; **those** things alone rising in price which **were in** demand **with the** classes whose pecuniary **incomes** were **increased**. While, **for instance,** the **coarser sorts of** clothing adapted to life at the **diggings** were fetching extraordinary prices, the **best** quality **of** cloth for a time was almost unsaleable. Moreover, **the** early rise in prices in the gold **countries was** not only partial, **but** only partially caused by **the** new **gold**. In the face of a rapidly increasing population, there **was an actual** decrease in the supply of labour and many of the **necessaries** of life. Farms and pastoral settlement were forsaken; the crops in many places **were lost** for want **of hands**; all building ceased in Melbourne **at the very time that crowds** were **arriving**; and the **vessels coming from Europe were too** full of emigrants to have room for considerable cargoes. **So far** too as the rise **of prices was** really caused by the increase **of gold**, and not by **the scarcity** of commodities, it should be **taken** into account that **a great part of the gold** current at first came not from the **new but from the old** mines of the world brought by immigrants **who did not come** empty-handed, and who were driven to spend **a good deal of old money** before they could make any new, or even get to the mines. Hence the first fall **in** the value of money in the gold countries was in **a** great measure **due to a temporary** and abnormal condition of things, and **not to** the fertility **of the mines. In** 1854, prices in Victoria were already **much lower than during** the two years before, and the following **table of prices**, published by the Registrar-General of the **colony**, shows **their** continuous descent **in subsequent** years:—

ESTIMATED WEEKLY EXPENDITURE OF AN ARTISAN, HIS WIFE, AND THREE CHILDREN.

	1854.	1857.	1861.
Bread, 28 lbs.	£0 12 6	£0 6 8¾	£0 5 3
Beef or mutton, 21 lbs. . .	0 15 9	0 12 3	0 6 10
Potatoes, 21 lbs.	0 5 10½	0 2 10½	0 1 0
Flour, 5 lbs.	0 2 2	0 1 2¼	0 1 0
Tea, 1 lb.	0 2 0	0 2 6	0 2 9
Sugar, 6 lbs.	0 3 0	0 2 6	0 2 3
Soap, 3 lbs.	0 1 0	0 1 0	0 0 9
Candles, 2 lbs.	0 1 6	0 1 4	0 1 2
Milk, 7 pints	0 7 0	0 3 6	0 2 4
Butter, 2 lbs.	0 9 0	0 5 6	0 3 0
Firewood, ¼ ton	0 12 6	0 6 0	0 4 0
Water, 1 load	0 10 0	0 5 0	0 2 0
Rent of cottage, per week .	2 0 0	0 10 0	0 6 0
Clothing	0 15 0	0 10 0	0 6 0
School fees	0 3 0	0 3 0	0 3 0
	£7 0 3½	£3 13 4½	£2 7 4

The reader will perceive in these figures a proof of the error of a method by which some writers have attempted to measure the permanent effect of the new mines on the value of money—that, namely, of taking an average of prices one year with another since their discovery. An average of prices for a succession of years hides the material point whether prices have continuously risen, or on the contrary have latterly fallen,—a point of great practical importance, since, as already observed, the general movement of prices has been very different in different places. As an illustration of this we beg attention to the following table of prices at Bilbao, in contrast with the previous table of prices at Victoria:—

	1854.*	1860.	1864.
Mutton, per lb.	£0 0 2¼	£0 0 4¾	£0 0 8½
Beef, do.	0 0 2½	0 0 4	5d. to 8d.
Veal, do.	0 0 3¼	0 0 8	8d. to 10d.
Butter, do.	0 0 5	0 0 9½	0 1 3
Eggs, per doz.	0 0 3¾	0 0 7½	0 0 10
Bread, per lb.	0 0 1	0 0 2	0 0 2
Common wine, two quarts. .	0 0 7½	0 1 3¼	0 0 10
Rent	£15 to £20.	£50 to £80.	£30 to £80.

* Prices in 1854 were the average prices of a long period anterior. The

It is evident from a comparison of the two tables, that persons intending to trade with or settle at either Melbourne or Bilbao, would make a serious mistake in averaging prices one year with another. The average would give a range more than three times too high at one of the places, and nearly three times too low at the other. Prices in Australia in the first years after the derangement of industry by the mines, and prices in Spain before the new gold had found entrance, are so far from affording a basis for calculations respecting the future probable value of money, that they ought rather to be excluded from the estimate. The contrast, however, between the descending movement of prices at one place, and their ascending movement at the other, indicates an important practical distinction. The causes which raised prices so high in Australia from 1852 to 1854 were in a great measure transitory and local; but those which have raised them in Spain are fundamental and permanent in their character, and extend in their operations over the whole area of commercial intercommunication. Mr. Windham has left the following note of Dr. Johnson's conversation on the effect of turnpike-roads in England:—'Every place communicating with every other. Before, there were cheap places and dear places; now, all refuges are destroyed for elegant and genteel poverty. Disunion of families by furnishing a market for each man's ability, and destroying the dependence of one man upon another.' The train of consequences described in these sentences has with extraordinary rapidity followed the recent increase in the communication between distant parts of the world, created by the knowledge and enterprise of our times, as well as by its better means of locomotion. Wherever these causes have acted may be seen the equalization of prices, the disappearance of comparative cheapness, the opening up of new markets for the special capabilities of each place and its inhabitants, and the rupture of ancient bonds of local dependence, of which Dr. Johnson saw, eighty years ago,

very high price of wine in 1860 was in part occasioned by scarcity; not so with the other articles. The harvests have been good, and although bread was at the same price at Bilbao in 1864 as in 1860, in consequence of railway communication with the interior, its price rose in the interior between those years.

almost the beginning in England. It is curious to observe how writers, at places the most remote from each other, fall naturally into the use of the very same words in describing the changes taking place under their eyes. Of Bilbao, the British Consul four years ago, when prices had not reached their subsequent pitch, reported—'The cost of living has risen enormously; and Bilbao, from being one of the cheapest towns in Europe, has become a comparatively dear place.' From Yokohama, in Japan, the Consul writes:—'From being one of the cheapest places in the East, it has become second only to Shanghai in expensiveness.' And from Alexandria we hear:— 'Egypt, which a few years ago was one of the cheapest countries, is fast rising to the Indian scale of prices.'

The rising prices in such places indicate, it should be particularly observed, not a mere fall in the local value of money, but a rise in the general as well as in the pecuniary value of their produce. If all the cattle in the pastures of South America could be carried rapidly and cheaply to Europe, their value in money might be more than decupled; but the change would not be a depreciation of money; for, on the contrary, money would have found an additional demand. Less than a generation ago, the Landes of the Gironde were a pestilential waste, covering 300,000 hectares, and valued at 900,000 francs on the whole, or three francs a hectare on the average. Partly by being brought nearer to markets by railways, partly by the mere fact of their capabilities becoming known, partly by drainage and cultivation, and partly, no doubt, through the general increase of money in France, the price of the Landes has risen in the extraordinary manner described in the British Consul's report, and more in detail by M. About, who relates that the tobacco crop of a single hectare was lately sold for more than a thousand francs, and that the wood alone, on a plot of 500 hectares only partly in plantation, will in less than twenty years be worth a million francs, being more than the worth of the whole territory of the Landes about the time that the mines of California were discovered. M. About adds:—'This enormous territory, which did not figure for a million francs when I was at College, will be worth six hundred millions in 1894.' In the same work from which these figures are taken,* M. About graphically describes some of the causes of the enormous advance in prices in Paris. It denotes, he observes, that Paris has become the metropolis of the business as well as of the fashion of the Continent; and rents are trebled because shops and hotels are crowded, and Paris is a city frequented by the rich. So far as it goes, this description is true, though it fails to allow both for the immense influx of gold shown in the official accounts of the foreign commerce of France, and for the expenditure in the metropolis of vast sums lent to the Government from the old hoards of the people. But we must differ entirely from M. About where he says that while Paris has become a place only for the rich, there remains, and will always remain, a refuge for poverty in the country. 'If the rise of prices in Paris terrifies you, there is the railway; it not only brings people to Paris, but takes them away. Live in the country.' We affirm, on the contrary, that just because the railway brings people and things from the metropolis as well as to it, it brings metropolitan prices into the country, and far more effectively than the old turnpike-road realizes Dr. Johnson's opinion of the results of easy communication between place and place: 'Before, there were cheap places and dear places; now, all refuges are destroyed for elegant and genteel poverty.' The price of eggs a few years ago at Bayonne was six or seven sous a dozen; now you will not get as good a dozen for fourteen; and the price of boarding in a pension at the same place has exactly doubled in the same period. In formerly less accessible places than Bayonne, the change in the cost of subsistence has been greater; and one cause of the concentration of the population of Europe in large towns—which is a fact of immense political significance in our times—is not only that access to them is easier, and employment in them is greater, but that railways are making the country as dear as the town. M. About recommends the country to the poor for its healthfulness and beauty as well as for economy; but modern means of locomotion, and the movement of which they are both cause and effect, tend to give all

* Le Progrès, 1864,

the advantages of each place a pecuniary value in proportion to their real utility and rarity, and to turn them to the utmost commercial account, thus finding new markets for the produce of the mines in the Pyrenees and the Alps. The same general tendency towards the commercial development of the natural wealth of such regions, which led to the production of the new gold, governs its distribution and effect upon prices. Buyers on the one hand, and sellers on the other, have gained, and are constantly gaining, access to new markets. The necessary consequence is to bring money in unusual abundance to places where prices were formerly low, and on the other hand, to bring the cheap produce of such places to the markets previously dearest, and to counteract more or less in the latter the fall in the value of gold which the increase in its quantity would otherwise have produced. And thus it is that stationary prices of commodities in general are the best marks of prosperity in one class of localities, namely, those in which money has always abounded, and where cheapness indicates improvement in production at home, and access to cheaper places of production abroad; while, in another class of localities, rising prices indicate improved means of exportation, better markets, and inducements for the ingress of capital and skill as well as money. For the rate of profit on capital and skill employed in the development of their resources, and bringing their produce cheaply to market, is in proportion to the increase of the quantity and price of the produce. If people can sell for £100 what cost them but £50, their profit in money is 100 per cent.; and the high profits and interest latterly yielded on capital employed in foreign trade and investments has arisen mainly from obtaining a share in the rising pecuniary value of the productions of regions whose commercial situation has been improved. This movement certainly tends to destroy the refuges of poverty, but it tends on the other hand to destroy poverty itself by 'furnishing a market for each man's ability.' It brings with it hardship to those whose condition is stationary, but it makes the condition of many progressive. A few years before Dr. Johnson's remarks on the effect of roads, Goldsmith made those excursions through the country which resulted in the poem of the Deserted Village, in which the features of the landscape, and something of personal incident, were drawn from his native village in Ireland ; but the picture of the intrusion of the wealth of towns and 'trade's unfeeling train' into remote parts of the country, was taken from England. The poet saw only the privation to the parson, who 'remote from towns' had been passing rich at forty pounds a year, and the sorrowful side of the migration of the peasantry ; Dr. Johnson saw also the market opened for each man's capacity by the union of localities, and the liberation of individuals from hereditary restraints and family dependence. This is exactly the movement which a philosophical jurist has pronounced to be the chief characteristic of progressive societies. Their movement is uniform, says Mr. Maine, in the substitution of the commercial principle of contract for the ancient family bond as the principle which associates men, and the amalgamation of isolated original groups into larger communities connected by local proximity.* This theory is equally true of the economic and of the legal and political framework of civilized society ; the migration of labour to new fields of employment, and of capital and wealth into the inmost recesses of the country or remoter regions, and of both money and commodities to new markets, are incidents of the better division of labour in which it results, by which the majority of men must be gainers ; and the working of the new gold mines is only a particular instance of the rapid development of the natural resources of each place, which must result in a vast increase of the aggregate of human wealth, although involving loss to particular classes. Considerable misapprehension has arisen with respect to the effects of the new gold, by attributing to it changes in prices due mainly to different causes. M. Levasseur, for example, concluded in 1857 that the mines had caused a monetary revolution in Western Europe very unfavourable to the wellbeing of the labouring classes. In the mining countries themselves, he observes that labouring men were the first to receive the gold, and the price of labour rose before that of commodities ; the latter rising only in consequence of the increased expenditure of the

* Maine's Ancient Law, pp. 168-70, and 132.

labouring class. But in countries like England and France, the new treasure was first received in exchange for commodities; the price of which consequently, according to this able writer, rose before labour; high profits preceded increased wages; the manufacturer, the merchant, and the farmer were gainers, but the labouring classes were losers. This, he says, is a repetition of what happened in the sixteenth century after the influx of money from the mines of America, when the labourers incessantly complained of the insufficiency of their wages. Happily, however, the historical parallel fails, for wages in the sixteenth century were kept down by law; and the modern changes in production and trade, of which the new gold is only an instance, tend rather to lower than to raise the price of corn in England and the districts of France in which it was formerly dearest. 'As commerce extends,' says Mr. Mill, 'and ignorant attempts to restrain it by tariffs become obsolete, commodities tend more and more to be produced in the places in which their production can be carried on at least expense of labour and capital to mankind.' We get corn from America and Russia for the same reason that we get gold from California and Australia, instead of from our own rivers and mountains—although there is gold in every stream that flows and on the side of nearly every hill —namely, that we seek the cheapest places for everything, and have access to cheaper places than formerly for many things, corn and gold included. Bad harvests, the Russian war, and speculation, and not the cheapness of gold, were the chief causes of the dearness of corn, and of several other important commodities, in England and France from 1853 to 1857. We have here another example of the error of measuring permanent prices by averages of foregoing years, without regard to their ultimate range, and the permanent or temporary character of the causes of a rise. It is on the reasons for prices, and not on mere prices themselves, that producers should found calculations for the future; and a farmer would be greatly in error in taking the price of corn from 1853 to 1857 as a safe basis for calculating the future profit and loss of its growth. The harvest of 1853 was almost the worst for a century throughout Western Europe; that of 1855 was very deficient; that of 1856 was under an average, while the war with Russia still farther shortened supply and added to the cost of importation; and the scarcity of corn, and not the abundance of money, was the **cause of the** sufferings of the labouring classes during the period. The relative price **of labour and bread in both countries** has really undergone an alteration in favour of those who purchase **the latter by the sale** of the former. Thus in France, while **corn** has considerably fallen, money wages have greatly advanced both **in** country and town, and the advance has been constant. In 1860, **the** average of wages in Paris was 4f. 55c., and is now computed at 5f.; and the pay of agricultural **labour in the country around** Bordeaux has risen in the same time from **40 to 50** sous a day. **In the** United Kingdom, money **wages have** also considerably risen; **and the rise** in the price of animal food, though greater **in remote rural** districts that in the large towns, and considerably greater on the average than is shown in any statistics on the subject, but little affects the bulk of the rural population, since agricultural labourers have never **been** accustomed to consume **much of it.** In towns, on the other hand, money wages **have risen** fully **as much as the price of** meat, the rise of which is, in fact, mainly due to an increased expenditure of **the** working population; and accordingly it is pork, **and** the inferior qualities of mutton and beef, which have risen most. The very causes which tend to raise wages and to cheapen corn, tea, sugar, and clothing, evidently tend to raise the price of animal food, by leaving the bulk of the people more **to** expend on it; it being a thing of which there are not the same means of increasing the supply as of clothing and corn. We cannot indeed exempt **the** owners of land from blame in **respect to** the dearness of meat and dairy produce, since **the** uncertain duration of tenure **has been, along** with some unfavourable **seasons, an obstacle** to the increase of the domestic supply, on which its price must chiefly depend. But the change in the relative prices of corn and fresh animal food, and the change in husbandry it is leading to, are mainly to be traced **to** the general movement of commerce, which it is the endeavour of this article to explain, and which is one certainly far from **injurious to** the labouring classes in its general results. The movement tends, as we have seen, to the production of everything, money included, in the cheapest accessible places, and its sale in the dearest accessible markets, and hence to equalize prices approximately in cheap and dear markets brought closer together, thereby raising considerably the price of each class of commodities, in the places connected, in which it was previously lowest, and, on the contrary, counteracting the effect of the increase of money in those in which it was previously highest. The price of corn has accordingly risen in many distant places nearly to its level in England; but in England its level has not been raised. But just as the **improvement** in communication **is** not the same between all parts of **the world** alike, and **the equalization of prices** is not universal for any commodities, so the improvement **is** not equal for all classes of commodities alike; and the **price of** commodities such as fresh butter and meat, which are portable only for a limited distance, has been equalized over a much smaller area than that of corn. The cheaper places to which London has access for fresh animal **food,** are only the remoter parts of the kingdom itself and the nearest parts of the Continent. Improvements in communication produce an approximation to equality in the prices of portable goods only in proportion to their portability, and hence a double change in relative prices ensues. In the **first** place, the prices of easily **portable articles approach to** a level in cheap and dear markets; **but, secondly, as all things** are not equally portable, a change is produced not **only in** comparative prices in different places, but in the comparative prices of different commodities; and both changes **result** in a disturbance of the profits of different occupations, **and a** change in the places of different industries. The same general cause tends to raise the **price of meat at** Athlone almost to the price it fetches in London, and to lower the price of corn in London almost to its price **at Odessa. And** the consequence is, that since labour and capital desert the occupations in which money returns are declining and stationary, for those in which **they** are increasing, the production of animal food is **taking the** place **of** the production of corn in this kingdom, and shepherds are increasing, and agricultural labourers decreasing in **number.**

But this internal change in our industrial economy is a small part of the change in the territorial division of labour which the changes in relative prices in the world of commerce are producing. For the very same reasons that the price of meat has risen in England, but not that of corn, and that the former has risen more in the remoter parts of the country than in the capital, and again, that the change in prices is producing the changes in the occupations of the people just stated, prices in general have rapidly risen in many foreign countries, and British industry and capital have been attracted from domestic to foreign employment. The pecuniary value of the produce of cheap places, rises in proportion as they are brought within reach of the best markets; and capital employed in the improvement of their commercial situation, the development of their resources, and the transport of their produce, obtains an extraordinary profit from sharing in the increase of its money value. If, for example, a cwt. of goods is worth £1 at one place, and only 5s. at a distance for want of communication, a railway company making the line of connexion may charge more for the carriage of goods, and buy the land and unskilled labour they require for its construction very much cheaper than if prices were near an equality at the two places already.

The great rise of prices in India and the enormous growth of its trade are regarded by many as passing results of the American war. And it is desirable, with reference to the future not only of India but of many other places under the same economic conditions, or which will soon be brought under them, and also with reference to the future outlets both for English capital and enterprise, and the produce of the new mines, to ascertain whether we ought really to regard the increase of money in India, and of English capital engaged in its foreign commerce or internal improvement, as a fortuitous and transitory event, or, on the contrary, as the result of permanent causes, which, upon the one hand, are continually investing with additional value the capabilities and productions of places circumstanced like India, and, on the other hand, are finding food and materials from the cheapest accessible quarters for countries like England, and new and remunerative employment for their accumulated capital and skill.

That the stream of the precious metals to India, and the rise of prices ensuing, are not solely attributable to the payments for cotton caused by the American war, is clear from the facts that the bulk of the treasure was imported before 1861, and that the balance of imports of specie above exports, reached fifteen and a half millions sterling in the year 1859-60, and has not reached twenty millions a year as the average since the war. It is an error to suppose we have paid the new cotton countries sums of money proportioned to the price of cotton in our markets, part of which has gone to our own merchants and carriers, and part has been paid in our own manufactures. The balance of trade is always considerably more in our favour than appears in the official reports of the value of our imports and exports respectively. We are ourselves the chief carriers both of our exports and imports, and foreign countries really pay more for our exports, and we pay them less for our imports than appears by our Custom-House valuation, since we receive ourselves a great part of the freight of cargoes both outwards and inwards, and of the mercantile profit on the exchange. The balance of trade, however, has been largely in favour of India for many years past, and the rise of prices was anterior to the war. In a speech at Calcutta, in February, 1860, Mr. Wilson, after referring to the rapid growth of Indian commerce, observed: 'It is notorious how much the price of all country produce has increased of late years, in consequence of the demand for exportation. I am thankful to know that the benefits thus conferred by our commerce upon the land have extended in no slight degree to the labourer. It is no exaggeration to say that the rate of wages has risen in many districts twofold, and in some threefold, during the last few years. In the face of evidence of this kind, can any one doubt that all classes in India are in a state of prosperity, unparalleled at any former time.'* A very different view of the matter has latterly been taken by several writers, who regard the rise in the price of all Indian produce as a calamity to India resulting from the growth of

---

* Economist, March 31, 1860. The following Table of prices of the chief articles of daily consumption in the 'Statement showing the Material and Moral Progress of India for 1860-61, pursuant to Act 21 and 22 Vic., c. 10,

cotton for Europe instead of food for the natives. The real increase in the cultivation of cotton in India has, however, been immensely exaggerated on the one hand, and the increase in the cultivation of crops for native consumption in numerous districts, has on the other hand been left out of sight. Our import of cotton from Bombay, Madras, and Bengal, amounted in 1860 to 570,000 bales, and in 1864 to 1,398,000, but the bales in 1864 were considerably lighter than in 1860, and a great part of their contents was not an additional growth, but cotton withdrawn from native manufacture and the markets of China. And there is copious evidence, that except in particular and exceptional localities, the dearness of food has not arisen from scarcity. In one of the principal new cotton districts—the Nagpore country, in the lake region of which 300,000 acres were under cotton—Mr. Temple's report on the trade and resources of the Central Provinces of India for 1863-4, states that 'agricultural produce abounds of all descriptions common to India.' General Mansfield, in his Minute on the Currency of India, March 8, 1864, observes: 'One great reason of the rise of prices in all descriptions of food, is the greater disposition to consume. The people, being richer, actually eat more than they did in the days of their poverty. Great tracts of land which for ages had lain waste, are being daily brought into cultivation.' In the papers relating to a Gold Currency in India, lately published by order of the House of Commons, there is a Memorandum by the Board of Revenue at Madras which states: 'Agriculture is extending everywhere. There is a great demand for cotton, and indeed for every product of the field. Prices are at the same time exceedingly high.' And the Madras Athenæum, not many weeks ago (March 4, 1865),

sec. 53,' shows the great rise of prices in Bengal before the cotton drain began:—

	1840				1859				March 1861			
	R.	A.		R.	A.	R.	A.		R.	A.	R.	A.	R.	A.
Grain,	1	2	to	1	4	1	11	to	2	2	2	6	to	2	7
Urrur Dhol,	1	7	to	1	10	2	2	to	2	12	2	8	to	2	9
Paddy,	0	7	to	0	11	1	2	to	1	4					
Ghee,	15	8	to	21	8	23	8	to	27	8	28	0	to	28	8
Oil,	6	12	to	7	0	9	4	to	9	6	17	0	to	28	8
Tobacco,	2	10	to	6	0	5	0	to	5	8	4	8	to	6	8

contained the following explanation of the rise of prices in that Presidency: 'The rise in the price of provisions has succeeded a general rise in the price of labour, skilled and unskilled. Men engaged in mercantile pursuits, from the lowest ryots and coolies, have been making money, and this has caused everything to be dear to those whose salaries were fixed in the good old times. Mutton is not dear solely because pasturage and grain are more costly, but because it has been eaten very much more largely. People took to it as soon as they could afford it. It has often been thought that religious prejudices among the natives would always preserve animal food for the Englishman at a cheap rate. But religious prejudices succumb under the influence of rupees, as they are dispelled by the light which rupees throw on the question.'

It is true that in particular places the dearness of the necessaries of life is partly the result of a failure of the crops, and is so far a misfortune; and in Bombay the late exorbitant prices of cotton have really led to a diminished production of food, and to a rise of general prices which cannot be regarded as entirely of a durable or beneficial character. But taking the upward movement of prices over India as a whole, we cannot consider it as otherwise than both beneficial and durable, and as being, like the rise of prices in the Landes of the Gironde and at St. Nazaire,* the result of a permanent improvement in commercial position, and in the means of turning to profitable account the great natural resources of the country and industrial powers of the people. In a speech at the opening of a railway two years ago, Sir Bartle Frere, the remarkably able Governor of Bombay, said:—'We all know what vast sums, chiefly of English capital, have of late years been spent in this country. Let us consider

---

* 'St. Nazaire, a small fishing-town seven years since, has attained a prodigious developement, equal to any American city. France, a short time since, did not possess a commercial port over an extent of 500 miles of coast washed by the Atlantic. The manufacturers of that part of France were consequently placed in a disadvantageous position in consequence of having no sea-port whence to ship their produce. The population has kept pace with the traffic. The value of ground has risen with the population. Ground sold formerly for sixpence the square yard is now worth almost £8.'—Times, April 29, 1865.

for one moment what has been the effect of giving a fair day's wages for a fair day's labour. As a rule, this was unknown before the railway period. Not only were wages in most parts of the country fixed by usage and authority, rather than by the natural laws of demand and supply, but the privilege of labour was in general restricted to particular spots, and nothing like the power of taking labour to the best market practically existed. The result was that the condition of the labourer was wretched in the extreme, and Government could do little to raise him above the status of a serf of the soil. All this has now changed, and for the first time in history the Indian coolie finds that he has in his power of labour a valuable possession, which, if he uses it right, will give him something better than a mere subsistence. As a general rule, the labourer works far harder and better, and acquires new and more civilized wants in proportion to the wages he receives.'

The whole population of India by no means indeed immediately shares in the gains arising from access to better markets and the ingress of European inventions, which on the contrary tend to deprive some classes of their former means of subsistence. 'The native handloom is collapsing in every part of India. The best wares of English manufacture are getting possession of the market, and in the form of utensils for cooking, eating, and drinking, are passing from luxuries into necessaries. Even Cheshire salt is supplied at prices which are obtaining for it a wide field of consumption in Northern India.'* This is part of the general change in the relative profits of different occupations, and the seats of different industries attending the altered distribution of money, produced by closer international commerce and the tendency of all things to be bought and produced in the cheapest and sold in the dearest places. Europe can now manufacture cheaper than Asia, which was once the manufacturer for Europe; the steel of Sheffield has supplanted that of Damascus; and the looms of Asia Minor and India are constantly decreasing in number. The same cause, however, which diminishes the earnings of Hindoo weavers increases the money

---

* Papers relating to a Gold Currency for India, p. 74.

incomes of the Hindoo population as a whole; for in proportion as they are enabled to buy and sell in the best markets, they get better prices for the numerous productions in which they excel. Mr. Senior pointed out that the comparative number of ounces of silver or gold the Indian and the Englishman can earn in a year depends on the comparative productiveness of their industry in exportable commodities. But an Indian labourer earned, when Mr. Senior wrote, only a ninth of the money earned by an English one, not because his labour was really less productive in that proportion, but because his means of exporting the produce were greatly inferior. The price of Indian cotton may decline; Bombay may cease to be England's principal cotton field; yet may it be safely predicted that the capabilities of India and its people for numerous other productions are such that, with the means of exportation henceforward at their command, prices in the three Presidencies will never subside to their former beggarly level. Future candidates for appointments and undertakers of industrial enterprises in India, would do well to include this result of the improved commercial situation of India in their calculations.

The monetary future of India has a more general practical importance for Englishmen. Mr. Fawcett remarked two years ago, that the question of a future depreciation of money in England, supposing the increase in the supplies from the mines to continue, is substantially a question as to the continuance of the drain of the precious metals to the East. We would expand Mr. Fawcett's proposition into the wider one, that it is a question as to the continued absorption of money in places in all quarters of the world, including Europe itself, in which the amount hitherto current has not been in proportion to their powers of production. India is only a representative of a large class of localities, whose industrial resources are providing new markets for the produce of the mines. In India itself, the Governor of Bombay observes in a Minute recommending a gold currency, 'Great quantities of silver absorbed in remote parts of the country go to furnish a currency where no general medium of exchange before existed. There can be no doubt rupees are now found in hundreds of small bazaars where all trade used to be conducted by barter.'*

Adam Smith has observed that the difficulties of land traffic are such that commerce settles first on the borders of seas and rivers, and is long before it penetrates into the inland parts even of the most opulent and mercantile countries. And notwithstanding the immense improvement in the means of land carriage, it is still true, not only of Asia but even of the most civilized countries in Europe, that there are inland districts in which prices are far below the surrounding level, because they cannot or do not sell in the best markets, or on the same terms as their neighbours. While some French writers expatiate on the rise of prices in the parts of France intersected by railways, others complain that in a country whose institutions are intended to favour equality, the railways promoted by Government have created a shocking inequality in local incomes and prices, by giving some places the power of transporting their produce cheaply to the capital, while others are not nearer to good markets than before railways were invented. A railway map of the world enables any one to predict that prices must rise greatly and soon in a vast number of places. However obvious the remark, it is one of great practical importance in trade, speculation, emigration, the purchase of land, and industrial enterprises of a hundred different kinds, that the price of labour and produce will eventually rise wherever the soil is productive, and the means of locomotion are defective; and will rapidly rise wherever those means are suddenly and greatly improved. But physical obstacles to traffic are by no means the only causes of low prices; ignorance is often the mountain to be removed, and it is one which still divides England itself into regions with different monetary rates. Mainly from the want of agricultural sta-

---

* Papers relating to a Gold Currency for India, p. 9. In page 89 of these Papers the following passage occurs:—'Partly owing to the change from a native to a European form of government, partly to the substitution of money for barter in remote districts, but chiefly to the general increase of prices and wages, and the vastly augmented amount and numbers of transactions, the requirements of India for coin are only beginning to be felt.'

tistics, the differences in the **wages** of farm-labourers, the profits of small shopkeepers, and the prices of produce in different counties are surprising. An excellent authority on this subject drew attention last winter to the fact that, **while in some** counties the farmers were paying ruinous prices for fodder, in **others,** hay, straw, turnips, mangolds, and carrots **were** selling at **much** the usual rates.* But these are inequalities which **cannot** continue; and the **fact of** their present existence enables us to foresee in a great measure the future movements **of** money and prices, and **the most** profitable **places for the** investment of capital. **Knowing** the places **where** prices **will** rise as soon **as** their resources are turned **to account, and their** markets **frequented,** the capitalist knows places **in which he** can get **a large** return for the **expense** of assisting **to** develop **these** resources, **or carry** the produce to the best **buyers.** For **example,** a considerable part of the enormous prices **paid in** Europe **for cotton** imported **from** the East, has really been **received by our own** merchants ; **and** the fact serves to explain **the** discrepancy between our own official accounts **of** the value **of our** imports from India, and those of India **itself as** to the value of its exports to us. And the enormous profits which have been **made of late years in our** foreign trade, and upon various investments **of capital in** regions the pecuniary value **of** whose produce **has** rapidly risen, **is** one principal **cause** of the high rates **of** interest latterly **prevailing.** A **high rate** of interest, **like a** high scale of prices, **may arise from** several causes. **It may arise** from a scarcity **of capital,** a great demand on the part of unproductive borrowers, **or high profits** which **enable producers to** borrow on liberal **terms to** the lender. **Governments may pay** a high interest out of taxes, but mercantile **men can only pay it out of profits,** and the maximum of profit fixes the maximum **permanent rate** of interest in trade. Mr. Mill is of opinion **that the** new mines have tended to lower the **rate of** interest. 'The masses of the precious metals which are constantly arriving from the gold countries are, it may be said, wholly added to the funds that supply the loan market.

---

* Daily News, November 19, 1864.

So great an additional capital tends to **depress** interest.'*
And there can be no doubt that a great portion of the new
gold received in this country did at first enter the loan market,
and tended to make interest low. The subsequent distribution
of the precious metals, however, seems to us to have tended in
the opposite direction. Money spent, for example, in improving
the Landes, in building at Bilbao or St. Nazaire, in cultivating
cotton in Egypt, and cotton, tea, oilseed, and other productions
in India, and in carrying such productions to the markets of
Europe, has reproduced itself with extraordinary profit, and
could be borrowed with profit at higher than ordinary interest.
In the future distribution of the precious metals, in like manner,
over markets in which prices will rise—thereby investing with
considerable pecuniary value resources which now have
scarce any pecuniary value at all—we may reasonably foresee a
source of high profit and interest for a long time to come. The
very spirit of mingled economy and enterprise, which adds to
the quantity of the capital in the loan market, by attracting
hitherto unemployed funds from the hoard, the till, and the
private account at the bank, tends to provide more profitable
employment for the capital seeking investment. 'It is,' in Mr.
Patterson's words, 'the utilization of hitherto useless things
which peculiarly characterizes our times. It is the utilization
of neglected resources, the accumulation and concentrated
appliance of a thousand forces or savings, which is the basis of
our extending power. We are economizing our money like
everything else; and this economy of capital, almost as much
as the new gold mines, is the agency which is giving to commerce its enormous expansion.'† In the production of gold in
mines utterly valueless less than a generation ago and now
worth twenty millions a year—in the reclamation of waste lands
and waste substances at home and abroad—in trade with new
markets and industrial enterprise in new regions—in the collection and subsequent diffusion of formerly unemployed money,
the same principle is operative throughout; a principle on which

---

* Principles of Political Economy, sixth edition, chap. 23.
† The Economy of Capital. By R. H. Patterson.

we may rely to find profitable use for the fresh produce of the mines, and for the savings of our incomes for an indefinite period.

The same economical movement has brought petroleum*—to take one of the latest examples of the redemption of wealth from the regions of waste—and the new gold into the market, and the former is a new demand for the latter. In every neglected or undervalued resource in the natural world or in human capacity, there is a profitable investment for money, and commercial enterprise is constantly finding fresh employment for money, both in the purchase of new articles of value, and in higher prices for things of which the value is enhanced by improvement. Speaking of the non-valeurs (a term for which we have no exact English equivalent) which still abound even in the most civilized countries, M. About remarks that among them should be classed not only things absolutely wasted and worthless from neglect, but also things whose value is only partially realized, like land under corn which would fetch more under grass. Such things M. About designates as non-valeurs relatives, including among them all the insufficiently exercised powers of humanity. An entire half of the French nation, he adds—the whole female sex—belongs to the category of non-valeurs relatives. But if women were enabled, by both custom and law, to realize the full worth of their powers, the higher prices their industry would obtain would denote, not a fall in the value of money, but a rise in the value of women. So the increase in the money earnings of coolies and ryots in India, and fellahs in Egypt, denotes not a mere doubling or trebling of counters of payment, but an elevation of the commercial status of two nations. There is thus an important distinction between the significance of a rise of prices in Calcutta and in London; in the latter it signifies generally either a scarcity of commodities or a depreciation of money, but in the former it

---

* 'Though petroleum has been but four years an article of commerce, it has already assumed the second place among the exports of the United States, and now ranks next to breadstuffs. In 1860 scarcely any was exported; last year the exports amounted to 32,000,000 gallons, while the domestic consumption was even greater.'—Times, April 27, 1865.

signifies trade on better terms with the world, as well as a change in the local value of money.

The question whether the new mines have lowered the value of money in England is one the more difficult to answer with precision, since, in addition to the absence of perfect statistics, causes, such as bad seasons and the Russian and American wars, have temporarily affected the prices of great classes of goods. Setting aside these disturbances, the truth seems to be, that while, on the one hand, such important commodities as corn, sugar, and coal* are cheaper than formerly, and the wholesale prices of textile manufactures, although higher than during the depression of trade, for some years before 1851, remained nearly stationary from that year until the American war,—on the other hand, the prices of animal food, of land, and of metal manufactures have considerably risen; and the result would appear to be, that in wholesale trade the general value of money was not sensibly altered in England before the American war. But, speaking of retail prices, into which higher rents, wages, and prices of animal food more or less enter, we should say that the cost of subsistence is decidedly greater to all classes, except agricultural labourers, whose chief expenditure is on bread, sugar, and tea; and that fixed incomes by no means buy as much as they used, especially in remote parts of the country. We believe, too, with an eminent economist, that the real rise of prices to consumers is partially disguised in a deteriorated quality of many things. The disguises which the fact that people are really given less for their money may assume, are numberless. For example, the prices were the same at the bathing establishments of Biarritz last autumn as in former years, but the visitor could often get nothing but a wet and dirty bathing dress for his sous. French gloves, again, are not only dearer than formerly, but seem made in order to tear; and both in England and France, washerwomen are apt to spoil linen now for the prices at which they used formerly to dress it.

---

* Average shipping price of Newcastle coal—1841, 10s. 6d. per ton; 1850, 9s. 6d.; 1860, 9s.—The Coal Question, by W. S. Jevons, Esq., p. 61.

But the effects of the new mines upon prices are far less obscurely and far more satisfactorily discernible in countries like India, where they have directly or indirectly furnished the means of raising the remuneration of industry, and circulating produce which had formerly little or no circulation. The result of this influx of money into India is by no means merely the trouble of carrying and counting more coins to do the same business as formerly; and so far as there has been such a result, it might have been in a great measure avoided had the Government allowed gold to pass current as money. By the exclusion of gold, India has been obliged to fetch a much bulkier material for its currency from a far greater distance, and to incur an unnecessary loss, first, on the freight from abroad; next, on the coinage at the mint; thirdly, on the carriage through the country; and fourthly, on the wear and tear of so many more new coins. The great mines of Australia seem to have been specially designed to provide, at a comparatively small cost, the additional money required by the increased trade of India, and its Government to have resolved to defeat the economy of nature. In contending, however, for all possible economy in the monetary system of India and every other country, we cannot adopt the opinion Mr. Patterson appears to entertain, that the economy might be carried so far as to dispense with the cost of metallic currencies altogether. Coin is better fitted for rough work and for the labourer's pocket than bank-notes. It cannot, like paper, be eaten by ants in the East, and is safer from water and fire. Nor can we conceive that a currency would be safe from depreciation by excess, unless based upon things possessing intrinsic value like silver and gold. Mr. Patterson argues that the value of money depends simply on its conventional use and acceptance. But limitation of supply is in all cases an indispensable condition of value; and the history of assignats in France, and greenbacks in America, shows that negotiability does not constitute the determining element of the value of a currency.* And taking this view of the monetary use and

---

* Mr. **Bonamy Price** says in a recent article: ' The peculiarity of this commodity (gold) consists only in this, that every man agrees to take it in

importance of the precious **metals, it** seems **to be** a question worth considering, whether the **future** supplies **are** likely to be sufficient to supply money **enough for** the rapid progress of the backward parts of the world, **and the** immense development their resources **seem** sure to obtain. Mr. Maine has remarked that investigators **of** the **differences between** stationary and progressive **societies** must, at the outset, realize clearly the fact that the **stationary** condition of the human race is the rule, the progressive, **the exception**; and when this reflection was made, the condition **of** the greater part of Asia and of Northern **Africa** might **even have** justified the proposition that **a** retrograde condition **of the human** race was the rule. **In** the wildest **regions** frequented **by the** nomad hordes of Central **Asia, the** traveller discovers the vestiges of former cultivation and **wealth.** But **he** can now perceive **in such** regions that while he **stands on the grave** of an old civilization he stands also on the borders **of a new** one. It seems certain, **at** least as regards Asia, which **contains** the bulk of **the human race,** that not only the stationary, but the **retrograde communities** will become progressive—will be **reached by roads, railways,** river navigation, and Western commerce, and obtain the aid of Western capital and skill. And **it seems** equally certain that the pecuniary value of their produce **will** immensly increase; **that** they will need vast quantities **of coin for** its circulation; **and that** the question

exchange for his goods. The general consent to make gold the medium of exchange constitutes the precise demand for gold, just as the general consent to make shoes of leather constitutes the demand for leather.' But the social **compact to** wear shoes does **not** determine what **they** are worth; that **depends** on the supply of leather **and** competent shoemakers. The public **consents** to take shillings as well as sovereigns, but it is not their consent that **makes a sovereign** worth twenty shillings, which it **would not be** if gold **were as easy to** get as silver. So the public may **consent** to take pieces of **paper for coins, but** how many must be given for a horse or a cow or a loaf depends **on the** comparative scarcity of each. **We** make this comment merely to illustrate the principle that the value **of** money depends on its rarity, and not on convention and custom, for we confess we do not see the drift of Mr. Price's arguments. He refutes some fallacies of the old mercantile school which hardly required fresh refutation, and which are not supported by any of the writers on currency he refers **to.** But he by no means makes it clear whether he objects only to the particular provisions of the Bank Charter **Act,** or to a metallic standard **altogether,** and to Sir Robert Peel's definition **of a pound.**

is one of importance, whether **coin enough** for the purpose **will be** easily obtained. The steady **decline** of the produce of some of the new **gold mines might seem to** justify a **doubt on** the **subject.** But from **Mexico and South America additional** supplies may be expected. **Of Peru the British Consul says:** '**Peru is one vast mine which the** hand of man has only hitherto scratched.' **To the produce** of the mines must be added **the vast sums** that **the progress** of commerce **will** restore **to** circulation from **the hoards of** Asia **and Europe**, which, even **in such** places as Lapland, are **great.** Large **sums of** Norwegian money are said by Mr. **Laing, in his Journal of a** Residence in Norway, **to** have disappeared in Lapland; **the wealthiest Laplanders having** always been accustomed to live, **like the poorest, on the produce** of the **reindeer, and to bury the money coming to them from** Norway **in places** where their heirs often **fail to discover it.**

The **movement we have** discussed **is one which tends to bring all buried and neglected** riches **to light; and we anticipate** from **it both an ample** provision **of** money **and an increasing demand for it;** although temporary **fluctuations in** both may **cause changes in prices.**

XXII.

PRICES IN GERMANY IN 1872.

(*Fortnightly Review*, November 1, 1872.)

The theoretical principles involved in what is called the gold question are matters, for the most part, about which little controversy exists, although there may be much respecting their application to facts, from the difficulty of ascertaining the real facts. The effect on prices of a great increase in the quantity of the precious metals in the world, depends on their distribution; on the proportions converted into money on one hand, and articles of use or ornament on the other, the latter constituting, in the hands of dealers, an addition to the demand for money, not to the supply of it; on the activity of the part converted into money, and the degree to which the volume of metallic circulation is swollen by instruments of credit; and, lastly, on the course which the additional expenditure takes in each country, and the conditions affecting the supply of the things on which it is laid out. The mere statement of these conditions shows such a multiplicity of agencies at work that the necessity of proceeding by observation to determine the actual movements of prices is evident; indeed, extensive and careful observation on the part of many inquirers is likely, after all, to leave us in ignorance or doubt on some points, but it cannot fail to afford much information, especially as foreign countries must be the principal field of inquiry. On the distribution of the precious metals, first of all, and the opening up of new channels for the new streams of treasure, hang the gravest issues affecting the classes with stationary incomes in this country. The rise of prices has for some months attracted considerable attention in England, and with good reason, but in many parts of the Continent it has been for more than a decade the subject of remark and complaint, and in the earlier attention to it abroad one may perceive the main reason why it has received comparatively little at home until now. A much rapider fall must have taken place in the value of money in England had there been no considerable fall in other parts of the world, had the chief part of the additional gold which has come into circulation in the last twenty-two years been poured into English markets; a matter in itself sufficient to show how deeply we are concerned in its distribution, and in the movement of prices in other regions. The movement in Germany in particular deserves investigation, as a country which has undergone great economic as well as political changes in the period of the new gold, and one in which several of the conditions determining its action on prices can be most advantageously studied. German statistics afford fuller information respecting local prices than are obtainable with respect to England or any other great country. But in every country the real movement of prices has been a number of different local movements, and in Germany we can trace the causes governing the modern changes not in German prices only, but in prices throughout the world. Wide miscalculations respecting the effects of the American silver mines on the value of money in the sixteenth and seventeenth centuries arose from attending only to some statistics of prices in a few principal markets. Even two centuries after the discovery of the American silver mines prices had not risen all over Europe in the manner commonly supposed. It was a partial, local, and irregular rise over a limited area, whence the prodigious effect of the streams of additional money in the localities which actually received them; prices rising enormously in London, for example, while wholly unaffected in part of the Highlands of Scotland and of the west of Ireland, and but little affected even, in some parts of England itself not far from the metropolis. The monetary phenomenon which now first strikes the eye on an inspection of German statistics is the extraordinary inequality of local prices, and it is one which throws a flood of light on both the past and the probable future distribution of the produce of the new mines of our own time.

In the month of December, 1870, to take official statistics published by Dr. Engel, Director of the Royal Prussian Statistical Office,* the price of beef, putting silbergroschen and pfennigen into English money, was 3d. a pound at Neidenburg, in the province of Prussia, at the east of the kingdom, while it was 8¼d. at Aix-la-Chapelle, in the Rhine province. In the same month butter was 9½d. at Neidenburg, 12½d. at Berlin, 14½d. at Magdeburg, in the province of Saxony, 15d. at Dortmund, in Westphalia, and 16d. at Aix-la-Chapelle. Straw was 10s. the shock at Braunsberg, in the province of Prussia, and £2 12s. at Saarbrücken, west of the Rhine. Take again the following statistics of a number of the most important articles at various towns. See table on next page. The prices are given in silbergroschen and pfennigen in Dr. Engel's tables, but the proportions will be sufficiently indicated by the figures.

Dr. Engel's tables give prices at other towns in each of the different provinces, the naked statistics being presented in all cases without theory or comment. The war in France may probably have disturbed the markets in the towns nearest the military operations during the latest period for which the official statistics are published, and the military element is one which we shall have to notice again as one of the conditions besides the new gold affecting the movement of prices in Europe. But it by no means accounts for the inequalities, as is evident from the statistics of a number of years before the war. Going back, for instance, to 1865, we find butter 7d. a pound at Neidenburg, 10d. at Thorn, in the same eastern province, and 13¾d. at Aix-la-Chappelle, at the extreme west of the kingdom. The value of money, in short, is a local affair, even in Prussia, though one of the most advanced countries in Europe, and one of the best provided with internal communications. Some of the differences are partially accounted for by differences in the fertility or in the harvests of different regions.

---

* 'Zeitschrift des Königlich Preussischen Statistichen Bureaus.' Elfter Jahrgang 1871. See also the statistics of prices in the volume published in 1867.

Average Prices in the Harvest Year, August 1, 1870, to July 31, 1871.

Town.	Province.	Wheat.	Rye.	Barley.	Oats.	Peas.	Potatoes.	Butter.	Beef.	Pork.	Straw.
Neidenburg	Prussia	82	48·9	34·1	30·5	54	15·1	6·7	2·8	3·8	180
Thorn	,,	91	58·6	49·1	39·8	62·9	22·10	10·3	4·4	5	308·8
Dantzig	,,	92·8	59·11	46·11	32·6	62·6	23·11	10·3	7·1	6·1	222·9
Berlin	Brandenburg	90·4	65	52·9	37·3	96	22·6	10·4	5·3	5·9	304·7
Magdeburg	Saxony	91·7	67·3	54·6	39·6	97·1	25·5	11·10	6·8	6·8	312·3
Münster	Westphalia	101·8	73·3	63·11	43·4	93·1	40·10	8·11	4·8	5	291·6
Dortmund	,,	105·5	74·9	58·7	41·11	108·6	37·3	10·9	5·7	6·3	406·7
Bochum	,,	104·6	76·11	63·2	41·8	109·7	40·9	11·9	5·4	6·6	437·6
Düsseldorf	Rhine Province	109·2	78	65·7	43·2	115·8	40·4	12·6	6·5	8·7	408
Aix-la-Chapelle	,, ,,	112·3	82	70·9	45·5	115	42	13·3	7·1	8·6	487·6

Great fortifications, as at Cologne, Coblentz, Mayence, Königsberg, Dantzig, and Stettin, obstructing the growth and business of towns, and raising the rents of houses, occasion other diversities. Other local causes affecting supply or demand were recently assigned on the spot at other places in reply to my own inquiry. But if special local causes alone were at work, the rise in some localities would be attended by a fall in others, because the same sum of money cannot be in two places at once, and if part of the money previously current had been drawn off to new localities, there would be less left in the old ones; whereas we find a higher range of prices than formerly everywhere throughout Germany, though the differences are surprising. In Germany, as in England, combinations and strikes are now often referred to as the chief cause of rise in the present year in the prices of many things, and of the greater cost of living at particular towns. But this explanation fails to account for a continuous rise of prices for twenty years before strikes or combinations (which are of very recent appearance in Germany) were heard of; nor could a rise of the mass of commodities take place without either an increase in the money demand, or a diminution, which is not pretended, of the supply. A rise in money wages at the expense of employers may cause a change in relative prices, and a rise of things produced mainly by labour, but in that case things produced mainly by fixed capital, and whose price consists largely of profit, would sustain a corresponding fall. An altered distribution of money to the advantage of the working classes, again, would lead to an increased expenditure on their part; their comforts and luxuries might accordingly rise. But this in turn would be met by a corresponding diminution of expenditure on the part of other classes, and a corresponding fall in some articles. A fall in the house-rents of the middle classes, for example, would ensue, whereas what is particularly complained of is a rise. The payments of France on account of the war are in some places spoken of as one cause of advanced prices in the present year. The chief part of the money coming from that source seems, however, as yet either to have been withheld from circulation by the Government, or to have been expended west of the Rhine, in Alsace and Lorraine; and in any case those payments afford no explanation of the continuous advance of prices before July, 1871, the last month to which **Dr.** Engel's statistics come down. There are, I must allow, anomalies in German prices which remain inexplicable to me after much recent local **inquiry**; but some general **results of** importance seem to emerge beyond doubt from their examination in a number of different places.

The lesson, it is true, which investigation of facts impresses more and more on one's mind is distrust of economic generalizations; still they are of use if we are careful both, as far as possible, to cover under them only the proper particulars, and also to use them as guides to, instead of as concluding inquiry. A generalization which may be advanced with reference to the present subject is that, in the first place, a much lower scale of the prices of land, labour, animal food, and other main elements of the cost of living to large classes, will usually be found to prevail in places without steam communication than in places similarly situated in other respects, but possessing railways or steam transport by water; in the next place, among **places possessing** steam communication, a considerably higher scale of prices of the staples referred to will for the most part be found in those which are centres of industrial or commercial activity or of foreign resort than in such as are of a stationary or colourless character; and, thirdly, **as a general rule, there is a marked** tendency to a higher elevation of prices in Germany as we travel from east to west. Hence Germany may be roughly divided into four monetary regions:—(1) places in arrear of the world's progress in respect of their means of locomotion as in other respects; (2) places communicating by steam with good markets, but not themselves the sites of much enterprise, or possessing any special attractions; (3) places which unite the best means of communication with local activity, or considerable resort from without; (4) among places falling within the last category, a higher scale of rents, wages, the price of animal food and other essentials will be found, **cœteris** paribus, in those which **lie** nearest **the** traffic and movement of Western Europe. **Of the** effect **of the** want of steam communication the reader may observe **an example** in the comparative prices given above, of

Neidenburg on the one hand, without either
transport by water, and Thorn on the other h
province, seated both on the Vistula and on a
for an example of the lower range of prices i
stationary places, though well provided with me
than in centres of industrial activity, comp
above, at Münster, in Westphalia, with those o
Bochum, in the same province, but among the
the Ruhr Basin. For an illustration, lastly,
prices as we move westward in Germany, com
chief towns of the province of Prussia with the
Westphalia, and these again with the prices of
on the borders at once of Belgium, Holland,
on the high road to France and to the Englis
upward movement of prices as we move west
connected both with proximity to the best inter
the increase of the manufacturing element and
commercial activity, and also with a third co
remotely allied to the two others—namely,
education. In the two most eastern provinces
Prussia and Posen, it appears that above twel
recruits annually enlisted are unlettered;
Saxony, and the Rhine Provinces, the percent
recruits is considerably below one per cen
some correspondence between this scale of e
following scale of the average prices, in the de
towns in the different provinces from Dr. Eng

Province.	Wheat.	Rye.	Barley.	Oats.	Peas.	Potatoes.	Butter.
Prussia	81.11	53.11	41.7	30.4	59.2	20.4	7.11
Posen	79.7	55.8	44.10	31.8	58.5	15.3	8.7
Brandenburg	83.7	59.11	47.4	34.1	73.2	18.10	9.8
Saxony	83.8	64.7	51.3	33.8	79.3	21.4	9.7
Westphalia	91.8	69.1	57.7	38.7	88.4	29.3	8.9
Rhine Province	98.6	67.11	56.9	35.6	90.10	27.10	9.5

The higher range of prices in western Ge
springs from the greater abundance of mone
and traffic are best situated and most active, t
element furthest developed, and general int

Knowledge, industrial energy, the value of land, labour, and time increase, and the commercial and money-making spirit becomes keener, for better for worse, as communication with the wealthiest and busiest countries of Western Europe becomes closer, and the German approaches the principal lines of western traffic, travel, civilization, and money expenditure.

Those who are conversant with the theory of the international distribution of the precious metals expounded by Mr. Senior and Mr. Mill, may find evidence in the local prices of Germany that the principles which govern the partition of the world's currency among different countries, and the scale of international prices, apply also to the distribution of a national currency and the comparative prices of different places in the same country. The more efficient, productive, and valuable the industry of any country, or of any locality, and the cheaper and faster its produce can be carried to the best markets, the higher will be the scale of pecuniary earnings and incomes, and the higher consequently the prices for the most part of things in great demand, such as labour, land, and fresh animal food, of which the supply is limited, and which make a great figure in the cost of living. The producers for the foreign market get higher profits and wages; money flows in from abroad, and producers for home consumption, though no such nice equality of wages and profits as book theorems assume really exists, earn more than can be earned in less active and less advantageously situated places. If Yorkshire cloths and Lancashire cottons, carried by steam, could be made to suit the convenience and taste and awaken a demand on the part of the whole population of European Russia and Asia, what would follow with respect to prices in England? Yorkshire and Lancashire would have a larger claim on the money of the world; there would be a rise in Yorkshire and Lancashire wages and profits in general, though by no means in the exactly equal ratio which economic fictions assume for wages and profits throughout the whole kingdom; both the working classes and their employers would have more to spend, and the comforts and luxuries of both, of which there was not a proportionately increased supply forthcoming, or not without additional cost, would advance in price. So in

Germany, although one cause of prices being higher in places of great industrial activity or resort than in more purely agricultural or less frequented localities, may be that the supply needed, or part of it, must be brought from a greater distance, yet the principal cause is the difference of money demand and expenditure. The great rise in the cost of living at Berlin in the last year and a half springs in the main from the fact that Berlin has become the capital not merely of Prussia, but of Germany, its political, intellectual, and financial centre. Hence a great influx of capital, people, and money, a great activity of business, an extraordinary demand for houses, building materials, and labour, an exorbitant rise in the prices of things into which they enter as principal elements, and a condition of the labour market which enables workmen in some trades to exact what are thought by employers exorbitant terms. The same monetary phenomenon presents itself likewise in small towns, which situation and local advantage have made places of much resort. At Heidelberg, for instance, I was lately told by a resident, who is a high authority with respect to German prices, that the cost of living to persons of moderate income, though rising many years before 1866, had advanced fifty per cent. since that date, and is still advancing, the main proximate cause in the last twelve months being the exactions by the working classes, in one trade after another, of a great advance in wages. But Heidelberg lies on the high road of travel, and almost at the intersection of the principal lines of European railway communication; it is one of a ring of towns of much resort, and itself possesses special attractions; the demands for higher wages have been grounded on the rise of commodities, and the increased pecuniary expenditure, of which the higher wages and prices afford proof, could not be forthcoming without a more plentiful circulating medium.

The comparison of local prices in Germany reconciles in principle two seemingly opposite theories respecting the international movement of prices consequent on the new gold mines, though neither theory is quite in accordance with facts. According to one theory, prices should have risen earliest and most in the countries whose industrial efficiency and whose means of communication were furthest advanced, and therefore more in England than in Germany or France. Another theory is that steam communication equalizes prices, raising them, therefore, most where they were formerly lowest, and therefore most in what formerly were backward and cheap countries and localities. Each theory contains a measure of truth, but the first overlooks the rapid diffusion of industrial inventions, activity, and improvements in transit, the consequent changes in the distribution of money and in the relative prices of different countries and different localities in the period of the new gold; while the second exaggerates the equalizing influences of steam locomotion. The real movement of comparative national and comparative local prices has not been a general equalization, nor as yet even a tendency towards it. What we find is, not a uniform elevation of the whole level, but the rise, as it were, of a great number of monetary peaks of different altitudes—a rise, that is to say, at a great number of points in continental countries to or near to the highest ranges in England, and again at a still greater number of other points to altitudes considerably below the pitch reached at the points of highest development, but much above the level of places without improved communication. Railways and steamers are said to equalize prices; and so they do, creating equalities and tendencies to equality of two kinds. They tend to raise prices at many of the most advanced places on the Continent to, or nearly to a par with those of the principal English markets, and again to bring prices in previously remote and cheap places up towards the range generally prevailing along the lines of steam transport. But they also create new inequalities, and these, too, of two kinds. They raise prices at places obtaining the new means of communication above the range prevailing at places obtaining no similar advantage; and again, they concentrate capital, business, and money expenditure plethorically, as it were, at particular spots with peculiar natural resources or advantages of situation, and thus elevate prices enormously there at a time when an unwonted abundance of money is in the world. Improvements in locomotion develop the resources of the world, but the resources of different countries and of different localities are unequal, on the one hand, and the new means of locomotion develop their actual resources unequally, on the other hand, because not equally distributed. It is not, we must remember, the mere acquisition of means of rapid communication that raises money-earnings to the highest point, or that makes the greatest change in habits of expenditure and the pecuniary cost of living; what does so is the ingress of wealth, enterprise, and outlay, the generation not only of opportunities for pecuniary gain, but also of the habit of taking advantage of them, the influx not only of money, but also of the money-making spirit, the creation of a custom of looking, not for customary prices, but for the highest prices to be got for everything, every inch of ground, every trifling exertion, every minute of time; while, at the same time, the habits of consumers naturally become costlier as their incomes as producers become larger. So far are railways and steamers from diffusing these causes of extraordinary pecuniary gains and extraordinary prices equally throughout all the regions they traverse, or even all the places they actually touch, that they often draw capital, business, and money, not to but from places on the very lines of steam communication, to others with greater advantages. Even at spots whose position and opportunities are such that the money-making spirit, the habit of seeking the utmost price, and the organization often necessary to obtain it, might be expected to develop themselves at once, they sometimes do not do so for years. In a district, for example, where the bulk of the inhabitants are owners of land, growing chiefly for their own consumption, they may not be tempted immediately by the offer which a new railway makes of high prices at a distance, to send their produce to market. People are often reluctant to change their ways of life, even where they would be great pecuniary gainers. A few weeks ago, at a place in the Ruhr Basin, which must soon be absorbed in the whirl of industrial activity round it, but where life is still comparatively cheap, tranquil, and old-fashioned, an hotel-keeper answered the question, whether there were any great factories or industrial establishments yet?—' No, thank God!' It must be confessed that the new movement does not always add to the comfort or happiness of the district it invades. Take those little hamlets which one sees from time to time nestling in a ravine on the side of one of the low mountains of Siegerland, where every householder has his twenty acres of land, his share in a wood, his three or four cows, his pig, and perhaps a few sheep, whose own land produces his food, and the sale of whose wood supplies all his other wants. The mountain has ribs and bowels of iron; tall chimneys and high prices will soon rise at its base; the peasant may find that his wood buys less than before; he may descend from the rank of a landowner to that of a labourer, and perhaps be tempted to begin a new, anxious, and uncertain career in a town. But there is another side of the picture. The progress of industrial and commercial activity is inseparably bound up with that of science and art, as both cause and effect; and it is the chief of the agencies which by a number of influences, direct and indirect, are elevating at last the condition of the toiling masses of Europe in one place after another.

The movement in place of prices in Germany, or of comparative local prices, is obviously connected with the movement in time, or the comparative prices of different periods, and therefore with the question concerning the changes in the value of money since the new mines were discovered, or the gold question. With a view to the solution of a different though closely related question to which we shall have to recur, and which the title of his essay explains,* an eminent German statistician has recently published an elaborate analysis of the prices of 312 commodities from 1846 to 1865 in the market of Hamburg. Among the results is a classification of the 312 commodities in eleven groups, with the comparative prices of successive quinquennial periods indicated in the following table, in which the prices of the first period, 1846-50, are represented by 100:—

---

* Welche Waaren werden in Verlaufe der Zeiten immer theurer? [What commodities become constantly dearer in the lapse of periods of time?] 'Statistische Studien zur Geschichte der Preise.' Von Dr. E. Laspeyres. Tübingen 1872.

Group.	Class of Commodities.	Number of commodities.	5 years, 1846-50.	5 years, 1851-55.	5 years, 1856-60.	5 years, 1861-65.	15 years, 1851-65.
I.	Products of South European plants—wines, fruits, &c.	23	100	121	143	136	133·7
II.	Agricultural products of Central Europe—corn, peas, beans, &c.	41	100	122	133	128	127·8
III.	Hunting and fishery products	19	100	116	135	131	127·8
IV.	Products of sylviculture	17	100	109	113	160	127·2
V.	Produce of European cattle rearing	29	100	113	137	125	124·1
VI.	Edible colonial products	44	100	110	125	129	121·8
VII.	Non-edible colonial products	44	100	105	115	123	114
VIII.	Fibrous manufactures—linen, woollens, spun silk, &c.	12	100	102	107	127	112·2
IX.	Chemical manufactures	40	100	111	117	102	109·9
X.	Mineral and metal manufactures	22	100	107	111	101	106·4
XI.	Products of mining and smelting—coal, iron, &c.	24	100	107	108	97	104·1
		312	100	111·2	122·1	123·3	118·98

If, however, the reader examines the prices of the particular articles comprised in the eleven groups, he will find that the average prices of the groups do not show the real rise, the greater number of the more important commodities having risen much more in the period subsequent to 1846-50 than the averages indicate. Unfortunately, too, the table stops at the end of 1865, while a great rise in some commodities has taken place in subsequent years. Group xi. in the table shows, in fact, a fall in coal and iron in 1861-65 compared with 1846-50, whereas those great staples are now at extravagant prices in Germany as in England. The statistics presented by Dr. Laspeyres[*] do not enable us to make any close comparison between the

[*] See p. 68 of his Essay.

movement of prices at Hamburg and at London, but so far as they go they indicate a considerably greater rise at Hamburg since the discovery of the new mines. On this point it seems to me that the reason assigned by Dr. Laspeyres for a greater rise of cereals, &c. (group ii.), at Hamburg than at London, namely, that England has derived greater benefit than Germany from improvements in transport and free trade in corn, hides the real distribution of benefits. Improvements in transport and trade tend to raise the pecuniary value of raw produce exported to the benefit of producers in the exporting countries, and to lower the price in the importing countries to the benefit of consumers. But Germany is an exporting, England a great importing country in the matter of corn, Germany being, in fact, one of the sources of the English supply. Dr. Carl Knies, the eminent professor of political economy at Heidelberg, pointed out in an essay on the Depreciation of Money in 1859, that there were causes tending to a greater rise of prices in Germany than in England. 'First and foremost,' he observed, 'among the agencies creating important changes in prices come railways, diminishing the differences in the local values of money, by causing its influx into places where prices were low from places where they were high. Germany may be classed among the former, England among the latter. At a time when a general fall in the value of money is taking place in consequence of the abundance of gold, the change is diminished in England and augmented in Germany by the change in the movement of money.' But the same movement which has given Germany railways and steamers has given it steam for manufacture and mining as well as for locomotion, and all the mechanical and chemical inventions of England and France in addition to its own. If we add great legal and administrative reforms removing obstacles to production and trade, and the spread of education, we may see reason for greater relative progress and a greater relative increase of pecuniary incomes in many parts of Germany than in England, though the actual scale of incomes and prices may still be higher in England. The prices of Hamburg, it should be added, must not be taken as representing the movement of prices throughout

Province.	Decade.	Wheat.	Rye.	Barley.	Oats.	Peas.	Potatoes.	Butter.	Tallow.	Beef.	Pork.	Hay.	Straw.
Prussia	1841—50 1861—70	67·4 81·11	42·1 53·11	31·11 41·7	22 30·4	46·7 59·2	15·9 20·4	5·5 7·11	4·6 5·2	2·4 3·7	3 4·8	19·1 24·8	143·11 188·3
Posen	1841—50 1861—70	66 79·7	44 55·8	34·5 44·10	24·4 31·8	47·8 58·5	14 15·3	5·10 8·7	3·9 5·3	2·9 3·10	3·4 4·10	22·8 25·7	166·4 194·2
Pomerania	1841—50 1861—70	68·8 85·10	45·7 59·11	33·4 46·9	24·7 33·7	48·4 64·7	16·1 19·4	6·7 9·3	3·10 4·4	2·9 3·11	3·4 5·4	19·7 22·3	172·3 232·1
Silesia	1841—50 1861—70	65·2 79·9	46·2 53·1	35·11 45·4	24·4 30·8	52·4 65·9	17·1 18·3	5·7 8·5	4·4 4·9	2·9 3·11	3·5 4·11	22·5 30·3	141·3 188·3
Brandenburg	1841—50 1861—70	69·9 83·7	46·3 59·11	47·4 35·10	26·6 34·1	56·9 73·2	14·6 18·10	6·9 9·8	4·6 6·2	3 4·7	3·6 5·2	22·7 27·7	181·9 249
Westphalia	1841—50 1861—70	76·4 91·8	56·6 69·1	42·10 57·7	28·9 38·7	68·5 88·4	20·9 29·3	5·5 8·9	4 5·8	2·11 4·8	3·9 5·5	29·6 31·1	169·3 275·4
Saxony	1841—50 1861—70	66·2 83·3	49·2 64·7	36·11 51·3	25·5 3·8	59 77·3	16·9 21·4	6·10 9·7	5·6 6·9	3·4 4·9	3·9 5·4	27·1 36·2	176·9 204·2
Rhine Provinces	1841—50 1861—70	82·1 93·10	61 67·11	46·2 56·9	28·7 35·6	72·5 90·10	20·9 27·10	6·1 9·5	4·9 5·8	3·2 5·3	4·2 5·11	28·1 37·3	201·4 275·4

Germany, where the real movement is made up of a number of different local movements. Hamburg, long one of the chief seats of German trade, has advanced much less in respect of industrial activity, means of communication, wealth, and the increase of money, than many other towns which have come to the front in the last twenty years. Dr. Engel's tables supply some additional information, showing, for example, the average prices of some important commodities in the chief towns of each province of Prussia in the two decades 1841-50 and 1861-70 respectively. (See table on preceding page.)

If, however, we compare the average prices of 1861-70 with those of the immediately preceding decade 1851-60, we find that while the rise in butter, tallow, beef, pork, hay and straw, has been a continuous one, wheat, barley, oats, peas, and potatoes were, on the contrary, on the average of years, higher in the decade 1851-60 than in 1861-70. The articles, however, which have risen continuously are much better measures of the purchasing power of money in Prussia than those which ranged higher in the first decade of the new gold period than in the second, above the prices of 1841-50. The prices of butter, tallow, beef, and pork are taken on a more uniform system throughout the different markets of the kingdom than those of the other articles. The seasons produce much more violent fluctuations in grain and potatoes than in animal food; and animal food is both a much more important item than bread and potatoes in the economy of the middle and wealthier classes, and one better adapted to test an increased expenditure on the part of the working classes—butter especially, on which the working classes in the mining and manufacturing districts at least of Prussia spend much more than on meat. Not to encumber our pages with too many figures on one hand, and because, on the other hand, butter, of all the articles in Dr. Engel's statistics, affords the best criterion of the movement of prices and the cost of living, let us take the price of that article during a succession of years at various towns; the year 1841 affording, as Dr. Engel's tables show, a fair standard of pre-Californian prices for comparison.

PRICE OF THE POUND OF BUTTER IN PFENNIGEN.

	Königsberg.	Dantzig.	Posen.	Stettin.	Berlin.	Breslau.	Magdeburg.	Münster.	Cologne.	Aix-la-Chapelle.
1841	73	71	70	96	84	64	81	64	75	75
1851	71	72	70	88	84	78	89	60	68	67
1852	80	80	84	95	86	90	89	64	77	93
1854	90	91	101	100	91	93	97	75	85	96
1855	95	103	106	110	91	98	104	82	93	100
1856	101	110	104	113	112	97	108	85	102	112
1857	104	104	102	117	120	102	118	88	113	129
1859	103	101	98	107	119	90	109	80	109	130
1860	92	95	88	104	108	82	95	75	91	111
1862	106	106	107	125	111	94	111	89	110	124
1863	105	107	109	120	114	102	108	73	104	122
1864	104	105	110	120	117	110	114	87	118	128
1865	110	112	116	125	118	113	120	92	125	137
1870	111	118	128	132	124	115	140	105	134	161

These statistics exhibit, amid some curious irregularities, a continuous rise at all the towns in the list, but a much greater rise at Aix-la-Chapelle, where the price has more than doubled, than at Königsberg, where the rise is a little more than 50 per cent. We have, however, no statistics of places where the rise has been greater; places, that is to say, which before 1850 had neither railway communication nor industrial activity, and **which** now are in the front rank with respect to both. Aix-la-Chapelle was a considerable town and had the advantage of a **railway** before the discovery of the new gold mines; but there **are** now mining and manufacturing centres which twenty years **ago** were not to be found on the map, and it is in such **places** that the scale of wealth, wages, rents, and the prices of animal food has changed most.

Dr. Engel's statistics do **not** come down to the present year, but Mr. Scott's report **on 'the** condition of the industrial classes, and the purchase **power** of money' in Würtemberg, supplies figures showing **a** continuous rise in that part of Germany since 1850 :—

	April, 1870.	April, 1872.
Beef	6d.	6¼d.
Pork	6d.	7d.
Veal	5¼d.	6¼d.
Butter	7¼d.	10¼d.
Milk	2¼d.	3¼d.

The recent advance in these articles has, I am assured, been greater in some parts of Germany, though I am not enabled to authenticate the results of personal inquiry by official statistics. It is more important to note that no statistics exhibit the real increase in the cost of living in many German towns, since they do not exhibit the increase of town wages and house-rents, and of the retail prices of many things into which wages and house-rent enter as principal elements. The practical change in the value of money varies, of course, for different classes and different individuals, according to the course of their habitual expenditure, since some things have risen more than others, and some, both imported and manufactured in the country, not at all. The classes who seem to be least affected by it as consumers, are those who have no wages to pay, while their own wages have risen considerably, and who have often a cottage, a garden, and cow of their own. The classes with stationary incomes, in whose expenditure house-rent, animal food, and the wages of servants form the chief items, are, of course, the chief sufferers.

On the whole, it is evident that there has been a great change in the value of money in Germany in the last twenty years, though it has been different in different localities, and we have no such array of statistics as would be necessary to determine the exact amount of the fall in any locality. Still less can we determine exactly the share of the new gold mines in the fall. There were causes tending to raise prices in Germany, though no new mines of extraordinary fertility had been discovered. One cause, altogether distinct from the mines in its nature, though indistinguishably associated with them in its operation, is the improvement in the industrial and commercial position of the Germans. In a country which has gold mines of its own, the production of gold depends partly on the powers and skill of the miners, and partly on the fertility of the mines. Let both the efficiency of the miners and the productiveness of the mines largely increase, and there will be a vast increase in the production of gold, but it will be impossible to say how much is due to the miners, and how much to the mines. Foreign trade, as economists put it, is the gold mine from which nations without actual mines of their own get their gold, and the fertility of the foreign mine and the efficiency of the Germans who work at it have increased together.

Both causes together, nevertheless, fall short of explaining the changes in German prices. Two other sets of causes have been at work at the same time; one augmenting the amount of the circulating medium and the rapidity of its circulation, the other affecting the supply of some of the chief articles on which the cost of living mainly depends. The improvements in locomotion and in commercial activity which have so largely augmented the money-making power of the Germans, have also quickened prodigiously the circulation of money; and the development of credit, likewise following industrial progress, has added to the volume of the circulating medium a mass of substitutes for money which move with greater velocity. You can send money by steamer and railway, but you can send credit by telegram, and a new million at New York may raise prices in a few hours at Frankfort and Berlin. A much smaller amount of money than formerly now suffices to do a given amount of business, or to raise prices to a given range; and to the increased amount of actual money now current in Germany, we must add a brisk circulation of instruments of credit. It is true that some of the principal means of substituting credit for coin, and economizing the use of the latter, have little or no operation in Germany. Cheques, strange to say, are hardly in use, and there is no Clearing House. But there is a mass of bank-notes; and bills of exchange, for very small as well as for large amounts, pass from hand to hand among people in business almost as freely as bank-notes; the same bill making often a great number of purchases before it reaches maturity. The transactions are, of course, liable to be reopened if the bills be not met in the end, but otherwise they answer as payment in cash. A small proportion of coin thus supports an immense volume of circulating credit. Were the circulating medium composed of coin alone, whatever the amount of the precious metals issuing from the mines or circulating in other countries, whatever the price of German commodities in the gold market abroad, no rise of prices of German commodities at home could take place without additional coin enough to sustain it. It might be the conviction of people in business in Germany, that, looking to international prices, and the relative cost of production of German exports and other German commodities, prices generally ought to be double their former amount; yet, in the absence of instruments of credit, only a doubled quantity of coin, or a doubled rapidity of its circulation could actually double prices, and give German labour and productions their due value in relation to money. But, when credit comes in as a substitute for coin, it may, with a small proportion of money as a support, raise prices at home to the pitch which equal amounts of labour and abstinence fetch in the foreign market.

There has, then, been a plurality of causes, besides the increased quantity of gold in the world, augmenting what for shortness we may call the money-demand for German commodities,—the increased industrial and commercial powers of the Germans, the more rapid circulation of money, and the rapid augmentation of the circulating medium by a volume of credit. But the question of prices is a question concerning the supply of commodities no less than the money demand. An increased money demand does not of necessity raise the prices of commodities. That depends on the conditions affecting the supply of each class of thing, for which there is a greater money demand. A nation like the United States, possessing a vast territory of prodigious fertility, might, with peace and free trade, see the prices of almost all things falling in the markets of California itself. An important class of considerations, connected with the rise of prices in both Germany and England, is contained in the question Dr. Laspeyres has raised: 'What commodities become constantly dearer in the lapse of periods of time?' Adam Smith has given an answer which at least points in the right direction, if it involves an erroneous distinction between corn and other sorts of rude produce in the case of old countries which do not import the former: 'If you except corn and such other vegetables as are raised altogether by human industry, all other sorts of rude produce—cattle, poultry, game of all kinds, the useful fossils and minerals of the earth, &c.—naturally grow dearer as the society advances in wealth and improvement.' Among the sorts of rude produce particularly referred to by Adam Smith in his elaborate exposition of the subject as naturally growing dearer in the lapse of periods of time is wood, and German statistics afford an illustration. In Professor Rau's 'Grundsätze der Volkswirthschaftslehre,' the following prices of a given measure of the same wood at Würtemberg, in successive periods, are given:—

	Fl.	Kr.
1640—1680	0	37
1690—1730	0	57
1740—1780	2	14
1790—1830	8	22

Dr. Engel, again, gives statistics which show the continuous rise of carpenter's wood in another part of Germany since 1830:

	1830	1840	1851	1860	1865
Carpenter's wood per klafter, in silbergroschen	50	75	102	130	180

Of course, the rise in price of things which grow naturally dearer in the progress of society is enhanced by any sudden increase of money and fall in its general value, and it then becomes impossible to apportion the influence of the different agencies—increased consumption with growing scarcity, or greater cost of production on the one hand, and greater abundance of money on the other. Every artificial obstruction to the supply of important commodities inflicts an aggravated loss on those whose money incomes remain stationary while money is falling in value. The rise in the price of animal food in Germany, where there is a wide distribution of landed property and a simple system of land transfer, may be ascribed mainly to natural causes; and a large part of the German population are either gainers by it as sellers, or unaffected by it as producers for their own consumption. It is otherwise in a country like England, in which laws in the supposed interest of an insignificant number limit the supply of land in the market, diminish its produce, and make food unnaturally dear. The gold question has added enormously to the importance of the land question in England, and the classes with fixed incomes are especially concerned in both.

Persons with stationary incomes in this country, are, as it were, between several fires. They suffer from high prices, whether they spring from abundance of gold, from natural dearth of commodities, or from the increase of population and wealth. They suffer along with other classes, and the prosperity of other classes is a calamity to them. The main resources they had to look to on the discovery of the new gold mines were reforms in the laws relating to land in their own country on the one hand, augmenting and cheapening the produce of land, and industrial and economical progress in other countries on the other, assigning to these the principal share of the new treasure. Of all parts of Europe, England is that in which the fall in the value of money, measured in commodities—I do not say measured in labour—ought to have been least sensible, on account of the nature of its imports, the natural cheapening of manufactures, the improvements in husbandry which legislation might have indirectly effected, the example which all the rest of the civilized world had set with respect to land laws, and the immense demand for the treasure from the new mines which peace, liberty, industry, and trade might have opened up in other countries to circulate a vast increase of produce at much higher pecuniary value than remoteness and poverty have hitherto allowed them to bear. The new area in Europe, not to speak of Asia, which civilization would open for the employment of new money is enormous. The inequalities in the local prices of Germany, the rise in its most progressive localities, the comparatively low prices in its backward localities, point to one of the chief outlets to which people here, with fixed incomes, might have reasonably looked for the absorption of the new gold. Low as prices still are in many places in Germany, they are lower over great districts of Austria, and yet lower over the greater part of Russia, two countries, moreover, where inconvertible paper currencies resist the circulation of the precious metals.

As matters stand, the increase of money in England has far outstripped the increase of some of the most important commodities. And when one reflects that the money comes from a new world of peace and liberty, in which production never flags, while the demand for it in **Europe is** limited by the policy of an old military **world,** and the supply of commodities by the law **of** an old feudal world, the prospect before those with whom money does not increase with house rent and the price of food, seems the reverse of encouraging.

XXIII.

PRICES IN ENGLAND IN 1873.

(Fortnightly Review, June 1, 1873.)

The movement of prices in England is a less simple matter than the reasoning of some eminent economists indicates. The advance in the cost of living is considerably greater than appears from their calculations, and the new gold is but one of the causes acting on prices. An attempt has been made to measure the effect of the gold by comparing the average prices of a number of important commodities during the period since the new mines were discovered, with the average prices of a previous period. Mr. Jevons, who adds rare mathematical powers to high economic attainments, has adopted this method; but in inquiries of this kind, the truth is seldom reached until several methods have been tried, and probable truth only, not mathematical precision, is attainable. The method of averages fails in several ways. It does not show the real movement of prices or the real depreciation of money; the tables omit some of the chief elements of the cost of living; the prices compared are wholesale prices, while the purchasing power of an income depends on retail prices; and, by ascribing the whole rise of prices to the new gold, this method conceals the material fact that the gold is only one of a plurality of causes lately tending to raise them.

A comparison of the average prices of successive periods of years may be useful to indicate the total profit and loss on transactions in the periods compared, but is delusive as a criterion of the change in the value of money. Suppose that in the first decade after the discovery of the new mines prices had risen twenty per cent., and in the second decade had fallen back to their old level, money at the end of the twenty years would be of the same value as at the beginning, yet the average prices of the whole twenty years would show a depreciation of twenty-five per cent. Suppose, on the other hand, that prices had risen steadily during both decades so as to range fifty per cent. higher at their close, the real fall in the purchasing power of money would be fifty per cent., yet an average would show a fall only of twenty-five, that is to say, only half the real fall. Take, as exemplifying the second supposition, the movement of prices in the sixteenth century, after the discovery of the American mines. Prices rose continuously in some parts of Europe until money had sunk to a third of its former value; here an average, including the lower prices of the earlier years of the movement, would far under-estimate the real depreciation. So in England now, if the cost of living to large classes be much greater than during most of the years since the new gold mines were opened, the average prices of the whole period afford no measure of the real diminution in the purchasing power of fixed incomes. If house rent, the wages of servants, indoor and outdoor, animal food of all kinds, coal, washing, many articles of clothing, horses and horse-keep, cost now in the aggregate, by a succession of rises, one half more than they did a generation ago, a householder would be a good deal out in his reckoning were he to measure the present and future purchasing power, say of a thousand a-year, by the average prices of the past twenty-five years. The averages referred to, moreover, omit some of the chief items in the cost of living. No account, for example, is taken of the great rise in house rent and wages in recent years, nor of the additional charges which retailers make to consumers, partly to cover higher wages, shop-rents, and other items in the cost of their own business. The recent prices of many important articles, e.g., butchers' meat, have risen far more than prices in the wholesale market. The actual increase in the cost of living to large classes, therefore, far exceeds the advance shown in tables which Mr. Jevons and the Economist have published. The living of the poorest class (of women especially), who pay no wages, rarely eat animal food, and whose chief expenditure is on bread, sugar, and tea, may, notwithstanding the rise of **coal**, cost no more than formerly; but where the scale of expenditure ascends to servants, meat and butter every day, and a tolerable **house,** the change for the worse in the purchasing **power** of **fixed** incomes makes itself more **heavily** felt than any **statistics** show.

Free trade created in this country a demand for a **larger** currency, **but** the chief cause which has prevented a ruinous rise **of** prices in England **is that** other parts **of** the world have absorbed the bulk of the gold **and** silver **sent into** circulation. Take a single fact. **In the twenty-two years, 1850-1871,** inclusive, the imports of **gold and silver into British India** amounted to **£235,000,000;** the amount exported **was** only £27,000,000, **and the mints of the** three Presidencies coined **upwards of £145,000,000.** In that period, therefore, India alone absorbed £208,000,000's **worth** of gold and silver for **currency and other purposes;** that is to say, an equivalent to **two-fifths of the addition made to the** stock of **the** precious metals by the new gold mines **in the** twenty-two **years.** What probability is there that the development of Indian trade will be such in the next twenty-**two years** as to absorb £208,000,000 more?* The question forms **part of a** larger one; what chance is there that, for **the** future, **the** progress of the **rest of the** world in **means of locomotion, production,** and trade will be such as **to divert from England all but a** small fraction **of** the new treasure the **mines may** yield?

The international and local distribution **of the** precious metals in the **last twenty** years has followed, **in the main,** the path of **the industrial** and commercial development abroad. Steamers, railways, **the** rise of manufactures, the growth of trade, internal and **external,** have **caused a** prodigious increase in **the** demand of foreign **countries for money to** carry on their increased business, and **represent the rise in both** the quantity and the market value **of their** productions. **The** same change in the distribution of money has taken place over **a great part**

---

* Sir Richard Temple's able financial statement for 1873-4, **shows** that in 1872-3 the influx of treasure had almost ceased. The Mints **of** Calcutta and Bombay were in **a state of** inaction.

of the world which took place earlier in England itself. Places formerly remote, undeveloped, and backward, ill-furnished with both means of locomotion and money, have gained access by steam to the best markets, have advanced in both industry and skill, have ceased to be poor and cheap, and have made vast additions to their currencies. But many of the foreign channels which railways and commerce have created for the streams of new money are now full—some full to overflowing. Many parts of the Continent, which not long ago were noted for cheapness, are now as notorious for dearness;* and although a great part of Europe has yet to be opened up by railways, it were rash to assume that the progress made in the next twenty years will be equal to that of the last twenty. The west of Europe is already reticulated with railways; the east will hardly in two decades overtake the west, and during their construction new railways raise the prices of English iron and coal, though when finished they find new outlets for money. An eminent authority points, indeed, to possible absorbents for much of the future gold in the resumption of payments in specie by France and the United States on the one hand, and the gold coinage of Germany on the other. The fact, however, which actually confronts us is, that France, the European country which had hitherto absorbed most of the new gold, is now driving it from its currency; and that Germany is exchanging silver for gold—the silver will be liberated for circulation elsewhere—but what we have to look to is, not the amount of gold only in the world, but the amount of gold, silver, and credit together, remembering that a great rise of prices in England can be brought about with a small importation of specie. Suppose that English iron and coal, for example, sell fifty per cent. dearer in the foreign market by reason of the abundance of the precious metals abroad, they may sell as much dearer in the home market, mainly by an expansion of

---

* See, as regards Germany, 'Prices in Germany,' Fortnightly Review, November, 1872. It is greatly to be desired that the eminent French economists who have discussed the effects of the new gold mines, M. Chevalier, M. Levasseur, and more recently M. Victor Bonnet, would resume the investigation in connexion with later changes of prices in France.

the credit circulation; and other English productions will then rise in price.

Other causes, besides the abundance of the precious metals, have raised the cost of living in England. The method of averages assumes the new gold to be the sole cause of the rise in prices arrived at, on the ground that 'the average must, in all reasonable probability, represent some single influence acting on all the commodities.' But why not a plurality of influences? Mr. Jevons's own work on coal proves the existence of one other cause besides the new gold. Mr. Tooke's History of Prices supplies a still more decisive example. The high range of prices from 1793 to 1815 was ascribed by many persons exclusively to the over-issue of notes, and the consequent depreciation of the currency. Mr. Tooke demonstrated that the main causes of the rise lay in conditions affecting commodities, not money, and that the depreciation of the currency never exceeded 30 per cent., while corn, to take one commodity, stood at one time at 177s. the quarter. Mr. Newmarch has done good service accordingly, by insisting from the first on an investigation of the conditions of demand and supply affecting commodities, before coming to any conclusion respecting the influence on prices of the increase of gold. By means of such an investigation only can we ascertain whether the causes of the rise of prices are permanent or temporary, and, what is more important, whether they are, as in the case of coal and animal food, to some extent within our control, or, like the fertility of the gold mines, altogether beyond it. It should, however, always be borne in mind, in speaking of demand and supply, that it is only in the shape of money-demand that the new gold can ever come into circulation, and that if there be independent conditions of supply and demand sufficient to cause a rise of prices, a great addition to the quantity of money in circulation must magnify the rise in proportion. But some reasoners go beyond this. They urge that since the demand which raises prices can be no other than a money-demand, to trace a rise of prices to an increase of demand is simply to trace it to the new gold. A rise of some commodities, it has been added, would, but for the new gold mines, have

2 A

been compensated by a fall of others, since the total amount of money expended would otherwise not have increased. It is not so, however. The total expenditure of money will naturally advance with the increase of population, though no new sources of money be discovered, and prices may rise without any discovery of more fertile mines. Suppose the population of England to grow from twenty to thirty millions, English exports and money returns increasing nearly in the same ratio, and the average money-income of the population continuing at, say, £10 per head. Though individual incomes will not rise on this supposition, yet the total money-income of the nation will increase with the population from £200,000,000 to £300,000,000. Suppose, then, that half the income of each individual, on the average, is spent on house-rent, animal food, leather, coal, and some of its products, not an acre of land will have been added to the island, and house-rents may rise; meat, butter, milk, and some other products of land may grow considerably dearer; coal may have to be fetched from greater depths or poorer mines at high cost. There may thus be a considerable rise in the cost of living, and a corresponding fall in the purchasing-power of fixed incomes, as the consequence merely of the growth of population. Let new gold mines of extraordinary fertility come at the same time into play—let money-incomes rise on the average from £10 to £15 per head, and the rise of prices may beggar the classes whose income are stationary.

The actual situation of matters in England is, then, that a number of causes, of which the new gold is only one, have raised the cost of living, and that the cause which has hitherto diverted from England the chief effects of the new gold mines can hardly be counted on. One result with which we may be threatened may be exemplified by the fact that the race of scholars in Germany is said to be in danger of dying out before the rise of prices and the diminished power of fixed incomes. We cannot, however, control the production of gold, we cannot hasten the development of foreign countries, and thus provide for its absorption. The more need, therefore, to do what lies in our power at home to check the increasing cost of chief staples of expenditure, such as coal and the produce of land. Even Lord Derby tells us that the produce of land is only half what it should be; and the bearing of our land system on the matter is sufficiently illustrated by the statement in the last Agricultural Returns of Great Britain, that a decrease of 3,592,600 sheep, or 12 per cent. in the whole stock of sheep in Great Britain, took place between 1868 and 1871, chiefly if not entirely through the want of irrigation and grass.

It is not in political economy to tell how the cost of extracting coal can be diminished, or how the enormous waste of fuel may be lessened. But it might at least be expected of economists not to foster extravagant prices by fictions and fallacies. The equality of profits is a fiction under which producers and dealers are enabled to hide inordinate gains; at one time by keeping down wages, at another by charging exorbitant prices. The assumption that an omniscient competition equalizes profits has done infinite mischief, both theoretical and practical, by checking inquiry into the actual phenomena of trade and the real distribution of wealth. The new gold itself is a novel condition from which an eminent economist anticipates a disturbance of relative prices and profits for thirty or forty years. What sort of equality is that which is liable to disturbance for more than a generation by even one of the numberless changes which industrial progress and discovery (to say nothing of political events) are perpetually importing into the conditions of trade? In London alone seventy-four new trades appear in this year's Directory, and it may be affirmed that before they were added not a capitalist in London knew so much as the names of the trades already existing. How then can it be maintained that capitalists are so well acquainted with the situation and prospects of every occupation that their competition equalizes profits? The truth is we are almost in total darkness respecting the profits of many long-established businesses, and this darkness (which is often the cover of exorbitant prices) is due in great measure to an influential school of economists who have taken away the key of knowledge—the investigation of facts—which Adam Smith and Mr. Mill had put into our hands.

XXIV.

THE MOVEMENTS OF AGRICULTURAL WAGES IN EUROPE.

(*Fortnightly Review, June* 1, 1874.)

THE question presenting itself in the Eastern Counties is really no mere local question or struggle, no mere trial of the right or power of English agricultural labourers to raise wages by combination, important and significant as is its assertion. It is a particular phase of a movement, or series of movements, general over Europe, arising everywhere mainly from similar causes, and exhibiting everywhere some similar phenomena, along with phenomena due to special causes in particular countries and localities. Farmers in the Eastern Counties no doubt imagine themselves in presence of an extraordinary difficulty. But there have been no combinations or strikes of agricultural labourers on the Continent, yet complaints of the rise of agricultural wages have been heard for years; it was one of the chief causes of the late French Enquête Agricole; a serious alarm on account of it is now felt in most parts of Germany (notwithstanding a recent general fall in the price of labour), and in some parts of Belgium. A survey of the principal facts in several representative countries may aid us to estimate the nature and strength of the forces with which the farmers in the Eastern Counties have to contend, and to judge how far general and permanent, how far local and temporary, causes are at work. The chief reason, however, for the present investigation is, that it is not an agricultural labour question only which is finding its issue at home and abroad, but one connected with all the most important economic phenomena and problems of the age, with the course of industrial and commercial development in Europe, the amount and distribution of money and its representatives, the changes in prices, the movements of population, the new ideas and powers of the working classes, and the operation of land laws and systems of rural economy; though some of these great subjects can only be glanced at in the following pages.

Two not unrelated phenomena in all the chief countries of Europe, are a remarkable rise in the money wages of agricultural labour in recent years, and prodigious diversities in the rates paid in different parts of each country.

In Belgium, where farm **wages had been rising** for twenty years, they have lately sprung in some districts from 2fr. 50c. to 3fr. 50c. and upwards. In France, M. de Lavergne estimated the general rise in the decade 1855-1865 at 20 per cent., but it was much greater in many places, and continued down to the war. **Dr. Baur** and Baron Von der Goltz put it at 60 per cent. in the north of France in the last twenty-six years; and one cannot doubt that the rise throughout the country would have been greater and would be still going on, **but for** the late war, the drain of money which has followed it, and the uncertain state of political affairs. In Germany there are four different classes of agricultural labourers (Dienstleute, Gesinde, Einlieger, and Haüsler), **and** a calculation of the rise in wages is much embarrassed by differences in **the modes** of payment, and payments in kind. For the present purpose **we need** concern ourselves only with the earnings measured in **money of the** two classes (called Einlieger and Haüsler, the **latter having** cottages of their own, and the former being lodgers) who **share** the designations of Tagelöhner and freie Arbeiter, day-labourers and free labourers. Baron Von der Goltz, Professor of Rural Economy in the University of Königsberg, a writer of great practical experience, in the new edition of his work on the German agricultural labourer's question, measures in money the rise of the wages of the classes of labourers referred to at 100 per cent. in the Rhine Province, and from 50 to 60 **per cent.** in the eastern province of Prussia, in the last ten to twenty years.* A table of agricultural wages in the last number of

---

* Die ländliche Arbeiterfrage. Zweite Auflage, 1874, p. 125.

the Journal of the Agricultural Society for Rhenish Prussia puts the rise in one district at from 75 to 100 per cent. in the last four years, in another district at **200 per** cent. in the last twenty years, and in a third at 200 per cent. in the last ten years.* At Tübingen in Würtemberg, Dr. Gustav Cohn tells me the rate was 1s. 2d. a day in 1850-1855; 1s. 4d. in 1860-1865; 1s. 8½d. in 1866-1870; and is 2s. 0½d. in 1874. At Wissen, in the Rhine Province, on the border of Westphalia, Mr. W. Wynne, a resident English engineer, states: 'Ten years ago agricultural wages were 1s. 2⅓d. a day, measured in money; about that time railway works commenced, and they rose very quickly. At present they are about 2s. a day—a fall after the exaggerated rates of last year.' Mr. White, British Consul at Dantzig, one of the best informed and most intelligent Englishmen in Germany, although remarking (April 27) that 'the price of labour in Germany has quite lately entered into a retrogressive stage,' measures the general rise in the price of agricultural labour at from 50 to 100 per cent. in the last twenty years, and speaks of great alarm on the part of farmers with respect to the future. The foregoing estimates are in accordance both with facts ascertained by myself in several visits to Germany, and with recent information from authorities so high as Professor Nasse of Bonn, member of the Prussian Parliament, Mr. W. T. Mulvany of Düsseldorf,† and Herr Bueck, formerly secretary to an East Prussian Agricultural Society, and now to an important society in Rhenish Prussia. It may be concluded from these authentic data that the rise of farm wages in some parts of Germany much exceeds the rise, according to Mr. Caird's estimate, in England.

A second European phenomenon is prodigious inequality in the prices of agricultural labour in different parts of each country. In England they varied at the end of 1873, according to Mr. Caird, from an average of 12s. a week in the southern

---

* Zeitschrift des landwirthschaftlichen Vereins für Rheinpreussen. Mai 1874, p. 158.

† Formerly Poor Law Commissioner in Ireland, but for many years past the chief of great mining and other industrial enterprises in the Ruhr Basin and the Rhine Province.

to 18s. a week in the northern counties; these averages, however, covering much greater local diversities. In 1870 they varied from 7s. a week in Dorsetshire to 22s. in Yorkshire and Northumberland, and they still vary from 11s. to 25s. In Belgium the actual diversities are thus described in a letter from M. Emile de Laveleye: 'In the Campine the rate of agricultural wages is 1fr. 25c. a day in summer, and 1fr. in winter, without food or other addition. This rate extends to the environs of Hasselt and St. Trond, four leagues from Liége. In Flanders the rate is 1fr. 50c.; in the Ardenne it is 2fr. 50c. In the coal and metallurgic basins of Liége, Charleroi, Mons, it is from 3fr. to 3fr. 50c.; and in a commune near Liége it is actually at this moment (May 1, 1874), 3fr. a day and the labourer's food into the bargain.' With respect to Holland I possess no more recent statistics than those given in the documents relating to foreign countries in the Report of the late French Enquête Agricole, where it is stated that the rate of wages varies from 1fr. in some provinces to 2f. in others. With regard to France, statistics exist in abundance. Dividing the country into six regions, M. de Lavergne, in 1865, estimated the earnings of the French agricultural labourer at 600fr. a year in the north-west and south-east, at 360fr. in the north-east, and only at 300fr. in the west, south-west, and centre. These figures, being averages struck over many departments, included much wider variations. According to the Enquête Décennale, published in 1868, wages were 3fr. 14c. a day, with 4fr. 35c. in harvest, in the Department of the Seine, 1fr. 14c., with 1fr. 68c. in harvest, in the Côtes du Nord. In 1869 Mr. J. S. Mill informed me that the rate about Avignon, where he resided, was 3fr. a day throughout the year. In the same year I found it as low as 1fr. a day in more than one place in Brittany; and Lord Brabazon's Report to the Foreign Office in 1872 gives an average rate of 2fr. 50c. in the Seine, 1fr. 13c. in the Côtes du Nord, and 1fr. 15c. in the Morbihan.* At present the tendency to a rise throughout France, which other-

---

* Further Reports, &c., respecting the Condition of the Industrial Classes and the Purchase-power of Money in Foreign Countries. 1872, pp. 43, 44.

wise might show itself, is arrested by political uncertainty; but at four or five leagues from Paris, as the eminent economist, M. Victor Bonnet, informs me, the rate is 3fr. 60c. a day; at from twenty to fifty leagues from Paris it varies from 2fr. 50c. to 2fr.; and in some remote parts of the country without a railway, it may perhaps be as low still as from 1fr. 25c. to 1fr.

In Germany the lowest rates of agricultural wages are found in the eastern provinces of Silesia and Posen. In one district of Silesia they averaged in 1873 only 8½d. a day in summer, and 7d. a day in winter; while in a district of the Rhine Province they were from 2s. 6d. to 4s. 6d. a day in summer, and from 2s. 2½d. to 3s. in winter, and by task-work the labourer in this district earned from 2s. 6d. to 6s. a day, according to the work and the season. In the Rhine Province itself prodigious diversities are found, for examples of which see the table of wages already referred to in the Zeitschrift des landwirthschaftlichen Vereins für Rheinpreussen for May, 1874. Even these instances fail to show the full extent of the inequality of the money earnings of an agricultural labourer's family in different parts of Germany. German women take an active part in farm work, and their wages vary from place to place, like the wages of their husbands and fathers. The number of working and earning days, again, is considerably greater in most parts of west Germany than in the north-east of the empire, although the length and severity of the winter in the latter region demands a larger expenditure in fuel and clothing. It is, too, much easier for the farm labourer in south-western than in north-eastern Germany to acquire a plot of land of his own, and the milder climate and better markets of the former enable him to make a larger addition to his wages by its produce than he could in the latter.

The inquiry follows, What are the causes of the two phenomena described—which might be easily shown to present themselves also in several other countries—the immense rise in the price of agricultural labour, and its prodigious local diversities?

The rise is supposed by many persons to be sufficiently accounted for by emigration and migration to towns—two agencies of great importance, but by no means adequate to account for the phenomenon. Emigration, in the first place, cannot have caused the rise in France or in Belgium, from neither of which has there been any emigration to speak of. From Germany the total emigration has been considerable, but the natural increase of population has more than replaced it; it has taken place chiefly in the parts of the empire where wages has risen least, and there has been but little emigration, if any, in recent years from the localities where wages are highest, and where they have risen most; in these localities immigration, in fact, not emigration, is the conspicuous movement. It is worthy of notice, moreover, that the chief emigration has been from provinces and districts where the population is thinnest, where large estates prevail, where little farms are fewest, and where the labourer despairs of getting a plot of land of his own.* In England, again, emigration has not hitherto much diminished the number of agricultural labourers, probably not at all in the districts where agricultural wages are highest; and though indirectly emigration from Ireland has had an appreciable effect on English wages by diminishing Irish immigration, the great recent rise in money wages in the southern counties certainly cannot be referred chiefly to that cause.

The migration of agricultural labourers to towns and mining and manufacturing districts is a more potent agent, the economic and social significance of which in several aspects can hardly be exaggerated. But it is demonstrable that it affords only a partial explanation of the rise in the price of agricultural labour. There has been no considerable migration from Flanders, yet agricultural wages have risen. In Germany, the migration of the rural population to Berlin and the chief industrial towns and districts in the west has been very great; but were that the sole cause of the rise in agricultural wages, how are we to account for the still greater rise of wages in those very towns and manufacturing districts? In France, likewise, a great rise of town wages preceded, and, indeed,

---

* Von der Goltz, Die ländliche Arbeiterfrage, pp. 114-121.

caused the migration of the rural population which continued down to the war. And in England, town, mining, and manufacturing wages have, although the movement is very unequal, on the whole risen greatly along with the price of agricultural labour; instead of sustaining a fall, as the migration theory, taken alone, would import. How is it, moreover, that farmers have been enabled to pay so much higher prices for labour in all the countries referred to? Whence has come the additional money to pay them, and to raise at the same time the prices of commodities all over Europe? The general rise in the money wages of agricultural labour must be connected with this general rise in the prices of commodities, and with the chief cause of the latter phenomenon, the immense augmentation and the more rapid circulation of money and its representatives since the new gold mines were discovered, and since railways and other inventions began to spread over Europe. To exemplify the rise in the prices of articles coming more or less within the consumption of the German labourer, Mr. W. Wynne has furnished me with the following table of prices, in silbergroschen, at Wissen in the Rhine Province (5 silbergroschen = 6d.):—

	1853.	1863.	1873-4.
Butter, per lb.	$3\frac{1}{2}$ sgr.	$4\frac{1}{2}$ sgr.	13—14 sgr.
Eggs, per dozen	2 ,,	3 ,,	9—10 ,,
Beef, per lb.	3 ,,	$4\frac{1}{2}$,,	7 ,,
Veal	$1\frac{5}{6}$—2 ,,	Not stated.	4— 5 ,,
Potatoes, per cwt.	10 ,,	—	25 ,,
Linen, per ell	$2\frac{1}{2}$,,	—	$4\frac{1}{2}$,,
Cloth ,,	30—35 ,,	—	60—70 ,,
Coffee, per lb.	5—6 ,,	—	10—12 ,,

As an instance of the rise of prices in north-east Germany, Herr Bueck states with respect to the district of Gumbinnen, in the province of Prussia, 'The Regierungsbezirk Gumbinnen obtained its first railway in 1860, and the price of one pound of butter was then 4 to 5 silbergroschen, whereas at present it is 10 to 13 silbergroschen; the price of beef, which was then $2\frac{1}{2}$ to 3 silbergroschen, is now 6 silbergroschen.' But although the rise in the prices of commodities, as well as in money wages, at home and abroad, and in both country and town, proves that one general agency is the increase and the greater activity of money and its representatives, the explanation thus afforded is by no means adequate to account for the movements of agricultural wages. The highest German authorities, scientific and practical, Professors Nasse and Von der Goltz, Mr. Mulvany, and Mr. Consul White, are agreed that the rise in money wages in Germany exceeds the rise in the price of the articles of the labourer's consumption.* The changes in wages, again, from year to year, and from decade to decade, do not correspond with the changes in prices. Not only has the price of rye, for example, which is the chief food of the German farm labourer, not risen in proportion to wages, but in the decade 1861-71 rye and all other cereals were cheaper than in 1851-61; yet money wages continually rose. Nor do the local variations of wages in Germany, or any other country, follow or correspond with the variations in the prices of commodities. Food and clothing are not dearer in the coal basin of the Meuse than in Flanders, yet agricultural labour is twice as well paid; and food is rather cheaper in the Ardenne than in Flanders, yet the farm labourer is paid about 75 per cent. more for inferior work. It is in fact impossible to get to the root of the rise in wages, without entering into the causes of the other striking phenomenon, their great local diversities.

The causes of this second phenomenon are both general and local; some common to all countries in Europe, some peculiar to particular countries, some to particular regions or districts. The most general causes are, first, the unequal natural advantages of different regions and localities for manufacture or trade; secondly, their unequal development, especially by means of locomotion, and, above all, railways. Capital, money and its representatives, and the demand for labour, have increased most

* Professor Nasse says, 'That the economic condition of the agricultural labourer has improved here, and that the rise of wages has surpassed the rise of prices of the necessaries of life, admit of no doubt. The condition of the labourers who, as here is often the case, have a little property in land, has especially improved.' From another part of the Rhine Province Mr. W. Wynne writes, 'The rise is to a considerable extent a real one, as the labourer now lives better, and clothes himself better, takes more holidays, gets oftener drunk, &c.'

where the means of production and the means of communication with the best markets have improved most, where coal, iron, and mechanical power have multiplied the produce of the human hand, and where railways and other modes of communication have made rapidest progress. Broad exemplifications of the influence of these two sets of conditions (which are closely related, for superior natural advantages attract the means of development) are to be seen on every side at home and abroad. Many years ago, Mr. Caird pointed out that a line 'following the line of coal' divided England into two regions of high and low agricultural wages, and his recent statistics show that the same line of division still exists:—

'Average weekly wages in England:	1850.	1873.
Northern counties	11s. 6d.	18s. 0d.
Southern counties	8s. 5d.	12s. 0d.'*

In Belgium a similar line divides a region without mineral wealth, including Flanders and the Campine, from one rich in coal, iron, and manufactures, where wages range from 100 to 300 per cent. above the rates in the former region. In Germany, the country above all others in which the study of the subject abounds in interest and instruction, the line between high and low agricultural wages drawn by Von der Goltz is one between northern and southern Germany;† the former being the region of low, and the latter of high agricultural wages. The rates of wages certainly justify this division, but they vary greatly from east to west in the north—from 1s. 8d. a day in Mecklenburg to 8d. a day in parts of Silesia and Posen—and a much more marked and characteristic division lies between north-eastern and south-western Germany. From Dresden westward, wages range higher than eastward, but the main region of high farm-wages is from the neighbourhood of Frankfort-on-the-Maine to

---

* Letter of Mr. Caird, Times, Jan. 3, 1874.

† In North Germany Von der Goltz includes the provinces of Prussia, Pomerania, Posen, Silesia, Brandenburg, Mecklenburg, Sleswig-Holstein, Brunswick, Oldenburg, Hanover, together with the northernmost parts of the Rhine Province and of Westphalia; the remainder of the present German empire forming South Germany, according to this division.

the Ruhr Basin, thence to Düsseldorf and Aachen, and southward through Rhineland to Baden.* In this region of high wages itself there are immense inequalities, but some of them form no exception to the principle of the division, others fall under another principle, likewise connected with natural advantages, which will be presently indicated. Speaking generally, the south-western region, whose boundary has just been roughly marked out, is the main region of German industrial and commercial enterprise, communication by steam, general activity, intelligence, and wealth. Vicinity to the chief countries and markets of western Europe, numerous lines of railway, a river crowded with steamers, coal, iron, and their products, cause a greater abundance and more rapid circulation of currency, a greater demand and competition for labour of all kinds, and a generally higher price for agricultural as well as town or mechanical labour, than is to be found in the north-east of the empire, which lies remote from the traffic, civilization, and progress of the western world, is much less completely provided with railways, and is in a more primitive condition as regards customs, ideas, and industrial life.† Take as an example of the influence of this diversity in the economic conditions of the two regions, the rates of agricultural wages in the districts of Düsseldorf on the Rhine, on the one hand, and Gumbinnen, in the province of Prussia, on the other hand, where the soil is good, but no manufactures or trade on a large scale exist:—

		Düsseldorf.		Gumbinnen.	
		s. d.	s. d.	s. d.	s. d.
Summer wages, per diem,—	Men	2 6	to 4 0	1 0	to 1 9¼
,, ,,	Women	1 6	to 2 0	0 6	to 0 9½
Winter wages ,,	Men	1 6	to 2 0	0 7¼	to 1 0
,, ,,	Women	1 0	to 1 6	0 4¾	to 0 6

* Mr. Consul White, who has an extraordinary knowledge of the industrial economy of Germany, remarks on this view, as to which I lately consulted him, 'What you say of the south-west is, I think, on reflection, the correct representation, and I quite agree in your delimitation. An English employer of labour, who has travelled over those parts quite lately, told me that at Nürnberg he found wages a trifle higher than at Dantzig, but from thence he found them highest at Frankfort-on-the-Maine, the Ruhr Basin, and Cologne. This tallies also with your views in the essay on "Prices in Germany" in the Fortnightly Review, November, 1872.'

† Low railway freights for raw material have been one cause of the indus-

The same principle shows itself in local inequalities within each of the two great regions. The price of farm labour is much higher close to Berlin than throughout the greater part of Brandenburg, and considerably higher about Dantzig than in most rural districts of the Province of Prussia. It is in like manner 75 per cent. higher in the Ruhr Basin, and near towns like Cologne, than in purely agricultural districts of Westphalia and the Rhine Province. One remarkable exception to the general principle (which, however, seems less real than apparent) is, that Silesia, the eastern province in which there is most manufacture and trade, and which possesses considerable mines, is also the province in which the price of farm labour is lowest. Mr. Consul White, remarking that 'it has always astonished him that Silesia, an industrial centre, has the lowest agricultural wages of all Germany,' adds, that he is told the cause lies in the cheap and thrifty modes of living of the peasantry, and suggests that the proximity of Poland and of Austria may also partly account for it in Upper Silesia. Von der Goltz also refers the low scale of Silesian wages partly to the low standard of expenditure of the inhabitants, partly to the relatively dense population. If, in addition to these conditions, we reflect that this immense province is for the most part untraversed by railways, is contiguous to a vast region backward in that as in other respects, lies remote both from maritime ports and from western markets, we may fairly consider the exception only a partial one; though it proves that there are economic conditions which no single generalization will cover, and the roots of which may reach far down in past history. 'Every province,' says the illustrious rural economist, M. de Lavergne, of his own country, 'has its history, which has powerfully acted on its economic development;'* and the observation is yet truer of Germany than of France.

But another potent cause of inequalities in agricultural wages alike in Germany and in many other countries, lies in local trial progress, wealth, and high wages of western Germany. Should the attempt to raise them which is now being made, be carried out, it is the opinion of high authorities that a serious decline in the rate of industrial progress will ensue.

* 'Economie Rurale de la France,' 3rd edition, p. 62.

diversities of climate and soil, a cause which the more merits attention that its operation is diametrically contrary to an old economic doctrine. It is where the work of cultivation has least variety and interest, where life has few charms, where winter is longest and coldest, where the wage-earning days are fewest, where the labourer finds it hardest to supplement his earnings by the produce of a little farm of his own, that the price of agricultural labour per diem is lowest in Germany, and Von der Goltz is certainly right in treating the climate as one cause of the low rate of wages in the north-east; though the chief cause seems, as certainly, the one previously pointed out, on which he does not dwell. In the south-western region itself we find this second class of natural causes in active operation, wages being usually much lower in barren mountainous districts than in those warm, fruitful valleys and plains which enable both the farmer and the labourer with a plot of ground of his own to rear close to excellent markets a variety of rich plants, tobacco, chicory, garden vegetables, hemp, which will not grow in less generous zones. After citing a number of local rates of agricultural wages in Würtemberg, Von der Goltz adds :—' From these data it follows that the rates in Würtemberg vary materially. In the least favourably situated districts they average from 47 to 49 kreuzers a day; in those most favourably situated they rise to 78-80 kreuzers. This fact meets one in all parts of middle and south Germany, in which climate and cultivation exhibit such diversities.' It is a fact to which an analogy may be found in these islands, in which wages and profit, as well as rent, cœteris paribus, usually are higher on exceptionally good land; all three, and not rent only, falling on barren and mountainous soils, whatever economic theories may suppose.* The great inequalities of wages hence arising in Germany are no doubt partially compensated by the descent of the mountain labourer into the plains and valleys at harvest and other seasons, when there is an unusual supply of work; but throughout the rest of the year his earnings are smaller, while his wants are greater,

---

* In the United Kingdom itself wages, profit, and rent are all three commonly highest, cœteris paribus, where the land is best.

on account of the cold, than those of the inhabitants of the lower districts. Baron Von der Goltz—almost the only economic defect of whose book is its tendency to sweep averages, the besetting sin of both statisticians and economists—seems much to overrate the compensatory influence of this periodical migration. The Irish labourer used, in like manner, to migrate to England for the harvest, but that did not raise his earnings to the English level; it only enabled him to exist for the rest of the year on Irish wages. Assuredly in Germany money wages have by no means followed the equitable principles of which economists, in their thirst after generalization rather than truth, and under the influence of eighteenth century notions of natural laws of equality and uniformity, have dreamt. It is where the skies are brightest, the air most genial, the work of husbandry pleasantest, life in every way most agreeable, that the price of farm labour is highest. It is here, too, that the labourer finds it easiest to get a property of his own, and that its produce is richest. 'The farther,' says Von der Goltz, ' we proceed from north and east to south and west, the more numerous is the class of landowning agricultural labourers, and the better is the condition of those who are so.' The fluctuations in the price of labour are no doubt greater in the industrial districts of the south-west than in north-east Germany, partly for a reason not referred to by Von der Goltz, but mentioned to me by Professor Nasse, that where small farming predominates, there is a less regular supply of labour in the market, and partly, I am disposed to think, because both demand and supply are here affected by the fluctuations in manufacture and trade. But it is beyond all question that the permanent influence of the causes which produce these variations has been favourable to the agricultural labourer, and that, notwithstanding them, his condition has been a continuously improving one. The remark which Consul White makes with respect to the farm labourer throughout Germany, is especially applicable to him in Rhineland and the Ruhr Basin: 'Improved civilization has produced greater demands and requirements in this class; all authorities agree that they live, on the whole, better than they used to, and insist on getting better paid.'

In France, as in Germany, the chief causes of high agricultural wages are proximity to great industrial centres or easy communication with great markets, but we find also local causes of diversity, such as differences of climate or soil. The high wages about Avignon, for example, are attributable partly to the high prices produced by markets such as Lyons and Marseilles, partly to the rich returns which the climate affords to cultivation, and partly to the skill of the cultivators. Writing in 1869 respecting the rise of wages there, above the rate ten years before, Mr. Mill said :—' All prices have risen at Avignon (which was already ten years ago a remarkably dear place), owing to the causes which made it then dear. There is a rapid sale for all agricultural produce in Paris, Lyons, and Marseilles ; consequently all the prices in the market are high. . . . The cultivation round Avignon is carried to a high degree of perfection, and seems to have been so for centuries. The system of irrigation is elaborate, ploughing deep, the clearing of the land from weeds very perfect, fallows unknown except in the poor mountain soil, and the whole country is covered with trees of some sort, under which there is cultivation. I have been told that, owing to the peculiar advantages of irrigation, climate, and position between large towns, with easy railway and river communication, there is a constantly increasing tendency towards the cultivation of early fruit and vegetables. Already the exportation of these is very considerable, and it seems as though this cultivation must be favourable to small properties.'

In Normandy the rate of wages is as two to one compared with the rate throughout a great part of Britanny; and there are several reasons for the difference. Normandy is much nearer to the market of Paris; it has great manufacturing towns, and Britanny none ; its soil is much more fertile, and the Norman population does not multiply like the Breton. Agricultural wages have greatly risen throughout France in the last twenty years, through the increase of French production and trade, the increased quantity and activity of money, railways, the demand for labour in the chief towns, the consequent migration of the rural population to the towns, their disinclination for large families, and the absorption of the peasantry (several millions of whom own small properties) in the cultivation of land of their own. But the local force of each of these causes varies, and the **prices of** agricultural labour are consequently very unequal.

In Belgium, again, although the principal cause (as in every progressive country in Europe) of diversity in the local rates of agricultural wages is the presence or absence of mines, manufactures, or commerce on a great scale, other causes are at work. Thus the low rate in Flanders and the Campine is due partly to the natural poverty of the soil; and the chief cause of the relatively high rate in the Ardenne, where the farm labourer earns twice as much as in Flanders (although his work is inferior, and the region has no manufactures or foreign commerce), is that there are 270 Flemings and only 100 Ardennois to the same number of hectares.

Thus there are various causes in each country for great local diversities of agricultural wages, but the most powerful and the most general cause is the unequal distribution of advantages for manufactures and commerce, and of good markets; and we can easily trace a close connexion between the great general rise in the price of agricultural labour in Europe in recent years, especially in parts of west Germany and Belgium, and the great local inequalities in its price in each country. The currency of all Europe has been vastly augmented by new mines and instruments of credit; the rapidity also of the circulation of money has multiplied, and the prices of all things, labour included, which have not increased in proportion, have by consequence risen. Secondly, money has increased most, and the price of labour has risen most, in the districts whose money-getting powers have increased most through industrial development and rapid communication with the best markets. Thirdly, our continental neighbours have acquired in recent years those new arms of industry and commerce, iron, coal, the steam-engine, steam-locomotion, which England possessed a generation earlier; prices consequently have risen in many parts of the Continent to the English scale from a much lower level; the demand and competition for labour, and the sums offered for its assistance, have increased abroad in proportion, and the French, German, and Belgian agricultural labourer has shared with the town workman in the new streams of money. An economist of merited parliamentary fame, lately spoke of machinery as one cause which has prevented a rise of wages in recent years in some trades in England;* and doubtless it sometimes has that effect, by superseding labour. Nevertheless the main cause of the comparatively high rate of wages throughout western Europe, and the main cause of high local rates of agricultural wages in each of its countries, is, in in one word, machinery, or the steam-engine—creating new industries and immense accumulations of capital, finding swift sale for their produce in markets where gold and its representatives abound, and augmenting the price of all kinds of labour in the vicinity.

The real movements of agricultural wages throughout Europe will be seen to be in striking contradiction to generalizations, such as the tendency of wages to equality, which have passed with a certain school of English economists for economic laws; generalizations not without a measure of truth as indicating one of several forces, but mistaken by that school for the actual resultant of all the forces; generalizations, one may add, which were once useful and meritorious as first attempts to discover causes and sequence among economic phenomena, but which have long ceased to afford either light or fruit, and become part of the solemn humbug of 'economic orthodoxy.' During the last two generations, while some distinguished economists were asserting, not merely a tendency towards it, but an actual equalization of wages, the real tendency in all countries making progress was towards inequality; a tendency which, in fact, already showed itself in a marked manner a century ago, with the advance of commerce and manufactures, in both Great Britain and France, as statistics collected by Adam Smith and Arthur Young prove. The 'law' which economists ought to have laid down for the age from those two great writers' days to our own, was the law of great inequality in the local demand for labour, by reason of great inequalities in the advantages,

---

* Mr. Fawcett, M.P., in an article in the Fortnightly Review; also in the new edition of his 'Manual of Political Economy.'

development, and money-making powers of different localities. But the conqseuent inequalities in the prices of agricultural labour in England, it is important to notice, were formerly compensated for in a good measure by corresponding inequalities in the prices of commodities; food was cheap where wages were low, food dear where wages were high. Prices rose around the great centres of mining, manufacture, and trade to a scale greatly above that prevailing in purely agricultural districts, just as they have risen in the industrial districts of West Germany above the scale in Pomerania, Silesia, and Posen. A new inequality in agricultural wages in England took place with the equalization of the prices of food by railways and roads. In not a few parishes in the southern counties money wages remained almost stationary, at 7s. to 8s., from 1770 to 1870, while meat rose in the interval from 2d., and in some places actually only 1¼d. a pound, to nearly the same price, say 10d., as in Yorkshire and Northumberland, and milk and butter in proportion. When Mr. M'Culloch was laying down in successive editions of Adam Smith's treatise, that canals, roads, railways, &c., had 'brought the prices of produce much nearer to a common level than at the period of the publication of the Wealth of Nations,' he was right enough about the prices of produce, but so wrong about wages that they varied in England at the time of his last edition from 9s. to 22s., not unfrequently with a cottage and garden in the latter case, and without either in the former. Moreover, on the rise in the prices of food in the southern counties, brought about by their equalization through the kingdom, supervened a succession of further rises caused by the general increase of population, the increased wages and consumption in the manufacturing districts, and the increase of both the metallic and the credit circulation of the country. The recent rise of money wages in the southern counties had in fact been preceded by a fourfold fall in real wages measured in the price of animal food, and a great fall measured in cottage rents. The rise, therefore, during the last three or four years in the wages of the southern farm labourer—though in some cases from 7s. and 8s. to 12s. and 13s.—is, compared with his real wages a century ago, almost a nominal one only.

Another inequality which the application of steam to manufactures and locomotion brought about, was a difference between the wages of mechanical and agricultural labour (unless in the manufacturing districts) out of all proportion to any differences in the severity of the employment and the skill and knowledge required. Adam Smith thought the ploughman in his time beyond comparison superior in skill, judgment, and discretion to the town workman or mechanic, and he certainly is not now inferior in the proportion of his pay. In so far as he is ignorant and inefficient, it is the effect, not the cause, of his low wages; and the groundlessness of a recent suggestion that the lower wages of the southern counties are attributable to an inferiority of race, is proved by the fact, which might have been learned from Mr. Caird, that a hundred years ago wages were higher in the southern than in the northern counties, in the proportion of 7s. 6d. to 6s. 9d. a week. The truth is that the sources of wages are unequally distributed by nature, but a more equal local development and a more equal distribution of labour might long ago have been brought about, had economists, in place of assuming equality, examined the facts, and ascertained the actual inequalities and their causes.

It remains briefly to indicate some of the conclusions to which the foregoing review of facts, and the present conditions of the situation, seem to point. A rise in the money wages of agricultural labour is a general European phenomenon, showing the operation of general causes. It is everywhere in part merely a nominal rise, but especially so in the southern counties of England, where a great fall in real wages, by reason of a continuous rise in prices, preceded it. In all countries in Europe there are great inequalities in money wages, but in most of them, Germany in particular, those inequalities are partially compensated by local differences in the prices of food, so that no such real inequalities in real wages exist there as in England; nor is it possible that such inequalities can continue here, now that the economic fictions which concealed them and their causes have been exposed. The future rate of money wages is indeed everywhere partly a question relating to the fertility of the gold mines and the abundance of money; but whatever may be the amount of money in circulation, it may be predicted that its distribution will be such as to secure a larger share than heretofore to the agricultural labourer in the southern counties of England. Temporary and local causes have lately checked the rise of agricultural wages in some countries, but all the permanent and general conditions tend to maintain it, especially in the lower levels. The recent decline in Germany is, in fact, a mark of the increasing influence of manufactures and trade on the price of agricultural labour, and of the disappearance of customary and stationary rates of agricultural wages, and of the excessive disproportion between them and the rates in other employments.* Everywhere in Europe farm labourers are breaking the bonds of tradition and habit, everywhere acquiring new powers; in England they have, moreover, gained those potent forces of union which have long been the monopoly of town workmen, and farmers in the depth of the country are beginning to feel at once the effects of the competition of distant employers in towns and in the new world, and of the combination of their own labourers on the spot. When one considers the number and strength of the causes tending to the elevation of the agricultural labourer, and the breadth of the area over which they are operating, one can hardly err in affirming the ultimate futility of a local effort to put a stop to a movement which, on the one hand, has what may be called universal and permanent forces on its side, and, on the other hand, is fortified by special local conditions. The dark part of the prospect is, that England, in the outcome, may lose the chief part of its rural population, for it seems too plain that nothing will awaken its legislature or its landowners in time to the importance of making it the well-grounded hope of the industrious and thrifty farm labourer to acquire a little farm of his own.

* Since this Essay was written, nearly five years ago, the diminished activity of manufactures and trade in Germany has been attended with a further decline in agricultural wages, which are not much higher in many places now than in 1867. Formerly the movements of trade did not affect German agricultural wages. January, 1879.

XXV.

ECONOMIC SCIENCE AND STATISTICS.*

(*Athenæum, September 27, 1873.*)

ECONOMIC SCIENCE was **not formally included** within the Statistical Section of the British Association until 1856; and even since then, addresses of distinguished Presidents of the Section have turned mainly on its statistical functions, and have been devoted principally to an inquiry into the nature and province of statistics. That the inquiry is neither so superfluous **nor so easy** as might at first appear, is sufficiently shown by **the fact that** there are, according to the great German statist, **Dr.** Engel, no less than 180 definitions of the term to be met with in the works of different authors. These various definitions may, however, be said to group themselves round one or other of three conceptions, of which one follows the popular view **of** statistics; the etymological and original meaning almost disappearing in the notion merely of tables of figures, or numbers of facts, of which the chief significance lies in their numerical statement. According **to another conception,** statistics, following etymology and the signification given to Statistik by the famous Göttingen school, should be regarded as equivalent **to** the science **of** States, or political science, but, nevertheless, as confining **itself to the** ascertainment and collection of facts indicative of **the** condition and prospects of society, without inquiring into causes or reasoning on probable effects, and carefully discarding hypothesis, theory, and speculation **in its** investigations. A third conception is, that statistical **science** aims at the discovery, not only of the phenomena of society,

---

* Written on the meeting of Section F of the British Association for the Advancement of Science, September, 1873.

but also of their laws, and by no means discards either inquiry into causes and effects or theoretical reasoning.

It is curious that some who give to statistics the first of these three meanings, and who regard the numerical statement of facts, and the marshalling of tables of figures, as the proper business of the statistician, nevertheless speak of statistics as a science. But, as the eminent economist, Roscher, has observed, numbering or numerical statement is only an instrument of which any branch of science may avail itself, and can never, in itself, constitute a science. No one, as he says, would dream of making a science of microscopics, or observations made through the microscope. The distinguished English statistician and economist, Mr. Jevons, has likewise condemned the misconception of statistics and the misuse of the term we refer to in language worth recalling :—'Many persons now use the word statistical as if it were synonymous with numerical; but it is a mere accident of the information with which we deal that it is often expressed in a numerical or tabular form. As other sciences progress, they become more and more a matter of quantity and number, and so does statistical science; but we must not suppose that the occurrence of numerical statement is the mark of statistical information.'

The doctrine that the consideration of causes and probable reasoning are excluded from the province of statistics, and that statisticians should confine themselves to the ascertainment of facts, is hardly more satisfactory. No branch of science, no scientific body, confines itself to the observation of phenomena without seeking to interpret them or to ascertain their laws. It is not, indeed, possible, at present, to explain all the phenomena which come within the observation of the statist, or to connect them with any law of causation; and even naked collections of statistical facts may be useful as aids to further inquiry, or as supplying links in the chain of observed effects. But serious error, and even practical mischief, have followed from attention merely to the recurrence of statistical facts without inquiry into their causes. A theory of a decennial recurrence of commercial crises, for example, was based on the occurrence of crises in 1837, 1847, and 1857. Had the causes of commercial crises been examined, it would have been discovered that they are extremely various and uncertain in their occurrence; that a war, a bad harvest, a drain of the precious metals, anything, in short, which produces a panic, may cause a crisis; and as there is no decennial periodicity in the causes, there can be none in the effects.

These considerations lead us to adopt the third conception noticed above, namely, that statistical science investigates the laws of social phenomena, as well as the phenomena themselves; and, if not co-extensive with sociology, or the science of society,—because not going so far back in its researches, and confining itself to the phenomena of modern society,—yet employs all available methods, inquiry into causes, theory, and probable reasoning for the interpretation of the facts it discovers. But it is not easy to give to a word a signification other than the one which long usage has put upon it; and, unfortunately, to the majority of persons the term statistics denotes simply dry figures and tabulated facts. The Statistical Section of the British Association has found a means to escape from the difficulty, in a great measure, by allying itself formally to Economic Science. It thus embraces definitely and expressly the whole economic side of the science of society, including the investigation of laws of causation as well as the observation of facts, and employing all the methods of scientific investigation and reasoning. But if it deals in this manner with economic facts, it can hardly fail to do so likewise with the other classes of social phenomena which it approaches. And thus, however narrow may be the sense in which the term statistics may be elsewhere employed, the Statistical Section of the British Association is free from all trammel, and unfettered by any exclusion of theory or even speculation in its investigation of political and social problems.

The formal incorporation of economic science with statistics has another great advantage: it tends to correct the error to which economists as well as that to which statisticians are specially prone. If the latter have been apt to think only of facts, it has been the besetting sin of the former to neglect facts altogether; if statisticians have often been content to collect phenomena without heed to their laws, economists more often still have jumped to the laws without heed to the phenomena; if statistics have lain chiefly in the region of dry figures and numerical tables, economics have dwelt chiefly in that region of assumption, conjecture, and provisional generalization, which other sciences, indeed—geology to witness,—have not escaped, but from which they are triumphantly emerging by combining the closest observation of phenomena with the boldest use of speculation and scientific hypothesis.

We may thus look for considerable benefit to both political economy and statistics from the combination of the methods to which the followers of each have been specially addicted. The subjects which occupied the principal place in Mr. Forster's address and in the attention of the Section, conspicuously illustrate the importance of combining statistical with economic inquiry, and the characteristic defects of the economic and statistical methods hitherto commonly followed. Take, for example, the question of wages. The relations of capital and labour, and the causes determining the rates of wages, are not to be summed up or disposed of in any brief formula or so-called 'economic law.' But much might have been done, by the collection of statistics and careful inquiry into facts, towards obtaining much closer approximations to truth than the generalizations which take the name of 'the wages fund,' 'the equality of profits,' 'the average rate of wages,'—generalizations of which the world generally has grown a little doubtful and not a little weary.

Economists have been accustomed to assume that wages on the one hand and profits on the other are, allowing for differences in skill, and so forth, equalized by competition, and that neither wages nor profits can anywhere rise above 'the average rate,' without a consequent influx of labour or of capital bringing things to a level. Had economists, however, in place of reasoning from an assumption, examined the facts connected with the rate of wages, they would have found, from authentic statistics, the actual differences so great, even in the same occupation, that they are double in one place what they are in another. Statistics of profits are not, indeed, obtainable like statistics of wages; and the fact that they are not so, that the actual profits are kept a profound secret in some of the most prominent trades, is itself enough to deprive the theory of equal profits of its base. Enough, however, is known or discovered from time to time by the working men in particular trades, to justify them in the conclusion, on the one hand, that profits will bear a reduction, and that wages may consequently receive an augmentation; and, on the other hand, that competition has not produced and will not produce those results. When, therefore, Mr. Forster assumes that the majority of working men are now disposed to admit as fundamental truths of economic science that the remuneration of labour can be raised only in three ways—by the increase of capital, the diminution of the whole labouring population, or the participation of labourers in capital,—we are reminded that not a few working men in certain trades believe there is another mode by which their remuneration might be raised, namely, by a participation in profits, which are enormously high; and that they believe, too, that this participation can be secured only by combination, not by competition. Not quite consistently with his own statement, that one of the methods by which wages may be raised is a diminution of population, Mr. Forster pointed to the increase of the population of England and Wales from $16\frac{1}{2}$ millions in 1831 to $21\frac{1}{2}$ millions in 1871, simultaneously with an increase of general prosperity, as militating against the theory of population advocated by Malthus and Mr. Mill, and the necessity those great writers contended for, of a prudential check to the potential rate of births. An unrestrained potential increase would have doubled the $16\frac{1}{2}$ millions about 1856; at the present time there would, at the same rate, be about 50 millions of people in England and Wales, and, before the end of the century, the population of that part of the United Kingdom would exceed 100 millions. Either, therefore, the prudential check has been firmly opposed by some classes of the population to the potential increase, and has permitted that increase of prosperity which Mr. Forster assumes, or other checks, in the shape of death and infirmity, have acted instead of the prudential check, and demonstrated the urgent necessity for it. Another point, in connexion with wages, on which Mr. Forster's reasoning seems to need some explanation, relates to the agricultural labourers. He seems to throw out an opinion that there is yet another source, besides those which have been named, from which the wages of labour may be raised, namely, rent; but his language on the subject leaves much to be desired, to use a Gallicism, on the head of clearness. He says it is well there is here 'a third class, namely, the landlords, who are able to enter into the question, and to act as mediators.' But then he adds that a paper might well be devoted in the Section to the question, how far the rent paid for land affects the question of wages? The innuendo would appear to be that an increase of rural wages may be brought about by an abatement of rent; and we fail to see how that prospect places the landlords in a position to qualify them for the position of impartial mediators between farmers and men. Another important subject discussed in the Section, the treatment of which was not exhaustive in respect of either the economic or the statistical methods employed, was that of prices, and the rise in the cost of living. Mr. Levi took the prices of the Metropolitan Meat Market for his measure with respect to that article, adding, indeed, the expression of an opinion, that the rise has been greater in the chief towns than in other parts of the kingdom. The fact is, that the diffusion of steam communication in the last twenty-five years has raised the price of meat in country places and remote parts of the kingdom much more than in the chief towns, because it has raised it from a much lower point in the former to something like the same price as in the latter localities. In many parts of Ireland and Scotland, where, thirty years ago, the price of butcher's meat averaged 3d. a pound, it is now not much below the London price; and this equalization of prices, where the means of communication have been equalized, is connected with the distribution of money over the world, in a manner very necessary to be borne in mind in estimates both of past and probable future changes in the cost of living. The prices of the Metropolitan Meat Market afford, for another reason, insufficient indications of what has actually taken place in respect of the purchasing power of money. The price of mutton per pound in that market has risen from 6·37, in 1863-7, to 7·62 in 1873. But in the same period the price of a mutton-chop in a London railway refreshment room has risen from 6d. to 1s.; and, in fact, the rise in retail prices, on which the cost of living really depends, is more accurately indicated by the latter figures than by those which Mr. Levi has cited. It is obvious, too, that the rise in wages is to a very large class, who have to pay servants' wages, an addition and not a counterpoise to the increased cost of living arising from the rise of commodities. Mr. Levi, we might add, seems to have caused some confusion of ideas, if he did not fall into it himself, with respect to the effect on the price of necessaries and ordinary comforts of an increased expenditure on luxuries. The consumption of better qualities of food and clothing would naturally tend to raise the cost of the particular articles on which the increased outlay took place. But an increased expenditure on luxuries, such as seal-skin jackets, carriages, wine, tobacco, would, cæteris paribus, diminish the outlay on other things, and would tend to a corresponding fall in the prices of the latter. Had we, however, much fuller statistics than are forthcoming respecting the changes in prices throughout the United Kingdom, we should still be unable to form a sound judgment respecting the most important part of the question, namely, the probable future range of prices, without a mass of additional information respecting the causes which have acted on the supply of each article, and on the distribution of money as well as on its amount. And we have in this matter an illustration of the defective character of that kind of statistical inquiry which confines itself to the collection of a multitude of instances of facts, without reference to causes. It must be allowed that the principles laid down by the illustrious Quetelet rather tend to foster the error to which we advert. He assumed that by enlarging the number of instances, we eliminate chance and arrive at general and stable laws or conditions. But a great number of instances does not give us their law, or justify us in any positive conclusion respecting the future. New conditions, for example, have been acting on prices during the last two years, and mere tables of prices for the last twenty or ten years, confound years in which those causes were in operation with years in which they **were not.**

We cannot close these few remarks and suggestions without thanking Mr. Forster, the eminent President of Section F, for the just, but not the less generous tribute which he paid to the great leader of economic science, whom the world has lately lost in Mr. John Stuart Mill.

XXVI.

POLITICAL ECONOMY AND SOCIOLOGY.*

(Fortnightly Review, February 1, 1879.)

PHILOSOPHICAL like religious and political history is the history of change and reform, of the decline of old and the rise of new systems, and the reformers encounter the same opposition in the world of philosophy as in that of religion and politics, being accused of attempts to destroy what they seek to regenerate and preserve. Those whose interest or pride is on the side of the old system resist the new one as an attack on themselves, but they call it an attack on religion, on the constitution, on science, or on some venerable name. The upholders of an ancient worship did not cry publicly that their craft was in danger to be set at naught, but 'great is Diana of the Ephesians.' So a cry is now heard in reply to Mr. Ingram from an old sect of economists of the greatness of Adam Smith. And it is well that the cry is now for him instead of Ricardo. Not long ago Adam Smith's name was seldom heard, his reputation was eclipsed by Ricardo's, the Wealth of Nations was treated as almost obsolete. A sort of mythical glory surrounded Ricardo, and we may realize in his instance the process by which the ballads of a number of singers came to be ascribed to one bard, and the exploits of a line of chiefs and warriors to a single hero. A theory to which a contemporary of Adam Smith was led by his own experience and observation of farming in Scotland, and which was afterwards reproduced by two contemporaries of Ricardo, came to be called 'Ricardo's Theory of Rent,' in spite of his own acknowledgment in his

---

* In connexion with this Essay, and the controversy referred to in it, see The Present Position and Prospects of Political Economy, by John K. Ingram, F.T.C.D., and an article in the Nineteenth Century, October, 1878, entitled Recent Attacks on Political Economy by the Right Hon. Robert Lowe, M.P.

preface and elsewhere that he took it from Malthus and West, and of the fact that only the exaggerations and inaccuracies were his own.* Mr. Mill's theory of international values has in like manner been traced to Ricardo, contrary to its author's own statement in his Autobiography of its independent origin. Mr. Mill himself, indeed, though he so qualified and amended the doctrines of his predecessor that the latter could scarcely have recognised them, and brought new elements and conditions within the field of political economy, sometimes spoke with the piety of a disciple, and has been represented by some of his own followers as little more; the giant thus standing on the shoulders of the dwarf to see over his head. It is a sign then that Ricardo has lost ground when his adherents fall back on Adam Smith, just as a victory was gained when theologians could no longer oppose a new doctrine as contrary to the Fathers, and were driven to contend that it was against the Bible, which they had before kept in the back-ground. A bold attempt may be made now and then hereafter to rehabilitate Ricardo, but practically he is given up. It is to be noted that the phrase 'desire of wealth,' which with some of his successors is made to bear the whole weight of political economy, was not used by Ricardo. But that is only because he dispensed altogether with psychology, and with all inquiry into the mental forces at work; setting out with naked assumptions such as that it is 'natural' that the value of things should be proportionate to the labour of producing them, and that the 'natural' rate of wages is the price of the labourer's subsistence. These nebulous assumptions are not only both false, but also contradictory, for if the cost of the labourer's subsistence determined the rate of wages, it could not vary in different occupations with the nature of the work. A deduction from the assumed relation between wages and food, on which much of his system was built, was that a tax on corn could not fall on the labouring class, and

* In all that I have said concerning the origin and progress of rent, I have briefly repeated and endeavoured to elucidate the principles which Mr. Malthus has so ably laid down, on the same subject, in his Inquiry into the Nature and Progress of Rent, a work abounding in original ideas.—Ricardo's Works, M'Culloch's ed., p. 374. Compare the Preface to Ricardo's Principles of Political Economy and Taxation. Ib.

this doctrine, as both Cobden and Sir Robert Peel have borne witness, was the main cause of the Corn Law. His theory that no improvement or economy in production can augment profit unless it lowers wages, has in like manner done incalculable harm. 'It **has been**,' he says in his treatise, 'my endeavour throughout this work **to** show that the rate of profits can never be increased but by a fall of wages.' Had he been an **English** Lassalle **or** Karl Marx, and his main object to sow enmity between **capital** and labour, **he could not have** devised a doctrine better adapted to the purpose. The notion too which his language did much to establish, that all wealth, including capital itself, is the produce of labour, in the sense of manual labour, exclusive of the capitalist's enterprise, invention, trouble and abstinence, is actually the corner **stone** of the creed of the German 'social democrat.' Political economy is then **emerging from a** cloud of petitio principii, **bad** generalization, **and** mischievous fallacy, when the controversy turns **on** the system of Adam Smith. **It** reminds one of the contest between the spirits of darkness and light for the body of Moses, to find the followers of Ricardo claiming Adam Smith for their prophet, and seeking **to** make his shrine the prop of a falling superstition.

The real issue of course is not what Adam Smith's system was, but **what is the true one**; the two questions however **are** not unrelated. 'Whom ye **ignorantly** worship, him declare I unto you,' the true disciple **of Adam Smith may say to** those who raise altars to his name, but **to whom he is** virtually an unknown being. Not only is the phrase **'desire of** wealth' not to be found in the Wealth of Nations, **and** Adam Smith guiltless of a vicious abstraction that has **done** much **to** darken economic inquiry; **he** introduced into his theory of the motives to exertion and sacrifice various desires and sentiments besides those which **have wealth for their object**. A writer from whom something more may **be** learned, **than** was known in the days of Plato respecting the philosophy of society, history, **and** law, has observed with respect to the deductive economists' practice of setting aside **a** number of forces as 'friction,' that the best corrective would **be a** demonstration that this so-called friction is capable of scientific analysis and measurement.* Friction is not, one may remark, a very appropriate or an adequate term, indicating neither the strength nor the mode of operation of the forces included under it. It would hardly seem correct to say that the earth is prevented by friction from falling into the sun. The motives too 'eliminated' in this fashion act in opposite ways, sometimes counteracting and sometimes stimulating by an additional object the love of gain. But Adam Smith was so far from 'eliminating' them, that he has set the example of an attempt to carry out Sir Henry Maine's idea of subjecting them not only to analysis but to measurement. The assertion of a recent advocate of the à priori and deductive method that the whole science of political economy is based on the desire of wealth and aversion from labour, is contrary not only to the spirit but to the letter of Adam Smith's Wealth of Nations. It is characteristic, indeed, of the laxity of the deductive method, in spite of its pretence of rigorous logic, that immediately after laying down the foregoing proposition Mr. Lowe drops one of the two abstractions contained in it and affirms that Adam Smith's method was successful because the subject admitted of the elimination of all motives save the single one of pecuniary interest. And at the centenary of the Wealth of Nations he pronounced that 'the result of Adam Smith's investigation amounts to this, that the causes of wealth are two, work and thrift, and the causes of poverty two, idleness and waste;' adding that in his own opinion no more need be known or perhaps could be known on the subject. Nearly three thousand years before Adam Smith, Solomon had said as much; summing up in his proverbs on the subject the results of sagacious observation and induction, while men in general sought to grow rich by shorter methods such as prayer to their gods, as in later times by the aid of human protectors.

But to set aside all other motives to exertion besides riches is quite opposed to Adam Smith's rationale of the choice of employments, and the different rates of wages and profit

---

* Village Communities in the East and West. Third Edition, p. 202.

Observing that these were everywhere in Europe extremely different in different occupations, he traced the diversities to various circumstances 'which either really or in imagination make up for a small pecuniary gain in some, and counterbalance a great gain in others'—the desire, for instance, of credit, distinction, or health, the love of independence, power, or country life, the interest in certain pursuits for their own sake, the dislike of others on various accounts. The cases in which such influences come into play in his system are by no means abnormal or uncommon. He examined their operation in many of the ordinary employments of life, the farmer's, the weaver's, the smith's, the collier's, the carpenter's, the painter's, the butcher's, the jeweller's, the soldier's, the sailor's, the barrister's, the author's; and sought to measure them by a pecuniary standard. Honour, he said, formed a great part of the reward of all honourable professions. The farmer's profit was lower than the merchant's or the manufacturer's in proportion to the other attractions of his business. So far from building a science of the production and distribution of wealth on Mr. Lowe's two abstractions, the famous tenth chapter of his first book involves a complete refutation of such a system; as it does also of the assertion that its leading principles were not obtained by induction. The notion of evolving from his own consciousness the circumstances and motives that diversify the employments of a nation, and the remuneration obtained in them, would be preposterous even if Adam Smith himself had not expressly stated at the beginning of the chapter that he had gathered them from observation. His exposition of the causes that lead men to accept a comparatively low rate of profit in farming, shows both the closeness of that observation, and the delicate analysis to which he subjected influences which have been either disregarded altogether, or lumped together as 'friction,' or 'disturbing causes' by the deductive school of his successors. 'The beauty of the country,' he said, 'besides the pleasures of country life, the tranquillity of mind which it promises, and wherever the influence of human laws does not disturb it, the independence which it really affords, are charms that more or less attract everybody, and in every stage of his existence man seems to retain a predilection for this primitive employment. Mr. C. S. Read, speaking the other day from practical knowledge, and without thinking of Adam Smith, of the reasons why men continue to hold farms at rents that leave little or no profit, fell into nearly similar language. The fact that Mr. Lowe with Adam Smith on his tongue, can think of no incentive to exertion save pecuniary gain, is enough to prove the inadequacy of the method he follows, of deducing the laws of political economy from his own mind instead of from careful induction. Even Mr. Senior, though ambitious to construct the science from the fewest possible principles, laid down several besides the two jumbled into one in his treatise as a desire to obtain wealth at the least possible sacrifice. Among these additional principles is that of population, and Mr. Lowe's mention of Malthus among the successors of Adam Smith, might have suggested to him the insufficiency of the foundation on which he builds a science of the production, accumulation, consumption, and distribution of wealth, as he defines political economy. Among the chief motives to production, the most powerful of all to accumulation, and deeply affecting consumption and distribution, are conjugal and parental affection. The family finds no place in a system which takes cognisance only of individuals, and of no motive save personal gain. Yet without the family and the altruistic as well as self-regarding motives that maintain it, the work of the world would come almost to a standstill; saving for a remote future would cease; there would be no durable wealth; men would not seek to leave anything behind them; the houses of the wealthiest, if there were any houses at all, would be built to last only for their own time. In order to solve the problem of political economy Mr. Lowe assures us that 'all that is wanted is the knowledge that the ruling passions of mankind are wealth and ease.' It does not appear whether, like Mr. Bagehot, Mr. Lowe excludes women from the sphere of the science; but the exertions of that hardest-worked of all labourers, the poor man's wife, can hardly be explained by the love of wealth and ease. Had not more than one of Mr. Ingram's opponents contended that the scientific character and the complete success of the method of eliminating all other motives is demonstrated by its enabling the economist to predict, it would seem too plain to need statement that just the opposite is the truth. If you know all a man's inclinations and motives, and their relative force, you may foretell how he will act under given conditions. But if you set aside all save the desire of pecuniary gain and aversion from labour, you will to a certainty go wrong about human conduct in general; you will not be right about even the miser, for he has sometimes some human affections, and on the other hand thinks nothing of trouble. Mr. Jevons, though favourably disposed by philosophical culture and tastes towards historical investigation in economics, has urged on behalf of deduction from the acquisitive principle, that even the lower animals act from a similar motive, 'as you will discover if you interfere between a dog and his bone.' A bone fairly enough represents the sort of wealth coveted by a dog, who has a comparatively simple cerebral system, and few other objects. Yet you cannot predict the conduct even of a dog from his love of bones, or not one would be left in the butchers' shops. The dog has a regard for his master and a fear of the police, and he has other pursuits.

All men, it may be said, desire health, 'and in the absence of disturbing causes' will seek it. But can a science of health be based on this assumption, or the conduct of mankind be predicted from it? Everybody, it might be affirmed, loves virtue 'in the abstract,' and 'in the absence of disturbing causes' would be virtuous; yet, policemen, prisons, and the Divorce Court show that no theory of morals, much less absolute predictions, can be drawn from this abstract principle. That the à priori method in political economy renders positive prediction possible, is indeed contrary to the doctrine of its most eminent expositors. Mr. Mill, though he subsequently much enlarged the scope and system of economic investigation, was in his earlier years an advocate of the à priori method, yet in the well-known essay in support of it, he emphatically insisted that the conclusions deduced from it are 'true only in the abstract,' and 'would be true without qualification only in purely imaginary cases.' Mr. Cairnes in like manner says, 'it is evident that an economist arguing from the desire of wealth and the aversion to labour with strict logical accuracy may be landed in conclusions that have no resemblance to existing realities;' adding that 'the economist can never be certain that he does not omit some essential circumstance, and it is indeed scarcely possible to include all, therefore his conclusions correspond with facts only in the absence of disturbing causes, and represent not positive but hypothetic truths.'*

The more sagacious adherents to the mere deductive method will therefore probably decline to accept Mr. Lowe as their representative, but his exposition is a reductio ad absurdum of their own system. He is only more thoroughgoing—one cannot say more consistent or logical, for he sometimes includes and sometimes discards the dislike of labour—in his elimination of all principles save the desire of wealth, which is the real backbone of their theory as well as his. The other motives and forces to which they nominally concede a place, are only admitted at the outset for form's sake, to be afterwards set aside as 'disturbing causes' in a manner without precedent or analogy in physical science. The last thing an astronomer would dream of, is that having admitted in general terms the existence of other forces besides those that were taken account of by the earliest observers, he need not concern himself with them further, and may calculate the movements of the heavenly bodies without reference to them. Nor is this the only fundamental objection. No such principle as 'the desire of wealth,' in the sense of a single, universal motive, whose consequences are uniform and can be foreseen, really exists. Adam Smith does not use the phrase, and his doctrine respecting the nature of wealth shows the impossibility of using it as a key to the movements of the economic world. Wealth, he says, 'consists not in the inconsumable riches of money, but in the consumable goods annually reproduced by the labour of the society.' It includes therefore food, drink, clothing, houses, furniture, plate, ornaments, books, works of art; in short, necessaries, comforts, luxuries, in all their varieties, and all the productions of nature or of human exertion and skill to be had in the

---

* Logical Method of Political Economy, p. 49.

market. It includes things which vary in different countries and different ages, and have very different economic effects; and which are objects not only of different but of antagonistic desires. The love of gin is the love of one kind of wealth which too often competes in the mind of a poor man with the love of a decent dwelling. There is a saying about a four-footed animal not without firmness of character but of limited ideas, between two bundles of hay both soliciting his choice. The decalogue shows that this animal was one of divers things which the Israelites were prone to covet. The ox, to which allusion is also made in the commandment, was, as Sir Henry Maine has explained, the kind of wealth most valued by early agricultural communities; yet even they desired some other kinds, and sometimes the reason why a man was without an ox for his plough, was that he was too fond of strong drink. In modern society there are countless varieties of wealth. Adam Smith has made some excellent remarks on the difference, in respect both of its amount and its distribution, of expenditure on different sorts. But expenditure is simply the method of acquisition by which, under a division of labour, the desires of men for different things are satisfied. Were there no such division, some would build houses and make clothes for themselves, while others in nakedness or rags distilled spirits or brewed ale in mud hovels or caves.

One of the most important economic inquiries relates to the changes which take place in the direction of the chief wants of mankind, and the species of wealth which they call into existence. The main object of industry and accumulation on the part of the French nation is landed property; the chief impulse determining the national economy is the desire of it; in England this desire is absent among the nation at large, and the one which takes its place with no small number of Englishmen is the love of beer. Happily in England there is a still more general object of desire in the house, and the house owes its structure, perhaps its very existence, to the institution of the family. Even in the matter of dress, the changes in the nature of the things constituting wealth deeply affect its economic condition. Richard II. wore a coat which cost more than £20,000 in modern money; the Prince of Wales would not take £20,000 to wear it. The stronger passion of women than men in our time for personal decoration is the result not of an original difference in the mental constitution of the two sexes, but of a different social and political history. The formula of demand and supply is still supposed by some economists to explain everything fully, but both demand and supply have in every case a long history. The demand for duelling swords and pistols in France is such that the supply makes no inconsiderable figure in the inventory of French wealth. Were they used only in duels, there would probably not be two swords or a brace of pistols in England. It is a misrepresentation of the Mercantile System that its adherents considered nothing but money as wealth, still they did attach undue importance to it; and the consequence of the excessive estimation in which they held it, demonstrates the absurdity of basing either the economic prosperity of nations or economic science on the abstraction which is the corner stone of both in the deductive system. The other principle which Mr. Lowe associates with it, the dislike of labour, involves an equal confusion. One might ask, when it is maintained that we can predict the conduct of mankind from these two principles, in what proportion are we to mix them for the purpose? The Jews were always a wealth-loving nation, and many of them industrious, yet there seem to have been not a few sluggards in Solomon's time who would go to no trouble to get it. Can employers tell whether higher weekly earnings or fewer hours of work will be the principal object of their workmen a year hence? The savage has a dislike for regular labour which only some form of slavery can overcome, but with the progress of civilization a love of exertion for its own sake grows up, and employment becomes necessary to the happiness of a great number of men. We are told somewhat abruptly in the Psalms that a man was famous according as he had lifted up axes on the thick trees, yet the most celebrated woodcutter of that period perhaps felled no more trees in a week than Mr. Gladstone will do for mere recreation. The German emperor replied to a deputation that he had felt the pain of his wounds less than the abstinence from his ordinary activity which they compelled. The love of several occupations for their own sake is one of the causes by which Adam Smith explains the small profit to be made in them. Had Mr. Lowe ever watched a French peasant at work in his vineyard, he could hardly have made a universal dislike of toil one of the two pillars of political economy.

Other motives, which eminent advocates of the deductive system propose to take into account, vary in like manner in force, direction, and consequence. Mr. Cairnes refers to the love of men for their own country as the main cause of the diversity of the rates of wages and profit in different countries, and it is a highly complex feeling, varying greatly in strength in different nations and ages. The Fleming was the great emigrant of the Middle Ages; now he can hardly be got to migrate to an adjoining province for double wages. Patriotism did not exist in England some centuries ago. Different races, nations, and clans had been too recently blended under one government for a strong feeling of nationality; a man belonged to his township, his borough, his guild, not to his country. Had Englishmen been as patriotic as they were brave, William of Normandy might never have got the title of Conqueror. The Germans when they invaded the Roman Empire knew no common fatherland. In 1870 they left lucrative employments in all parts of the world for a soldier's perils and pay, in a manner that shows how much there is on earth that is not dreamt of in Mr. Lowe's philosophy. And this is far from exhausting the principles entitled, even on the admission of distinguished adherents of the deductive method, to a place in the science of wealth. Mr. Cairnes asks, for example, 'how far should religious and moral considerations be admitted as coming within the province of political economy?' His answer is that 'they are to be taken account of precisely in so far as they are found in fact to affect the conduct of men in the pursuit of wealth;' and one need only allude to the influence of mediæval religion on both the forms and the distribution of the wealth of the community, the changes in both with the change in religion after the Reformation, in proof of the impotence of the à priori method to guide the economist in relation to this class of agencies. Yet a few pages after recognising their title to investigation, Mr. Cairnes argues that induction, though **indispensable** in physical, is needless in economic science, on the ground that 'the economist starts with a knowledge of ultimate causes,' and 'is already at the outset of his enterprise, in the position which the physicist only attains after ages of laborious research.'* The followers of the deductive method are in fact on the horns of a dilemma. They must either follow Mr. Lowe's narrow path, and reason strictly from the assumption that men are actuated by no motive save the desire of pecuniary gain, or they must contend that they have an intuitive knowledge of all the moral, religious, political, and other motives influencing human conduct, and of all the changes they undergo in different countries and periods.

Shut out by their own method from the investigation of the true problems of political economy, the deductive school have devoted themselves to a fictitious solution of others which the ablest among them have nevertheless admitted to be insoluble. 'If you place a man's ear within the ring of pounds, shillings, and pence, his conduct can be counted on to the greatest nicety,' according to Mr. Lowe. Mr. Cairnes on the other hand, as we have seen, concurs with Mr. Mill that positive, unconditional, conclusions are beyond the reach of the economist, since he does not take into account, or even know all the forces at work, much less can measure them with precision. An entire lecture in Mr. Cairnes's Logical Method of Political Economy is devoted to proof that quantitative exactness is unattainable in the science, and that its conclusions being only hypothetically true, and representing only several tendencies 'in the absence of disturbing causes,' ought not to affect the semblance of numerical exactness. Mr. Lowe's proposition is nevertheless true in the sense that the deductive system does affect the power not only of absolute prediction, but of prediction with mathematical accuracy. Take any treatise following the deductive method, and it will be found to consist mainly of propositions respecting wages, profit,

---

* Logical Method of Political Economy, p. 75.

prices, rent, and taxation, which profess to determine with arithmetical exactness on whom a given tax, say on a box of lucifer matches, will fall, how much it will add to the price of the box, and what profit both the manufacturer and the retailer will net on its advance. In a previous article* the present writer has exposed the fallacies involved in the whole chain of reasoning, and shown that it cannot be foreseen whether a trader will ever recover a so-called indirect tax at all; that it may be a direct tax on himself, may drive him and all other small capitalists from the business, and ultimately give a lucrative monopoly instead of 'average profit' to a few great capitalists—half-a-dozen distillers and brewers for example. The deductive theory of wages, profits, prices, rent, and taxation is substantially a set of predictions respecting the distribution of wealth, which affect to foretell exactly the gain in every business, and the rates at which goods of every kind may be sold. It has been well said that before predicting the future, we must learn to predict the past; and before predicting the past, it might be added, we should learn to predict the present, by studying the forces at work in the world around us, the conditions under which they operate, and their actual results. A striking instance of the failure of the deductive economist to predict even the present, is Mr. M'Culloch's assertion in several editions of the Wealth of Nations that the local inequalities of wages, of which Adam Smith spoke, had almost disappeared with the improvement in the means of communication. In point of fact they had greatly increased; agricultural wages varying from 6s. to 16s. a week when his first edition was published, and from 9s. to 22s. at the date of the last, varying too from causes which inductive investigation had enabled Adam Smith to discover, namely, the unequal local development of manufactures, commerce, the greater demand and competition for labour in some places than in others, and the obstacles to its migration.

The history of the last few years gives disastrous proof of the falsity of the predictions of both present and future

---

* Fortnightly Review, February, 1874.

involved in the theory of the equality of profits, which assumes that the gains in different employments can be foreseen with a close approximation to accuracy, and that competition accordingly keeps them nearly at a level. If there was a man in the country who might have been supposed capable of foresight in such matters, by reason of the widest information and great financial skill, it was Mr. Gladstone when a few years ago he described the trade of the country as advancing by leaps and bounds. Did he see that they were leaps in the dark? Did the capitalists who rushed into the businesses in which prices and profits were trebling, see that they were bounds that would end in a fall on the other side? Have the capitalists in other businesses, who were heavily mulcted by the rise of coal and iron, recovered their losses 'with average profit'? Adam Smith, reasoning from observation, rigorously and emphatically confined the tendency of profits to equality to long-established well-known trades in the same neighbourhood, unaffected by new discoveries, by speculation, fluctuations of credit, accident, or political events, carried on, not by directors and shareholders with other business to mind, but by persons whose sole occupations they were. In other words, from an induction he predicted inequality where the deductive economist predicts equality. Mr. Cairnes, indeed, though adhering to the general truth of the doctrine of equality, was of opinion that the new gold would, by its unequal distribution over different trades, disturb the level of profits for many years. The actual course of the distribution was however very different from that which à priori reasoning led him to predict, the chief rise of prices being in foreign countries where railways, industrial progress, and the opening of the English market raised them suddenly from a low scale towards the English range.*
The new gold was only one of many new conditions of modern trade. In an age of companies there is a very

---

* An example of this was cited lately by the eminent French economist, M. Leroy-Beaulieu, in the Economiste Français, from statistics compiled by Mr. Newmarch, showing that between 1830 and 1870 the price of corn fell 14 per cent. in England, while it rose 17 per cent. in France, 88 per cent. in Belgium, 133 per cent. in Hungary, 142 per cent. in Austria.

imperfect division of labour; credit and speculation have made trade a lottery in which 'the absurd presumption of every man in his own abilities, and the still more absurd presumption in his own good fortune,' of which Adam Smith speaks, have full play.

The recurrence of commercial crises alone defeats all attempts to predict the course of prices and profits, and would do so even if the doctrine of decennial cycles had a solid foundation; for if the periods of inflation and depression could be foretold, and the occurrence of each crisis timed with precision, the particular movements of credit, speculation, and prices, and the gains and losses in each business could not. The theory of a decennial cycle, like that of the equality of profits, and the whole à priori system, with its seeming simplicity, symmetry and roundness, owes its attractions to that idol of the tribe which, as Bacon says, leads the spirit of man to suppose and feign in nature a greater equality and uniformity than is in truth, and to mark the hits of his system but not the misses. An ingenious attempt has lately been made to account for the imaginary decennial cycle by the supposition that about every ten years there is a change in the management of business through a younger generation taking the place of the older, as though the commercial world were composed of successive ranks of men born together at the beginning of successive decades, and all in each rank reaching sixty and retiring together. But the commercial class, like the army, the bar, and the whole nation, is recruited with fresh blood every year, not only every tenth year. Lord Bacon himself showed a strong tendency to believe in both a political and an economical cycle, and supposed his own age of the world on the descent of the wheel, though he judiciously thought it 'not good to look too long on these turning wheels of vicissitude, lest we become giddy.' Adam Smith too leaned to the notion of a code of nature regulating the movement of the economic world with perfect equality and uniformity. Perhaps therefore one need not wonder that Mr. Jevons, whose philosophical powers have enabled him to make real discoveries, should be fascinated by the idea of commercial cycles recurring with the regularity of astronomical phenomena, and traceable to astronomical causes. But one is driven to suspect that Mr. Lowe can never have made a discovery, when he argues that Adam Smith's method was wholly deductive, because in the Wealth of Nations he puts his conclusions first; supporting them afterwards by the instances which he deems most convincing, instead of setting before his readers a vast number of historical and statistical facts, and working out the principle which they establish under their eyes. A library would not contain the books he would have written, had he attempted to convey to other minds by such a method the knowledge he had himself reached by long and laborious investigation. A discoverer would be avoided like a pestilence or the ancient mariner, were he to relate all the steps by which he got to his journey's end, after many misfortunes and failures it may be, and often burning his fingers in the crucible. Results, it is well said, not processes are for the public eye. How little Adam Smith was disposed to publish all his processes, appears from his direction to Hume in 1773 to burn all the papers, with one exception, found in his house at his death, and from his own destruction of them a few days before his end. The advantage of the division of labour—to which Mr. Lowe refers as a proof that he proceeded by assumption, because the number of examples he gives is small—was not a new doctrine, but his chapter on its limitation by the extent of the market bears all the marks of wide research and induction. The work of induction in relation to the division of labour is moreover by no means complete. There are plain symptoms in modern economy of tendencies to an amalgamation instead of a division of occupations. And the most arduous problem respecting the separation of occupations has never even occurred to the deductive school; namely, what are the causes governing its actual course, determining the directions of the national energies, the employments of different classes and of both sexes, in different countries and ages?

The human being or 'individual' from whose assumed tendencies the conclusions of the deductive system are drawn and its predictions made, is a fiction not a reality, a personification of **two** abstractions, the desire of wealth and aversion for labour; feelings differing, as has been shown, in different countries, ages, and persons, differing much, for example, in men and women. Mr. Bagehot felt so strongly the inapplicability of the assumptions of the system to the greater part of the world, that he actually limited political economy to England at its present state of commercial developement, and to the male sex in England. Such a limitation involves a complete surrender of the position that the system is based on universal laws or principles of human nature,—it involves also an admission that it is only by inductive investigation that we can determine what the actual **economy of** society is, and what the causes **that govern its structure and movement.** Enough has been said **too to** show that **the** fundamental assumptions of the deductive economist are really as fallacious in reference to modern Englishmen as to Frenchmen, Germans, Asiatics, or Africans. **The** economy **of** English society can no more than that of any other nation be explained by assuming that Englishmen are personifications of the love of wealth and ease. But this is only one of the fundamental shortcomings of the system. Looking only to the assumed motives of individuals, it ignores altogether the collective agency of the community, through its positive institutions as an organized political body or state, its history and traditions, and the social environment with which it encompasses every man and woman within it from the cradle to the grave.

Adam Smith's philosophy was not, **like the** little system that pleases some of his successors, if I may use **a** Horatian phrase, 'complete in itself, smooth, and round.'* **There was, it** is true, in his mind an ideal order of things which he called 'natural,' as **being** that **which** would take place **if** certain tendencies of human nature **were** allowed **to** operate without interference. Even in this ideal world however he saw that there must be laws relating to property, **succession,** tenure, and other **subjects,** although, in accordance with both the political **and** the theological philosophy of his time, there was a 'natural' type

---

* 'In se ipso totus, **teres** atque rotundus.'—Hor.

to which these institutions ought to conform. Mr. Macleod has urged on behalf of confining the scope of political economy to commercial exchange, that the 'distribution' of wealth contemplated by the French Physiocrates was that effected by exchange, or by the process of distribution as distinguished from that of production. The Physiocrates, it may be observed, were not the first to use the term in this sense; it was so employed by English writers on commerce a hundred years earlier. But one might as reasonably exclude all agencies save water from geology on the ground that Werner did not take them into account, as limit the investigations of the economist to the mode of distribution taken cognisance of in either the seventeenth or the eighteenth century in either England or France. The very word 'distribution,' moreover, which Adam Smith applies in his first book to the partition effected by exchange, is in his third book applied to that effected by succession; though in both cases we may perceive the influence of the ideal code of nature on his opinions and language. Long before his time indeed the term was applied to the distribution of wealth by law, as the Statute of Distributions shows. He sets before us both the 'natural,' as he called the ideally best, order of things, and the actual order resulting from positive institutions, historical events, and the constitution of human nature with its various and conflicting propensities; among which, as he points out, the love of dominion is apt to prevail over the desire of gain. The third book of the Wealth of Nations is mainly an investigation into the action and reaction of political and economic history, the progress of agriculture, manufactures, and commerce, and of the different classes of society in both country and town, until out of mediæval, Catholic, and feudal Europe had issued the Europe of his own time with an economy moulded and fashioned by centuries. The word evolution had not come into use in Adam Smith's day, and social philosophers did not call the historical order of events the natural order, or the actual sequences resulting from the whole constitution of human society and the surrounding world the results of natural law; the word Nature in their terminology having a purely ideal meaning. Yet in substance Adam Smith shows that the economic condition of the nations of modern Europe was the outcome of a long historical evolution, and could not otherwise be accounted for or understood, although a better state of things, which in the language of his time he called the natural state, would have resulted from better human government and institutions. Whoever compares the last three books of the Wealth of Nations with the announcement, at the end of the Theory of Moral Sentiments, of the author's intention 'in another discourse to give an account of the general principles of law and government, and of the different revolutions they have undergone in different ages and periods of society, not only in what concerns justice, but in what concerns police, revenue, arms, and whatever else is the subject of law,' will find evidence that political economy was not the only branch of political science in which Adam Smith had advanced beyond Plato, in whose days Mr. Lowe affirms that knowledge in all other branches of moral and political philosophy came to a standstill. Adam Smith saw that 'the revolutions of law and government' had followed a determinable order, that the whole movement of society, including even that of positive law, was subject to law in the scientific sense of regular and intelligible sequence, and that the economic state of a nation at every period of its history was only a particular aspect of the whole social development. This is the fundamental conception on which the Science of Society rests, although the modern social philosopher calls the actual succession of social phenomena the natural one, while Adam Smith used the word 'natural' in a different sense.

'In love, or war, or politics, or religion, or morals,' Mr. Lowe argues, 'it is impossible to foretell how men will act, and therefore it is impossible to reason deductively;' whereas, 'in matters connected with wealth, deviations arising from other causes than the desire of it may be neglected without perceptible error.' The truth is that all these causes, war, love, religion, morals, and politics, do profoundly influence the conduct and condition of mankind in relation to wealth, and the economic structure of society. It is one of Mr. Buckle's incorrect generalizations that in the middle ages there were but two engrossing pursuits, war and religion, and only two professions, the Church and the army. It is, on the other hand, a no less superficial philosophy that overlooks the influence of war and religion on the economy of modern Europe, the occupations of its inhabitants, and the nature, amount, distribution, and consumption of their productions. At no period of the middle ages was so large a proportion of the population of the Continent trained to war as at the present day. An immense part of the wealth of modern Europe, England included, consists of weapons, warlike structures and stores, and the appliances of armies and fleets. What would be the worth of a treatise deducing the economy of Germany from the assumption that every man is occupied solely in the acquisition of wealth, 'the actual deviations being so slight that they may be treated as practically non-existent'? Were astronomers able to discover certain indications of human life in another planet, on Mr. Lowe's principle we should know all that need interest or could instruct us respecting the economy of the planetary world from 'the two ruling passions of mankind, wealth and ease.' Would not the questions arise, Does war exist, and, if so, is every man a soldier, or is there a distinct military profession? Have the inhabitants of the planet any religion, and, if so, is there a wealthy priesthood? Are the institutions of marriage and the family established? What are the checks to the increase of population? Is land held in common, or does private property in it exist? What are the laws and customs with respect to succession? Have the people of this planet the same kinds of wealth as those of the earth, and have different countries in it different kinds, as in our own world? It has been shown that the mundane economist possesses no such powers of prediction as Mr. Lowe ascribes to him, just because politics, war, religion, morals and love do all powerfully affect human conduct in matters connected with wealth. Nevertheless the philosophy of society is not so undeveloped that no regular sequence or natural law is discoverable in these very influences, or prediction altogether impossible in relation to them. It can be foretold with a close approximation to accuracy how many marriages there will be between the 1st of January, 1879, and the next census. A well-known economist is said to maintain that marriage is nothing but a commercial contract, but Edmund Burke's complaint that the age of chivalry was gone, and that of economists and calculators had succeeded, was not quite so well grounded. Love, chivalrous sentiment, morals, religion, do still deeply affect marriage, even among a nation of shop-keepers; and it is because they do, that we can nearly foretell the number of such unions, and the number of children born and reared. We should be altogether without data for calculating the advance of population, the supply of labour, the movement of rent, the accumulation of capital, and its distribution by marriage and succession as well as exchange, if men and women, or even men alone, were influenced by no other than mercantile motives.

The economic structure of any given community, the direction taken by national energies, the occupations of the different classes, and of both sexes, the constituents and the partition of movable and immovable property, the progressive, stationary, or retrogressive condition in respect of productive power and the quantity and quality of the necessaries, comforts, and luxuries of life, are the results not of special economic forces, but of all the social forces, political, moral, and intellectual as well as industrial. The very wants and aims summed up in 'the desire of wealth' arise not from innate, original, and universal propensities of the individual man, but from the community and its history. Hunger and thirst, desire of shelter from cold and heat, are probably the only forms of the economic impulse that a human being isolated altogether from social influences would feel. The very kinds of food sought in civilized society are determined by a long national history, and are not the same in England and France. The predominant form which the love of wealth takes in the last country is, as already said, the love of landed property, a form non-existent in primitive humanity; and which in civilized countries is so much the result of national history that it is extinct in our own as a motive to labour and thrift on the part of the nation at large, though once widely diffused through all classes in both country and town.

Political economy is thus a department of the science of society which selects a special class of social phenomena for special investigation, but for this purpose must investigate all the forces and laws by which they are governed. The deductive economist misconceives altogether the method of isolation permissible in philosophy. In consequence of the limitation of human faculties, not that the narrowing of the field is in itself desirable or scientific, it is legitimate to make economic phenomena, the division of labour, the nature, amount, and distribution of national riches, the subject of particular examination; provided that all the causes affecting them be taken into account. To isolate a single force, even if a real force and not a mere abstraction, and to call deductions from it alone the laws of wealth, can lead only to error, and is radically unscientific. The development of the positive law of a nation, for example, is in all its bearings on industry, commerce, accumulation, and the distribution of property, a subject demanding the economist's investigation. The primitive ownership of things in common, the evolution of the separate possession of both chattels and land, of slavery, serfdom, and free labour, the changes in the law of intestate succession, the growth of the testamentary power, and of the law of contract in its different forms, are at once jural and economic facts, which the jurist regards from one point of view and the economist from another. The field of human society is so large and complex, man's capacity so limited, that it is by a number of investigations in relation to different aspects of the subject, that the science of society as a whole, is most likely to be advanced, and its ultimate generalizations and laws at last reached. The history of political economy is a warning against all attempts to reach them per saltum, and to construct at once a complete and symmetrical system. A radical error with respect to the history of both science in general and political economy in particular, lies at the root of Mr. Lowe's notion, that 'science means knowledge in its clearest and most absolute form, the test of which is prediction;' and that the fabric of economic science, under the hand of Adam Smith, 'rose up, like Jonah's gourd, in a single night.' If science meant only knowledge in its clearest and most absolute **form,** no science could have a beginning or a youth; it must spring into life fully grown and armed, like Minerva from the head of Jove; and only a science founded, like deductive political economy, on fiction, could do so. Had political economy grown up, like Jonah's gourd, in a night, it would like it have perished in a day, and could not have borne the light. A long line of inquirers had preceded Adam Smith, to some of whom he has acknowledged his debt. Nearly a century before the publication of the Wealth of Nations, Dudley North, himself a merchant, had expounded the policy of commercial liberty, going on some points even beyond his illustrious successor. Adam Smith's own language respecting the French Economists **answers** a question raised by Auguste Comte's remark, that he made no pretence of founding a new and special science of wealth. He did not pretend to be its founder, but he did regard such a science as not only founded, but far advanced by Quesnay and his followers, whose system of political economy he describes as, 'with all its imperfections, the nearest approach to perfection that had yet been made in that important science.' At the same time, like his French contemporaries, he regarded it as **a branch of** a wider science which they called Physiocratie, or the science of the government and laws of nature, and which he called Moral Philosophy.

Science is patient and progressive, never therefore reaching perfection; its essence consists in a right method of investigation more than in the extent of its progress. The same misconception that leads Mr. Lowe to admire the à priori political economy, with its fictitious completeness, symmetry, and exactness, **and to deny a** science of society, because it is yet in an inchoate state, shows itself in his assertion that no more is known now in psychology, morals, or politics, than was known in **the** days of Plato. No such realistic abstraction as the Ideas of Plato now deludes the psychologist, though something akin to it lingers in the deductive economist's notion of 'the desire of wealth.' The association of ideas is a psychological law which alone places mental philosophy far beyond the point it had reached with the Greeks; and the change in the course of social progress, on the one hand, and the inheritance, on the other, of cerebral qualities, can hardly be known to Mr. Lowe, or he could not refuse to admit a great recent advance in our knowledge of the laws of the human mind. In the science of law and politics the superiority of Adam Smith himself over Plato is evident. His remarks on the Athenian tribunals show that he could have saved Pericles from a blunder which not only deprived Athens of a system of jurisprudence, but did much to corrupt and undermine the State; yet Plato failed to discover it, though its consequences were under his eyes, and the constitution of courts was one of the subjects that engaged his attention. And the perception of revolutions in law and government following a regular sequence, and evolving successive economic as well as political states, to which Adam Smith attained, not only never dawned on Plato's mind, but may be said in itself to be a long step towards the foundation of a true science of society. The attempt to raise a prejudice against such a science on account of the difficulty of naming it otherwise than sociology, a compound of Latin and Greek, is not only captious and frivolous, but displays an extraordinary forgetfulness of scientific nomenclature. To say nothing of the admission of such combinations in Germany, the fatherland of philology, in words such as Socialpolitik, English philosophical terminology itself abounds in them. Natural philosophy, moral philosophy, are names compounded of Latin and Greek, which according to German usage would be written in one word, like Socialpolitik; and the term natural law is a mixture of Latin and English. One wonders indeed that Mr. Lowe, who is so shocked at sociology, does not shudder at the name of Adam Smith, as a combination, not from cognate tongues like Latin and Greek, but from Hebrew and English.

Yet although neither the objection that sociology has not attained to the perfection of astronomy, nor that it is a hybrid word, is entitled to a serious consideration, it would be a grave error to regard it as otherwise than a science still in its infancy. Its students should take warning from the history of political economy against hasty induction, and attempts to rise at once to the deductive stage. Two men of extraordinary genius, Auguste Comte and Herbert Spencer, though differing considerably on some points, have struck out some luminous generalizations and aperçus; but great circumspection and caution are needed in their application; they cannot safely be made to support trains of deduction, still less can they be treated as constituting the supreme inductions and fundamental laws of a science of society. Mr. Spencer's theorem, for example, that 'a movement from the homogeneous to the heterogeneous characterizes all evolution,' in both the physical and the social world, is true in a number of instances; and he has connected it with veræ causæ, with ascertained **natural** forces and conditions indubitably creating diversity where there had been similarity, and evolving new kinds and species of phenomena. Yet it is not a universal law, or an invariable truth from which inferences respecting the course of social development can with certainty be drawn. The movement of language, law, and political and civil union is for the most part in an opposite direction. In a savage country like Africa, speech is in a perpetual flux, and new dialects spring up with every swarm from the parent hive. In the civilized world the unification of language is rapidly proceeding; probably no Celtic tongue will be spoken in any part of Europe, Brittany or Wales not excepted, in a few generations; the diversities of English speech were so great four hundred years ago that Caxton found them a great obstacle to printing; four hundred years hence the same English will be spoken over half the globe, and will have few competitors, there is reason to believe, over the other half. The movement of political organization is similar; already Europe has nearly consolidated itself into a Heptarchy, the number of States into which England itself was once divided; and the result of the American war exemplifies the prevalence of the forces tending to homogeneity over those tending to heterogeneity. Two systems of civil law, again, the French and the English, now extend over a great part of the civilized world, and Sir Henry Maine has established many grounds for the proposition that 'all laws, however dissimilar in their infancy, tend to resemble each other in their maturity.' In customs and fashion civilized society is likewise advancing towards uniformity. Once every rank, profession, and district had a distinctive garb; now all such distinctions, save with the priest and the soldier, have almost disappeared among men; and among women the degree of outlay and waste is becoming almost the only distinction in dress throughout the west. In the industrial world a generation ago a constant movement towards a differentiation of employments and functions appeared; now some marked tendencies to their amalgamation have begun to disclose themselves. Joint-stock companies have almost effaced all real division of labour in the wide region of trade within their operation. Improvements in communication are fast eliminating intermediate trades between producers and consumers in international commerce; and the accumulation and combination of capital, and new methods of business, are working the same result in wholesale and retail dealing at home. Many of the things for sale in a village huckster's shop were formerly the subjects of distinct branches of business in a large town; now the wares in which scores of different retailers dealt, are all to be had in great establishments in New York, Paris, and London, which sometimes buy direct from the producers, thus also eliminating the wholesale dealer. These changes are among the causes that baffle the supposed prevision on which the doctrine of the equality of profits rests.

In the early stages of social progress, again, a differentiation takes place, as Mr. Spencer has observed, between political and industrial functions, which fall to distinct classes; now a man is a merchant in the morning and a legislator at night; in mercantile business one year, and the next perhaps head of the navy, like Mr. Goschen or Mr. W. H. Smith. There is even a strong tendency to sink the representative into the delegate, and to give every male householder a direct and immediate part in the government of the country. Improvements in both manufactures and the art of war seemed to Adam Smith with good reason to necessitate a separation between the military and industrial occupations; now every able-bodied man is a soldier on the continent. And here one of Auguste Comte's great generalizations also comes into question. Were a tendency to division of labour, and differentiation of functions, still to display itself on all sides, it would not give us a fundamental law determining the directions of human energies and their actual occupations. To take the case of another planet inhabited by human beings, astronomers might conceivably discover marks of a diversity of employments, and yet get no clue to the nature or course of the division of labour. We should need to know, for example, whether war and religion had any influence on their occupations. One of Comte's inductions affords an example of the kind of fundamental law needed to give us an insight into the causes and directions of the movement. Theology and war, according to Comte, are the ruling powers governing in the early stages of society human energies and employments; science and industry the chief powers in the more advanced stages. Undoubtedly the grounds on which this induction rests go to the root of the matter, and bring some great changes in the political, moral, and economic state of society under scientific law. Theology has long been a declining force, and though its indirect influence is still great, has now little direct control over the economic structure of western society. But the military element is more powerful now in Europe, and its power rests on less accidental causes than in Auguste Comte's own day. The very improvements in manufacture and the military art which tended in Adam Smith's view to wean the mass of mankind from war, the very agencies represented by steam and gunpowder to which Buckle triumphantly traced its extinction in the civilized world, have brought nations so close together, and armed them with such deadly weapons, that every man may almost be said now to sleep with arms at his side, ready to do battle in the morning. Science and industry themselves, along with pacific tendencies, have others of the opposite character, both in the effects already referred to, and in the higher pride, rivalry, ambition, and patriotism of nations developed by intellectual and industrial progress. When Buckle pointed to the Russians as the only warlike people in Europe except the Turks, because the least civilized, they were really a most unwarlike people under a warlike government. Now a military spirit is fast rising among them. Who shall say too that when the people of the United States have fully assimilated their present territory, and are at the same time brought into close proximity to the old world, their energies may not take a military direction for a time? 'The Americans,' said Tocqueville, 'have no neighbours, consequently no great wars to fear; they have almost nothing to dread from military glory.' When they are within four days of Europe they may find they have neighbours beyond sea; but, without crossing it, the whole continent north and south of the isthmus may tempt their ambition. Although a fundamental truth underlies the generalization referred to, it is not then a law from which deductions can be made. There are moreover diversities in the course of social evolution in different countries, which must be closely investigated before the sociologist can be in a condition to lay down universal canons; and after these are reached, much will remain for inquiry respecting the special development of particular races and nations.

A science of society thus does not exist in the sense of 'knowledge in its clearest and most absolute form, of which the test is prediction.' That however is not a scientific definition of science, and the sociologist may answer it with Bacon's words, prudens interrogatio dimidium scientiæ. Nor is it the science of society in its entirety only that is yet in its youth, and has a long and arduous future before it; it is so also with the department of it relating to the economic condition of mankind in different countries and ages. The labourer in this field too must go to work in a modester frame of mind than that of 'the Political Economist,' as he called himself in capitals, of twenty years ago. Mr. Lowe arrogates 'triumphs' for his own economic method; those he refers to were achieved by the opposite method of reasoning from observation and experience. But the scientific spirit is not a triumphant and boastful one, fired with a sort of intellectual Chauvinism, seeking polemical distinction and a path to promotion in the field of party war. A cavalry officer of the period before the Crimean War, when that branch of the army was distinguished by the glory of a moustache, used to say that no man could conceive the pitch to which human conceit could soar, unless he had served in a light dragoon regiment. **He was** however mistaken. There was a being yet more elate **with a sense of** superiority over his fellow-creatures in the economist who had Bastiat at his finger's ends, and who looked on political economy as a weapon by which he could discomfit political adversaries, and on **free** trade as a personal **triumph;** though he had as much claim **to** renown for it as a passenger in a Cunard steamer to the fame of Columbus.

Some **of the** earlier economists, Adam Smith, Malth**us,** Tooke, **and** John Mill, had a true claim to honour and reputation as discoverers. But the generalizations **and** conceptions that do credit **to one** period may discredit the next, just as it would disgrace the navigators of our time to follow the same **course,** and **sail in the same kind** of ship, as Columbus. **The** deductive economists of the present generation have contented themselves with the repetition of doctrines and formulas which once caused the light of science to dawn where all **had** been confusion and darkness. Clouds of abstraction and à **priori** reasoning nearly extinguished the promise of day, but fresh light is beginning to break. A few years ago Mr. Ingram's Address could hardly have been delivered, and the 'orthodox' economist, who now receives it with sullen respect, would have scoffed at it. It is suggested indeed, by way of diminishing its effect, that its author is a follower of Auguste Comte, but it expresses the views **of** many who, like the present **writer,** are not, however highly some of them like him may think of **Comte's genius.**

XXVII.

AUVERGNE.*

Fortnightly Review, December, 1874.

In the magnificent picture of the physical geography of France, with which the genius of Michelet has illustrated its history, only a few harsh touches are given to the province of Auvergne, depicted briefly as a land of inconsistencies and contradictions, cold beneath a southern sky, and inhabited by a southern race shivering on the ashes of volcanoes; a land of vineyards, whose wine does not please, of orchards, of which distant strangers eat even the commonest fruits, and one to whose mountains thousands of emigrants yearly return without a new idea. It is, in fact, a land of contrasts, physical and moral; containing regions whose features, social and economic, as well as geological, are widely dissimilar. Yet the contrasts involve no real contradictions. The chief physical contrast is between mountain and plain, and remarkable economic and social diversities spring

---

* Some controversy exists on the point whether, in translating the name l'Auvergne, the English article should be used, as in the case of the Bourbonnais, the Lyonnais, the Vivarais, the Ardennes, the Seine, the Creuse &c., or whether we should say simply Auvergne, as in the case of Normandy, Brittany, Picardy, Flanders, &c. A German philologer whom I consulted on the point, and in whose opinion a French philologer, also consulted, concurs, draws the following distinction between the cases in which the article should be used in English, and those in which it is more idiomatic to discard it :—' The Bourbonnais, the Lyonnais, the Vivarais, are adjectival formations, and therefore naturally take the article in English. The French departments, again, being the names of rivers and mountain chains, take the article in English just as we say the Seine, the Loire, the Alps, the Pyrenees, of the rivers and mountains themselves. But the only French province which could properly take the article in English would be such as La Marche, where English idiom too would require us to say the March, or the Border. There is nothing to distinguish the case of Auvergne from that of Normandy and Brittany, where the article is omitted in English, though used in French.'

from it. But mountain and plain are correlatives and complements, not contradictions, to one another; and differences of life, occupation, usage, thought, and feeling in their inhabitants are but consequences of the same laws of human nature, operating under diverse conditions, and afford excellent illustrations of the mode in which differences of structure and character in human societies, often superficially attributed to diversity of ancestral origin or race, are really produced.

It is not the scenery of Auvergne that this essay seeks to describe, but some of its chief economic and social phenomena; they are, however, so related to some of its physical features, that the latter cannot be left altogether unnoticed. Of the two departments into which the ancient province once called Arvernes, from the Arverni, is now divided, that of the Cantal, formerly La Haute Auvergne, is wholly a mountainous region; while the richer, more populous, and far more important department of the Puy-de-Dôme—so named from the huge mountain overhanging Clermont-Ferrand, its capital—contains both mountainous districts, and also the famous plain or valley named the Limagne, traversed by the railway from Gannat to Issoire; of which, thirteen hundred years ago, King Childebert said, 'there was but one thing he desired before he died; that was to see the beautiful Limagne of the Auvergne, which was said to be the masterpiece of nature, and a land of enchantment.' A century earlier Sidonius Apollinaris wrote from a country-seat in this rich valley, 'The Auvergne is so beautiful that strangers who have once entered it cannot make up their minds to leave it, and forget in it their native land.' The strangers who enter Auvergne at the present day are for the most part either geologists about to inspect its extinct volcanoes and other similar phenomena, or invalids on their way to the mineral waters of Royat, La Bourboule, or Mont Dore, or ordinary tourists coming to see both its exhausted craters and its baths. The geologists and the tourists usually make up their minds to leave the province after a few days; and a few weeks at the baths generally suffice to give the invalids strength and resolution to return home. Least of all, perhaps, is the visitor who comes (as has happened more than once to the present writer) fresh from Switzerland to the Limagne, likely to be moved to the enthusiasm of Sidonius Apollinaris by its scenery; especially just after the harvest, when its corn-fields, like shorn sheep, are bare and unpicturesque. But the ancient could as little have sympathized with the modern traveller's admiration for Switzerland. What he loved was a land of corn and wine and fruit, and that the Limagne is. His associations with gigantic mountains, frowning rocks, tremendous precipices, deserts of ice and snow, were horror, hunger, danger, and death. Auvergne itself has mountains and rocks, which, picturesque as they are, have few charms for those to whom they are associated only with privation and hardship. A woman, of whom I asked my way a few weeks ago in the highlands of Mont Dore, said, 'This is not a nice country, with all these mountains and rocks,' adding with a horizontal movement of her hand, 'I like a flat country.' Her associations with mountain scenery were black bread with a few chestnuts and potatoes, water unreddened with the wine at which Michelet sneers, hard times in winter, and hot and weary work in summer, with only one preservative from thirst, not to have a habit of drinking. 'Je n'ai pas l'habitude de boire, ainsi je n'ai pas soif,' she replied to a question suggested by my own feelings under a burning sun. In the plain of the Limagne she knew that the labourer often owned the ground on which he worked, might, if he pleased, drink the juice of his own grapes, and might, if he sold, as Michelet says, the common apples from his orchard in a distant market, instead of eating them himself, get 450 francs to the hectare for them, with as much more for the grass amidst which they grew. Having heard an old woman in a cottage in the Limagne say to a visitor, to whom she offered a slice off a huge melon, that she was very fond of melons, which are cheap in that region, I asked my friend on the Mont Dore mountain if she liked them. 'Je les aimerais mieux,' she replied, 's'ils venaient dans les montagnes.'

A contrast full of instruction and interest, when viewed in relation to its causes, between the mountain and the plain in Auvergne, is the different distribution of landed property. In the mountainous districts of the Puy-de-Dôme, the term large property—'la grande propriété'—is applied, as a general rule, only to properties of a hundred and fifty acres and upwards; properties under forty acres being there classed as 'la petite propriété,' and those between forty and a hundred and fifty acres as 'la moyenne propriété.' In the Limagne, on the other hand, from twenty to five-and-twenty acres make a large property in popular thought and speech, and a multitude of the small properties do not exceed a quarter of an acre. The soil in this fertile plain has in the last two generations, especially the last twenty years, passed almost wholly out of the possession of wealthier and larger owners into that of 'petits propriétaires,' who cultivate it with their own hands. The Report on the the Puy-de-Dôme, contained in one of the twenty quarto volumes of the 'Enquête Agricole,' after referring to the want of capital in the mountainous parts of that department, says, 'In the plain, the want of capital does not make itself felt, in consequence of the sale of land in small lots, which has permitted of the liquidation of property by paying off mortgages; but the species of proprietors has changed, and the man of means, the former proprietor, has become a capitalist, who has invested the proceeds of his land in securities.' This diversity in the distribution of landed property results partly from economic causes, partly from profound differences in the feelings and ideas generated by opposite conditions of life in mountain and plain. The economic causes are by no means the most interesting, but they must not be overlooked. In the mountains, on the one hand, both the comparative infertility of the land and the nature of pastoral husbandry tend to maintain comparatively large farms, and to prevent their being broken up by sale in small parcels. In the Limagne, on the other hand, the aptitude of the soil and climate for the production of rich plants, the vine, for example, requiring minute cultivation, and peculiarly suited to spade-husbandry,—the rise in the price of such productions in recent years,—the rise, moreover, of wages, adding nothing to the expenses of the cultivator who employs no hired labour, but heavily to those of the large farmer,—the increased gains and savings of both small cultivators and labourers, and their consequently increased purchases of land,—make a combination of causes tending to minute subdivision. Adam Smith, remarking that it was a matter of dispute among the ancient Italian husbandmen whether it was advantageous to plant new vineyards, adds that the anxiety of the owners of old vineyards in France in his own time to prevent the planting of new ones indicated an opinion that the high profits of vine-growing could last no longer than the restrictive laws which they had **procured for that** purpose. The increased growth of the vine around Clermont-Ferrand in the last five-and-twenty years shows what the small proprietors in the Limagne now think on the subject. In the arrondissement of Clermont alone, between thirty and forty thousand acres of both hill-side and plain are now covered by **vineyards,** which **formerly** were to be seen only on certain slopes **with the best aspects.**

Yet, after allowing **all due weight** to the causes referred to, it remains **certain** that causes of a totally different **order** have powerfully contributed to the maintenance of larger properties in the mountainous **districts than** in the plain; namely, the greater strength **in the** former **of** ancient usage, old family feeling, **and** religious sentiment in both **sexes.** In the plain, both the sale of land in small plots and the partition of inheritances by the law of succession tend to break up family properties; **in the** mountain neither has hitherto operated considerably. **The** Report of the 'Enquête Agricole' on the Puy-de-Dôme makes **no attempt to trace to** their sources the curious diversities of usage and sentiment **which** it describes; but the description itself is worth citing. 'The transmission of property takes place in **a** manner essentially different in **the** plain and the mountain. **In the** plain, an inheritance is almost always partitioned or sold **when a** succession (**of** more than one **child**) takes place; if partitioned, each of the heirs takes a part of **each parcel;** if it is sold, it is so in detail, and by the smallest fractions, **in** order the more readily to find buyers. Everything thus contributes to indefinite subdivision in the plain. In the mountains they cling **to the** conservation **of** the inheritance unbroken, and do all that is possible in order not to destroy the work of the family, and not to divide the paternal dwelling. The daughters willingly consent **to** take religious vows, and renounce the patrimony of their parents; those who contract marriage agree to leave to the head of the family their share of the inheritance. It is the same with the sons, of whom some become priests, others emigrate, consenting not to claim their share of the property; and it is one of the sons who remains at home, working with the father and mother, who becomes in turn proprietor of the paternal dwelling. Thus the principle of the law of equal partition is eluded, and it comparatively seldom happens that the other children assert their claims, so accepted is the usage in the manners of the mountain.'

In Auvergne, as in the department of the Creuse, one reason for the great annual migration of the peasants to the towns, which, in France, where there is no exodus to foreign countries, goes by the name of emigration, is doubtless the comparative unproductiveness of mountain land. It cannot give bread to all the young men born on it. But a more potent reason, in Auvergne, though one less in accordance with old economic hypotheses, is that the younger sons, as the 'Enquête Agricole' states, seek a subsistence elsewhere in order to leave the property undivided to the elder brother; or occasionally it is the elder brother who emigrates, relinquishing his share to a younger one remaining at home. Thousands of Auvergnats are consequently to be found labouring in remote cities, as masons, sawyers, porters, water-carriers, blacksmiths, chimney-sweeps; and it is a saying in the surrounding provinces, when some hard work has to be done, 'Il faut attendre le passage des Auvergnats.'

They have a character in French towns, and French novels, for clownishness and stupidity, derived doubtless from the nature of their occupations, as hewers of wood and drawers of water. But they show no lack of native shrewdness, according to my observation, when questioned on any subject. And M. de Lavergne remarked to me lately, that the Auvergnat displays more sagacity in timing his migration than the peasant of his own department, the Creuse—M. de Lavergne is deputy for the Creuse—does. The Auvergnat leaves his home at the beginning of winter, when the country is buried in snow, returning in summer, when work of different kinds is going on.

2 E

The Creuse peasant, on the other hand, goes to Paris, Lyons, or some other town, when summer is coming on, and comes back in winter, when there is nothing to do. Michelet taunts the Auvergne emigrants with bringing back some money, but no new ideas. The sum they bring to the poor department of the Cantal is put at five million francs (200,000) a year, in the report of the 'Enquête Agricole' on that department—a sum hardly to be despised. But the renunciation by the emigrants of their share in the family property certainly shows, if not an extraordinary imperviousness to new ideas, an extraordinary tenacity of old ones, and in particular of two ideas which are among the oldest in human society—subordination to the male head of the family, and conservation of the family property, unalienated and unpartitioned. The number of younger sons from these mountains who become priests is a still more remarkable phenomenon, though traceable in the main to the same causes. M. Bonnet, of Clermont-Ferrand, being asked in the course of his evidence before the 'Enquête Agricole,' what was the proportion of young men in the plain and the mountains, respectively, of the Puy-de Dôme, who devoted themselves to the clerical profession, replied, 'In the Limagne, very few young men devote themselves to the religious profession. It is from the mountains they come. Half the clergy of the diocese come from the arrondissement of Ambert.'

A few weeks ago, I happened myself to sit beside a party of priests at dinner, and learned that four out of the six were born in the Auvergne mountains, which likewise contribute largely to recruit the convents with nuns. M. Bonnet, being asked whether the mountain families do not induce the daughters to take religious vows, in order to prevent the partition of the family estate, replied, 'To that I answer in the affirmative. The parents, in consequence of the piety which reigns in the mountains, are not sorry to see their daughters embrace the religious profession, and at the same time to see the family property thereby less divided. In general, the eldest son remains at home, and the father frequently leaves to him the part disposable by will. And when a daughter enters a convent, if the portion she brings to it does not absorb her share in the inheritance, she on her side usually makes her will in favour of the already favoured brother.'

Thus in the Auvergne mountains at this day, 'the younger brother sinks into the priest,' just as Sir Henry Maine describes him as doing under the influence of primogeniture in feudal society. The daughter, too, enters the convent just as she did in the middle ages, and from the same causes which actuated her then—family sentiment and male primogeniture on the one hand, and 'the piety which reigns in the mountains' on the other hand, which is in fact a survival of mediæval piety, preserved by certain conditions of life and environment. A reason, it is true, sometimes assigned for the number of young women who become nuns in the department of the Puy-de-Dôme is that there are no girls' schools in the mountains; the daughters of parents who can afford it are, therefore, sent to convents to be educated, and the education they receive both unfits them and gives them a distaste for the rude life of a mountain farmhouse. They learn to make lace and embroidery, but not to mend stockings or to make butter or cheese. It is neverthless undisputed that religious feeling and family ideas fill the chief place among the motives which lead both the daughters to take vows, and the younger sons to become priests.

I have nowhere met with any attempt to trace to their ultimate causes the curious social phenomena just described; but one may, I think, point with certainty to the difference of environment and conditions of life in the mountain and in the plain, as the source of the superior force of religion, family feeling, and ancient usage in the former. On its moral and social side, the contrast between mountain and plain is the contrast between the old world and the new; between the customs, thoughts, and feelings of ancient and modern times. The principal sources of change and innovation in the plain— towns, manufactures, trade, easy communication with distant places, variety of occupation and manner of life—are inoperative in the mountains. Even in summer, the mountain lies aloof from the town and its life, communication between them is tedious for people on foot; the country carts are of the most primitive make, and drawn by slow oxen or cows; where a heavy load has to be brought up hill on the best roads in the department, for instance, from Clermont towards Mont Dore, I have seen six horses yoked in a curious order to draw it—first one wheeler, then two abreast, with three leaders in tandem. In winter the whole mountain region is under snow, the roads are often impassable, and the members of the mountain family are shut up together with their dumb companions, the cattle. Then the life of the mountain pastoral farmer is the same from father to son, and from age to age; the whole neighbourhood too follows the same occupation, and leads the same life, so that there is a surrounding mass of uniform and primitive usage and thought. But the family is the earliest of social bonds, and it is by studying it as it survives in places such as the Auvergne mountains, that we can best realize something of the force of that ancient bond, and something of the nature of the sentiments which led to the patriarchal authority of the elder brother, on the one hand, and the conservation of the family property under his guardianship and control on the other. Sir Henry Maine calls the origin of primogeniture, as affecting the devolution of land in the middle ages, one of the most difficult problems of historical jurisprudence; and it has a peculiar difficulty in England to which he has not referred. How was it that during a period when society was decidedly becoming more orderly, and patriarchal rule was giving place to regular government, the division of socage lands among all the sons was superseded by primogeniture, the principle already established in the case of land held in military tenure? A tendency to uniformity in the law, produced by the institution of itinerant royal courts, and the bias of the judges, contributed probably to the change; but something more is required to explain it. The courts proceeded to make custom, instead of the old law of gavelkind, determine the succession to socage lands; but the question follows, how did a custom come into existence contrary to the old law, and to the apparent interest of the majority of the family? And the existence at this day, in the Auvergne mountains, of a custom directly opposed to the positive law of the land helps us to understand how the English courts were supported by family feeling in assuming a custom of primogeniture contrary to the old law of division.

The force of religious feeling, 'the piety which reigns in the mountains,' as M. Bonnet calls it in a passage cited above, has its root, doubtless, partly in the same conservation of ancient sentiment, thought, and belief, which gives the family property to one son, partly in other ideas and feelings generated by the conditions of mountain life. As the difference between the mountain and plain is a phase of the difference between the old world and the new, so is it a phase of the difference between country and town. The mountain is as it were the country in its rudest primitive form, while the plain is as it were a great suburb of the towns it contains and has continual intercourse with. The 'petit propriétaire' in the Limagne has the money-making spirit as strongly developed as the town tradesman; sometimes he himself lives in the town, and in any case he has frequent transactions of buying, selling, and other relations with it. But the money-making and commercial spirit evidently tends to individualism, and to the disintegration of the family; and it has ever been found also to foster a secular spirit and repugnance to sacerdotal dominion. In towns, moreover, and also (though in a smaller degree) in the surrounding plain, men see chiefly the power of man, and unconsciously gather confidence from their own numbers against both the powers of nature, which are supreme in the mountain, and those supernatural powers which the powers of nature suggest to rude minds. The difference between the force of religious sentiment and reverence for the clergy in town and country in Catholic countries is striking. One has but to look at the way in which a Flanders priest is saluted in the streets of Ghent, for instance, and at some miles distance in the country, for evidence of the opposite influence in this respect of town and country life. At Clermont-Ferrand, the respectable working-man commonly holds aloof from the clergy, declines their aid, even when in need, and is averse from joining societies for the mutual benefit of the members, because the clergy take a part in their management. Indications of the prevailing disposition in that town towards ecclesiastical authority, have repeatedly come under my notice. One day, last September, I was reading a newspaper in a café, when an old woman going by observed in the most sarcastic manner and tone in reference to a person beside me, 'Ce monsieur appartient à Monseigneur l'Evêque, puisqu'il a acheté la Gazette d'Auvergne.' Pointing to another person, she continued, 'Ce monsieur-là appartient à Monsieur le Préfet, puisqu'il a acheté le Journal du Puy-de-Dôme.' Then seeing both journals in my hand, 'Voilà un monsieur qui a acheté tous les deux. Il ne sait pas encore à qui appartenir. C'est une question difficile.' No old woman in the mountains of a diocese which draws half its clergy from their youth, could have spoken with such levity of an episcopal dignitary. The persistence in the Auvergne mountains of ancient ideas and feelings on such subjects as both the clergy and family property, notwithstanding that thousands of their peasants spend half the year in large towns, affords an instructive example, on the one hand, of the profound influence of physical geography on the mental constitution of man, and the history of the different branches of the race, and, on the other hand, of the operation of laws of human nature and motives to human conduct, powerfully affecting the economic structure of society, the division of occupations, the amount and the distribution of wealth, which are absolutely ignored in what still passes with some professed economists for a science of wealth.

Among the most active agencies in the town which rarely reach the mountains in Auvergne, is the newspaper, the influence of which at Clermont-Ferrand I have heard ecclesiastics deplore, although they themselves employ it to the utmost of their power. Arthur Young tells that he could not find a single newspaper in a café in that town in the autumn of 1789, though the air was alive with revolutionary rumours. In the autumn of 1874 he might have found half-a-dozen in any one of several cafés, besides having them pressed upon him by newsvendors incessantly passing by. The local journals are not sparing of rhetoric, or lacking in party spirit. The number of the journal which the old woman called the organ of Monseigneur l'Evêque, contained a furious article against

radicalism, of which the following passage is a specimen:—
'The radical lives on hatred. Irritated against authority, irritated against society, irritated against God, he hates everything, he hates even himself. Hatred devours him, and hatred supports him. To glut his hatred he would give his life, and he wishes to live only to glut it. He breeds, imbibes, and feeds on hatred; and, like the garment of Nessus, it burns him, being in that respect an anticipation of eternity.' If the Auvergne radical is a good hater, it seems that the Auvergne ecclesiastic is so **too**. M. de Lavergne, speaking of **the** immense subdivision **of landed** property **in** the Limagne since 1789, and the vast **increase in the** number of spade-cultivators, remarks **in his 'Rural Economy of** France' that the prevalence of such severe manual labour has a tendency to produce rough and violent **manners.** Such manners certainly are sometimes exhibited in the Limagne, but not by spade-cultivators only.

The minute subdivision of land during the last twenty-five years in the Limagne, whatever may be its tendencies for good or for evil in manners and other respects, assuredly cannot be ascribed to over-population, once regarded in England as the inevitable consequence of the French law of succession. It is true that between 1789 and the middle of this century, the population of the Puy-de-Dôme increased, as M. de Lavergne says, from 400,000 to 600,000.* But later statistics supplied to me by M. Adolphe F. de Fontpertuis, an economist well known to English readers of the Économiste Français and the Journal des Économistes, exhibit an opposite movement—

	1851.	**1866.**	1872.
Population of the Puy-de-Dôme	601,594	**571,690**	566,463

And the Report of the Enquête Agricole on the department states, 'All the witnesses have declared that one of the principal causes of the diminution of the population is the diminution of children in families. Each family usually wishes for only one child; and when there are two, it is the result of a mistake (une erreur), or that, having had a daughter first, they desire to have a son.' A poor woman near Royat, to

---

* 'Économie Rurale de la France,' p. 371.

whom I put some questions respecting wages and prices, asked whether my wife and children were there, or at one of the other watering-places, and seemed greatly surprised that I had neither. She thought an English tourist must be rich enough to have several children; but when asked how many she had herself, she answered with a significant smile, 'One lad; that's quite **enough**.' Our conversation on the point was as follows:—

'Votre **dame et** vos enfants, sont ils à Royat?'

'Non.'

'Où donc? à Mont Dore?'

'Moi, je n'ai ni enfants ni femme.'

'Quoi! Pas encore!!'

'**Et** vous, combien d'enfants avez-vous?'

'Un gars; c'est bien **assez. Nous** sommes pauvres, mais vous êtes riche. Cela fait une petite différence.'

If over-population gives rise to tremendous problems in **India,** the decline in the number of children in France seems almost equally serious. If two children only are born to each married couple, a population must decline, because a considerable number **will** not reach maturity. If only one child be born to each pair, a nation must rapidly become extinct. The French law of succession is producing exactly the opposite effect to what was predicted in this country. Had parents in France complete testamentary power, there would not be the same reason for limiting **the number of children.** M. Léon Iscot, accordingly, in his evidence on this subject before the '**Enquête** Agricole' on the Puy-de-Dôme, **said,** 'The number **of** births in families has diminished one-half. **We must** come **to liberty of** testation. In countries like England, where **testamentary** liberty exists, **families** have more children.'

Whatever may be thought **of the** change which is taking place in France **in** respect of the numbers of the population, there is one change **of** which no other country has equal reason to be proud. Its agricultural population before the Revolution was **in** the last extremity of poverty and misery, their normal condition was half-starvation; they could scarcely be said to be **clothed,** their appearance in many places was hardly human. No other country in Europe, taken as a whole, can now show upon the whole so comfortable, happy, prosperous, and respectable a peasantry. The persons examined before the 'Enquête Agricole' on the Puy-de-Dôme, a department with many disadvantages of situation and climate, grumbled about many things, as landowners and farmers universally do; but they were unanimous **on the** point that the peasantry and labouring class were 'better fed, better clothed, and better lodged' than **a** generation ago; and in all these respects **a** visible improvement has taken place, even within the last ten years. You still, it is true, often see boys and girls in the Puy-de-Dôme without shoes and stockings, but rarely ever otherwise than comfortably clad in all other respects. The absence of shoes and stockings is a sign, **not of** poverty, but of the retention of ancient custom. **In the** north of Ireland it is still not uncommon to **see girls on the** road in a smart dress and bonnet, and holding a parasol over their heads, with their shoes not on their feet, but in their hands. And in a good many parts of the south of France a century has made no great change since Adam Smith **wrote**, 'Custom has rendered leather shoes a necessary of life in England. The poorest person of either sex would be ashamed to appear in public without them. In Scotland, custom has rendered them a necessary of life to the lowest order of men, but not to the same order of women, who may, without any discredit, walk about barefooted. In France, they are necessaries neither to men nor to women; the lowest ranks of both sexes appearing there publicly, without any discredit, sometimes in wooden shoes and sometimes barefooted.' That it is no discredit either to boys and girls in the Puy-de-Dôme to go barefooted, and, on the other hand, that modern fashion is beginning to creep even into the mountain villages, I saw evidence the other day in the village of La Tour d'Auvergne, **where** children smartly chaussés in the latest style were playing with others without shoes or stockings. The Auvergne children, one may observe, do play; they are not, like the children in Swiss villages, serious little old men **and** women, too busy and grave for laughter or play. Children and adults alike in Auvergne seem for the most part in rude health, though in the mountains they may sometimes owe more to the air than to the food; and in some villages crétins are still to be seen—a consequence doubtless of the filthy condition of the cottages within and without. The horrid malady of crétinisme has lately been driven from some Swiss valleys by an improvement of the houses. In the Puy-de-Dôme this autumn, I saw many instances of a change which is the **sure** precursor of an elevation of the standard of habitation, namely, the substitution of tiled for thatched roofs. One hears people say there, indeed, that **this** change is no improvement; that **the** thatch is not only cheaper, but warmer in winter and cooler in summer. **It is**, however, a source of constant danger from **fire to the** whole village; and in every country in western Europe the change from the straw roof to **tiles or** slates is found to be accompanied **by** material progress. **M. L. Nadaud puts** into the mouth of an interlocutor in his '**Voyage** en Auvergne,' 'You will never **make of an** Auvergne village a Flemish village. Climates form the habits and tastes.' Climate certainly plays a great part in determining the **economic condition of** mankind; and its agency, along with other physical influences, has been too generally overlooked by economists in **their** eagerness to explain the whole economy of society by reference to the single assumption of **a** desire of every one to obtain additional wealth. But climate did not make the Flemish village. It grew up by degrees in the middle ages **out of** liberty, manufactures, and markets for village productions. And the fact that the Auvergne villager is beginning to **roof** his dwelling **with** tiles from another province shows that liberty and **facilities** for trade may yet make a Flemish village of the **Auvergne** one. Even of the remote and mountainous Cantal, M. de Lavergne said several years ago, 'The discoveries of modern civilization have been long unknown in Upper Auvergne; its towns are but rude villages, and its rustic dwellings have but too often the repulsive aspect of extreme poverty, yet competence and comfort are making their way into them by degrees.'

A general rise of wages has taken place in Auvergne in the **last** fifteen years, but the rise **has** been very unequal. The demand for labour has increased much more in some communes than in others, and, on the other hand, **the** supply is much scantier in some than elsewhere. 'In one commune,' says the Report of the Enquête Agricole, 'there are but **four** labourers; every one therefore fights for them, and when they **work for one** employer, it is impossible for the others to get their **work done.**' At Saint Maude, near Issoire, **M.** de Saint-Maude stated to **the** commission that it was out of the power of large proprietors there to farm their own land, on account of the scarcity of labour and its extravagant price. 'The price of a day's labour is from **4 to** 5 francs, and a meal **besides,** with wine. Wages have more than doubled since 1852. **Women,** above all, have seen their wages trebled.'* In another place, however, the rate was shown to be only **1 fr. 25 cents** in winter, and 2 fr., with food, in summer; **and in a** third, 1 fr. 50 cents, without food, during the greatest part of **the** year, with 1 fr. 25 cents, and food, in harvest. **In the** autumn of the present year, after the harvest, I found 3 francs a day the rate in several parts of the Limagne, and a person from Normandy, who was present when I made **some** inquiries on the subject, remarked that this was more than is paid in that wealthy province—a statement quite in conformity with M. Victor Bonnet's statistics.† The assertion of M. de Saint-Maude respecting the rise of women's wages is likewise in accordance with a statement of a high authority on French economics, M. Paul Leroy-Beaulieu, that the pay of women for agricultural labour has risen more than that of men in recent years—a fact, he adds, only to be rejoiced at, women having formerly been much underpaid in comparison with men. With respect to the relative movement in recent years of agricultural and town wages in Auvergne, the following figures are taken from some unpublished statistics, which Mr. Somerset Beaumont, **late** M.P. for Wakefield, collected **at** the close of last year, showing the comparative rates in agriculture and several other employments in 1868 and 1873, at Clermont-Ferrand and in its neighbourhood :—

---

* 'Enquête Agricole, **Puy-de-Dôme,**' p. 296.
† 'Agricultural **Wages in Europe,' Fortnightly** Review, June, 1874, p. 708.

		1868. fr. c.	1873. fr. c.
Agricultural Wages, per diem, without food	(during the harvest	3 17	4 0
	(in ordinary seasons	2 24	2 50
Masons		3 0	3 50
Carpenters		3 0	4 50
Joiners		3 0	3 50
Locksmiths		3 25	3 50
Servants, per annum,	men	300 0	400 0
	women	150 0	200 0

The reader will observe that these variations are by no means in harmony with the old assumption of abstract political economy, that the diversities of wages in different employments correspond to diversities in the nature of the work; as though all the poor workmen throughout every country could know exactly all the differences of wages and work in all occupations, and choose their own trade accordingly. The wages of carpenters at Clermont were lower in 1868 than those of locksmiths; in 1873 they were much higher, and were so, not because the nature of either employment had changed, but simply for the same reason that agricultural wages had risen in some communes much more than in others, namely, that the local conditions of demand and supply had changed.

Among causes both of a rise and of local inequalities in wages, prices, and the cost of living in Auvergne are its watering-places, Royat, Mont Dore, and La Bourboule, which may be classed together as constituting a third social and economic region. Auvergne, as already said, is a land of contrasts, and the contrast which this third region presents to the two others already described is worth notice, not only as contributing to a description of the province, but also as illustrating the influence of local physical conditions on social phenomena, and exemplifying the causes which produce distinct types of human life, character, and pursuit.

One difference which strikes the eye at once between the watering-place and the two other regions is, that while the latter display dissimilar social and economic features, yet those features are in both cases indigenous; it is the Auvergnat you see, unlike as he appears in mountain and plain. But the watering-place, though in Auvergne, is not of it, socially speaking. You find yourself, on entering it, among Frenchmen from every part of France, except the province in which it is situated; its chief social phenomena are exotic, not native. The only pervading **type** of character here is also altogether unlike the types which the two other regions develop. The representative man of the Limagne is the spade-husbandman wringing the uttermost farthing from his little property; **the** patriarchal head of the pastoral household, the priest, the nun, the emigrant labourer, are the representatives of the mountain. But in the watering-place the only representative character is the invalid; the people round you differ in every respect but one, that they are almost all seeking the cure of some malady. In the mountain, family sentiment, religion, ancient usage, are the dominant principles; in the rich agricultural plain, the paramount object is to make money wherewith to buy land; at Royat, **Mont** Dore, and Bourboule the dominant motive which determines the occupations of producers and the demand of consumers is the desire, not of wealth, but of health. But this desire brings wealth to the watering-place, which thereby becomes a monetary region in which the cost of living is higher than in other parts of the province, and is so in conformity with the main principle governing the diffusion of money and the movements of prices. The general principle traceable throughout the immense monetary changes of our time—one which the assumption that wages **and** profits are equalized by competition has led not a few economists to miss—is that the distribution of the increased currency of the world has followed the path of local progress, and of the development of local resources or advantages, of whatever kind. Superior local advantages for manufactures and trade in one place, for scenery or amusement in another, for the cure of disease in a third, cause a relatively large influx of money, and send up the prices of labour and important commodities above the rates prevailing in places making inferior progress, or offering no special attraction to money. Only one classification, as already said, fits the majority of the visitors to the watering-places of Auvergne, namely, that they are for the most part invalids; but whatever they are, and however they spend their lives, they spend here in the mass a great sum of money at hotels, and on baths, carriages, saddle-horses, sedan-chairs, shops, the casino, &c.; and as their numbers yearly increase, local prices rise. Not many years ago, Royat, Mont Dore, and Bourboule were three villages of no reputation, with village prices. Bourboule, in particular, was then a mere hamlet of the meanest order; now the visitor forgets the old hamlet in a cluster of new hotels, and villas, with rows of smart little shops, which disappear at the close of the season. Bourboule was mentioned in guide-books not long ago as having from seventy to eighty visitors in the season; this autumn it had several thousands, most of whom remained for several weeks. There were members of the National Assembly, authors, country gentlemen, Parisians, provincial townspeople, military men, ecclesiastics, besides a multitude of nondescript young gentlemen and ladies. Eminent above all was a writer of European fame, M. Léonce de Lavergne, especially entitled to mention here, not only as having described the rural economy of both the Limagne and the mountains of Auvergne, but also as having foretold the growth of its watering-places in one of the celebrated works by which he is best known to most English readers, 'L'Economie Rurale de la France.' In his own country, he has long held a high place both in the world of letters and in the political world, having formerly occupied a considerable post in M. Guizot's government, and being now one of the most influential and respected members of the National Assembly, although the infirmity of his health has prevented his taking a conspicuous part in its public proceedings. His presence at Bourboule this autumn may be instanced as an example of the operation of the physical causes which are giving both wealth and celebrity to places formerly as poor as unknown, and changing the scale of prices in proportion. The charge for pension this autumn at Bourboule was from twelve to fifteen francs a day, according to the length of the stay—a rate, perhaps, not immoderate, considering that it included wine, but one which would have seemed incredible a few years ago. At Clermont-Ferrand, the passing and uncovenanted stranger still pays only four francs for an excellent dinner in the principal hotels, with wine and fruit unlimited. Clermont, indeed, with the other chief towns of the Puy-de-Dôme, might fairly be classed together as constituting a fourth region with distinct social and economic phenomena; one indication of this being that, close as are the commercial and other relations between the towns of the Limagne and the surrounding plain, the villagers in the latter generally regard the townspeople with a feeling approaching to hostility. It was, however, the aim of this essay to sketch only some of the most striking and distinctive social and economic features of a province as yet little known in those respects in England; and its towns, though not without peculiar characteristics, seem hardly to call for a special description. The sketch which has been given of the phenomena of the rest of the province may suffice to illustrate the importance of taking account, in economic investigations, of physical geography and environment, and the necessary fallaciousness of a theory which professes to account for the division of labour in every country, the amount and distribution of its wealth, and the movements of money and prices, by deductions from the principle of pecuniary interest.

What do we learn respecting the real division of employments in Auvergne, the motives which determine it, the distribution of landed property and other wealth, the scale of wages and prices, from the assumption that every individual pursues his pecuniary interest to the uttermost? Is it simply the desire of pecuniary gain which makes one Auvergnat a porter at Lyons, another a priest at Clermont, and the sisters of both perhaps nuns, while an elder brother of each has the whole family property? In one only of the three regions described is pecuniary interest the dominant principle; and even in that region there are inequalities of wages and profits, with other economic phenomena utterly at variance with doctrines which, by a curious combination of blunders, have been called by some writers 'economic laws.' The faith of a school of English economists removes mountains. In France, where labour moves from place to place, and from agriculture to other employments, much more freely than in England, mountains certainly do not prevent the migration of labour.

Yet even in France the migration by no means takes place on such a scale, or with such facility, as nearly to equalize wages; and in the places from which it is greatest, the department of the Creuse and the province of Auvergne, the main cause is not pecuniary interest. The younger brother in Auvergne goes from his home to a distant city in obedience to traditional family sentiments; and the peasant goes from the Creuse to Paris as a mason, not because he has calculated the difference of earnings in the two places, and in different employments (for he could make more in many cases by remaining at home), but because his father went to Paris before him, and his comrades do so around him. The relation of the economic phenomena of society to its moral, intellectual, and political condition is undreamt of by the old school of economists. Even in the case of men, it is manifestly vain to look for an explanation of the causes which determine the economic condition either of individuals or of classes, without reference to laws, customs, moral and religious sentiment; how much more is it so in the case of women? Let me adduce one instance, showing how, even in the smallest details, the economic structure of society, as regards the occupations and earnings of women, is influenced by moral and other causes, quite apart from individual pecuniary interest. At a hotel in Clermont-Ferrand, in which, as is commonly the case in large French hotels, a man does the work of housemaid, a Swiss visitor remarked to me lately, that you will rarely find perfect cleanliness and neatness where such is the case; yet in France, he added, 'it is a necessary evil. A young or good-looking housemaid has no chance of keeping her character in a French hotel; in Switzerland she is as safe as in a church.' I answered that possibly she might be as safe in the mountains of Auvergne as of Switzerland; for climate is certainly one of the causes which produce a difference in this respect between French and Swiss morals. Other causes too might be assigned, but I refer here to the moral difference in question only as exhibiting the influence of moral causes on the economic structure of society down to the minutest details.

There is another subject on which the social and economic phenomena of Auvergne may be seen to throw considerable light, namely, the mode in which diversities of human character and life are produced, and the real origin of differences of national character, customs, and condition, which are vulgarly attributed to difference of race,—that is to say, to ancestral and inherited differences of physical and mental constitution. Greater differences of human life, motive, and pursuit are to be found in parts of the province of Auvergne, a few miles from each other—in adjacent districts of mountain and plain, for example—than some which are often pointed to between Frenchman and Englishman as the consequences of an original difference of race. The people of every country like to be told that they possess an inherent superiority to every other, and the doctrine of race flatters every race and every nation. The Englishman, the Frenchman, the German, the Spaniard, the Jew, above all the Chinaman, each thinks himself of a superior race. When we descend from nations to smaller divisions of mankind, to provinces for example, the same claim is commonly set up by each to superiority over the other divisions. An Auvergnat lately asked me if I did not observe that the Auvergnats were a finer and more vigorous race than the rest of Frenchmen, and the question reminded me that a Comtois once asked me the very same question in favour of the men of his own province, la Franche Comté. Divide provinces into departments or counties, and one finds that county pride can soar quite as high as provincial or national pride. Descend further from counties to yet smaller divisions, to villages for instance, and you will find neighbouring villages in Germany with a profound contempt for each other, and an exalted consciousness of their own hereditary superiority. Take still minuter groups, and you may discover in every country many thousands of families, in all ranks of life, the members of each of which believe that they come of a better stock, and possess finer natural qualities than their neighbours. From the family come down to the individual, and the real root of the popular doctrine of race in all its forms is reached, being no other than individual conceit. The doctrine of race not only does not solve the problems which really arise respecting national diversities of character, career, and condition, but prevents those problems from being even raised. And it is impossible to acquit a dogmatic school of economists of all blame in respect of the ignorance of ascertainable causes of social diversities which the vulgar theory of race exhibits. The method of abstract reasoning from crude assumption, in place of careful investigation of economic phenomena and their causes, has prevented the discovery of a mass of evidence respecting the real origin of differences in the aims, qualities, and circumstances of mankind in different countries and situations, such as the mountain and the plain of Auvergne for example, upon which a true theory of the causes of the diversities commonly attributed to race, might have been built.

XXVIII.

M. DE LAVELEYE ON PRIMITIVE PROPERTY.*

M. DE LAVELEYE's present work has two distinct aspects, historical and practical. On the one hand, it investigates the early forms of landed property in a number of societies, European, Asiatic, African, and American. On the other hand, it raises a practical problem, the importance of which will be admitted by readers who may dissent from M. de Laveleye's views with respect to its solution. A study of the course followed by the development of property from the infancy of society has led to two opposite lines of inference and thought—represented respectively by Sir Henry Maine and M. de Laveleye—with regard to its present forms in most civilized countries; but the historical researches of both these eminent writers coincide in establishing that the separate ownership of land is of modern growth, and that originally the soil belonged in common to communities of kinsmen.

The property of which M. de Laveleye treats in this volume is property in land; of all kinds of property that which has most deeply affected both the economic condition and the political career of human societies. In one sense indeed land was not primitive property; it was not man's earliest possession or wealth. The first forms of property are lost in the mist that surrounds the first infant steps of the human race. Wild herbs, fruit, berries, and roots were probably the earliest acquisitions, but the food thus obtained was, doubtless, devoured at once. When at length providence was developed so far as to lead to the laying by of some sustenance for the future,

---

* This Essay formed an Introduction to the English edition of M. de Laveleye's Primitive Property, published at the beginning of last year by Messrs. Macmillan and Co., and is reproduced here with their permission.

the inference to which the earliest developments of movable wealth of which we get glimpses, unmistakably point, is that the store which individuals might thus accumulate would not have been regarded as their own absolute property, but as part of the common fund of the community, larger or smaller according to circumstances, of which they were members. Before land had been definitely appropriated by tribes or smaller groups, movables of many sorts had been successively added to the stock of human possessions—new descriptions of food, implements and weapons, ornaments, the rudiments of clothing, fuel, captured and domesticated animals, human slaves, vehicles, boats, tents, and other movable dwellings. The importance of some of these early kinds of property to the progress of mankind is illustrated by the probability that the domestication of animals, and the acquisition thereby of a constant supply of animal food, contributed more than any other agency to the cessation of cannibalism. And a mass of evidence converges to the conclusion that the chief of these various chattels were possessed in co-ownership by families or larger communities, held together by blood or affinity. The bearing of this proposition on the nature of the ownership of land in early societies is obvious, and it has also a relation to the practical aspects of the subject which M. de Laveleye discusses. Some evidence in support of it may therefore be appropriately adduced in the present Introduction; the more so that an opinion seems to prevail, even among scholars familiar with the true beginnings of property in land, that movable property in primitive society belonged, from the first to individuals.

In the ancient laws of Ireland the whole tribe has both 'live chattels' and 'dead chattels.' Among the Eskimos of Greenland, according to Dr. Rink's account of their ancient usages, a house was the joint property of several families; a tent, a boat, and a stock of household utensils and articles for barter were owned in common by one or more families; the flesh and blubber of captured seals belonged to a whole hamlet, while larger animals such as whales were shared among the inhabitants of neighbouring hamlets; and custom strictly limited the quantity of clothes, weapons, tools, and other articles of personal use, that a single individual could keep to himself. 'If a man had anything to spare, it was ranked among the goods possessed in common with others.' Among the Nootkas of North America, we are told by Mr. Bancroft, though food is not regarded as common property, 'any man may help himself to his neighbour's store when needy.' Sir Henry Maine and M. de Laveleye have shown that a joint table, with meals partaken in common by several families, is an archaic usage once prevalent throughout Europe and not extinct at this day among the Southern Slavs; and M. de Laveleye, with great probability, traces to it the common repasts in ancient Greece which historians have been accustomed to ascribe to the policy of legislators. Again, down at least to the fourteenth century, groups of English peasants, sometimes a whole village, had chattels such as horses, oxen, ploughs, boats, in common; a joint proprietorship which to the modern eye may look at first like a species of co-operation for convenience, but which it is more in conformity with the ideas and practices of early society to regard as a survival of the co-ownership of movables by kinsmen settled together, as we know the inhabitants of English villages in many cases originally were. Another fact pointing in the same direction is that in ancient Germany the compensation in cattle for a homicide or outrage went to the kindred, and the eric-fine of Irish law went partly to the whole sept, and partly to the chief as its head. Much evidence collected by recent inquiries into the usages of uncivilized communities at the present day, seems to lead us back to a stage of human development at which women not only were considered as chattels, but were themselves owned as such in common by clans, septs, or smaller groups of kinsmen; and the ancient Irish laws contain indications to the same effect. The honour price of an abducted woman was paid, according to the Book of Aicill, in part to her chief and her relatives; and her children belonged to her family, who might sell them or not as they pleased. The infrequency of exchanges, the absence of coin and other divisible currency for small individual purchases, the use of cattle and slaves in the earlier stages of society, as a medium of payment, point in like manner to the absence of individual property in chattels. Commercial transactions took place between groups, or at least whole families, not between individuals. We may find here, I venture to suggest, the true explanation, though Mommsen gives a different one, referred to by M. de Laveleye, of the distinction, so long maintained in Roman law, between Res Mancipi, requiring a solemn ceremonial for their transfer, and those later or less important kinds of property called Res nec Mancipi, which were transferable by simple delivery. Res Mancipi included slaves, horses, asses, mules, oxen, lands in Italy, but not coin, jewels, lands beyond Italy, and many other possessions, either entirely unknown to the primitive Romans, or not deemed of such importance as to require the forms of Mancipatio for their transfer. The original distinction, I apprehend, lay between things that were common property, and things that were allowed to belong to individuals.* A limited stock of certain things for personal use was early permitted, and accordingly weapons, food, and other articles for his journey to another world, were placed in the warrior's grave, though it is a curious inquiry whether similar provision was made for a woman on her departure. This explanation of the formalities accompanying the transfer of Res Mancipi is quite in harmony with Sir H. Maine's exposition of the solemnities accompanying the commercial transactions of primitive associations. 'As the contracts and conveyances known to ancient law are contracts and conveyances to which not single individuals, but organized companies of men are parties, they are in the highest degree ceremonious; they require a variety of symbolical acts and words intended to impress the business on the memory of all who take part in it, and they demand the presence of an inordinate number of witnesses.'†

No mere psychological explanation of the origin of property is, I venture to affirm, admissible, though writers of great

[* Dr. Hearn (Aryan Household, pp. 422-4), probably without previous knowledge of this explanation, has arrived at one closely resembling it. 1879.]
† Ancient Law, p. 271.

authority have attempted to discover its germs by that process in the lower animals. A dog, it has been said, shows an elementary proprietary sentiment when he hides a bone, or keeps watch over his master's goods. But property has **not its** root in the love of possession. All living beings like and desire certain things, and, if nature has armed them with any weapons, **are** prone to use them **in** order **to** get and keep what they **want.** What requires explanation **is not** the want or desire of certain things on **the** part of individuals, but the fact that other individuals, **with** similar wants and desires, should leave them in undisturbed **possession, or allot** to them a share, **of** such things. It is the **conduct of the** community, not the inclination **of individuals,** that needs investigation. The mere desire for **particular articles, so** far from accounting for settled and peaceful ownership, tends in the opposite direction, namely, **to conflict and the** right of the strongest. No small amount of **error in several** departments of social philosophy, and especially **in political** economy, has arisen from reasoning from the **desires** of the individual, instead of from the history **of** the community.

A more promising line of inquiry might at first sight appear to be one **to which Sir Henry** Maine has alluded in Ancient Law. **Observing that the question** proposed by many theorists respecting **the origin of property** is—what were the motives which **first induced men to respect each** other's possessions?— he adds that '**the** question may still be **put,** without **much** hope of finding an answer, in the form **of an inquiry into the** reasons that led one composite group to keep **aloof** from the domain of another composite group.'* Within each composite group men originally, **it may be** affirmed, did not 'keep aloof from each other's domain,' **for** there was in fact no such separate domain. The idea, so far as **any** definite **idea on** the subject was dimly conceived, could only be that the group was an indivisible corporation, one in blood, property and customs. Nor was **it** until a great advance in civilization had been made, that one community recognized any right whatever, collective or individual, on the

---

* Ancient Law, p. 270.

part of the members of another community of different blood or origin, to their domain or other possessions, or even to life or liberty. Property in the infancy of social progress consisted, one may say, simply in a feeling of unity and consequent co-ownership on the part of the men of a tribe, horde, clan, sept or family; the size of the group being conditioned in a great measure by the means of subsistence and other environing circumstances. So long as such a community led a wandering life, the co-ownership would be felt only in movables. But as its boundaries became circumscribed by its own growth, or by the neighbourhood of other communities, and its place of habitation in some degree fixed by the needs of incipient agriculture, landed property began to develop itself in the primitive forms set before us by M. de Laveleye in the present work, which affords one of the most brilliant examples in literature of the application of the comparative method to historical investigation.

Sir Henry Maine in his lectures at the Middle Temple was, I believe, the first to lay down with respect to landed property the general proposition, afterwards repeated in his Ancient Law, that 'property once belonged not to individuals, nor even to isolated families, but to larger societies.'* But proof of this proposition in detail exceeded the powers and opportunities for research of any single inquirer, and needed a number of original investigations in different parts of the world. One link in the chain, unknown to Sir Henry Maine, had already been forged by some profound Danish scholars, especially Oluf Christian Olufsen, who discovered from ancient legal records the original co-ownership and common cultivation of the soil of Denmark and Holstein by village communities. Their investigations were followed by the celebrated researches of Haxthausen, Hannsen and Georg L. von Maurer, in Germany. Professor Nasse, of Bonn, is entitled to the renown of having been the first to prove that in England, as in the German fatherland, groups of husbandmen cultivated the ground and fed their herds and flocks on a co-operative system which bears all the marks of descent

---

* Ancient Law, p. 268.

from the primitive communal usages of the Teutonic race. Domesday had been so imperfectly studied before Mr. Freeman's day, and other English documentary records had preserved so few traces of the primitive co-ownership and common use of land by village communities, that historians had been accustomed to follow the assumption of lawyers, that the rights of common surviving to modern times, grew up by sufferance on the part of the lords of Manors. Mr. Freeman has cited an instance from Domesday, of the men of a village community or township holding common land at Goldington in Bedfordshire; adding that such cases must have been far more usual than the entries in that great survey would lead us to think.* Professor Nasse has reproduced the rural economy and system of common husbandry that grew in some cases out of such common proprietorship, in other cases out of the common tenure of lands granted to individual owners in chief, but settled and cultivated on the same plan as those which belonged at first to the members of whole townships in common. Meanwhile Sir Henry Maine's residence for several years in India, had enabled him to collect fresh evidence from existing forms of Hindoo property and social organization, in support of his original doctrine, that the collective ownership of the soil by communities larger than families, but held together by ties of blood or adoption, was in eastern as well as in western countries the primitive form of the ownership of the soil. Sir H. Maine's conception of ancient society and its institutions, it may be observed—and the observation applies also to the theory which M. de Laveleye illustrates by so many striking examples in this work—is nowise invalidated by proof on the part of other investigators like Bachofen, Herbert Spencer, Sir John Lubbock, Mr. Tylor, Mr. McLennan, M. Giraud-Teulon and Mr. Lewis Morgan, of antecedent states of human association, before the earliest stage of inchoate civilization had been reached, or the family, as we understand the term, had been formed. The institutions that Sir H. Maine and M. de Laveleye call primitive, are so in the sense at least of being the earliest usages of society emerged from savagery,

---

* History of the Norman Conquest, v. 463.

and in some degree settled. And M. de Laveleye's work affords a magnificent example of the immense range of investigation for which there was room in respect of one of the chief of those institutions. However widely some of his readers may dissent from his views with respect to the modern distribution of landed property, there will be but one opinion respecting the breadth of research and learning with which he has illustrated its primitive forms. To the evidence previously collected by Sir H. Maine and the Danish and German scholars already referred to, he has added proofs gathered from almost every part of the globe. Ancient Greece and Rome, mediæval France, Switzerland, the Netherlands. Russia, the southern Slav countries, Java, China, part of Africa, central America, and Peru, are among the regions laid under contribution. Slavs, says M. de Laveleye, 'boast of the communal institutions of the village community as peculiar to their race, and destined to secure its supremacy, by preserving it from the social struggles impending over the States of Western Europe; but when it is proved that similar institutions are to be found in all ages, in all climates, and among the most distinct nations and races, we must see in their prevalence a necessary phase of social development and a universal law, as it were, presiding over the evolutions of the forms of landed property.' It should not, however, be overlooked that the stage of development in which such institutions are natural, is a primitive one, and that their retention may be a mark not of superiority, but of backwardness, like the retention of those first implements to which M. de Laveleye alludes, and which in the age of stone were universal.

The term 'natural' has been indeed a source of so much confusion and error in both the philosophy of law and political economy, that it might be well to expel it altogether from the terminology of both; but it could not be more legitimately applied than in the proposition that there is a natural movement, as society advances, from common to separate property in land as in chattels. This movement is perceptible among the Slav nations themselves, and it is closely connected with the movement from status to contract which Sir H. Maine has shown to be one of the principal phases of civilization. Since the emancipation of the Russian peasantry, as M. de Laveleye observes, 'the old patriarchal family has tended to fall asunder. The sentiment of individual independence is weakening and destroying it. The married son longs to have his own dwelling. He can claim a share of the land, and as the Russian peasant soon builds himself a house of wood, each couple sets up a separate establishment for itself. The dissolution of the patriarchal family will perhaps bring about that of the village community, because it is in the union of the domestic hearth that the habits of fraternity, the indifference to individual interest, and the communist sentiments which preserve the collective property of the mir, are developed.' And in like manner M. de Laveleye ends a highly interesting description of the structure and life of the family communities among the Southern Slavs as follows: 'The flourishing appearance of Bulgaria shows decisively that the system is not antagonistic to good cultivation. And yet this organization, in spite of its many advantages, is falling to ruin, and disappearing wherever it comes in contact with modern ideas. The reason is that these institutions are suited to the stationary condition of a primitive age; but cannot easily withstand the conditions of a state of society in which men are striving to improve their own lot as well as the political and social organization under which they live. I know not whether the nations who have lived tranquilly under the shelter of these patriarchal institutions, will ever arrive at a happier or more brilliant destiny; but this much appears inevitable, that they will desire, like Adam in Paradise Lost, to enter on a new career, and to taste the charm of independent life, despite its perils and responsibilities.'

Familiar as Englishmen are with Switzerland in its physical aspects, and with those features of its social life that meet the eye of the visitor, the very name of the Swiss Allmend, originally signifying the property of all, is probably known only to those who have studied M. de Laveleye's works. A large part of the land of each Swiss commune is preserved as a common domain, called the Allmend, respecting which the reader will easily obtain from M. de Laveleye's pages information which is not to be got elsewhere. M. de Laveleye points to it as an example of the possibility of reconciling the primitive system of common property and equality of wealth, with the modern system of individual ownership and great inequality of fortune. The chapters in the volume on this subject will repay careful study, but there are two points that ought not to escape observation. One is that there are indications of a tendency even in Switzerland—which stands alone in the world as a land that has maintained both the free political institutions and the communal system and property of the times before feudalism—towards a disintegration of the Allmend. Thus in the canton of Glaris 'at the present day, the commonable alps are let by auction for a number of years: and in complete opposition to ancient principles, strangers may obtain them as well as citizens.' The other point is one which the last words of the passage just cited suggest. Some of M. de Laveleye's expressions might convey the idea that an original instinct of justice, and a respect for 'natural rights' and equality, are discoverable in the primitive usages of society relating to property. Yet such language needs some interpretation to make it appropriate. The only rights which men in early society recognised were those of the community to which they belonged. These rights ran in the blood, as it were, and were confined to fellow-tribesmen or kinsmen. The stranger had no share in the common territory, no natural right as a fellow-man to property of any kind or even to liberty. And within the community, equality was confined to one sex, even after the family, as we know it, had been founded, and a partition of arable land had been made. 'Everywhere,' in M. de Laveleye's words, 'the daughters are excluded from the succession. The reason of this exclusion is manifest. If females inherited, as by marriage they pass into another family, they would effect a dismemberment of the joint domain, and the consequent destruction of the family corporation.'

Modern communism finds no precedent in the institutions of early society, its conceptions and aims are of purely modern origin; and it neither can justify them on the ground of conformity with original sentiments of justice, nor, on the other hand, can be charged with going back to barbarism for its theory of rights. The original ownership of movables by communities shows that the early usages of mankind are not models for our imitation. If separate property in land is contrary to primitive ideas and institutions, so is the separate ownership of chattels and personalty of every description. If indeed we ought to revert to common property in land because it is primitive, why not also to communism in women, if that too can be shown to have been the primitive system? The truth is that the early forms of property were natural only in the sense of being the natural products of an early state of the human mind. The forms natural in the present state of society are those in conformity with the development of human reason and with modern civilization. Some phrases in the present work might seem to indicate a desire on M. de Laveleye's part to return to the primitive co-ownership of the soil, but this he expressly disclaims. The real ground on which he builds his practical doctrines is the modern one of policy and expediency. He sympathizes with the equality of fortunes maintained in early society, but his counsels to modern society are based on the dangers that threaten it from enormous inequality of property in an age in which all men are becoming equal in political power, and sovereignty is passing into the hands of those who possess least, because they are the most numerous. Nor can it be denied that the unequal distribution of landed property in the British Islands especially, has been the result, in no small degree, not of social development or natural evolution in that sense, but of violence and usurpation in past times, and the maintenance down to our own time of a system of law derived from them.

The fact that Sir H. Maine and M. de Laveleye look with different eyes on the primitive usages of society is easily intelligible. The tendency of agriculture, commerce, and invention, of the development alike of human wants and aspirations, and of human faculties, is not only towards individual property, but towards inequality of property; and for my own part I see no greater injustice in unequal riches than in unequal strength or intellectual power. But the actual inequalities of fortune, and of landed property especially, have sprung also from other very different causes which M. de Laveleye describes. The result of the combined operation of both sets of causes is that where Sir H. Maine sees progress and civilization, M. de Laveleye sees formidable dangers to society. The owners of property are on the eve of becoming a powerless minority, and the many, to whom the whole power of the State is of necessity gravitating, see all the means of subsistence and enjoyment afforded by Nature in the possession of the few.

Readers who incline more to Sir H. Maine's point of view may therefore find much to concur with in some of M. de Laveleye's practical conclusions. The course of English legislation with respect to commons, for example, would, one may safely assert, have been materially different had M. de Laveleye's book been published two generations ago; and even now it may not be without influence on the side of those who resist further usurpation under the cloak of improvement: the pretext urged from the days of Henry III. when the statute of Merton was passed, to those of Victoria. The subject, again, has a practical importance in relation to two opposite types of society, represented on a great scale within the limits of the British empire; namely, ancient communities like those inhabiting India, and new communities at the beginning of their career, like those of Australia and New Zealand. As regards the first, it cannot be doubted that a knowledge of the early forms of land ownership would have preserved English administration from some of the worst blunders ever committed in the history of the government of dependencies. In the case of young colonies, on the other hand, it is no invasion of the principles on which individual property properly rests, to concede to writers like M. de Laveleye and Mr Pearson,* that a few score of the first comers into an immense territory ought not to be suffered to engross to themselves and their descendants the greater part of the land.

Great changes in English ideas with respect to the

---

* The reference is to Mr. C. H. Pearson, the historian, who is now resident in Australia, and has written powerfully on the subject.

devolution and distribution of landed property will doubtless follow sooner or later a great change in the distribution of political power. The history of political ideas is the history of change; and the ideas of the dominant classes become the dominant ideas in politics. No right is now held more sacred in England than the right of unrestricted bequest; and the same sentiment supports the right of settlement and entail; both are regarded here as natural rights, although at the other side of the English Channel the prevailing opinion is that a child has an indefeasible right to a share of the property of his parents. Both conceptions are of historical origin; the first descends from the early code of the Twelve Tables, the second has come down from the code of Justinian. 'In France,' says Sir Henry Maine, 'the change which took place at the first Revolution was this: the land law of the people superseded the land law of the nobles. In England the converse process has been gone through; the system of the nobles has become in all essential particulars the system of the people.'* When the people shall have the dominion in England, what shall become of the system of the nobles?

There is no path of historical research that does not lead to some practical conclusions, but some of its paths end as it were in cross roads, going different ways, between which the choice may be difficult. It is however one great advantage of the historical method that it has attractions and instruction apart from the practical inferences of particular authors. The historical part of Auguste Comte's Positive Philosophy, for example, may be studied with profound admiration by readers who wholly repudiate his system of polity. In like manner M. de Laveleye's work on primitive property cannot be read without interest and benefit even by those who most firmly refuse to accept some of the doctrines that it upholds.

* Early History of Institutions, 2nd Ed., p. 124.

XXIX.

MAINE'S EARLY HISTORY OF INSTITUTIONS.*

(Fortnightly Review, March 1, 1875.)

A PHILOSOPHICAL work may be regarded from two points of view, with reference, namely, to the additions which it makes to our knowledge within its special department, and to its bearing on other subjects. The special subject of Sir H. Maine's book is archaic law, but the results of his researches derive additional value from their relation to some of the chief social and political problems of our time. The early history of law is full of interest, the curiosity it excites is ever increasing; and to Sir H. Maine belongs the whole credit of arousing attention to it in this country. But modern questions respecting the capacities of different races and sexes are among those on which his Lectures throw light; and his historical method is applicable to other than the legal phenomena of society. As to one class of early institutions, his present work may be considered as complementary to his two previous ones, Ancient Law and Village Communities, together with M. de Laveleye's De la Propriété et ses Formes Primitives. The extraordinary extent of M. de Laveleye's researches in both hemispheres made the lacuna in respect of Celtic institutions more remarkable. This could be filled only by the study of ancient Irish usages, and Sir H. Maine's present work may be said to complete the proof of the collective ownership of land in early society by groups of kinsmen. But his investigations have a much wider range,

---

* The Early History of Institutions. By Sir Henry Sumner Maine. London: Murray.

covering the whole field of the primitive institutions of men arrived at the social stage. Some English scholars have looked askance at the Celtic nations, and shown a manifest reluctance to admit them on equal terms within the pale of historical inquiry, as though the Greek, the Roman, and the Teuton had almost an exclusive claim to the philosophic historian's attention. The chief place in Sir H. Maine's book is assigned to the ancient Irish, the most unfortunate of the Celtic nations.

The early history of Ireland—of the events of which it is made up—is buried in darkness and disaster, but something may be recovered through the study of the native institutions of the Irish people. It would, however, be a misapprehension of Sir H. Maine's chief object in investigating Irish law, and of the point of view from which he examines it, to suppose that he is concerned with the legal history of Ireland simply as such. He considers it in connexion with the general problems of historical and comparative jurisprudence. He takes Irish law as an example of an archaic legal system, and proceeds to ascertain its characteristics as such, the degree of its archaicism, if we may so speak, or the stage of early progress to which it belongs, the mode of its development, its analogies to other bodies of primitive law, its peculiar features, and the causes of those peculiarities. The inquiry is one as to which on many points only probable, on some only conjectural conclusions can be reached, and on not a few doubt and diversity of opinion may always exist. It is said in the Senchus Mor that the ancient poets of Ireland were 'deprived of' the judicature' because 'obscure indeed was the language which they spoke, and it was not plain what judgments they had passed.' If the judgments of the Brehons who succeeded to the poets were no clearer than are the tracts which go by their name, they too might fairly have forfeited the judicial office. Sir H. Maine's acuteness and learning afford a clue through much which before was a pathless maze, but no genius could extract from the tracts as yet published or accessible a decisive answer to several inquiries which present themselves. One of these relates to the mode in which the ancient laws of Ireland were developed. A legal system may be developed in several ways, by the spontaneous growth of popular usage, by the interpretation of lawyers, by the judgments of regular tribunals, and by legislation. Sir H. Maine, who traces to primitive Aryan usage the original elements of Irish law, inclines to refer its subsequent development chiefly, if not exclusively, to juridical interpretation.* A class of writers, on the other hand, of whom Dr. Sullivan is at once the latest and the ablest, attribute to Ireland at a very early period a central government with a complete legislative and judicial organization for the enactment and administration of law, and to this period they refer the institutions described in the so-called Brehon law tracts. A third view which seems to the present writer most in conformity with the evidence will subsequently appear.

A preliminary question is, what authority are we to ascribe to the tracts just named? Can we accept them, according to the title officially given to them and under which they are published, as the Ancient Laws and Institutes of Ireland? Ought they in strictness to be even called Brehon law tracts? O'Curry, one of the translators, when citing them, used the phrase, 'the law says,' and Dr. Sullivan attributes to part of them the authority of statute law. A material observation is that they ought not to be taken in the lump as entitled uniformly to the same character and authority; a consideration of the more importance, since besides those already published and hereafter to be published by the Brehon Law Commission, others, such as the Crith Gablach and the Book of Rights, are sometimes cited as authentic records of Irish law. There is for the most part no unity of authorship even in the case of each tract singly. An original text is in most cases imbedded in glosses and commentary, written by different and unknown hands at different periods. 'On its face, the commentary,' in the language of the learned editors, 'bears the appearance of a work which has grown up under the hands of successive generations of lawyers,'† with frequent variations and contradictions. Sir H. Maine traces an analogy in several respects between the writers of these Irish tracts and the authors of the

---

* Early History of Institutions, pp. 10, 11; 42, 43; and 286-290.
† 'Ancient Laws of Ireland,' vol. iii., General Preface.

Brahminical jurisprudence, at the same time observing that it is often doubtful how far the latter can be accepted as truly representing the old customary law of India. But we do not even know that the writers of the so-called Brehon law tracts were all Brehons, and are not without reason for supposing that some of them were not. Sir H. Maine suggests that the compiler of the Corus Bescna may have been an ecclesiastic, or, if a lawyer, was one writing in the interest of an ecclesiastical client. He finds evidence of bias, mere speculation, triviality and silliness in the tracts; and in truth there are passages which it is impossible to regard as the utterances of expert judges, legal practitioners, or professors of law, and which must be the work of mere tiros and dabblers. The tracts moreover appear not to have been in the hands of the Irish lawyers generally; each appears, in Sir H. Maine's words, to have been 'the property and to have set forth the special legal doctrines of a particular family or law school.'* He remarks that Shane O'Neill's view of the Irish law of legitimacy was directly contrary to the legal doctrine of the Book of Aicill, and that it would seem to follow that this book had not an universally recognised authority. The Book of Rights, according to Dr. Sullivan, contains the law regulating the relations between the local authorities and the different kingdoms; but this book is really a book of the claims of the Munster dynasty, and its authority could hardly have been recognised by a rival dynasty. The editors of the tracts officially published, in their preface to the third volume, compare the Corus Bescna with Chitty on Contracts, as the work, not of a legislator or a judge, but of a private lawyer without official authority. But, apart from the possibility that the compiler was not even a lawyer, there is the essential difference that Mr. Chitty's treatise was written for, and has circulated as a standard work among, the whole English legal profession, whereas the Corus Bescna may have been unrecognised by, and even unknown to, the majority of the profession in Ireland. Edmund Spenser evidently had never heard of the Brehon law as being in

---

* Lecture i. p. 16. Compare pp 21, 33, 280.

writing, and defines it as 'a rule of right unwritten, delivered by tradition from one to another.' Some written texts of law may have been in the possession of Irish lawyers in general, but the tracts as a whole, with their glosses and commentaries, seem certainly not to have been so. Sir James Ware appears to have been as ignorant as Spenser of any written corpus of Irish law, and states that the Brehons in their judgments were guided by aphorisms taken partly from the Civil and Canon laws, and partly from certain Irish rules and customs.*

A fresh set of difficulties arise with reference to the period to which the tracts belong. Most of the extant MSS. appear to have been written in the fourteenth and fifteenth centuries, but when were they originally composed? Mr. Whitley Stokes ascribes the Senchus Mor to the eleventh, and the book of Aicill to the tenth century, but this opinion is understood to refer only to the text, with perhaps the oldest part of the glosses and commentary. From the differences in substance, as well as in language, between the text of the tracts and the commentary and glosses, it is plain that the latter are often of much later date than the former; and it is hardly conceivable that the transcribers of the fourteenth and fifteenth centuries added no glosses or comments of their own. But were we able to fix the time of the composition of every part of each of the tracts, the inquiry would in many cases remain, were the writers describing a past, a present, or an ideal state of things? It is impossible to answer this question with respect to the Book of Rights, much of the Crith Gablach, and various passages in the Senchus Mor and the Book of Aicill. In some cases a sufficient answer may be arrived at. We know, for instance, that the eric-fine for murder and other offences was an existing institution in the time of Edmund Spenser, and we may be certain that it had existed for many centuries. We may, again, feel assured that the Irish process of distress, with the practice of fasting on debtors of rank, is older than any known event in Irish history, and was a primitive Aryan institution. But there are not a few cases

---

* Antiquitates Hiberniæ, cap. viii.

where we are left in doubt as to the period, and even as to the real existence at any period, of the customs and rules which the tracts describe. The conclusion to which all these considerations conduct us is, that the tracts are not properly entitled to the name of 'the Ancient Laws of Ireland,' and that even 'the Brehon law tracts' is an inaccurate and misleading title, though one probably now irrevocably attached to them. They are not the Laws of Ireland, but only evidence respecting them, evidence of great importance, yet needing to be scrutinized at every step with the utmost caution. No one would give the titles of the Laws of England to all the books, tracts, and unpublished manuscripts that have been written about English law. We may accept the Senchus Mor as unimpeachable evidence of the nature of the Irish remedy of distraint, because the learning of scholars like Sir H. Maine and Mr. Whitley Stokes has established the close analogies between it and ancient Roman, Germanic, and English remedies on the one hand, and the Hindoo custom of 'sitting dharna' on the other. We may further accept some, perhaps nearly all, of the tracts as sources of law, through the influence they exercised on the Brehons who had access to them, but this influence must have been in a great measure local, since as a body they were not in the hands of the legal profession throughout the country.

The question then arises, was there no source of law in Ireland of a more authoritative kind? Dr. Sullivan, in his very learned and ingenious treatise, asserts that during two or three centuries previous to the invasions of the Danes, Ireland was far advanced in civilization, material and moral, and possessed a complete legislative and judicial organization. But after the eighth century, through the anarchy resulting from the incursions of the Northmen, this organization was, in his view, broken up; and such continued to be the condition of things after the English invasion, by reason of 'the isolation of the numerous small states into which the country was divided, and the continuous feuds between their chiefs.'* The

---

* Introduction. O'Curry's Lectures, pp. xvi., xvii., cclii.

assumption of a complete legislative and judicial organization in the seventh and eighth centuries is founded mainly on the Crith Gablach, though apparently a composition of comparatively modern date, and one or two other tracts; but Dr. Sullivan attributes it chiefly to the influence of the Christian Church, together with peace, extensive commerce, industry, wealth, and learning. If, however, we are, with Dr. Sullivan, to take the Senchus Mor and the Book of Aicill as recording the usages of that early period, they certainly do not bear out his conclusions respecting the powerful influence of the Church, or the high civilization of the country. The lax relations of the sexes which they disclose and sanction, the rules respecting divorce, legitimacy, and abduction, are as incompatible with his theory of the state of religion and morals, as the archaic character of some of the customs of which they are evidence is with his supposition of a very advanced economic development. The composition for injuries in the primitive form of payments in cattle exists; no coin is current, notwithstanding the assumed wealth and commercial development of the island; and, notwithstanding the learning of monks and missionaries, the Senchus Mor describes the education of sons of chiefs as confined to chess-playing, riding, swimming, and shooting. Had so martial a people, one may add, as the Irish been so perfectly organized under a central government as Dr. Sullivan supposes, it seems certain that they must have easily driven the Danes back into the sea in the ninth century. 'I have heard,' says Edmund Spenser, no panegyrist of the Irish, 'some great warriors say that in all the services which they had seen abroad in foreign countries, they never saw a more comely man than the Irishman, nor that cometh on more bravely in his charge.'

On the whole, Dr. Sullivan seems much to exaggerate the social, political, and legal development of Ireland in the seventh and eighth centuries. But the chief defect in his representation is, that it leaves us in the dark with respect to the government and judicial institutions of Ireland during a much longer and more important period—the period to which the tracts really belong—namely, the eight hundred years from the beginning of the ninth to the end of the sixteenth century. With respect both to this and to the antecedent period, the learned editors of the third volume of the tracts conclude that the authority of the Brehons depended merely on public opinion and the voluntary submission of the litigants, and that the Irish people were altogether without legislative and judicial institutions. 'The total absence,' they say, 'of such institutions is the most remarkable point in the Brehon law.' This view is, however, contrary to many passages in the tracts referring to courts of justice and their procedure.* Citing one of these passages, Sir H. Maine indicates the importance of the question involved:—'The Brehon lawyer who ought to accompany the distrainor is expressly stated by the Senchus Mor to aid him 'until the decision of a Court.' What was the proceeding here referred to. What authority had the Irish courts at any time at which the Brehon law was held in respect? To what extent did they command the public force of the sovereign State? Was there any sovereign power established in any part of Ireland which could give operative jurisdiction to Courts of Justice and operative force to the law? All these questions—of which the last are in truth the great problems of Irish history—must in some degree be answered before we can have anything like a confident opinion on the working of the Law of Distress set forth at such length in the Senchus Mor.'

To these questions Sir H. Maine makes no positive answer, but suggests that if any such courts as the Senchus Mor assumes really existed, their jurisdiction may have been voluntary like that of the ancient Frankish courts. His remarks on the subject, however, seem to relate chiefly to the early period which Dr. Sullivan represents as one of such advanced and elaborate organization. Respecting the period from the reign of Henry II. to that of Elizabeth, Sir John Davis, Sir James Ware, and Edmund Spenser give decisive answers to Sir H. Maine's questions; and the governmental and judicial institutions which Sir John Davis describes must obviously be taken as having

---

* Senchus Mor, vol. i. pp. 85, 121, 201, 203, 294; vol. ii. p. 89.

existed before the reign of Henry II. 'To give laws,' he says, 'unto a people, to institute magistrates and officers over them, to punish and pardon malefactors, to have the sole authority of making war and peace, and the like, are the true marks of sovereignty, which King Henry II. had not in the Irish countries, but the Irish lords did still retain all these prerogatives to themselves. For they governed the people by the Brehon law; they made their own magistrates and officers; they pardoned and punished all malefactors within their several countries; they made war and peace without controlment; and this they did not only during the reign of King Henry II., but afterwards in all times even until the reign of Queen Elizabeth.' He relates, too, that when Sir W. Fitzwilliams, the Lord Deputy, told Maguire that he was about to send a sheriff into Fermanagh, Maguire replied: 'Your sheriff shall be welcome to me, but let me know his eric, or the price of his head beforehand, that if my people cut it off, I may cut the eric upon the country.' Spenser's View of the state of Ireland contains evidence to the same effect.* And Sir James Ware has graphically described the tribunal in the open air, and the rude seat of judgment from which the Brehons of the king or lord of the local territory at fixed times administered justice to the suitors litigating before them.† The editors of the tracts speak as though the existence of law in the proper sense of the term depended on the existence of a supreme central government; but there were laws in England before the States of the so-called Heptarchy were consolidated into a single kingdom, and Ireland, as a polyarchy of petty States, may well have had regular courts of justice in which the laws were expounded and administered by Brehons sitting as judges. And the judgments of such Brehons constituted, it is submitted, the true 'Brehon law.' The view which Sir H. Maine takes, that the Brehons succeeded to the Druids as judges, is strongly borne out by

---

* 'The judge, being as he is called the Lord's Brehon, adjudgeth for the most part a better share (of the eric fine) unto his Lord, that is the Lord of the soil or the head of the sept, and also unto himself for his judgment, a greater part than unto the parties grieved.'—View of the State of Ireland.

† Antiquitates Hiberniæ, cap. viii.

analogies, but the conclusion which the evidence seems to establish is that Irish law was developed in a great measure by their decisions in courts, and not solely, as Sir H. Maine rather inclines to believe, by 'the opinions of lawyers.' 'The ultimate criterion of the validity of professional opinion' in Ireland as at Rome* seems to have been 'the action of courts of justice.' The constant internal warfare in which the Irish were involved is by no means incompatible with the regular working of tribunals. 'The Norse literature,' as Sir H. Maine himself observes, 'shows that perpetual fighting and perpetual litigation may go on side by side;' and the Paston Letters prove that such was the state of things even in England so late as the fifteenth century. It is not improbable that there were suits where no public authority intervened, and the Brehons acted as arbitrators chosen by the suitors; but in large classes of cases the language of the Senchus Mor respecting the procedure of courts appears to be amply warranted. There were, it would follow, at least two sources of Irish law, doubtless acting on each other; the authoritative judgments of courts on the one hand, and the theoretical jurisprudence of lawyers and law schools on the other. There is some ground also for thinking that down to the time of Spenser, decisions on both public questions and private controversies were arrived at in local assemblies such as Mr. Freeman describes as among early Teutonic institutions.† 'There is a great use among the Irish,' says Spenser, 'to make great assemblies together upon a rath or hill, there to parley about matters and wrongs between township and township, or one private person and another.' Decisions thus arrived at may have constituted a third source of Irish law, and several passages in the tracts support the supposition.

The point of principal importance is the stage of political and legal development which Ireland had reached prior to the establishment of English law over the whole island. And the conclusion to which the evidence points, is that the native Irish

---

* **Early** History of Institutions, p. **42**.
† Comparative Politics, pp. 242, 243.

were not in the anarchical and utterly barbarous condition commonly supposed. Their judicial system seems to have reached a considerable development, and to have been such that the establishment of a native central government (which Sir H. Maine believes the English settlement prevented*) would have rapidly led to a complete national system of legislation and judicature. To judge of the stage of social and legal progress to which the Irish institutions belong, we must, however, look, not only to the external machinery for the enunciation and administration of law, but also to the nature of the laws maintained. The question thus arising is one of general importance in historical and comparative jurisprudence, over and above its interest in relation to the history of Ireland. For we have to inquire what are the institutions belonging to different stages of development? By what marks are we to determine whether laws or customs are of an archaic, a modern, or a transitional type? Are the institutions of the ancient Irish those of an advancing, a retrograde, or a stationary society? In the third volume of the tracts, the editors specify various tests of the more or less archaic character of a body of laws, and a number of others might be suggested. For the present inquiry it may be sufficient to instance the predominance of collective or of separate property; the existence or non-existence of wills, of individual contracts, and of powers of alienation of land inter vivos; the classifications of property; the nature of legal remedies and penalties, especially in the case of wrongs known in modern jurisprudence as crimes; and the proprietary and other legal rights and the social status of women. Some, however, of these tests are not decisive. In the earlier stages, the institutions of a people have one common bond, a tie of blood connects them all. Tribal or family ownership in common, the absence of testamentary and other powers of alienation, the exclusion of women from property, the blood feud (which passes subsequently into fines to the kindred of a slain or injured person), the absence of the legal remedies which regular tribunals confer, are closely related

---

* Lecture ii. pp. 54, 55.

phenomena. Thus the absence of the will, and other modes of alienation, and of proprietary rights on the part of women,* keep the tribal or family property from being broken up; and the blood feud, and its successor, the eric-fine to the kindred, grow out of and mark the same unity founded on kinship which makes the tribe, clan, sept, or other group of relatives, an indivisible corporation in respect of the ownership of land. But an advanced society may long retain some of its early institutions, as the Romans did in the patria potestas, the distinction between Res Mancipi and Res Nec Mancipi, and the treatment of theft as a **tort**; and as English law does to this day in the distinction between real and personal property, the laws relating to the property of married women, and the rights of inheritance of women in general. On the other hand, a people **whose** legal system is fundamentally archaic, may have imported from without some advanced institutions, such as the will, which Roman example, or the influence of the Christian Church, introduced among nations of mediæval Europe whose usages were in other respects of the archaic **type.**† Nevertheless we are not without decisive tests, both positive and negative. Thus, although the existence of the will is not conclusive, its absence is. In two words, nullum testamentum, Tacitus enables us to pronounce as to the primitive character of the institutions of the Germans; and he does so in nearly as few words when he states that the penalty for crimes was a fine in horses and cattle, although we may perceive a step onwards in the payment of part of it to the king or the State. Passing to Irish institutions, we find tribal ownership of both land and chattels; an eric-fine in cattle for crimes (though here, too, part of the fine goes to the chief, marking the interposition of public authority); and a process of distress with the most archaic features. On the other hand, testamentary and other powers of alienation of property exist;

---

* See on the connection between the joint ownership of kinsmen and the exclusion of women from property, M. de Laveleye's 'De la Propriété et ses Formes Primitives, pp. 172-5. (An English translation with large additions, was published in **1878**.)

† **Early History of** Institutions, pp. 56, 61-3, 104, 105.

and the modern character of the doctrines relating to contract, partnership, contributory negligence, and the measure of damages, is emphatically noticed by both the editors of the tracts and Sir H. Maine. The former, indeed, observe that it is doubtful whether such advanced doctrines corresponded with popular usage; but, even in that case, they would indicate an advance in the legal mind.

The conclusion to which these opposite characteristics point is, that while the native customs and jurisprudence of the Irish exhibit the marks of a state of society retaining many primitive features, they reveal also not only the germs of potential advancement, but evidence of actual progress in certain directions, in spite of obstacles which might well seem insuperable. In this view, one of the most interesting departments of Irish law and usage is that relating to the rights and condition of women, though it is one, the difficulties surrounding which are greatly augmented by the circumstance that Sir H. Maine's luminous researches into the history of the property of women relate almost exclusively to other communities. Nevertheless we may discover unmistakable indications in the Irish institutions of that improvement in the legal and civil condition of women which he characterises as a test of advancing civilization.* The societies which he takes up for examination on this subject are the Roman and the Hindoo, and at the patriarchal stage. Indications, however, of an earlier stage, even among communities of the Aryan stock— the ancient Irish, for example—seem clearly discernible. Sir H. Maine may fairly treat the stage at which the family is constituted as that at which the history of human society, in the proper sense of the term, begins; and he seems justified in calling the usages of that stage the primitive institutions of society. But he sometimes too narrowly circumscribes, both in space and time, the investigations of juridical history. He limits (Lecture ii., p. 65), the inquiries of the student of jurisprudence to two or at most three great races; and he somewhat curtly dismisses the evidence of practices at one period on the part of those

---

* Pp. 326, 339-41.

races themselves, resembling in respect of the relations of the sexes those of most of the lower animals. Yet his own researches show that the domain of historical and comparative jurisprudence ought to include every section of mankind in every stage of progress, since he illustrates the growth of the power of the feudal lord by the customs of African tribes. And the farther we go back in human history, and the lower the condition of the primitive human being, the greater will be seen to be the progress achieved, and the more encouraging is the evidence of human capacity for improvement. It is only in this way that we can regard with any satisfaction or hope the career of mankind. The Germans of the age of Tacitus were farther advanced than those whom Cæsar knew; in the eleventh century the English were in many respects far more civilized than their forefathers who landed in Britain; and the progress of all Western Europe since the eleventh century has been prodigious. Other parts of the world, however, have receded; all the regions under the sway of the Turk have retrograded since the Romans governed them; ruin and desolation have succeeded to wealth and prosperity over a great part of Asia. It is only by going back to the earliest condition of mankind that we discover the real movement of humanity. All mankind were once savages; savages are now to be found only in parts of the globe which have been until recent times shut out from intercourse with the progressive regions. And thus it is by taking into account evidence of usages on the part of Irish tribes of a pre-patriarchal period, that we perceive the real movement of Irish history in relation to women. Dr. Sullivan gives no reason, and there is none, for attributing 'to prejudice rather than accurate information' the description which he cites from St. Jerome (who speaks as an eyewitness), of communism in wives and the practice of cannibalism among the ancient Scoti and Atticotti.* That down to the seventeenth

---

* 'Scotorum natio uxores proprias non habet, set ut cuique libitum fuerit pecudum more lasciviunt.... Scotorum et Atticottorum ritu ac de Republicâ Platonis promiscuus uxores communes liberos habeant.... Ipse adolescentulus in Gallia vidi Atticottos, gentem Britannicam, humanis vesci carnibus.'

century the relations of the sexes in Ireland were not regulated by Christian morality appears clearly from a comparison of the Irish law tracts with the statements of Sir John Davis. Nevertheless there is decisive evidence of an immense advance beyond the state of morals and habits described by St. Jerome; and Sir H. Maine himself suggests that the rules of the tract on Social Connexions, lax as they are, may indicate a social advance. Lawful marriage has been instituted, and is held in honour. Marriage is not indeed the only recognised relation between the sexes, but the concubine or mistress is regarded as holding a position very inferior to that of the wife; her connection, moreover, is with only one man, and her industrial services are a principal reason for the connection which actually subsists, and for its recognition by the law. Another proof of a rise on the part of women is that a bondmaid has ceased to be the common medium of exchange, and the original term 'cumhal' has come to signify a value in cattle. The abduction of women continues to be a frequent occurrence in the society portrayed in the tracts, but it is visited with heavy fines; and it is moreover a practice which points to the earlier and ruder usage of marriage by capture described by Mr. McLennan. According to the original law of Irish gavelkind, males alone shared in the repartition of a deceased tribesman's land, and Dr. Sullivan adduces no authority for his statement that ultimately daughters appear to have been admitted to succeed in the absence of sons. But whatever may have been the law of succession, the women of the period to which the tracts relate have become largely possessed of separate property, by marriage portions from their own family and marriage gifts from their husbands, by their own earnings, and probably also by bequest. The proprietary rights of the wife are considerable, much exceeding, as Sir H. Maine observes, those conceded by the English common law. The rights of women, both married and single, are in many respects equal to those of men. They can sue and be sued; they may give evidence and go security; and from a comparison of the glosses and commentary with the original text of the tracts, their power of making contracts uncontrolled by husbands or guardians appears to have undergone a considerable expansion.

disabilities which in the text seem imposed on women in general, are treated by subsequent commentators as applying only to women cohabiting without lawful marriage, and even the latter are invested with certain contractual powers. An especially remarkable feature of ancient Irish society is the important place in its industrial economy which both the law tracts and later testimony exhibit women as filling. Edmund Spenser describes them as having 'the trust and care of all things both at home and in the field;' the tracts represent them as both superintending and sharing the work of the farm out of doors, and spinning and making linen and cloth in the house; and this was evidently a principal reason for the temporary cohabitation of women as mistresses, and for the care of the law to secure to them the value of their services. Women of high birth, again, had several of the privileges of chiefs; and among these the Crith Gablach states, according to the translation, that the wife of an Aire-Tiusi, a chief of high rank, had the right to be consulted on every subject.'

On the other hand, there are proofs of the long continuance, among the Irish, of some very early usages in relation to women. Part of the bride's dower or marriage gift went, if her father were dead, to the chief of her sept. Part of the honour-price of an abducted woman went to her chief and her family; her children were the property of her family, who might sell them if they liked, according to the Book of Aicill, though it is not improbable that this custom became at a later period obsolete. In one particular women appear from the tracts to have lost ground; several women being mentioned as having anciently been judges. Dr. Sullivan suggests, with considerable probability, that these traditionary female judges were Druidesses. The entrance of the Christian Church on the stage would, of course, account for the loss of the priestly functions which, in the age of the Druids, were blended with the judicial. But throughout Europe the mediæval clergy exerted their influence against the exercise of public functions by women. There is a passage in the Senchus Mor in which the hand or the inspiration of the Churchman clearly appears, at the same time that it contains a remarkable recognition of women as law-worthy.

'What is the reason that it is called the Senchus of the men of Erin, since it does not treat more of the law of the men of Erin than of the law of the women? It is proper indeed that it should be so called, that superiority should be first given to the noble sex, that is to the male, for Christus caput viri, et vir caput mulieris—Christ is the head of the man, and the man is the head of the woman; and the man is more noble than the woman, and it was on account of man's dignity it was ascribed to him.'

Sir H. Maine shows how injurious priestly prejudices and interests have been to women in India, but credits the mediæval clergy with having done much to improve their position in Europe in relation to property. The subordination of women was, nevertheless, a prime object of ecclesiastical policy, and in his Ancient Law, Sir H. Maine has shown us how, by proprietary disabilities consequent on the complete subordination of the wife, the canon law deeply injured civilization. But the influence of the Church over Irish law was comparatively slight, and this probably explains the comparatively independent position of married women prior to the establishment of the English common law, which instantly lowered the position of the Irish wife.*

On the whole, the movement towards the emancipation and elevation of women, which Sir H. Maine regards as part of the general movement called civilization, is distinctly visible in Irish legal history. Its features in this respect corroborate evidence previously adduced, that the state of society exhibited in the native institutions of Ireland during many centuries prior to the establishment of English law, is not one of utter anarchy and barbarism, but one grievously hindered in its development, and retaining many traces of archaic usage, yet exhibiting marked tendencies to improvement, and in some important points great actual progress. It is not to the past, but to the future, that eminent Irishmen like Dr. Sullivan should teach their countrymen to look for proof of Irish capacity for civilization. More hope, however, for the future is to be gotten

* Early History of Institutions, p. 324.

from St. Jerome's description of the Scots and Atticotti in the fourth century, than from Dr. Sullivan's picture of the high civilization of their descendants in the seventh and eighth centuries. The idea presented by a comparison of St. Jerome's account with the evidence respecting the condition of Irish society in later ages is one of remarkable progress in the face of enormous obstacles; the picture which Dr. Sullivan holds up is that of a precocious social maturity, followed by rapid decay.

An important conclusion which Sir H. Maine has established in relation to Irish institutions is, that some of the rudest of them are of the genuine Aryan type, exhibiting the closest analogies to early Roman, Teutonic, and Hindoo customs. Few chapters in historical jurisprudence are more instructive than the Lectures in which he compares the Irish process of distress with the Roman pignoris capio, the pignoratio of the Leges Barbarorum, the English remedy of distraint and replevin, and the Hindoo custom of 'sitting dharna.' Irish customs which Sir J. Davis denounced as 'lewd and unreasonable,' were virtually the same institutions out of which 'the just and honourable law of England' grew; only without the development which English law owed to the establishment of a strong central government, introducing general legislation, effacing ancient tribal and local usage, taking on itself the redress of wrongs and jurisdiction over all controversies, terminating feuds and private war, and promoting the substitution of contract for kinship and status as the basis of rights.

One striking analogy, however, between Irish and ancient Teutonic institutions, of which Sir H. Maine may claim to be the original discoverer, is to be contemplated with small satisfaction—the growth, namely, in Ireland, as throughout most of Western Europe, of feudalism, in the sense of the transformation of the chief of the tribe or the clan into the lord of its territory; a change which involved the sinking of the tribesmen among whom the chief had been only primus inter pares, into dependents and serfs, and the conversion of the patrimony of the many into the estate of the one. Nor does the economic compensation to which Sir H. Maine points, appear to have really followed. Property in land, he points out, has had a twofold origin, having arisen partly from the disentanglement of the individual rights of the tribesmen from the collective rights of the family or tribe, and partly from the growth of the dominion of the tribal chief. 'The English conception,' he states, 'of absolute property in land is really descended from the special proprietorship enjoyed by the lord, and more anciently by the tribal chief in his own domain;' and he adds that 'we are indebted to the peculiarly absolute English form of ownership for such an achievement as the cultivation of the soil of North America.' Whether absolute individual property in the soil be the best political and economic institution, or, as M. de Laveleye thinks, the reverse, there seems, in the first place, no necessity for tracing it to the proprietorship of either the chief or the feudal lord; it finds its archetype in the absolute property of the tribesman in his own dwelling and surrounding plot of ground. Nor is it plain why the English form of property, descended from the dominion acquired by the lord, should be described as peculiarly absolute. The same process which transformed the chief of the village community into the lord of its land, subjected him to an overlord, and one of the fundamental doctrines of English real property law is, that the idea of absolute ownership is unknown to English law. Sir H. Maine himself contrasts socage tenure, 'the distinctive tenure of the free farmer,' which he traces to the ownership of the tribe, with military tenure descending from the suzerainty of the lord; and it was only by transforming itself into socage tenure that military tenure relieved itself of burdens most obstructive to good husbandry and improvement. Seignorial proprietorship hindered, as Adam Smith has pointed out, improvement on the part of both landlord and tenant; and it was one of the main causes of the backwardness of English agriculture at a time when the humbler forms of proprietorship and tenure descending from the village community had converted the swamps and sandbanks of Flanders into richly cultivated gardens.* M. de Laveleye doubtless errs on the

---

* Economie Rurale de la Belgique, Par E. de Laveleye. 2nd ed., p. 16.

other side, in attempting to trace the instincts of justice, and a beneficent natural law, in the original common proprietorship of the tribe and the village group of kinsmen. It involved the exclusion of men of different blood, and of women even of the same blood; it was closely connected with slavery; and Sir H. Maine is obviously justified in objecting to descriptions which represent the communism of the primitive cultivating groups as an anticipation of modern democratic theories. Nor is the statement groundless, that 'the transformation and occasional destruction of the village communities was caused, over much of the world, by the successful assault of a democracy on an aristocracy.' This description, however, is not applicable to either England or Ireland. In both the assault was made by an aristocracy or a plutocracy; and in both the economic results to the cultivators of the soil were disastrous.

Works of genius and learning not only convey new information to other minds, but also stir them to reflection and further investigation, sometimes resulting in difference of conclusion. And especially where the subject is one, like the laws and legal history of Ireland, bristling with points respecting which much is necessarily open to conjecture and doubt, one of the uses of a work such as Sir H. Maine's is to excite controversy. But it establishes many important conclusions incontrovertibly, and does so not only with respect to its special subject, the early history of institutions, but also in respect of several social problems of our own day. One of these is the great question of race, and the causes of diversities of national character and career. Edmund Spenser, and Bishop Berkeley after him, saw in the manners and customs of the Irish, and the state of Irish society, the traits of a race naturally repugnant to civilization. Sir H. Maine teaches us to regard them as the characteristics of an early phase of social progress, presenting manifest germs of and proofs of capacity for improvement. Sir John Davis denounced Irish institutions as 'lewd and unreasonable;' Sir H. Maine shows that they belong to a stage of development through which the laws of all civilized nations have passed. It is needless to say how the lessons which Sir H. Maine deduces from the history of law tend to diminish national prejudices, to improve international relations, and to facilitate the government of different nations and races under the same empire, or how hopeful they are in respect of the aptitudes of all races for civilization under propitious conditions. His investigations have likewise the merit, seldom possessed by the researches of scholars, of taking both sexes into account; and of showing that the same process of social development which displays itself in the transformation of archaic into civilized institutions, tends to raise the legal condition of women to the same level with that of men, leaving individual position to individual powers.

The method of investigation, it ought to be added, which Sir H. Maine has done more than any other writer to introduce into England, is applicable to other departments of social philosophy besides jurisprudence; and it is not a rash prediction that one of the results of his works on the history of law will be the application of the historical method to political economy.

XXX.

HEARN'S ARYAN HOUSEHOLD.

(*Athenæum, January* 25, 1879.)

THE opening sentences of the introduction to Mr. Hearn's learned and interesting work* remind one of the beginning of Macaulay's History of England, and it may be regarded as an indication of the progress of research into the structure of archaic society that so good a scholar as Mr. Hearn feels the ground firm enough under his foot to tread with the confident step of a narrative historian. He does not, it should be understood, profess to investigate the primitive condition of human beings, or broach any theory respecting it. His inquiries relate to the institutions and social life of the so-called Aryan branch of the human race at a stage at which the family, or, as he prefers to call it, the household, and the clan, together with an intermediate group which he calls the near kin, mæg, or joint family, were constituted. He pronounces no opinion on theories such as M'Lennan's or Mr. Lewis Morgan's respecting a communistic state anterior to the institution of marriage, though his own view of the relation between the clan and the family would hardly be accepted by those authors. Archaic society means in Mr. Hearn's book, as it does in Sir Henry Maine's Ancient Law, patriarchal society, composed of families akin to each other, and each held together by the patria potestas, with a chief at the head of the whole community or clan, who represents the common ancestor, and is assumed to

---

* The Aryan Household: an Introduction to Comparative Jurisprudence By William Edward Hearn, LL.D. **Longmans & Co.**

be his nearest descendant in the male line. It is, too, society at the settled and agricultural stage, at which the arts of building substantial houses and ploughing are practised. Mr. Hearn's clan is, in fact, the village community which Sir Henry Maine's researches have made known, in its original purity. Yet there is a difference, although not so wide or so deep as Mr. Hearn himself seems to suppose, between his view and Sir Henry Maine's. Their theories bring out different aspects of the same structure, and at first sight may seem built on different foundations, as Mr. Hearn represents them to be. Among the Aryán nations the basis of human association was, in his view, religion. The members of the community were kinsmen, but kinship, according to him, consisted not in common descent but in community of worship. Those who worshipped the same gods were kinsmen, although no common blood flowed in their veins, and those who did not were not of kin, although according to the flesh they may have been brother and brother and parent and child. But when we ask what the religion of these fellow-worshippers was, Mr. Hearn answers, the worship of forefathers. Archaic religion was, he says, domestic, and consisted of two closely related parts—the worship of deceased ancestors and the worship of the hearth, the latter being subsidiary to and consequent on the former, for the deceased forefather was buried, or assumed to be buried, under the hearth; though some superstition relating to fire probably entered into the rites. 'The spirit of the house father hovered round the place he loved in life, and, with powers for good and evil preternaturally exalted, still exercised unseen the functions which in his life he had performed.'

It follows that the root of the religion was reverence for forefathers, that the common worship was the effect of common descent, and that the fundamental bond of association, alike in the case of the family and the clan—for the clan, too, worshipped a common ancestor—was actual kinship. A time came, indeed, when the family no longer counted some who were related to it in blood, and reckoned among its members some who were not, but the exclusion of emancipated and the admission of adopted sons were certainly later developments which, by a natural consequence, excluded the former from and admitted the latter to the worship of the ancestral gods. Ruth clave to her mother-in-law, and therefore to her people and gods, forsaking, consequently, her own people and gods. 'Thy people shall be my people, and thy gods my gods.'

Mr. Hearn brings out with skill and effect the potent influence of this form of religion on social life and sentiment—on the authority of the house father, the solemnity of the common meals at which he was spiritually a partaker, the sacredness of the common property, the importance of an heir to preserve the memory of the dead and their place and offerings among the living, and the strength therefore of the tie of kinship by adoption as well as by blood. He looks, in short, at archaic society on its religious side, shows what its religion was, how powerful an agent it was, how it helped to bind the property of the family to the male line, because otherwise the ancestral spirits would lose their home, their altar, and their sacrifices, and how these spirits became in imagination the guardians of the house and its precincts, and a terror to marauders. He follows here a line of inquiry of great interest and instructiveness, from which light may hereafter be thrown on modern ideas and usages that are supposed to have a very different origin. It is, too, a line of inquiry which Sir Henry Maine, whose subject was archaic law, not archaic religion, has but lightly and occasionally touched. None the less is this archaic religion a branch from the stem of the patriarchal family, not the root of that grand factor of human society. The religion, too, which Mr. Hearn describes is manifestly not a primitive product of the human mind, but the growth of time and of family traditions and feelings. There is, indeed, reason to suspect that it had succeeded earlier superstitious ideas, and that the ancestral gods who in later times were expelled as false idols had themselves dethroned objects of a more primitive worship.

An author naturally inclines to attach chief importance to the side of a subject that has engaged his own chief attention, and to which he has contributed most, but when Mr. Hearn says of the household or family that 'its one great aim was the **perpetuation of** the sacra,' a correction may be found in his **own pages,** which afford **ample proof that** it had other ends. The **worship** of forefathers became doubtless an object of sedulous care; yet though we cannot penetrate into all the **secrets** of the patriarchal dwelling, **we may take it for** certain that conjugal, parental, **and filial** feelings, marital jealousy, the services of wife, children, and dependents, **contributed to the** institution **and** organization of the **household.** Patriarchal society **had,** moreover, what in modern language would be called economic, civil, and military ends. The **clan, as already** said, **was** constituted **and** settled, and agricultural **life had begun at** the earliest stage to which Mr. Hearn's investigation goes back. **The** clansmen **lived in villages,** had landed property **both** collectively **and by** households, and a regular system, **though not** reduced to formal rules, with respect to its distribution **and** management. Each family had **its own** dwelling **and garden,** with an allotment **of arable** land, and shared in the use **of** the natural **pasture and forest.** Subsistence **and** certain **kinds of wealth were thus among the** objects of the little society, **and it was in** one aspect an **industrial** organization. **It was also** an organization for war and defence. The kinsmen **avenged each** other's wrongs, defended their common property, **and** went forth **to battle** and on forays together. The religious observances **which** Mr. Hearn represents could not have **been the exclusive or** even the primary objects of the association. They presuppose the house, the **hearth,** and possessions **of** various kinds, movable and **immovable.** He lays great **stress** on philology as one of the **main sources of** light respecting archaic Aryan life, and it does not suggest that the first **use** of the house was to serve as a domestic temple or place **of** worship, though it became one.

Mr. Hearn's explanation of **the** origin of archaic property shows how it gained an additional security besides that which the strong arms of its joint owners afforded, but does not account for its existence. Commenting on Sir Henry Maine's view, that the problem respecting the first institution of property is indissolubly connected with one of which no solution has been given respecting the origin of the family, Mr. Hearn expresses his own conviction 'that Sir Henry Maine understates the resources of the science of which he is so distinguished a student, and that historical jurisprudence is not silent in the presence of this great problem.' His own answer is that 'as the household depended on the house spirit, so the respect for another's property depended on the respect for the spirits that guarded the property.' But the rejoinder is obvious, that the supposed existence of invisible defenders of the property of the kinsmen in archaic society no more accounts for their joint ownership than the actual existence of policemen accounts for the institution of individual property in modern society. Another great problem in historical jurisprudence, that respecting the origin of promogeniture, finds its solution, according to Mr. Hearn, in the succession of the eldest son to the domestic priesthood in the room of the last house father. But he overlooks the established fact that the texts of Hindoo law which he cites in support of his view of this and other points have undergone manipulation by comparatively modern Brahminical expositors, who, as remarked by Sir Henry Maine in his Early History of Institutions, show a visible desire to connect property with sacrificial duties, in the interest doubtless of their own order. Mr. Hearn seems, too, to forget that the description of the usages of the Tencteri, which he cites in proof that 'the eldest son was in ancient times the heir among the Teutons,' occurs in the second part of the 'Germania,' where, as Tacitus formally warns his readers, the customs described are those peculiar to particular tribes; and that the language of the first part with regard to the general custom of succession is different, and, though not perhaps absolutely incompatible with the existence of primogeniture, certainly does not suggest it.

Mr. Hearn's investigations do not end with the household and the clan. At the outset he proposes 'to describe first the clan system, which was the original type of Aryan society, and next the rise of political society and its relation to the earlier system.' Accordingly the last seven chapters of his work are devoted to tracing the growth of the State and of law—if, indeed, the process, as he views it, can be called growth, for he draws a sharp line of division between the clan, with its body of customary rules, and the State, with its system of positive law. The State, in his words, 'was not a spontaneous growth, like a natural household, it commenced in a voluntary association.' Yet his own account of the clan shows that it had already a polity, and that it might be developed into a State answering Austin's definition by a natural process. It was, as we have seen, at the stage at which Mr. Hearn's investigation begins, a village community, and, in his own words, 'the development of the village gave the πόλις or city state.' The members of the clan, he says, exercised full powers of self-government, and maintained for the purpose a suitable organization, acted together in avenging wrong done to any of their members, obeyed and honoured a common head, and in the course of time branched out into numerous sub-clans. Again, he says, there was an organization common to the household, the clan, and the State. Each of these bodies had its chief and its council; and in their external relations the same resemblance may be traced. The chief of the clan 'was the natural leader of his kinsmen in war, and the administrator of their customs in peace. In all external relations he was the spokesman and representative.' Surely we have here distinctly the beginning of political organization and of the functions of the head of a State. And he shows how naturally 'as the household expands into a clan, so the clan expands into a people.' At this point, however, he assumes that 'with the increase of its numbers the simple homogeneous body becomes in the usual way a collection of heterogeneous related bodies;' elsewhere he says that when a clan branched out into sub-clans, each of them tended to become a separate and independent community. Mr. Hearn seems here to reason not from historical evidence, but by deduction from Mr. Herbert Spencer's generalization that evolution is everywhere a movement from the homogeneous to the heterogeneous. There is no reason to suppose that the German civitates described by Tacitus were generally formed by 'voluntary association' as opposed to 'spontaneous growth.' A number of blood-related clans might tend either to dispersion and separation, or to coalescence, according to surrounding conditions. Under external pressure, and with constant necessity for common action, they might naturally maintain a close connexion and a common government for certain purposes. And a government once formed has a strong tendency to grow, and to extend the sphere of its jurisdiction and intervention, as Roscher points out in a work which Mr. Hearn, wide as his studies have been, seems not to have examined.* The truth is that the State arose in several ways; sometimes by the growth of a clan, with the increase of numbers, into a people who held together instead of dispersing; sometimes by conquest and the forcible annexation of other tribes and their territory; sometimes by voluntary alliance. But in every case it was by degrees only that it extended the sphere of its action so as to answer fully Austin's definition.

Mr. Hearn's account of the rise of positive law is open to like criticism. Objecting to Sir Henry Maine's view that Austin's definition of law is strictly applicable only to the rules by which society is controlled in states of a type which is exceptional in the world's history, and not to Asiatic empires such as Runjeet Singh governed, Mr. Hearn observes: 'The difficulty which presses Sir Henry Maine arises, if I may venture to say so, from his failure to appreciate the broad distinction between law and custom. It is true that Runjeet Singh ruled extensive territories, and never made a law in his life. But there was no law in Runjeet Singh's dominions. His subjects, or rather his tributaries, lived according to their customs.'

The real failure, if we may venture to say so, appears to lie in Mr. Hearn's inability to conceive law as passing through stages of development, like the State itself, and only at an advanced stage becoming fully conformable to Mr. Austin's formula. It is, Mr. Hearn himself remarks, 'the main error of the analytical jurists that they in effect admit no intermediate

---

* Nationalökonomik des Ackerbaues, von Wilhelm Roscher. Siebente Auflage. Einleitung.

condition between law and anarchy.' We should add that his own main error on the subject is that in effect he admits no intermediate condition between mature law and no law, and does not see that law may begin in custom, as the State may begin in the clan, and with the advance of political organization and the extension of the activity of the central government may come to rest expressly or tacitly on its authority. 'In its earliest sense,' Mr. Hearn says, 'Jus Privatum meant clan custom, Jus Publicum meant State law.' The Jus privatum, which regulated family relations, property, succession, contract, and wrongs against individuals was, we should say, at the stage at which it was clan custom, also law at an early stage. The difference is not a mere verbal one; it involves the question whether both the State and law are sudden and artificial formations or natural growths; and whether they have not stages of development, to the latest of which only Mr. Austin's formulas can properly be applied.

Throughout his work Mr. Hearn appears to have been unconsciously biassed by a tendency to magnify the points of difference between his own views and Sir Henry Maine's; and this tendency has led to some errors, and to a one-sided treatment of several subjects. He cites Sir Henry Maine frequently and respectfully, but expresses chief obligation to M. de Coulanges, while we should say that he owes most to Sir H. Maine, though he has looked at the structure of archaic society also with the eyes of M. de Coulanges. Yet it were unjust not to admit that Mr. Hearn's work is one of great learning, ability, and value, and that it does honour to the University of Melbourne, in which he now holds office, as well as to the author's Alma Mater, the University of Dublin.

APPENDIX.

TWO BOOKS ON INTERNATIONAL LAW.*

(Athenæum, May 18, 1878.)

THE appearance of a work on International Law, like a petrel on the wave, is usually the harbinger of a storm. The treatise of Grotius, 'De Jure Belli ac Pacis,' was a product of the early years of the cruelest war of modern times, and was followed by a continuance of it for a generation. The last two words of its title were an afterthought; the author had originally a commentary on the laws of war only in view. More than half of the earlier editions of Wheaton's work related to war. The first volume of Sir Robert Phillimore's Commentaries was published in the first year of the Crimean war. General Halleck's work was a result of the war between the United States and Mexico, and the first edition appeared in the same year which saw the beginning of the American Civil War. The hostilities, past and prospective, arising out of the Eastern Question had, it may be conjectured, something to do with the new editions of Wheaton and Halleck before us, and they certainly help to make their appearance well timed. Such facts are enough to demonstrate that it is only by a metaphor the name of Law can be applied to the doctrines of publicists respecting international relations, and that the language of

---

* Elements of International Law. By Henry Wheaton. English Edition. By A. C. Boyd. (Stevens & Sons.) Halleck's International Law. A New Edition. By Sir Sherston Baker, Bart. (C. Kegan, Paul & Co.)

Hobbes is still true of independent commonwealths, that 'they live in the condition of perpetual war, with their frontiers armed, and cannons planted against their neighbours round about.'

Men, however, as statesmen sometimes needlessly assure us, are not governed by logic, while they are very much governed by words, and the name of Law has, on the whole with happy results, given no little practical authority to the dicta even of private text writers respecting the rights and obligations of States. Legal fictions have played a great part in the history of civilization, and of all the fictions of jurists the grandest, looking to the magnitude of its effects in both ancient and modern times, is that of a code of natural law. The law of nations, in the modern sense, is an offshoot of the same law of nature which the Roman jurists thought they saw in their Jus Gentium, a phrase which General Halleck has grievously misunderstood. And although some of the modern writers on international law repudiate the authority of the code of nature in its earlier shape, they have been unable to shake off allegiance to it, or to dispense with it as a foundation for the rules they lay down. Wheaton, for example, accuses Grotius of having founded the laws of nations on fictions, and affirms that his supposed state of nature never existed. Yet we find Wheaton himself stating that 'the law of nature has not precisely determined how far an individual is allowed to make use of force,' basing natural proprietary rights on the 'law of nature,' and professing to determine particular international controversies which are not without practical importance and interest at the present moment by reference to natural rights.

Thus the old claim of the Baltic powers to treat the Baltic Sea as mare clausum has lately been mooted in some German and Russian journals, and related to it is a wider question respecting the claims of nations to exclusive dominion over portions of the sea. There are, according to Wheaton, 'two decisive reasons applicable to this question;' first, that 'things which are originally the common property of all mankind can only become exclusive property by means of possession,' and, secondly, that 'the sea is an element which belongs equally to all men, like the air.' Both these reasons are derived from the fiction of a code of natural, inherent, original, and universal rights. Nothing whatever was originally the common property of all mankind; **whatever** property mankind first possessed belonged, if not to particular individuals, to particular groups of **men.** Did the sea really belong equally to all mankind, it could not be the property of particular States, even in bays, harbours, ports, and other places where Wheaton allows it to be so Jure Gentium. The air, on the other hand, often actually is private property. 'Cujus est solum ejus est usque ad cœlum' is an **old** maxim of law, and the high rent of many **sites** depends on **the** purity of the air their owners are enabled to let. Mr. Boyd refers to **a curious** question that **arose during** the Franco-German war as to what treatment persons should receive **who** ascended in balloons in order to reconnoitre the enemy's forces. **Those who** were captured by the Germans were imprisoned, **and** afterwards tried before a council of war. According to **some** authorities aëronauts of this class are to be treated as prisoners of war. Mr. Boyd observes that although they ought not to be treated as spies, a general is justified in threatening to treat them severely. It is not easy to see how, if all men have a natural right to the air, a general could be justified in punishing any one for moving **about** in it. The truth is that 'international law' is based simply upon the usage and conventions of States, the principles of conduct they recognise, and the dictates of policy, reciprocity, and humanity; and so far as it is so, it may be regarded as containing the germ of law, in the strict sense of the word. The Baltic Sea is not mare clausum, simply because the Governments of the civilized world have never admitted it to be so. The King's Chambers, on the other hand, are portions of the sea under the exclusive territorial jurisdiction of the British Crown, because Great Britain has immemorially maintained dominion over them, and other States have conceded it. So, again, the principles applicable to the treatment of persons surveying the operations of an army in the field from a balloon, should be based partly on belligerent usage in analogous cases, and partly on the milder sentiments and more enlightened ideas governing the conduct of modern Governments and generals than those which dictated the practices of warfare before balloons were in use for the purpose. No 'decisive reasons' applicable to any question concerning either the sea or the air can be drawn from such sources as Wheaton appeals to.

Considering how largely the international code of war has been made, not by neutral powers or impartial judges, but by the conduct of the commanders of hostile armies, one might well be astonished at first sight that it is not more cruel and tyrannical than it is. How it actually grew up; how it gradually softened as civilization advanced, and as the perceptions on the part of sovereigns, statesmen, and generals of the interests of their own armies and countrymen became finer, and how far, again, it is from being founded on the recognition of any original or natural rights of mankind, is admirably illustrated by passages in the Duke of Wellington's despatches, which authors of works on international law would do well to study. We find him calmly stating that he always treats his French prisoners with the utmost humanity and attention, and that his only reason for doing so is that the enemy may treat his soldiers well when they become captives in turn. He protects the French peasantry from pillage, not on the ground that, by a law of nature, private property on land is entitled to such immunity, but because if his troops plunder 'they will ruin us all;' and because the result of paying for everything was that the peasants drove their flocks to seek protection within the lines of the British army, while the French troops were almost starving.

The confusion with which the attempt to deduce a code of belligerent rights from great original and fundamental principles, instead of from the actual usages of war, has surrounded the subject, is exemplified in the two books before us by the discussions relating to the exemption of private property from capture. If the two works be compared, it will be seen that it is not clear whether the general principle from which we are to set out is that a belligerent has a right to use every means to subdue his enemy and to deprive him and his adherents of everything that might enable him to resist, or that no use of force is legitimate unless it be necessary to secure victory. If, again, we accept it as a general rule, however arrived at, that private property is exempt from confiscation, we presently find that the exceptions are so sweeping that the general principle appears to be wholly set aside by them. Not only may private property be taken from enemies in the field, or in besieged towns, but military contributions at discretion may be levied on the inhabitants of the enemy's country. Whatever ministers to the strength of the enemy and enables him to continue the contest may be seized. Thus, during the American Civil War the Supreme Court decided that cotton could be lawfully captured on the ground that 'any property which the enemy can use, either by actual appropriation or by the exercise of control over its owner, or which the adherents of the enemy have the power of devoting to the enemy's use, is a proper subject of confiscation.' It is 'lawful' also to ravage or lay waste the enemy's country, 'if it be necessary to accomplish the just ends of war.' General Halleck thickens the confusion by the statement that 'some modern text writers—Hautefeuille for example —contend for the ancient rule that private property on land is subject to seizure and confiscation,' adding that 'they are undoubtedly correct with respect to the general abstract right, as deduced from the law of nature and ancient practice; but while the general right continues, modern usage and the opinions of modern text writers of the highest authority have limited this right by establishing the rule of general exemption.' The truth of the matter is that the law of nature is a mere dream; that not ancient but modern practice, not ancient but modern sentiments and ideas, should guide the policy and conduct of governments and generals and the principles of publicists in the matter. But the same consideration shows, on the other hand, the fallacy of the reasoning of writers who, starting from the position that international law is so called only by a fiction or a metaphor, and that no legal rights or obligations, in the strict sense, are established even by the most solemn treaties of independent states, conclude that a treaty is consequently binding only so long as each of the parties chooses to be bound by it, or as the circumstances which led to it remain unaltered. Doubtless neither usage nor convention can, where there is no lawgiver or legislature, create legal rights or impose legal obligations, in the strict sense of the words, but the matter is one of morality, reciprocity, and the welfare of the civilized world. And the faithful observance of international compacts is of the utmost consequence for the settlement of international differences, the conclusion of actual hostilities when they arise, and the establishment of confidence instead of continued suspicion and jealousy between States on the close of disputes.

We believe in the possibility of a work on international jurisprudence of a character different from that of either of those before us, one which, while boldly setting aside the fictions on which celebrated publicists have hitherto built, shall yet lay a solid foundation for the best parts of the system they have expounded. Both Mr. Boyd's edition of Wheaton and Sir Sherston Baker's of Halleck, however, undoubtedly meet an existing demand, and they supplement one another. Sir Sherston Baker, we must at the same time observe, has in one instance done his author no service by respecting his original text. General Halleck's work was written before the publication of Sir H. Maine's Ancient Law; had he been acquainted with that work he could hardly have committed the blunder of describing the Jus Gentium of the Romans as 'a civil law of their own, made for the purpose of regulating their own conduct towards others in the hostile intercourse of war.' Such a misconception ought not at any rate to have been left standing without correction or comment, and it shows the uncritical frame of mind in which Sir Edward Creasy pronounced, in a passage quoted in the editor's preface, that 'the only fault' of General Halleck's work was that it had no index. Neither Wheaton's nor Halleck's work, considerable as their merits are, deserves the commendation of being faultless. Nevertheless, new editions of both were a desideratum, and the present state of European politics adds to their timeliness. Nor will they lose their utility by a settlement of the Eastern Question. Points of international law now frequently start up unexpectedly in time of peace before British tribunals in the remotest parts of the world. The Japan Gazette has reported interesting cases of this sort tried before Mr. H. Wilkinson in the British Court at Kanagawa, and, if our memory serves us, some questions of the same class deserving the consideration of the law officers of the Crown in this country, came not long ago before Mr. James Russell as Acting Attorney-General at Hong Kong. Nor is it British civil servants only who find editions of works like Wheaton's useful in China. It would not be easy to name a fact putting in a stronger light the increased activity of international relations and the constantly increasing need of a body of principles and rules for their adjustment than the one mentioned in Mr. Boyd's preface, that the last edition of Wheaton by Mr. Lawrence was a translation of the work into Chinese by order of the Chinese Government.

www.ingramcontent.com/pod-product-compliance
Lightning Source LLC
Chambersburg PA
CBHW021417300426
44114CB00010B/538